Reading STREET

Grade 6

Pearson

Reader's and Writer's Notebook

PEARSON

Glenview, Illinois • Boston, Massachusetts • Chandler, Arizona • Upper Saddle River, New Jersey

PEARSON

ISBN-13: 978-0-328-47677-0
ISBN-10: 0-328-47677-3
15 16 17 V011 18 17 16 15

CC1

Unit 1: Loyalty and Respect

Unit 2: Space and Time

Unit 5: Resources

Unit 6: Exploring Cultures

Name ______________________________

Unit 1 Independent Reading Log

Reading Time	Title and Author	What is it about?	How would you rate it?	Explain your rating.
From ______ to ______			Great 5 4 3 2 1 Awful	
From ______ to ______			Great 5 4 3 2 1 Awful	
From ______ to ______			Great 5 4 3 2 1 Awful	
From ______ to ______			Great 5 4 3 2 1 Awful	
From ______ to ______			Great 5 4 3 2 1 Awful	

Name ______________________________

Unit 2 Independent Reading Log

Reading Time	Title and Author	What is it about?	How would you rate it?	Explain your rating.
From ______ to ______			Great 5 4 3 2 1 Awful	
From ______ to ______			Great 5 4 3 2 1 Awful	
From ______ to ______			Great 5 4 3 2 1 Awful	
From ______ to ______			Great 5 4 3 2 1 Awful	
From ______ to ______			Great 5 4 3 2 1 Awful	

Name ______________________________

Unit 3 Independent Reading Log

Reading Time	Title and Author	What is it about?	How would you rate it?	Explain your rating.
From ______ to ______			Great 5 4 3 2 1 Awful	
From ______ to ______			Great 5 4 3 2 1 Awful	
From ______ to ______			Great 5 4 3 2 1 Awful	
From ______ to ______			Great 5 4 3 2 1 Awful	
From ______ to ______			Great 5 4 3 2 1 Awful	

Name ______________________________

Unit 4 Independent Reading Log

Reading Time	Title and Author	What is it about?	How would you rate it?	Explain your rating.
From ______ to ______			Great 5 4 3 2 1 Awful	
From ______ to ______			Great 5 4 3 2 1 Awful	
From ______ to ______			Great 5 4 3 2 1 Awful	
From ______ to ______			Great 5 4 3 2 1 Awful	
From ______ to ______			Great 5 4 3 2 1 Awful	

Name ______________________________

Unit 5 Independent Reading Log

Reading Time	Title and Author	What is it about?	How would you rate it?	Explain your rating.
From ______ to ______			Great 5 4 3 2 1 Awful	
From ______ to ______			Great 5 4 3 2 1 Awful	
From ______ to ______			Great 5 4 3 2 1 Awful	
From ______ to ______			Great 5 4 3 2 1 Awful	
From ______ to ______			Great 5 4 3 2 1 Awful	

Name ____________________

Unit 6 Independent Reading Log

Reading Time	Title and Author	What is it about?	How would you rate it?	Explain your rating.
From _____ to _____			Great 5 4 3 2 1 Awful	
From _____ to _____			Great 5 4 3 2 1 Awful	
From _____ to _____			Great 5 4 3 2 1 Awful	
From _____ to _____			Great 5 4 3 2 1 Awful	
From _____ to _____			Great 5 4 3 2 1 Awful	

Name ______________________________

Selection Title ______________________ **Author** ______________

Historical fiction, like realistic fiction, is a made-up story that may include both real and imaginary characters and events. Characteristics of historical fiction include the following:

- The story takes place in the past.
- The setting is a place that still exists or existed in the past.
- Authentic details about the characters and setting help the reader understand what it was like to live in that place at that time.

Directions As you read *Old Yeller,* look for examples of the time and place in which the story is set and the authentic details that make this story historical fiction. Write those examples below.

Time ______________________________

____

____

Place ______________________________

____

____

Authentic Details ______________________________

____

____

Explore the Genre

Think about the time, place, and authentic details in another story you've read that's historical fiction. What similarities and differences do you find between that story and *Old Yeller?* Write about them. Use a separate sheet of paper if you need more space.

____

____

____

____

____

Name ______________________________________

Selection Title ______________________________ **Author** ____________________

When we **infer,** we use our background knowledge with information from the text to come up with our own ideas about what we're reading. To infer, or make inferences, try the following steps.

- Think about what you already know about the topics.
- Combine what you know with information from the text to make inferences.
- Based on your inferences, think about ideas, morals, lessons, or themes in the text.

Directions As you read the selection, use your background knowledge and clues from the text to make inferences. Use the chart below to show how you made your inferences. Then write a statement that summarizes the theme, moral, or lesson from the selection.

What I Know	Information from the Text	What I Infer

Statement that summarizes the theme, moral, or lesson ______________________________

____

____

____

Name ______________________________

Selection Title ______________________ **Author** ______________________

Realistic fiction tells a story about fictional characters whose actions and situations are believable. Characteristics of realistic fiction include the following:

- The characters seem like real people that you might know.
- The setting is realistic, such as a city or town, a school, or other places you might know.
- The plot is possible and could happen in real life.

Directions As you read *Viva New Jersey,* look for examples of character, setting, and plot that make this story realistic fiction. Write those examples below.

Character ______________________________

____

____

Setting ______________________________

____

____

Plot ______________________________

____

____

Explore the Genre

Think about the characters, setting, and plot in another story you've read that's realistic fiction. What similarities and differences do you find between that story and *Viva New Jersey?* Write about them. Use a separate sheet of paper if you need more space.

____

____

____

____

____

____

Name ______________________________

Selection Title ______________________________ **Author** ____________________

Important ideas in nonfiction texts are the main ideas and details about a topic that the author wants the reader to understand. You can do the following to help identify important ideas and details as you read.

- Preview the selection and read the title, headings, and captions.
- Look for words in special type such as italics, boldface, and bulleted lists.
- Watch for signal words and phrases such as *for example* and *most important*.
- Use text features including photographs and illustrations, diagrams, charts, and maps.

Directions As you read the selection, use the chart below to write down any important ideas and details that you find. List any text features or signal words you used to locate these ideas. Use the important ideas and details to write a short summary of the selection.

Important Ideas	Details

Write a Summary ______________________________

____

____

____

Name ______________________________

Selection Title ______________________ **Author** ______________________

Good readers ask questions as they read. **Questioning** helps us monitor our comprehension and clarify anything that's confusing. Questioning also helps to make inferences, interpret the texts we read, and promote discussion. As you read, use the following questioning strategy.

- Preview the selection and think about any questions you have about the topic.
- Read with a question in mind and make notes when you find information that addresses the question.
- Write down other questions that come up as you read and look for answers in the text.
- Remember that not all questions are answered in the text. Sometimes we have to make inferences or interpretations based on the information the author provides.

Directions As you read the selection, use the chart below to write down any questions that you have about the text in the column on the left. Write down any answers you find or inferences or interpretations you make in the right-hand column.

Questions	Answers, Inferences, Interpretations

Name ______________________________

Selection Title ______________________ Author ______________

Strategic readers **monitor** their understanding of what they've read and use fix-up strategies to **clarify** understanding. Ways to monitor and clarify include the following:

- Ask questions during and after reading and summarize to check your understanding.
- Adjust your reading rate, read on, or reread the section that caused confusion.
- Visualize what you are reading.
- Use text features and illustrations to help clarify the text.

Directions As you read, write down the page numbers of places that you had trouble understanding. Then describe each fix-up strategy you used to clarify the meaning.

Where in the Text I Had Trouble: ________ ________ ________

Fix-Up Strategies I Used:

Selection Summary

Write a two- or three-sentence summary of the selection. Use a separate sheet of paper if you need more space.

Name ______________________________

Selection Title ______________________ **Author** ______________

Expository text tells about real people, objects, ideas, or events. Expository text is a type of expository nonfiction. Characteristics of expository text include the following:

- The topic provides information about the real world and people.
- The information in the text is factual.
- Selections often include text features such as diagrams, maps, charts, and graphs.

Directions As you read *The Emperor's Silent Army,* look for examples of expository text. Write those examples below.

Selection Topic ______________________________

____

____

Facts ______________________________

____

____

Text Features ______________________________

____

____

Explore the Genre

Think about another selection you've read that is expository text. What similarities and differences do you find between that selection and *The Emperor's Silent Army?* Write about them. Use a separate sheet of paper if you need more space.

____

____

____

____

____

____

Name ______________________________

Selection Title ______________________ **Author** ______________

Text structure refers to the way an author organizes a text. Cause and effect and compare and contrast are two types of text structure. Knowing how a text is structured can improve our comprehension. Here are ways to identify text structure.

- Before you read, preview the text. Make predictions; ask questions; and use titles, headings, and illustrations to try to identify the structure.
- As you read, look for language that gives clues to the organization.
- After reading, recall the organization and summarize the text.

Directions As you preview and read the selection, write down features of the text that help you identify the text structure. Remember to ask questions, use text features, and look for language clues to identify the text structure. After reading, write the name of the text structure and a brief summary of the selection.

Before Reading ______________________________

____

____

____

During Reading ______________________________

____

____

____

Text Structure/Summary ______________________________

____

____

____

____

Name ______________________

Selection Title ______________________ **Author** ______________________

Science fiction is a made-up story that usually tells about life in the future or in another world. Characteristics of science fiction include the following:

- Events and plot may be based on real laws, theories, and beliefs of science.
- Some characters and events may be fantastic and not based on scientific fact.
- Descriptions of the setting may include details about what the future or another world might be like.

Directions As you read *Good-bye to the Moon,* look for examples of real laws of science, fantastic elements such as characters and events, and details about the future or another world that make this story science fiction. Write those examples below.

Real Science ______________________

Fantastic Elements ______________________

Details of Future or Other World ______________________

Explore the Genre

Think about another story you've read that is science fiction. What similarities and differences do you find between that story and *Good-bye to the Moon?* Write about them. Use a separate sheet of paper if you need more space.

Name ___________________________________

Selection Title ______________________________ **Author** ______________________

When we **summarize,** we capture the important ideas or events of a selection in a few sentences. Good readers summarize what they've read to check understanding and improve comprehension. Keeping important ideas and events in a logical order also improves comprehension. To summarize, do the following:

- In fiction, look for the important events of the plot, including the climax.
- In nonfiction, look for the important ideas that the author presents.
- Jot notes as you read to help you summarize, keeping events in a logical order.
- Restate important pieces of information in your own words.

Directions As you read the selection, write down any important ideas or plot events. Remember to record events in a logical order. When you're finished reading, use your notes to summarize the selection.

Important Ideas or Events

____

____

____

____

Summary

____

____

____

____

Name ______________________________

Selection Title ______________________ Author ______________________

Background knowledge is what we already know about a topic. Using background knowledge can help us better understand what we're reading. Activate your background knowledge by doing the following:

- Preview the selection to find out what it's about.
- Think about what you already know about the topic.
- Connect the selection to your own world—to people, places, and events you already know.

Directions Use the KWL chart below to chart your background knowledge about the selection. List what you already know in the K column. Then list what you want to learn in the W column. After reading, list what you learned in the L column. Write a brief summary of the selection on a separate sheet of paper.

What We **K**now	What We **W**ant to Know	What We **L**earned

Name ____________________

Selection Title ____________________ **Author** ____________________

A **biography** tells the story of all or part of a real person's life, written by another person. Events in the person's life are generally told in the order that they happen. Characteristics of a biography include the following:

- The subject is part or all of the life of a real person.
- The events in the person's life are generally told in the order that they happen.
- Events are told in a third-person narration using *he, she, him,* or *her* when referring to the person.

Directions As you read *When Marian Sang,* look for examples of who the subject is, events in order, and third-person narration that make this selection a biography. Write those examples below.

Subject ____________________

Events ____________________

Third-Person Narration ____________________

Explore the Genre

Think about another selection you've read that is a biography. What similarities and differences do you find between that biography and *When Marian Sang?* Write about them. Use a separate sheet of paper if you need more space.

Name ______________________

Selection Title ______________________ **Author** ______________________

An **autobiography** is a form of literary nonfiction. Like a biography, it tells the story of all or part of a real person's life. But with an autobiography, a person tells his or her own story. Characteristics of an autobiography include the following:

- The subject is part or all of the life of a real person.
- The events in the person's life are usually told in the order that they happen.
- Events are told in the first-person point of view.

Directions As you read *Learning to Swim,* look for examples of who the subject is, events in order, and first-person narration that make this selection a biography. Write those examples below.

Subject ______________________

Events ______________________

First-Person Narration ______________________

Explore the Genre

Think about another selection you've read that is an autobiography. What similarities and differences do you find between that autobiography and *Learning to Swim?* Write about them. Use a separate sheet of paper if you need more space.

Name ______________________________

Selection Title ______________________________ **Author** ____________________

Folk tales are stories that were created by an unknown storyteller and handed down orally from generation to generation until someone wrote them down. Characteristics of folk tales include the following:

- The subject matter is often the customs or beliefs of a particular culture.
- Human and animal characters usually represent some human trait or aspect of human nature.
- Themes about human nature are expressed.

Directions As you read *Juan Verdades,* look for examples of subject matter, characters, and theme that make this story a folk tale. Write those examples below.

Subject Matter ______________________________

____

____

Characters ______________________________

____

____

Theme ______________________________

____

____

Explore the Genre

Think about another story you've read that is a folk tale. What similarities and differences do you find between that story and *Juan Verdades?* Write about them. Use a separate sheet of paper if you need more space.

____

____

____

____

____

Name ________________________________

Selection Title ______________________ **Author** ______________________

Story structure is the important parts that happen at the beginning, middle, and end of a story. To identify story structure, strategic readers do the following:

- Look for the conflict, or problem, at the beginning of the story.
- Track the action as conflict builds.
- Recognize the climax when the characters face conflict.
- Identify how the conflict gets resolved.

Directions As you read *Morning Traffic,* chart the story structure using the plot map below. When you are finished, briefly retell the story on a separate sheet of paper.

Title ______________________________________

Characters

Setting

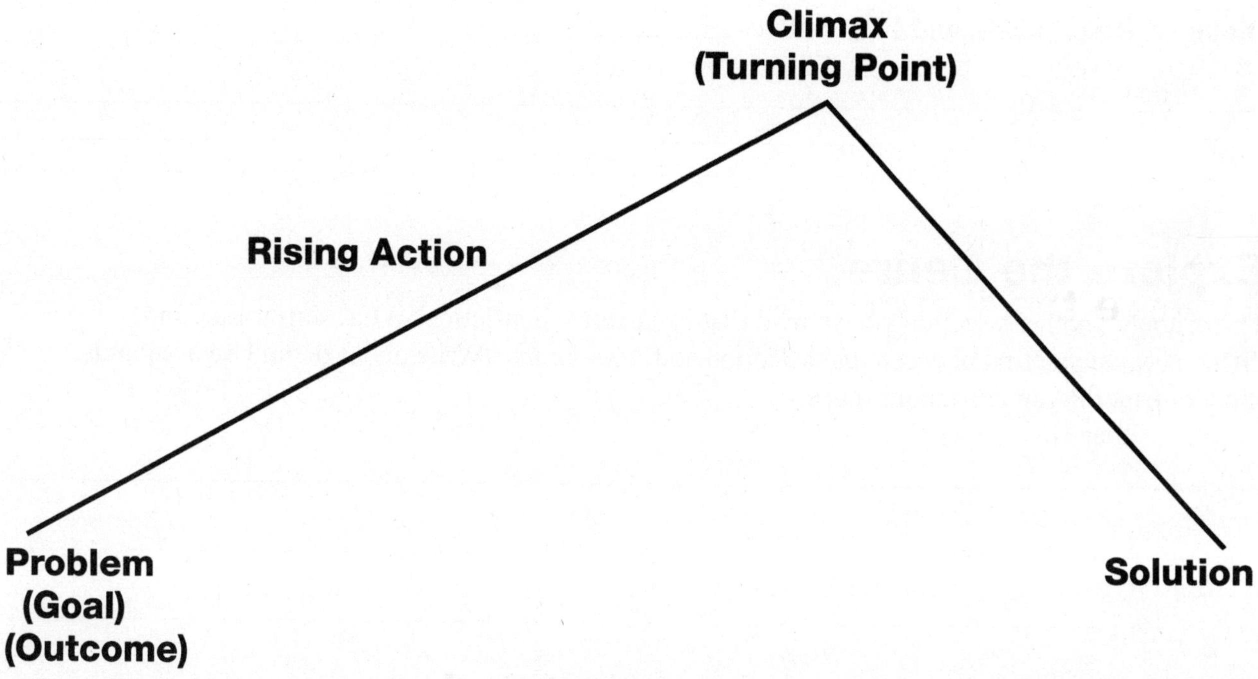

Name ________________________________

Selection Title ____________________ Author ____________________

Narrative nonfiction tells the story of a true event or events. Elements that are found in fiction may be used in narrative nonfiction as well. Characteristics of narrative nonfiction include the following:

- The plot centers around true events.
- Characters may include people who really existed at the time that the events took place.
- The story may include fiction elements such as dialogue, descriptions, and illustrations.

Directions As you read *Into the Ice,* look for examples of true events; real people; and dialogue, descriptions, and illustrations that make this selection literary nonfiction. Write those examples below.

True Events ________________________________

____

____

Real People ________________________________

____

____

Dialogue, Descriptions, and Illustrations ________________________________

____

____

Explore the Genre

Think about another selection you've read that is narrative nonfiction. What similarities and differences do you find between that selection and *Into the Ice?* Write about them. Use a separate sheet of paper if you need more space.

____

____

____

____

____

Name ______________________________

Selection Title ______________________________ **Author** ____________________

Text structure refers to the way an author organizes a text. Cause and effect and compare and contrast are two types of text structure. Knowing how a text is structured can improve our comprehension. Here are ways to identify text structure.

- Before you read, preview the text. Make predictions, ask questions, and use titles, headings, and illustrations to try to identify the structure.
- As you read, look for language that gives clues to the organization.
- After reading, recall the organization and summarize the text.

Directions As you preview and read *Chimpanzees I Love,* write down features of the text that help you identify the text structure. Remember to ask questions, use text features, and look for language clues to identify the text structure. After reading, write the name of the text structure and a brief summary of the selection.

Before Reading ______________________________

____

____

____

During Reading ______________________________

____

____

____

Text Structure/Summary ______________________________

____

____

____

____

Name ______________________________

Selection Title ______________________________ **Author** ____________________

When we **infer,** we use our background knowledge with information from the text to come up with our own ideas about what we're reading. To infer, or make inferences, try the following steps.

- Think about what you already know about the topics.
- Combine what you know with information from the text to make inferences.
- Based on your inferences, think about ideas, morals, lessons, or themes in the text.

Directions As you read *Black Frontiers,* use your background knowledge and clues from the text to make inferences. Use the chart below to show how you made your inferences. Then write a statement that summarizes the theme, moral, or lesson from the selection.

What I Know	Information from the Text	What I Infer

Statement that summarizes the theme, moral, or lesson ______________________________

____

____

____

Name ____________________

Selection Title ____________________ **Author** ____________________

When we **predict,** we tell what we think might happen in a selection. Predictions are based on our preview or what we've already read. We **set a purpose** to guide our reading. We can do the following to predict and set a purpose:

- Read the title and the author's name. Look at the illustrations and other text features.
- Think about why you're reading and set a purpose.
- Use your prior knowledge—what you already know—to make a prediction.
- As you read, check and change your prediction based on new information.

Directions Preview *Deep-Sea Danger*. Make a prediction and set a purpose for reading the selection. As you read, check your predictions and set a new purpose as necessary. When you finish reading, write a summary of the selection.

Before Reading

Make a Prediction ____________________

____

Purpose for Reading ____________________

____

During Reading

Check and Change Prediction ____________________

____

Set a New Purpose ____________________

____

After Reading

Write a Summary ____________________

____

____

____

Name ________________________________

Selection Title ________________________ **Author** ____________

A **photobiography,** like a biography, tells the story of all or part of a real person's life. In a photobiography, the author uses many photographs to help tell the story. Characteristics of a photobiography include the following:

- The subject is part or all of the life of a real person.
- The events in the person's life are usually told in the order that they happen.
- Photographs are used to help tell the story.

Directions As you read *Inventing the Future,* look for examples of who the subject is, events in order, and photographs that make this selection a photobiography. Write those examples below.

Subject ________________________________

Events ________________________________

Photographs ________________________________

Explore the Genre

Think about another selection you've read that is a biography. What similarities and differences do you find between that biography and *Inventing the Future?* Write about them. Use a separate sheet of paper if you need more space.

Name ______________________________

Selection Title ______________________ Author ______________________

Humorous fiction tells about characters in funny situations. Like realistic fiction, the characters, setting, and events are believable. Characteristics of humorous fiction include the following:

- The characters may be amusing in how they look, act, or talk.
- The setting is realistic, such as a city or town, a school, or other places you might know.
- The plot is about humorous events that are believable.

Directions As you read *The View from Saturday,* look for examples of character, setting, and plot that make this story humorous fiction. Write those examples below.

Character ______________________________

____

____

Setting ______________________________

____

____

Plot ______________________________

____

____

Explore the Genre

Think about the characters, setting, and plot in another story you've read that's humorous fiction. What similarities and differences do you find between that story and *The View from Saturday?* Write about them. Use a separate sheet of paper if you need more space.

____

____

____

____

____

Name ____________________

Selection Title ____________________ **Author** ____________________

Text structure refers to the way an author organizes a text. Cause and effect and compare and contrast are two types of text structure. Knowing how a text is structured can improve our comprehension. Here are ways to identify text structure:

- Before you read, preview the text. Make predictions; ask questions; and use titles, headings, and illustrations to try to identify the structure.
- As you read, look for language that gives clues to the organization.
- After reading, recall the organization and summarize the text

Directions As you preview and read *Harvesting Hope,* write down features of the text that help you identify the text structure. Remember to ask questions, use text features, and look for language clues to identify the text structure. After reading, write the name of the text structure and a brief summary of the selection.

Before Reading ____________________

____

____

____

During Reading ____________________

____

____

____

Text Structure/Summary ____________________

____

____

____

____

Name ______________________

Selection Title ______________________ **Author** ______________________

Myths are old stories that have been passed down through word of mouth for hundreds of years. Some myths have many different versions depending on the culture. Characteristics of myths include the following:

- The beliefs of a particular culture are reflected in the story.
- Characters are usually gods, goddesses, and humans interacting with natural forces.
- The plot often centers around events that try to explain a force of nature.

Directions As you read *The River That Went to the Sky,* look for examples of a particular culture; characters such as gods, goddesses, and humans; and events that try to explain nature that make this story a myth. Write those examples below.

Culture ______________________

____

____

Characters ______________________

____

____

Events ______________________

____

____

Explore the Genre

Think about the culture, characters, and events in another myth you've read. What similarities and differences do you find between that story and *The River That Went to the Sky?* Write about them. Use a separate sheet of paper if you need more space.

____

____

____

____

____

Name ______________________________

Selection Title ______________________________ **Author** ____________________

Background knowledge is what we already know about a topic. Using background knowledge can help us better understand what we're reading. Activate your background knowledge by doing the following:

- Preview the selection to find out what it's about.
- Think about what you already know about the topic.
- Connect the selection to your own world—to people, places, and events you already know.

Directions Use the KWL chart below to chart your background knowledge about the selection. List what you already know in the K column. Then list what you want to learn in the W column. After reading, list what you learned in the L column. Write a brief summary of the selection on a separate sheet of paper.

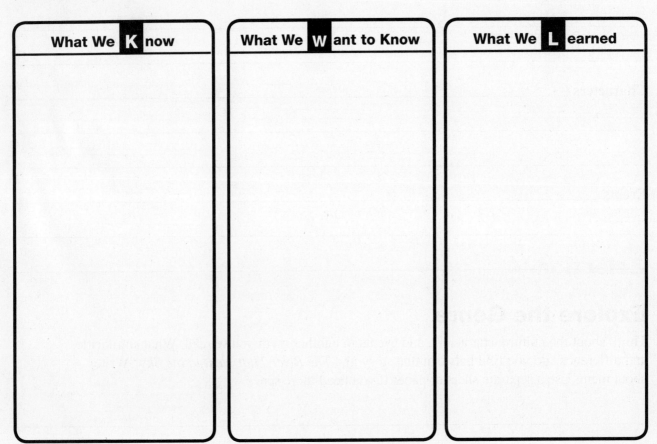

What We **K**now	What We **W**ant to Know	What We **L**earned

Name ______________________________

Selection Title ______________________ **Author** ______________

Strategic readers **monitor** their understanding of what they've read and use fix-up strategies to **clarify** understanding. Ways to monitor and clarify include the following:

- Ask questions during and after reading and summarize to check your understanding.
- Adjust your reading rate, read on, or reread the section that caused confusion.
- Visualize what you are reading.
- Use text features and illustrations to help clarify the text.

Directions As you read *Greensburg Goes Green,* write down the page numbers of places that you had trouble understanding. Then describe each fix-up strategy you used to clarify the meaning.

Where in the Text I Had Trouble: ________ ________ ________

____

Fix-Up Strategies I Used:

____

____

____

____

____

Selection Summary

Write a two- or three-sentence summary of the selection. Use a separate sheet of paper if you need more space.

____

____

____

____

Name ______________________________

Selection Title ______________________________ **Author** ____________________

Good readers ask questions as they read. **Questioning** helps us monitor our comprehension and clarify anything that's confusing. Questioning also helps to make inferences, interpret the texts we read, and promote discussion. As you read, use the following questioning strategy:

- Preview the selection and think about any questions you have about the topic.
- Read with a question in mind and make notes when you find information that addresses the question.
- Write down other questions that come up as you read and look for answers in the text.
- Remember that not all questions are answered in the text. Sometimes we have to make inferences or interpretations based on the information the author provides.

Directions As you read *Don Quixote and the Windmills,* use the chart below to write down any questions that you have about the text in the column on the left. Write down any answers you find or inferences or interpretations you make in the right-hand column.

Questions	Answers, Inferences, Interpretations

Name ______________________________

Selection Title ______________________________ Author ____________________

When we **predict,** we tell what we think might happen in a selection. Predictions are based on our preview or what we've already read. We **set a purpose** to guide our reading. We can do the following to predict and set a purpose:

- Read the title and the author's name. Look at the illustrations and other text features.
- Think about why you're reading and set a purpose.
- Use your prior knowledge—what you already know—to make a prediction.
- As you read, check and change your prediction based on new information.

Directions Preview *Ancient Greece*. Make a prediction and set a purpose for reading the selection. As you read, check your predictions and set a new purpose as necessary. When you finish reading, write a summary of the selection.

Before Reading

Make a Prediction ______________________________

____

Purpose for Reading ______________________________

____

During Reading

Check and Change Prediction ______________________________

____

Set a New Purpose ______________________________

____

After Reading

Write a Summary ______________________________

____

____

____

Name ______________________________

Selection Title ______________________________ **Author** ____________________

When we **infer,** we use our background knowledge with information from the text to come up with our own ideas about what we're reading. To infer, or make inferences, try the following steps:

- Think about what you already know about the topics.
- Combine what you know with information from the text to make inferences.
- Based on your inferences, think about ideas, morals, lessons, or themes in the text.

Directions As you read *The All-American Slurp,* use your background knowledge and clues from the text to make inferences. Use the chart below to show how you made your inferences. Then write a statement that summarizes the theme, moral, or lesson from the selection.

What I Know	Information from the Text	What I Infer

Statement that summarizes the theme, moral, or lesson ______________________________

____

____

____

Name ________________________________

Selection Title ________________________ **Author** ________________

Informational text is text that is based on factual information. Characteristics of informational text include the following:

- The topic provides information about the real world and people.
- The information in the text is factual.
- Selections often include text features such as headings, charts, illustrations, etc.

Directions As you read *The Aztec News,* look for examples of informational text. Write those examples below.

Selection Topic ________________________________

____

____

Facts ________________________________

____

____

Text Features ________________________________

____

____

Explore the Genre

Think about another selection you've read that is informational text. What similarities and differences do you find between that selection and *The Aztec News?* Write about them. Use a separate sheet of paper if you need more space.

____

____

____

____

____

____

Name ______________________________

Selection Title ______________________________ Author ______________________

We **visualize** to create pictures in our minds as we read. Creating pictures can help us better understand what we're reading. To visualize, try the following:

- Combine what you already know with details from the text to make a mental image.
- Think about the events of the story or selection. Use your five senses to create pictures and to try to put yourself in the story or selection.

Directions As you read *Where Opportunity Awaits,* use your senses to help you visualize what's happening or the information the author provides. Write down what you can see, hear, taste, smell, and touch.

See ______________________________

____

____

Hear ______________________________

____

____

Taste ______________________________

____

____

Smell ______________________________

____

____

Touch ______________________________

____

____

Name ____________________________________

Book Talk Tips

- Speak clearly.
- Make eye contact.
- Talk about a book YOU liked reading.
- Don't give away the ending.
- Talk for 2–4 minutes, sharing amusing or important information from the book.

Directions Use the talking points below to help organize your book talk.

1. What is the title of the book?
2. Who is the author?
3. What is the genre?
4. What other book has the author written?

If your book is fiction . . .

5. What is the most exciting part of this book? the plot, characters, theme? Explain why.
6. Briefly describe a setting, scene, or character from this book.

If your book is nonfiction . . .

7. What important information did you learn from this book?
8. Briefly describe an interesting part of the book.

9. Do you have a personal connection with the story or topic? Explain.
10. Explain why your listeners should read this book.

Name ______________________________

Before writing

- Help your partner brainstorm ideas for writing.
- Discuss the writing topic with your partner. Does he or she need to narrow the topic or expand it?

After the first draft

- Before you exchange papers, tell your partner what you would like him or her to look for when they read your writing.
- Using sticky notes or a piece of notebook paper, note any questions or comments you have about your partner's writing.
- Point out the information or ideas that are well written.
- Discuss any information that seems unneeded or confusing, but make sure your comments are helpful and considerate.

Revision

- Read your partner's paper out loud to listen for strengths as well as places for improvement.
- Always tell your partner what you think works well in his or her paper.
- Start with a compliment, or strength, and then offer suggestions for improvement. For example, "I liked how you ____________. What if you also ____________?"
- Remember also to look for correct spelling and grammar.

Other areas you might comment on:

- Title
- Introduction
- Conclusion
- Descriptions
- Examples
- Use of verbs, nouns, adjectives, or adverbs

Name ______________________________

Name of Writing Product ______________________________

Directions Review your final draft. Then rate yourself on a scale from 4 to 1 (4 is the highest) on each writing trait. After you fill out the chart, answer the questions.

Writing Traits	4	3	2	1
Focus/Ideas				
Organization				
Voice				
Word Choice				
Sentences				
Conventions				

1. What is the best part of this piece of writing? Why do you think so?

____

____

____

____

2. Write one thing you would change about this piece of writing if you had the chance to write it again.

____

____

____

____

Name ____________________

Setting and Plot

- The **setting** is the time and place in which a story occurs. Usually, the author tells you the setting, but sometimes you have to figure it out from clues in the story.
- The **plot,** or story line, is the sequence of events in a story. The plot usually starts with some *background,* or what the reader needs to know about the characters, setting, and situation.
- The main character or characters experience a *conflict,* or *problem,* which sets the rising action of the plot in motion.
- The setting can determine what kind of events happen in a story.

Directions Read the following passage. Then fill in the chart below with elements of the story's setting and plot.

It had rained all night long and it was still raining in the morning. Nick called his sheep dog, Jake, to help him move the sheep to the north pasture. He needed to hurry because the stream in the south pasture would soon turn to a raging river. Already, the rain had washed out a part of the main path to the north pasture, so they would have to take the forest path to get to the north pasture.

The gold and red trees along the forest path drooped under the heavy rain. The passage between the trees was muddy and slowed their progress. It would take another hour to lead the sheep to the higher ground.

Setting (Time and Place)	Plot (Series of story events)
Morning, South Pasture	**1.** All night long, it ____________________ ____________________
2. ____________________ ____________________	**3.** The rain ____________________ ____________________
4. ____________________ ____________________	**5.** The problem Nick faces is ____________________ ____________________

School + Home **Home Activity** Your child described the setting and plot in a reading passage. Choose a favorite book or film with your child and work together to describe the elements of the setting and how they affect the story's events.

Writing • Personal Narrative

Key Features of a Personal Narrative

- focuses on a real event from the writer's life
- uses the first person, "I"
- uses appropriate sensory details

Rocking and Rolling

It happened when I was eight. My cousins and I were at my grandfather's house. While the adults cooked and talked inside, we were outside, sniffing the wonderful aromas and having a blast playing tag.

There's a wall made of huge, round, gray rocks in my grandfather's yard. My cousin Leo was on top of the wall, and I was on the grass below, daring him to tag me. Suddenly, I heard a grinding, rumbling sound, and, in what seemed like seconds, my arm was pinned beneath a gigantic rock! "Arghhh!!!" I screamed, tasting rock dust. "A loose rock rolled on top of me! I can't move!"

Leo jumped down to rescue me, but the rock was too heavy. My other cousins raced to the house for help.

Within a minute, my grandfather and two uncles were standing over me. They pushed mightily, and at last the menacing rock rolled off. "Thank you!" I gulped, trying to be brave even though my arm was throbbing.

An ambulance arrived with its siren blaring, and I was off to the bustling hospital emergency room. Three hours later my bone had been set and I was ready to go home.

I wore my cast for the rest of the summer. My family and friends decorated it with colorful autographs, and I retold the exciting story—again and again—of how I broke my arm and learned to expect the unexpected!

1. Why do you think the author chose to write about this event?

____

____

2. Underline as many examples of the author's use of sensory details as you can find.

Name ____________________

Vocabulary

Directions Choose the word from the box that best matches each definition. Write the word on the line shown to the left.

Check the Words You Know
___lunging
___nub
___romping
___rowdy
___slung
___speckled

____________ **1.** a lump or small piece

____________ **2.** moving forward suddenly

____________ **3.** covered with small spots

____________ **4.** thrown, cast, or hurled

____________ **5.** rough and disorderly

Directions Choose the word from the box that best completes each sentence below. Write the word on the line shown to the left.

____________ **6.** At the end of the school day, Susan ____ her books into her locker.

____________ **7.** The bird's nest held three pale, ____ eggs.

____________ **8.** The boys liked ____ around during recess.

____________ **9.** The ____ neighborhood kids ran down the block, shouting and laughing.

____________ **10.** The pencil eraser was worn down to a ____.

Write a Journal Entry

On a separate sheet of paper write a journal entry you might make after you hiked in the woods and saw a bear. Use as many vocabulary words as you can.

School + Home **Home Activity** Your child identified and used vocabulary words from *Old Yeller.* Work with your child to identify familiar people or things to whom each word might be applied.

Four Kinds of Sentences

A **declarative sentence**, or statement, tells something. It ends with a period.

Joey is reading the autobiography of his favorite baseball player.

An **interrogative sentence** asks a question. It ends with a question mark.

Have you ever written a story about your life?

An **imperative sentence** gives a command or makes a request. It ends with a period. *You* is the understood subject.

Keep a journal of your daily adventures.

An **exclamatory sentence** shows strong feeling. It ends with an exclamation mark.

How funny my autobiography would be!

An **interjection** is a word or a group of words that expresses strong feeling. It is not a complete sentence.

Wow! Hooray! Ouch!

Directions Write *D* if the sentence is declarative. Write *IN* if the sentence is interrogative. Write *IM* if the sentence is imperative. Write *E* if the sentence is exclamatory.

1. Many famous people have pets. ________

2. What is a pet license? ________

3. Find the groomer's number in the phone book. ________

4. You can adopt a pet from an animal shelter. ________

5. Wow! I never knew Spot could run so fast! ________

Directions Put a period, a question mark, or an exclamation mark at the end of each sentence to show what kind of sentence it is.

6. Have you taken the dog for a walk ________

7. My mom plans to surprise my dad with a new puppy ________

8. Oh, no! The lizard escaped from its tank ________

9. Megan's baby sister is allergic to dogs and cats ________

10. How did your kitten climb onto our roof ________

School + Home **Home Activity** Your child learned about the four different kinds of sentences. Have your child name the four kinds of sentences and write an example of each one.

Name ______________________

Adding *-ed* and *-ing*

Spelling Words				
answered	answering	traveled	traveling	chopped
chopping	qualified	qualifying	panicked	panicking
interfered	interfering	omitted	omitting	magnified
magnifying	patrolled	patrolling	skied	skiing

Words in Context Write the list word that completes each sentence.

1. When I heard the warnings about the tornado, I almost ___. 1. ____________
2. Charlie spent the whole day ___ wood. 2. ____________
3. I ___ the phone as soon as it started ringing. 3. ____________
4. Ellen hopes she will be ___ for the state finals in the spelling bee. 4. ____________
5. The explorers ___ the world in search of the lost ancient city. 5. ____________
6. The karate expert ___ through a board with his bare hand. 6. ____________
7. Stella used a ___ glass to take a closer look at the ant. 7. ____________
8. I wish my sister would stop ___ with my studies. 8. ____________
9. Juan has been on the slopes taking ___ lessons. 9. ____________
10. The helicopter ___ the area, looking for lost hikers. 10. ____________
11. This summer my family will be ___ to California by car. 11. ____________
12. Lia realized she was ___ some important facts from her report. 12. ____________

Word Groups Write the list word that fits into each group.

13. upsetting, distressing, ___ 13. ____________
14. responding, replying, ___ 14. ____________
15. competent, prepared, ___ 15. ____________
16. enhanced, enlarged, ___ 16. ____________
17. disrupted, disturbed, ___ 17. ____________
18. skated, slid, ___ 18. ____________
19. guarding, inspecting, ___ 19. ____________
20. left out, skipped, ___ 20. ____________

School + Home

Home Activity Your child used words with *-ed* and *-ing* endings. Say a list word and have your child use it in a sentence.

Outline

Title ______________________

A. ______________________

1. ______________________
2. ______________________
3. ______________________

B. ______________________

1. ______________________
2. ______________________
3. ______________________

C. ______________________

1. ______________________
2. ______________________
3. ______________________

Name ____________________

Vocabulary • Synonyms

- A **synonym** is a word that means the same or almost the same as another word.

Directions Read the following passage. Circle the synonym that *best* replaces each **boldfaced** word or phrase.

If you ask an American to imagine a bear, the black bear is almost certainly the one they will picture. Black bears are not seen **much** in American forests. Since Colonial times, their numbers have been **shrinking** because humans have hunted them and moved into their **land.** But it is still a good idea to avoid them.

Films often show bear cubs romping in the woods. However, brown bears are much more dangerous than they are **cute.** They eat everything from grass to animals and are very **protective** toward their **young.** Food left lying around campsites may attract them.

If you do see a bear, **moving** away is not a good idea. Any sudden movement will cause the bear to chase you. Park rangers often recommend loud singing or **rowdy talk** while you are hiking. Bears avoid humans when they can. If a bear hears you coming, it will **vanish** into the woods before you arrive.

1. **much:**	often	highly	considerably
2. **shrinking:**	hiding	dwindling	shriveling
3. **land:**	nation	property	territory
4. **cute:**	attractive	adorable	pretty
5. **protective:**	caring	anxious	defensive
6. **young:**	babies	offspring	children
7. **moving:**	relocating	fleeing	stirring
8. **rowdy:**	noisy	rude	disorderly
9. **talk:**	conversation	lecture	gossip
10. **vanish:**	disappear	fade	evaporate

School + Home

Home Activity Your child identified synonyms that could replace words in a passage. Read a newspaper or magazine article with your child. Find two or three words that could be replaced with synonyms. Have your child name the synonyms.

Name____

Graphic Organizer

- **Graphic organizers** are story maps, semantic maps, pictorial maps, webs, graphs, frames, charts, time lines, and other devices that help you to view and construct relationships among events, concepts, and words.

Directions Complete the graphic organizer to understand the setting of a story by using the following information.

The story you read is set in a log cabin in the 1800s. A fireplace is used for heat and a cast iron wood stove for cooking. The furniture includes a straw bed and a table with four chairs.

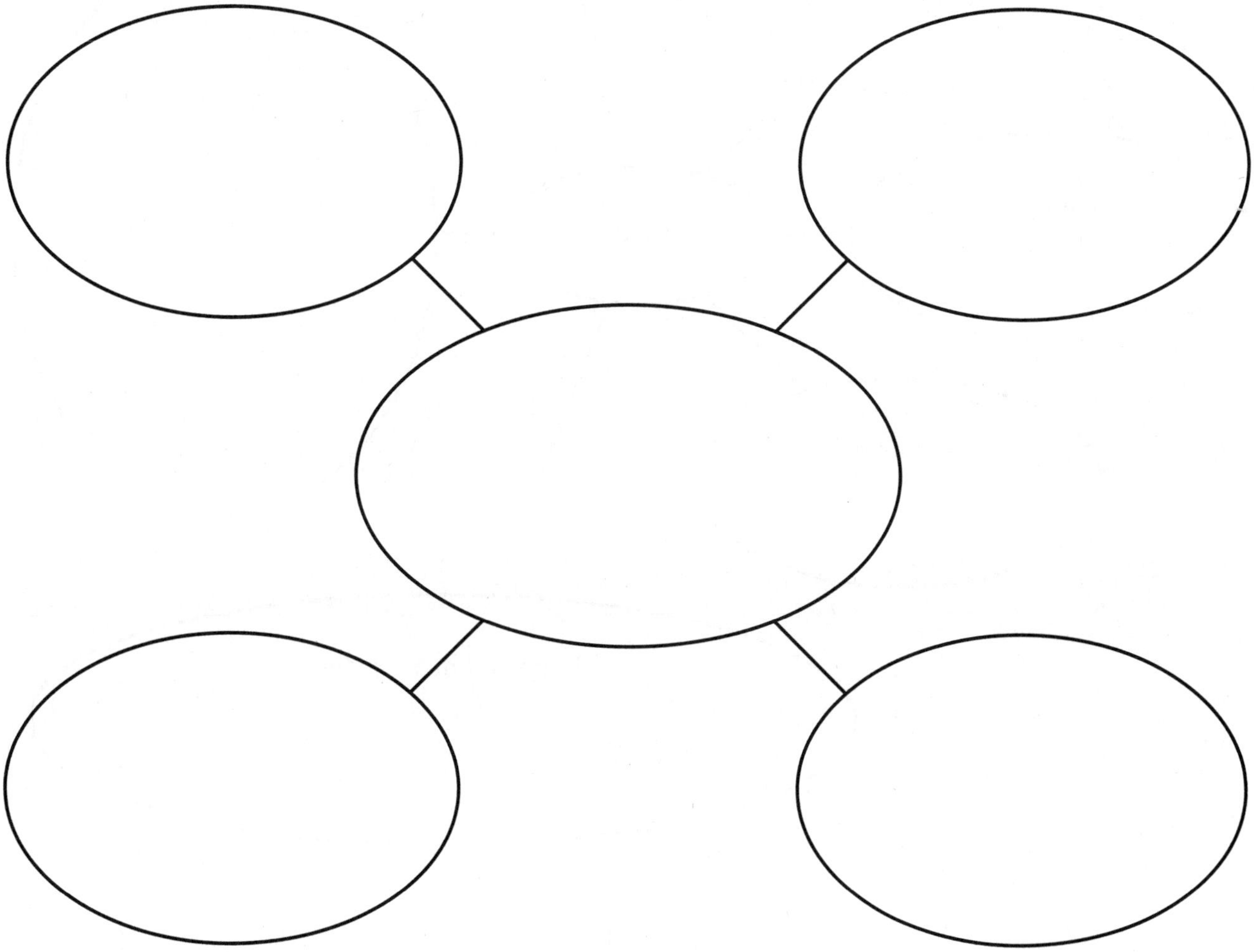

Name ____

Directions Fill in this graphic organizer with information about the vocabulary word ***speckled.***

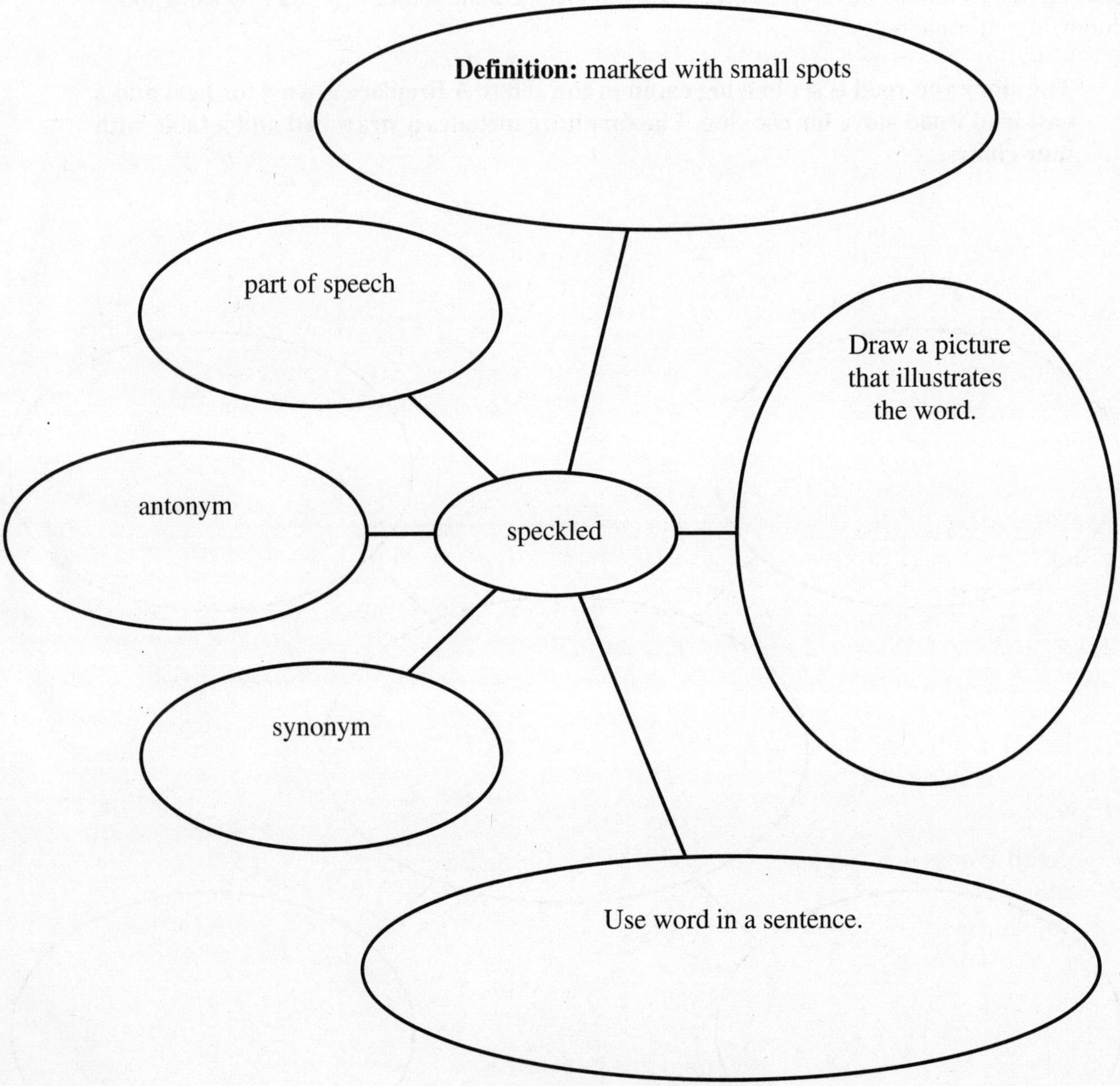

Home Activity Your child learned about using graphic organizers as a way to organize and understand information. Read a story with your child and create a graphic organizer to help him or her visualize and understand the setting or characters of the story.

Name ______________________________

Adding *-ed* and *-ing*

Proofread a Report Circle five words in this report that are spelled incorrectly. Write them correctly on the lines. Find a sentence with improper capitalization. Write it correctly on the line.

Spelling Words

answered
answering
traveled
traveling
chopped
chopping
qualified
qualifying
panicked
panicking
interfered
interfering
omitted
omitting
magnified
magnifying
patrolled
patrolling
skied
skiing

Frequently Misspelled Words

grabbed
swimming

Hybrid Cars

Some people think the efficiency of hybrid cars has been magnified. A hybrid car uses more than one source of energy while travelling. It combines a gasoline engine with a rechargeable electric battery.

Because a hybrid uses electricity for extra power, its gas engine is smaller and lighter. When stopped at a red light, the battery takes over, omiting use of the engines.

Some people think the efficiency of hybrid cars has been magnifyed. however because, they get better gas mileage, they save fuel. Hybrid cars give off fewer exhaust fumes, which avoids interferring with our air quality. This is one way technology is answerring our pollution problems.

1. ______________ 2. ______________

3. ______________ 4. ______________

5. ______________

6. ____

____

Proofread Words Circle the word in each pair that is spelled correctly. Write the word.

7. skiing	skeing	**7.**	______________
8. patroled	patrolled	**8.**	______________
9. interfered	interferred	**9.**	______________
10. chopping	choping	**10.**	______________
11. travled	traveled	**11.**	______________
12. magnifying	magnifing	**12.**	______________

School + Home **Home Activity** Your child identified misspelled words with *-ed* and *-ing* endings. Ask your child to spell the list words he or she did not write when answering the questions on this page.

Name ____________________

Four Kinds of Sentences

Directions Read the passage. Then read each question. Circle the letter of the correct answer.

Looking for a Pet?

(1) Many people consider owning a pet at some time in their lives! (2) Dogs and cats are generally considered the most sociable animals. (3) They usually can be trained to live happily with children, and with other animals. (4) When choosing a pet, a family should consider how much living space they have? (5) Will this animal live comfortably in their house? (6) Families must also decide whether they can afford to pay the food and medical expenses for their pet. (7) Many exotic animals require considerably more care than cats and dogs. (8) Useful information about a wide variety of animals can be researched on the Internet.

1 What change, if any, should be made in sentence 1?

A Change the exclamation point to a question mark

B Change the exclamation point to a period

C Change ***Many people*** to **Many People**

D Make no change

2 What change, if any, should be made in sentence 3?

A Remove the comma

B Change ***can be*** to **were**

C Change the period to a question mark

D Make no change

3 What change, if any, should be made in sentence 4?

A Change ***When*** to **when**

B Remove the comma

C Change the question mark to a period

D Make no change

4 What change, if any, should be made in sentence 6?

A Change the period to a question mark

B Change ***can afford*** to **afforded**

C Remove ***must***

D Make no change

5 What type of sentence is sentence 8?

A Interrogative sentence

B Declarative sentence

C Imperative sentence

D Exclamatory sentence

School + Home

Home Activity Your child prepared for taking tests on kinds of sentences. With your child, look through a newspaper or magazine article and find examples of different kinds of sentences.

Name ______________________________

Character and Theme

- **Characters** are the people or animals who take part in the events of a story.
- You can understand the **characters** by examining their words and actions and the way other characters act toward them.
- The **theme** is the main idea or central meaning that the author wants you to learn. The theme may be stated directly in the text, but usually the reader has to figure it out. The theme may be thought of as a broad one- or two-word concept, or as a complete one-sentence statement.

Directions Read the following passage. Then fill in the chart below with elements of the story's characters and theme.

Margie dreamed of playing for the Olympic softball team someday. Her brother hid when she called him because she always wanted him to play catch with her. If no one was around to play with her, she would throw the ball up and catch it or hit it by herself. Margie's dad pitched to her whenever he had time. As she cooked dinner every night, her mom looked through the kitchen window and watched Margie play ball in the backyard.

Margie	Brief story summary	Theme
1. What word describes Margie?	4.	5.
2. What is Margie's goal?		
3. How does Margie try to reach her goal?		

Home Activity Your child read a passage and identified the theme and details about the main character. Describe the personality of someone you both know and ask your child to identify this person.

Name ______________________________

Writing • Thank-You Letter

Key Features of a Thank-You Letter

- begins with a greeting
- expresses thanks
- includes personal details
- ends with a closing

Dear Uncle Jack,

I want to thank you for your birthday gift of tennis lessons. My game has gotten so much better and I enjoyed spending time with you those four Saturday afternoons.

You are a natural teacher. Your calm manner helped me get over my initial nervousness. Your endless patience allowed me to take as much time as I needed to learn to hit the ball. And your sense of humor helped me remember not to take things too seriously. You reminded me that tennis is a game and that I should be having fun.

And did I learn the value of hard work! You encouraged me to practice hitting tennis balls a few times a week on my own. When I did that, it definitely paid off. My friends Leslie and Becca often practiced with me. They benefited from my lessons because I shared your tips with them. They thank you, too!

This was one of the best birthday gifts I've ever received. I hope that you can still make time to play tennis with me. You always say that I'd get better by playing with better players. And you're the best!

Your grateful niece,
Abby

1. Who is writing this letter to Uncle Jack?

____

____

2. What is Uncle Jack being thanked for?

____

____

____

Vocabulary

Directions Choose the word from the box that best matches each definition. Write the word on the line shown to the left.

Check the Words You Know
___apparently
___fixtures
___flimsy
___incident
___subscribe
___survive

________________ **1.** to continue to exist; remain alive

________________ **2.** things put in place to stay

________________ **3.** to give your consent or approval; agree

________________ **4.** easily torn or broken

________________ **5.** something that happens

Directions Choose the word from the box that best completes each sentence. Write the word on the line shown to the left.

________________ **6.** His ____ hat fell apart the first time he wore it.

________________ **7.** Maddie reported the ____ to the principal.

________________ **8.** After my brother finished the sixth grade, he told me I would ____ it too.

________________ **9.** The bathroom's ____ needed to be cleaned.

________________ **10.** The janitor had ____ fixed the window in the classroom because the room was now warm.

Write a Scene from a Play

On a separate sheet of paper write a scene from a play about a police officer. Your scene may involve your main character talking with members of the community or with other officers. Use as many vocabulary words from this week as you can.

School + Home **Home Activity** Your child identified and used vocabulary words from *Mother Fletcher's Gift.* Write a story with your child including as many of the vocabulary words as possible.

Name ______________________________

Subjects and Predicates

A sentence must have both a subject and a predicate. The **subject** is the part of the sentence that tells whom or what the sentence is about. All the words in the subject are the **complete subject**. The most important word in the complete subject is the **simple subject**. A simple subject can be more than one word, such as *Officer Wagner*.

Many police officers are working hard to protect our city. The simple subject is *officers*.

The **predicate** is the part of a sentence that tells what the subject is or does. All the words in the predicate are the **complete predicate**. The most important word in the predicate is the **simple predicate**, or verb. A simple predicate can be more than one word, such as *has worked*.

Many hard-working police officers protect our city. The simple predicate is *protect*.

A **fragment** is a group of words that lacks a subject or a predicate.

The police station in our neighborhood. This fragment lacks a predicate.

A **run-on** is two or more complete sentences run together.

The police station is on Green Street it is next to the library.
Officers sometimes patrol the area on foot, we feel safe.

Directions Draw a line between the complete subject and the complete predicate in each sentence.

1. Everyone in our neighborhood knows Officer Wagner.
2. Mr. Clement complained about damage to his grocery store.
3. Officer Wagner caught the vandals in one day!
4. A lost kitten was found by the thoughtful police officer.

Directions Underline the simple subject and circle the simple predicate.

5. Many people will visit one another on holidays.
6. Grandpa Johnson is cooking a giant turkey for the whole family.
7. Holidays are a special time for our family.
8. Mrs. Sanders gives food to the needy.

Directions Write *F* after fragments. Write *R* after run-ons. Write *S* after sentences.

9. Helping others. ________
10. Many ways to do that. ________
11. Mr. Smith cleans up garbage in the park. ________
12. You can clean up garbage around the neighborhood you can recycle too. ________

School + Home

Home Activity Your child learned about subjects and predicates. Have your child write several sentences describing your neighborhood. Ask your child to circle the complete subject and the complete predicate in each sentence.

Vocabulary • Greek and Latin Roots

- Many words in English are based on Latin and Greek words. Recognizing a word's root will help you figure out its meaning.
- For example, the word *vivid* contains the root *viv-*, from the Latin word *vivere,* meaning "to live." *Scribe* is in the Latin word *scribere,* meaning "to write." *Appear* comes from *apparere,* the Latin word meaning "to come into view."

Directions Read the following passage. Then answer the questions below. Look for root words as you read.

Kiran was reading an article in the local magazine. Apparently, some new students from other countries at a local school did not yet speak English well. A group of students at the school worked with their teachers to put together a program to help these new students survive the first few months of school. It wasn't a flimsy program either. A lot of work was required of both groups of students. They were all pleased with the program's progress. It went forward without incident. After reading the article, Kiran hoped programs like this would become fixtures at the school. She also decided to subscribe to the magazine.

1. What does *apparently* mean?

____

2. The Latin word *subscribere* means "to write beneath," as when you sign your name to the bottom of a document. How does this help explain the meaning of the word *subscribe* in the passage?

____

____

3. What does *survive* mean in the passage?

____

4. What does *fixtures* mean in this passage?

____

5. Write two other words with Latin or Greek roots. Tell what each means, and then use them in sentences.

____

____

Home Activity Your child used context clues and root words to understand new words in a passage. Show your child some words from a newspaper or magazine that have root words. Ask your child to identify the root word and look up its definition.

Name ______________________________

Thesaurus

- A **thesaurus** is a kind of dictionary that lists **synonyms** (words with the same or similar meanings), **antonyms** (words with opposite meanings), and other related words. Because not all synonyms have exactly the same meaning, you should check their meanings in a dictionary.
- Entry words are arranged in alphabetical order. Parts of speech are listed to show how an entry word is used. If an entry word has more than one meaning, a thesaurus provides synonyms for each meaning.
- Sometimes a thesaurus includes sentences to illustrate the meanings of synonyms.
- One type of thesaurus provides an index in which you can look up the word for which you want synonyms.

Directions Read the following entry from a thesaurus. Then answer the questions below.

> **survive** (v) **1. endure:** live on, persist, continue, last, exist, remain: *Some holiday customs from 100 years ago survive to this day.* **2. live through:** come through alive, stay alive: *Because they were wearing seat belts, the passengers were able to survive the accident.* (ant) perish, disappear, succumb to, die from.

1. Would the entry above appear before or after the entry for the word *subscribe*? Explain.

____

____

____

2. List two synonyms for the first meaning of *survive*.

____

3. List two synonyms for the second meaning of the word *survive*.

____

4. How would you describe the difference between the first group of synonyms and the second group?

____

____

____

5. List two antonyms for the word *survive*.

____

____

Directions Read the following thesaurus entry. Then answer the questions below.

> **flimsy** (adj) **1. thin:** slight, frail, fragile, delicate, diaphanous, sheer, filmy, gossamer, shoddy, ill-made, jerry-built, insubstantial: *This old shirt has grown too flimsy to wear.* **2. weak:** feeble, inadequate, poor, worthless, trivial, petty, superficial, shallow: *The suspect provided only a flimsy alibi.* (ant) sturdy, strong, well-made, sound, substantial, solid.

6. How many synonyms for *flimsy* appear on this page? What part of speech are they?

____

7. How would you describe the difference between the first group of synonyms and the second group?

____

____

____

8. Which numbered list of synonyms would you use for *flimsy* as it is used in this sentence: "The girl's shoelaces had grown worn and flimsy." Why?

____

____

____

9. Which list would you use for *flimsy* as it is used in this sentence: "The judge ruled that the evidence was too flimsy to send the man to jail." Why?

____

____

____

10. Which antonyms would be good choices to use in a sentence about a shirt that was *not* flimsy? Why?

____

____

____

____

School + Home **Home Activity** Your child learned about using a thesaurus as a resource. Look at a thesaurus together. Ask your child to locate several entries. Then ask him or her to find a synonym for each of these words.

Name ______________________________

Short Vowels

Proofread a Letter Circle six words in this letter that are spelled incorrectly. Write them correctly. Find a sentence with improper punctuation. Write it correctly on the line.

Dear Editor,
I'm sorry, "but" I have to disagree with your writer's review, of the recent concert. He wrote that the show wasn't worth seeing. In my honest opinion, the show was fantastack. The fake cannan explosion at the end was great, the backdrop of a huge ancient palice was beautiful, and the music was the best. At the end of the concert we expressed are appreciation with loud cheers. In all honisty, I think your writer should modafy his review.

1. ____________ 2. ____________

3. ____________ 4. ____________

5. ____________ 6. ____________

7. ____

____

Spelling Words

damage
gentle
injury
palace
cottage
honesty
mustard
legend
clumsy
message

modify
ruffle
glimpse
strict
dungeon
fender
fantastic
dignity
property
cannon

Proofread Words Circle the word in each group that is spelled correctly. Write the word.

8.	dungin	dungun	dungeon	dungen	8. ____________
9.	damage	damege	damige	dammage	9. ____________
10.	mustird	mustard	musterd	moustard	10. ____________
11.	message	messege	messige	messidge	11. ____________
12.	gentel	jentle	gentle	gentell	12. ____________
13.	dignity	dygnity	dignty	dignety	13. ____________
14.	proprty	propertie	proparty	property	14. ____________
15.	glympse	glimps	glimpse	glimpce	15. ____________
16.	fender	finder	fendir	fendere	16. ____________

Frequently Misspelled Words

our
we're

School + Home **Home Activity** Your child identified misspelled words with short vowels. Say a list word and ask your child to use it in a sentence.

Subjects and Predicates

Directions Read the passage. Then read each question. Circle the letter of the correct answer.

Safety First

(1) The Hillsdale Police Department provides important bicycle safety programs for students of all ages. (2) Friendly police officers give presentations to each grade in the elementary schools. (3) The youngest children learn about basic bicycle safety. (4) They learn to make a habit of wearing a bicycle helmet. (5) Older students study the rules of the road. (6) They learn to obey traffic signs and signals. (7) Members of the Parents' Council set up small traffic courses on the school parking lots. (8) Children on bikes (9) The mayor of Hillsdale gave the Police Department a major award for service to the schools.

1 What is the complete subject of sentence 1?

A Hillsdale
B bicycle safety programs
C Police Department
D The Hillsdale Police Department

2 What is the complete predicate of sentence 3?

A learn
B learn about
C learn about basic bicycle safety
D basic bicycle safety

3 What is the complete subject of sentence 7?

A Parents' Council
B Members of the Parents' Council
C Members
D set up small traffic courses

4 How can you best describe sentence 8?

A Run-on sentence
B Has a complete subject
C Has a subject and a predicate
D Sentence fragment

5 What is the complete predicate of sentence 9?

A of Hillsdale
B gave the Police Department a major award for service to the schools
C a major award for service to the schools
D gave

School + Home

Home Activity Your child prepared for taking tests on subjects and predicates. Find five sentences in a magazine article. Ask your child to underline the complete subject and circle the complete predicate in each sentence.

Name____

Compare and Contrast

- To **compare and contrast** is to tell how two or more things are alike and how they are different.

Directions Read the following passage. Then complete the diagram by listing Jenny's and Elena's similarities in the intersection of the circles and their differences on the outsides.

Jenny met Elena at dance class at the local community center. Although Jenny was two years older than Elena, they were in the same dance class because they were both beginners. Jenny was only taking the class because her mother made her take it. Her mother hoped Jenny would meet people and make some friends. They had just moved into the neighborhood three weeks ago.

On the other hand, Elena loved to dance and dreamed of becoming a dancer. She had finally convinced her mother to let her take dance lessons after begging her for months. On the first day of class, both Jenny and Elena were nervous. Now, after three weeks, they were pleased with their class and looked forward to seeing each other every week.

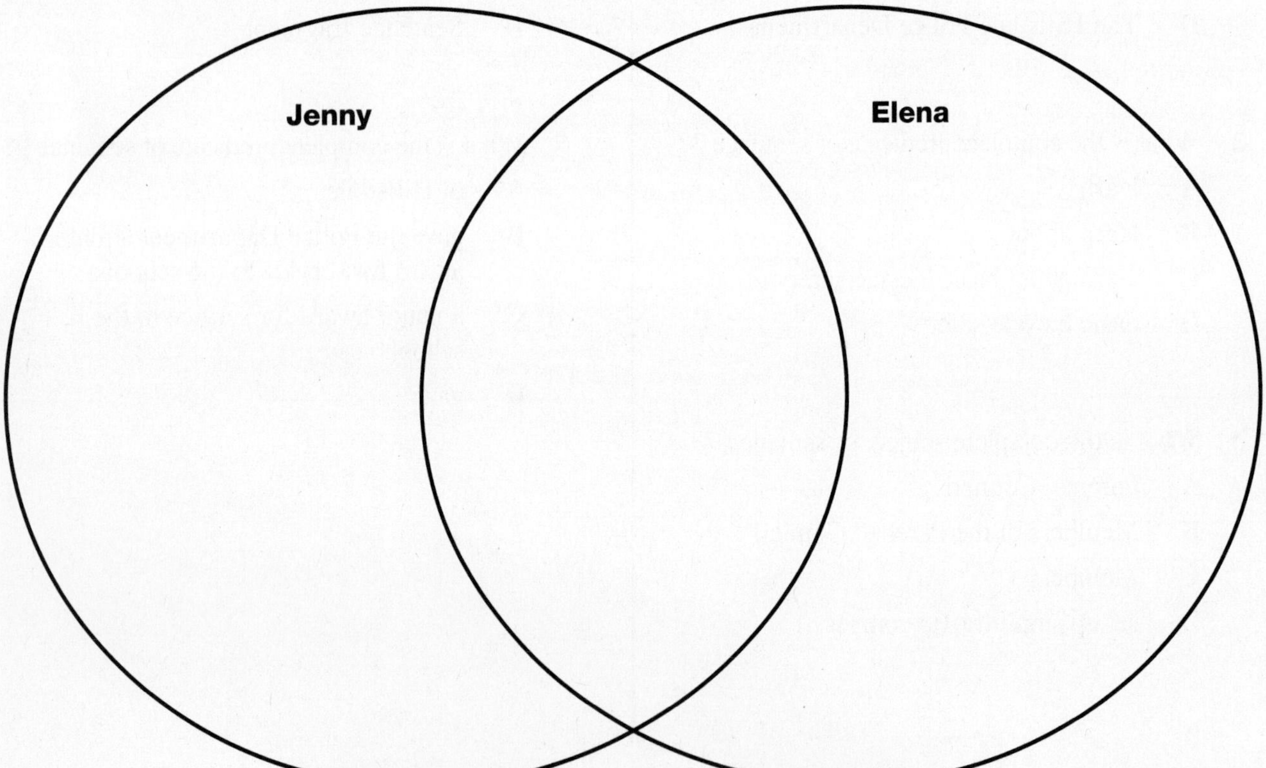

Home Activity Your child identified the similarities and differences between two characters in a short passage. Read about two animals in an encyclopedia or other book and have your child identify the similarities and differences between the two animals.

Writing • Poem

Key Features of a Poem

- uses verse to communicate ideas
- may use poetic techniques, such as rhyme or sound patterns
- includes carefully chosen words to create a strong effect

An Autumn Day When I Was Ten

I raked the leaves into a mountain of yellow and red.
With no cloud in the sky and the sun shining,
I lay on the soft peak like a climber going to bed.

Then I swish and shuffle fast and furious with my feet,
The leaves crackle and crunch like brown burnt paper.
Dizzy, I dance on the leaves until I feel weak and beat.

Now, fiery, bright sun explodes through maple, oak, and pine.
Leaves float down from their homes on long branches,
Soon to be part of this golden mountain of mine.

1. List three examples of alliteration used in the poem.

____

____

____

2. What words in the poem create a strong effect?

____

3. What is an example of assonance used in the poem?

____

Name____

Vocabulary

Directions Choose the word from the box that best matches each definition. Write the word on the line.

Check the Words You Know
___corridors
___destination
___groping
___menacing
___mongrel
___persisted
___pleas

______________________ **1.** long hallways

______________________ **2.** requests or appeals

______________________ **3.** threatening

______________________ **4.** the place to which one is going

______________________ **5.** an animal of mixed breed

Directions Choose the word from the box that best fills in the blanks.

It was nearly midnight, and Paul was **6.** ______________________ through the darkness along a path through the campground. He **7.** ______________________ in his idea of scaring his friends even though it was late. The large tent at the outskirts of the campground was his **8.** ______________________. His **9.** ______________________ growl echoed off the nearby boulders. When he heard his friends' **10.** ______________________ for help, he knew he had succeeded.

Write a Newspaper Article

On a separate sheet of paper write a newspaper article about a lost dog that finds its way home after several months of travel. Use as many of the vocabulary words as you can.

School + Home **Home Activity** Your child identified and used vocabulary words from *Viva New Jersey.* Make up a story with your child about a mongrel dog. Use as many of the vocabulary words as you can.

Name ______________________________

Independent and Dependent Clauses

An **independent clause** has a subject and verb and can stand alone as a complete sentence. A **dependent clause** has a subject and a verb but cannot stand alone as a complete sentence. In the following sentences, the independent clause is underlined once; the dependent clause is underlined twice. The dependent clause is followed by a comma when it comes before the independent clause.

Lucinda took the dog home because she was lonely.

Because she was lonely, Lucinda took the dog home.

Directions Write *IC* after each independent clause and *DC* after each dependent clause.

1. Because she was friendly. _______
2. Lucinda ran to the basement and found it empty. _______
3. Jan bathed Shadow in the backyard. _______
4. When the power went out. _______
5. After they crossed the Mississippi River. _______
6. If Carmen had not seen it. _______
7. Tenants mingled outside their apartments. _______
8. The boys won the baseball game. _______
9. As she called from the window. _______
10. They were eating dinner. _______

Directions Underline the independent clause and circle the dependent clause in each sentence.

11. Because the dog was abandoned, Lucinda had to take care of him.
12. The dog caused problems when it ran away.
13. Although she was shy, Lucinda talked to Ashley.
14. While Lucinda was gone, her parents almost called the police.
15. Ashley read many books because she wanted to be a writer.

School + Home **Home Activity** Your child learned about independent and dependent clauses. Have your child tell you what independent and dependent clauses are and give you an example of each.

Name ______________________________

Vowel Sounds with *r*

Spelling Words				
porch	servant	shore	disturb	market
margin	worth	purchase	kernel	perhaps
ignore	concern	attorney	barge	detergent
corridor	ornament	artistic	particle	nervous

Definitions Write the list word that matches the definition.

1. a lawyer 1. __________
2. a small piece or bit of something 2. __________
3. a type of soap 3. __________
4. to pay no attention to something 4. __________
5. creative and interested in various art forms 5. __________
6. to buy something 6. __________
7. area where water meets land 7. __________
8. a type of boat used to haul cargo 8. __________
9. a hallway 9. __________
10. monetary or other value 10. __________
11. a seed or piece of grain 11. __________
12. to bother or annoy 12. __________
13. a large, open place to buy things 13. __________
14. another word for *maybe* 14. __________
15. a decorative item 15. __________
16. open structure on the front or side of a house 16. __________

Antonyms Write the list word that is the opposite of each word.

17. calm 17. __________
18. indifference 18. __________
19. center 19. __________
20. master 20. __________

School + Home **Home Activity** Your child wrote words with vowel sounds with *r*. Say a list word and ask your child how it is different from its antonym.

Name ______________________________

Three-Column Chart

Name ____________________

Vocabulary • Unfamiliar Words

- When you are reading and see an unfamiliar word, use **context clues**, or words around the unfamiliar word, to figure out its meaning.
- Context clues include definitions, explanations, and synonyms.

Directions Read the following passage about dogs. Then answer the questions below. Look for context clues as you read.

Walking down one of her usual streets, Officer Laura heard the whimpering pleas of a puppy. She looked around and realized the puppy had fallen into a storm drain. She reached down but found that she could not reach down far enough. Officer Laura persisted and kept groping for the puppy, but it was just out of reach.

She called the fire department for more help. When the firefighters arrived, they lowered a special hook with a looped rope to lift the puppy. The puppy did not like the rope, and everyone heard its menacing growl. They carefully worked the rope around the puppy, and it was finally lifted to safety.

The mongrel pup was wet and dirty and looked like a cross between a cat and a poodle! Officer Laura laughed at the sight. She held the puppy up to show the crowd who had gathered to watch. The crowd applauded and continued on to their final destinations. Officer Laura and the puppy walked together down the street. Officer Laura realized she had found a new partner.

1. What are *pleas?* What sound did this puppy make?

____

2. What does *persisted* mean? What clues help you to determine the meaning?

____

3. What does *groping* mean? What clues help you to determine the meaning?

____

4. What does *mongrel* mean? What clues help you to determine the meaning?

____

____

5. What word in the passage is a synonym for *threatening?*

____

School + Home **Home Activity** Your child identified and used context clues to understand new words in a short passage. Work with your child to identify unfamiliar words in an encyclopedia article about dogs.

Name ______________________________

Magazine/Periodical

- **Magazines** contain an **index**, which is much like a table of contents. The index is usually in the first few pages.
- Many magazines also have recurring **sections** devoted to certain subjects (news, entertainment, fashion, sports, or finance, for example).
- Magazines present information by order of interest and present important articles of high interest first. Article titles are like chapter titles, letting readers know what they are about. Most magazine articles follow the five W's and H format. A reader learns the Who? What? When? Where? Why? and How? in the first few paragraphs.

Directions Use this index from a news magazine to answer the questions below.

1. What are the titles of the three main sections?

____

2. What are the titles of the two articles in the NATION section?

____

____

3. On what page is the article about car leases?

____

4. What is the title of the article in the BUSINESS section?

____

5. The YOUR TIME section contains two articles. What are their titles?

____

Name______________________________

Directions Read this article from a news magazine. Then answer the questions below.

Village at Risk

Shishmaref is melting into the ocean. Since the mid-1970s, this Inupiaq village, perched on a slender barrier island 625 miles north of Anchorage, has lost half its coastline. As Alaska's climate warms, the permafrost beneath Shishmaref's beaches is thawing, and the sea ice is thinning, leaving its 600 residents increasingly vulnerable to violent storms. One house has collapsed, and eighteen others had to be moved to higher ground, along with the town's bulk fuel tanks. Giant waves have washed away the school playground and destroyed $100,000 worth of boats, hunting gear, and fish-drying racks. The remnants of multimillion-dollar sea walls, broken up by the tides, litter the beach. "It's scary," says a village official. "Every year we agonize that the next storm will wipe us out."

6. **Who** is this article about?

____

____

7. **What** is this article about?

____

____

8. **Where** does this take place?

____

9. **When** do events in this article take place?

____

10. **Why** is this happening?

____

____

School + Home **Home Activity** Your child learned about using magazines as resources. Look at a magazine index together. Ask your child to locate an article you are both interested in. Then read the article and find the five W's and H in each.

Name ____

Vowel Sounds with *r*

Proofread an Article Read this article about yard sales. Circle five words that are spelled incorrectly. Write them correctly on the lines. Find a sentence with a capitalization error. Write it correctly on the line.

Having a Yard Sale

Choose a date and start gathering all your items together. Tools, ornaments, clothing, and toys are faverite items to sell. put a price tag on everything. Put an advertisement in the local newspaper. Post artistick signs around your neighborhood advertising the sale. Every body loves a bargain, so people may arrive early hoping to make a good purchas. Perhaps your ad should specify that there will be no sales before the time the sale starts. Remember that some communities have laws about yard sales. Find out about the local rules before you put your items on the markit.

1. ________________ 2. ________________

3. ________________ 4. ________________

5. ________________

6. ____

Proofread Words Circle two list words in each sentence that are spelled incorrectly. Write the words correctly on the lines.

The servent used detrgent to wash the sheets.

7. ________________ 8. ________________

The atturney told her client to sit in the coridor outside the courtroom.

9. ________________ 10. ________________

Please don't ignor my consern.

11. ________________ 12. ________________

Spelling Words

porch
servant
shore
disturb
market
margin
worth
purchase
kernel
perhaps

ignore
concern
attorney
barge
detergent
corridor
ornament
artistic
particle
nervous

Frequently Misspelled Words

favorite
everybody

School + Home

Home Activity Your child identified misspelled words with vowel sounds with *r*. Say a list word, spell it incorrectly, and ask your child to spell it correctly.

Independent and Dependent Clauses

Directions Read the passage. Then read each question. Circle the letter of the correct answer.

Escape from Danger

(1) A blazing fire started at 10:15 this morning. (2) When Mr. Boyle smelled smoke, he immediately called the local fire department. (3) He was very concerned about his two children, who were sleeping upstairs. (4) He raced to their bedrooms to wake them. (5) They knew they had to leave the house quickly when they smelled the smoke traveling up from the basement. (6) The fire department was already dousing the fire with water. (7) The Boyle family felt there were not enough words of thanks to give the fire department when the fire was out and everyone was safe.

1 What is the dependent clause in sentence 1?

A A blazing fire
B started at 10:15 this morning
C A blazing fire started at 10:15 this morning.
D None of the above

2 What is the independent clause in sentence 2?

A he immediately called the local fire department
B When Mr. Boyle smelled smoke,
C smelled smoke
D None of the above

3 ***who were sleeping upstairs*** in sentence 3 is

A an independent clause.
B a dependent clause.
C both an independent and a dependent clause.
D None of the above

4 Which word identifies a dependent clause in sentence 5?

A *when*
B *leave*
C *knew*
D None of the above

5 Sentence 6 has

A one dependent clause.
B one independent clause and one dependent clause.
C one independent clause.
D None of the above

School + Home **Home Activity** Your child prepared for taking tests on independent and dependent clauses. Have your child look through a newspaper or magazine article and find sentences with independent and dependent clauses.

Name ____________________

Fact and Opinion

- A statement that can be proved true or false is called a **statement of fact.**
- A statement that tells a person's thoughts, feelings, or ideas is called a **statement of opinion.** Statements of opinion cannot be proved true or false.

Directions Read the following passage. Then complete the graphic organizer below.

Rain forests make up only 7 percent of the land surface of our planet. However, some scientists say they think that they contain more than half of Earth's plant and animal species. A large percentage of rain forest animals are insects, and a large percentage of those insects are beetles. Scientists are still not sure how many animal species exist on Earth because they have only been able to identify a small fraction of rain forest insects. One scientist said, "I believe that as many as thirty million kinds of insect live in the rain forests."

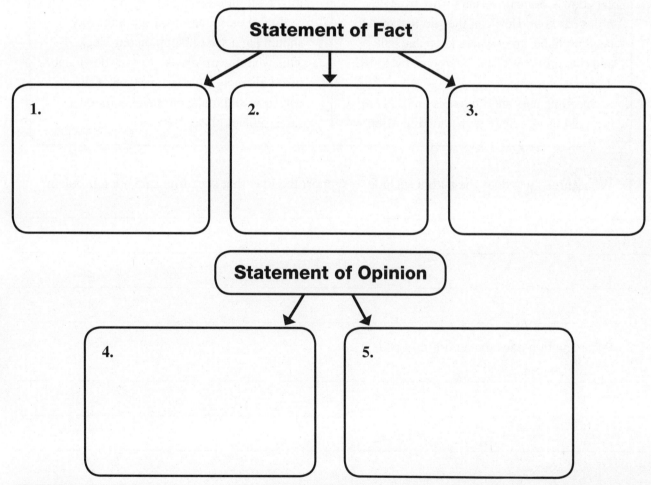

Statement of Fact

1.

2.

3.

Statement of Opinion

4.

5.

School + Home **Home Activity** Your child identified statements of fact and opinion in a short passage. Tell your child a story about a friend or family member that contains both statements of fact and opinion. Have him or her tell you which statements are which.

Name ____

Writing • Problem-Solution Essay

Key Features of a Problem-Solution Essay

- follows a problem-solution text structure
- may persuade readers
- gives an opinion supported by facts

Give Us a Bump!

Cars speed down LaCienega Street. This is especially dangerous because kids often play there. Something needs to be done!

LaCienega is a busy street, and there are no stop signs or speed bumps to slow cars down. Sometimes cars whiz by at 40 miles per hour. How can they do that on a neighborhood street where kids play ball and ride bikes? When a car zooms by, kids dash out of the way.

Speeding cars are often noisy too. There is an old black Chevy with a loud muffler. It roars by many nights around 6 P.M. and invades our "peaceful" dinner hour.

A speeding car could hit the parked cars. People who park in the street shouldn't have to worry about their cars' safety. My mom is afraid that our car might get hit.

For all these reasons, I think the city should put a speed bump on our block. This would warn drivers to slow down and give kids more time to move out of the way. It would make our neighborhood a safer, quieter place.

1. What three facts does the author include to support the idea that speeding cars are a problem?

____

____

____

____

2. What solution does the author propose?

____

____

____

____

Name____

Vocabulary

Directions Choose the word from the box that best matches each definition. Write the word on the line.

Check the Words You Know

- ___basin
- ___charities
- ___equator
- ___erosion
- ___evaporates
- ___exported
- ___industrial
- ___recycled
- ___tropics

________________________ **1.** an imaginary line around the middle of Earth

________________________ **2.** changes from a liquid to a gas

________________________ **3.** regions of the world near the equator

________________________ **4.** processed to be used again

________________________ **5.** sent to a different country for sale or trade

Directions Circle the word or words that have the same or nearly the same meaning as the first word in each group.

6. charities	organizations that help	groups of writers	clubs for children
7. basin	hill near the sea	land drained by a river	mountain with snow
8. erosion	building up	covering over	wearing away
9. industrial	for use in business	for help in education	for ideas at home
10. evaporates	disappears	melts	boils

Write a Weather Report

On a separate sheet of paper, write a weather report for a tropical area. Include as many vocabulary words as you can.

School + Home **Home Activity** Your child identified and used vocabulary words from *Saving the Rain Forests.* Have a discussion with your child about the selection. Encourage him or her to use the vocabulary words during the discussion.

Compound and Complex Sentences

A **simple sentence** has a complete subject and a complete predicate.

The clouds gathered quickly.

A **compound sentence** has two or more simple sentences joined by a comma and a conjunction such as *and, but,* or *or.*

The clouds gathered quickly, and the leaves rustled in the wind.

A **complex sentence** has one independent clause and one or more dependent clauses.

Although it was sunny just a moment ago, the clouds gathered quickly.

A **compound-complex sentence** has more than one independent clause and at least one dependent clause.

Although it was sunny just a moment ago, the clouds gathered quickly, and the leaves rustled in the wind.

Directions Identify each sentence as *simple, compound, complex,* or *compound-complex.*

1. The forest ranger is speaking at my school, and I can't wait to hear him. ______________
2. When it rains, it pours. ______________
3. When they got back from the boat tour, Donna took a nap, and Terry read the paper. ______________
4. Paul looked up at the tree, and he saw a huge fern. ______________
5. Many species of plants and animals live in the rain forest. ______________
6. Although I have a map, I can't find the camp. ______________

Directions Complete each compound sentence with the conjunction *and, but,* or *or.*

7. She loved to hike, ______________ she loved to camp.
8. Some animals live among the leaves, ______________ some live on the tree trunks.
9. We must protect the rain forests, ______________ they will disappear.
10. Larry loved the rain, ______________ Darla did not.
11. Forest fires are common, ______________ they endanger the rain forest.
12. You need to hurry, ______________ I'll leave you behind.

School + Home

Home Activity Your child learned about compound and complex sentences. Have your child tell you what compound and complex sentences are. Then ask your child to find one example of each kind of sentence in a magazine article.

Name ________________________________

Difficult Spellings

Spelling Words				
fierce	weird	piece	perceive	perfume
preserve	soldier	model	multiple	fuel
briefcase	retrieve	deceit	perception	vegetable
preferable	rectangle	bushel	pinnacle	preliminary

Complete the Sentences Write the list word that completes each sentence.

1. My favorite ___ is celery. 1. ______________
2. Uncle Tony picked a whole ___ of tomatoes. 2. ______________
3. My mother left her ___ full of papers at her office. 3. ______________
4. My dog loves to ___ sticks that I throw in the pond. 4. ______________
5. I dislike dishonesty and ___. 5. ______________
6. I would like to achieve the ___ of success as an athlete. 6. ______________
7. I came in first in the ___ competition. 7. ______________
8. My sister wants to be a fashion ___ when she gets older. 8. ______________
9. She wears so much ___ that I can smell it from the next room. 9. ______________
10. My uncle is a ___ serving in the armed forces. 10. ______________
11. I can't find the last ___ of this jigsaw puzzle. 11. ______________
12. Lions are ___ and deadly predators. 12. ______________
13. Food is like ___ for your body. 13. ______________
14. I have ___ copies of the same comic book. 14. ______________
15. A square and a ___ have four sides. 15. ______________

Classifying Write the list word that belongs in each group.

16. desirable, better, superior, ___ 16. ______________
17. idea, sensation, vision, ___ 17. ______________
18. conserve, save, keep, ___ 18. ______________
19. observe, notice, comprehend, ___ 19. ______________
20. odd, strange, peculiar, ___ 20. ______________

School + Home

Home Activity Your child wrote words with difficult spellings. Ask your child to pick a word group and explain why the list word belongs in that group.

Name ________________________________

Outline

Title ________________________________

A. ________________________________

1. ________________________________
2. ________________________________
3. ________________________________

B. ________________________________

1. ________________________________
2. ________________________________
3. ________________________________

C. ________________________________

1. ________________________________
2. ________________________________
3. ________________________________

Name ______________________________

Vocabulary • Word Endings *-ed, -s*

- An **ending** is a letter or letters added to the end of a base word.
- The ending *-ed* is added to a verb to make it past tense. The ending *-s* is added to a verb to show present action in the third person.
- The ending *-s* is added to most singular nouns to make them plural.
- Recognizing an ending will help you figure out a word's meaning.

Directions Read the following passage. Then answer the questions below.

Many people in the United States eat bananas. A banana plant needs a hot, wet climate to grow. That is why they grow in the tropics near the equator. Millions of tons of bananas are exported and are shipped to the United States every year. Many doctors recommend eating bananas because they are a good source of vitamin C, fiber, and potassium.

1. *Bananas* and *tropics* both have the same ending. What are their base words? How does *-s* change the meanings of their base words?

____

2. What is the difference in meaning between *-s* at the end of *tropics* and *-s* at the end of *needs*?

____

____

3. If the last sentence began with "A doctor," what would you have to do to *recommend* to make the new sentence correct?

____

4. *Exported* and *shipped* both have the same ending. What are their base words? How does *-ed* change the meanings of their base words?

____

5. Choose a noun or a verb from the passage. What is its base word? Add a new ending to it. How has the meaning of the word changed?

____

____

School + Home **Home Activity** Your child identified endings to understand new words in a passage. Write a note with him or her to another member of your family. Have your child identify the *-s* and *-ed* endings of words used in the note.

Name ____

Graph

- A **graph** is a pictorial representation of data. Graphs show how any one piece of information compares with other pieces. A graph can show information more quickly than a verbal explanation and can reveal how something changes over time.
- There are bar graphs, circle graphs, line graphs, and pictographs. Titles and labels on a graph will help you interpret the data in the graph.

Directions Use this bar graph to answer the questions below.

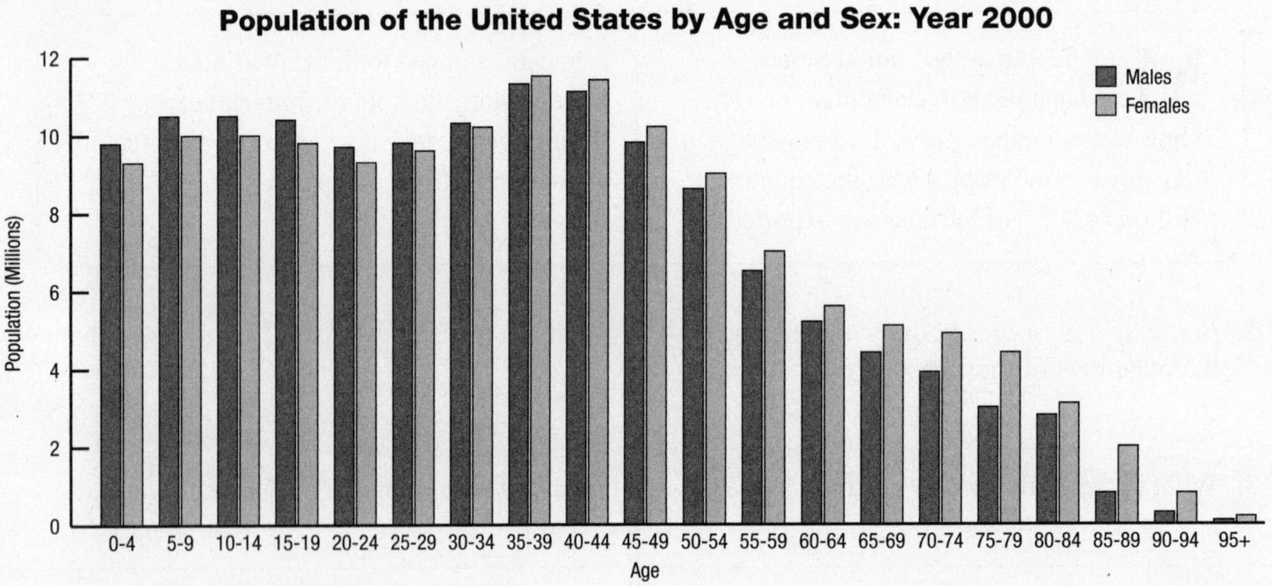

1. What information is given in this graph?

____

____

2. What two groups are compared in this graph?

____

3. Which group had a greater population from birth to age 4?

____

4. Using the data in this graph, what conclusion can you draw about people over 60 years old?

____

____

5. What generalization can you make about human lifespans based on the data in the graph?

____

Name ____

Directions Use the following graphs to answer the questions below.

Monthly Rainfall in a Coniferous Forest

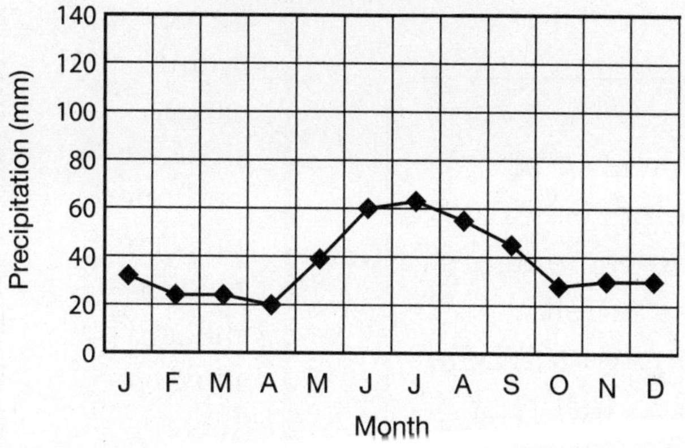

Monthly Rainfall in a Temperate Deciduous Forest

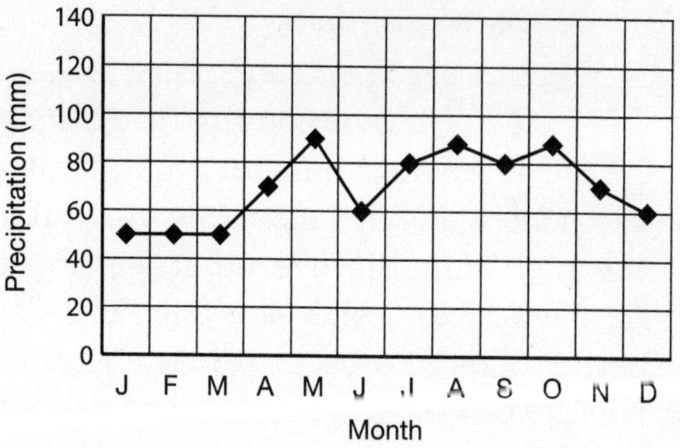

6. Which forest has more rain in May?

____

7. In which month do both forests have the same amount of rain?

____

8. Which is the rainiest month in the coniferous forest? the temperate deciduous forest?

____

9. What conclusion can you draw about precipitation in the coniferous forest for October, November, and December?

____

____

10. What conclusion can you draw about precipitation when you compare the data from both forests?

____

____

School + Home **Home Activity** Your child learned how to read and understand data on graphs. Find a graph in a newspaper or magazine. Discuss it with your child and draw conclusions about the data.

Name ______________________________

Difficult Spellings

Proofread the Story Circle five words in this story that are spelled incorrectly. Write them correctly. Find a sentence with an incorrect verb form. Write the sentence correctly.

Overcoming Stage Fright

Lisa is excited but nervous about performing at the school talent show. She has vivid memories of the night she discovered stage fright. She remembers how wierd and sick she felt. She knows she felt better once she began to dance, and she gave a modle performance. However, she never wants to feel that horrible again.

So she research stage fright. She learned that many of the world's top performers get stage fright and that it can be prefrable to overconfidence. Stage fright heightens purception and helps performers reach the pinacle of their ability. This time she will prepare herself by recalling happy moments from her past. She will gain confidence from knowing that she never looks as nervous as she feels.

Spelling Words

fierce
weird
piece
perceive
perfume
preserve
soldier
model
multiple
fuel

briefcase
retrieve
deceit
perception
vegetable
preferable
rectangle
bushel
pinnacle
preliminary

Frequently Misspelled Words

field
don't

1. ______________ 2. ______________

3. ______________ 4. ______________

5. ______________

6. ____

Proofread Words Circle the word in each group that is spelled correctly. Write the word.

7. modle model modal 7. ______________

8. preserve perserve presurve 8. ______________

9. peice peise piece 9. ______________

10. pinacle pinnacle pinnakle 10. ______________

School + Home

Home Activity Your child identified misspelled words. Say a list word and ask your child to spell the word aloud.

Name ______________________________

Compound and Complex Sentences

Directions Read the passage. Then read each question. Circle the letter of the correct answer.

The Wealth of the Rain Forest

(1) The Amazon rain forest provides a strong link between humans and nature. (2) Because the rain forest supports millions of plant species, native healers have looked to nature for cures to diseases. (3) Today the rain forest is one of the richest resources on our planet. (4) Many new drugs have been developed from the plants and trees of the rain forest, and we expect many more will be discovered. (5) The rain forest is a likely source of new drugs as we try to cure cancer, diabetes, AIDS, Alzheimer's, and other diseases. (6) Over 100 pharmaceutical companies are funding projects in the rain forest, and the United States government encourages companies to study the natives' knowledge of the plants.

1 Sentence 1 is which type of sentence?

A Simple sentence
B Compound sentence
C Complex sentence
D Exclamatory sentence

2 Sentence 2 is which type of sentence?

A Simple sentence
B Compound sentence
C Complex sentence
D Interrogative sentence

3 In sentence 4, which word is a conjunction?

A Many
B from
C more
D and

4 In sentence 5, ***The rain forest is a likely source of new drugs*** is what?

A Dependent clause
B Independent clause
C Compound sentence
D Complex sentence

5 Sentence 6 is which type of sentence?

A Compound sentence
B Simple sentence
C Complex sentence
D Exclamatory sentence

School + Home **Home Activity** Your child prepared for taking tests on compound and complex sentences. Together look through a newspaper or magazine article. Ask your child to find and circle three compound sentences and three complex sentences.

Name ___________________________

Fact and Opinion

- **Statements of fact** can be proved true or false. Facts can be proved by a reliable reference source, by observation, or by asking an expert.
- **Statements of opinion** are judgments or beliefs. They cannot be proved true or false, but they can be *supported* by facts and logic.

Directions Read the following passage. Then complete the diagram by identifying statements of fact and statements of opinion.

Golden retrievers, the best choice of pet, are less popular than Labrador retrievers. People love goldens because with proper training they are patient and gentle with children. Golden retrievers seem to want to do nothing but please their owners. They also make good watchdogs because they bark when a stranger approaches. Golden retrievers make excellent pets when they are well cared for. Daily exercise and proper training help the dog manage its behavior. Occasional grooming keeps the dog's coat free of tangles and looking great.

Statement: Golden retrievers, the best choice of pet, are less popular than Labrador retrievers.

1. Which part of the statement is opinion?

2. Which part of the statement is fact?

3. How to support?

4. How to prove?

School + Home **Home Activity** Your child read a short article and identified statements of fact and statements of opinion. One way to check facts is to look on Web sites. Talk with your child about how to tell whether the information on a Web site can be trusted.

Writing for Tests

Prompt: Write a journal entry about a time when things did not turn out as you had hoped or planned.

March 19, 20__

This morning as I read the local paper, a story on the front page caught my attention. The headline read, "Local Farm Appeals for Help." Since I love animals of all kinds, I was immediately drawn to the story.

It seems that this week's heavy rains flooded a nearby farm. The family that owns the farm was reaching out to find temporary homes for some of its animals. We already have two dogs, three cats, a parakeet, and a guinea pig, so I wasn't sure that Mom and Dad would be willing to take in a short-term farm animal. But, we do have a big yard. We could easily keep a horse out back, and maybe even a chicken or two.

After breakfast, I asked Mom whether she had read the article. She hadn't read the paper, yet, but she promised she would get to it later. I asked her, polite as can be, to *please* read the article now because it was very important to me. Mom knows how much I adore animals, so she read the article right then and there. When she finished, she looked up at me, and I gave her my sad puppy-dog eyes, hoping she would know exactly what I was thinking. "Well" she said. "We don't have room for another animal. If you want to help, you could always volunteer at the farm. It says in the paper that they need people to help clean up damage caused by the flood."

I definitely would have preferred a horse, but I suppose it's good to help in any way I can. And who knows? Maybe when the farm is up and running again, I will be able to visit the animals I helped!

1. What experience does the writer describe in this journal entry?

____

____

____

2. Underline the sentence that tells you how the writer feels about animals.

3. Circle three different pronouns that show that the entry is written in the first person.

Name ______________________________

Vocabulary

Directions Choose the word from the box that best matches each definition. Write the word on the line.

Check the Words You Know
___fixed
___furious
___morsel
___nudge
___quietly
___ruff
___stooped
___vigil

_______________ **1.** in a quiet way

_______________ **2.** push gently

_______________ **3.** a small bit of food

_______________ **4.** held steady

_______________ **5.** a time of watching

Directions Choose the word from the box that best matches each clue. Write the letters of each word on the line. Take the circled letters to make a word below.

6. marked by excitement and activity ___ ___ ___ ___ ___ ___ (___)

7. hunched over ___ (___) ___ ___ ___ ___ ___

8. without noise ___ ___ ___ ___ (___) ___ ___

9. a fringe of fur growing around the neck ___ (___) ___ ___

10. held steady ___ ___ ___ (___) ___

___ ___ **a** ___ ___ ___

Write a Description

Using a separate sheet of paper, describe what a hungry dog might do or look like. Use as many vocabulary words as you can.

School + Home **Home Activity** Your child identified and used vocabulary words from *Hachiko: The True Story of a Loyal Dog*. Read an article about dogs with your child. Have him or her point out unfamiliar words. Try to figure out the meaning of each word by using words that appear near it.

Scoring Rubric: Journal Entry

	4	3	2	1
Focus/Ideas	Clear, focused composition with effective supporting details	Mostly clear and focused composition; some supporting details	Composition somewhat unfocused; insufficient supporting details	Composition with no clarity or development
Organization	Organized logically; ideas are coherent and focused	Organized logically, few gaps; ideas fairly focused and coherent	Organization attempted, but not clear; some ideas unrelated to subject	Poor organization; ideas lack focus
Voice	Engaging; clearly expresses writer's thoughts	Evident voice; shares some thoughts and feelings	Weak voice; does not share many thoughts and feelings	Lacking clear voice
Word Choice	Vivid, precise word choice	Accurate word choice	Limited or repetitive word choice	Very limited word choice
Sentences	Varied sentences	Not as much variety	Too many similar sentences	Many fragments and run-ons
Conventions	Excellent control and accuracy; common and proper nouns used correctly	Good control, few errors; common and proper nouns generally correct	Weak control; errors with common and proper nouns	Serious errors that obscure meaning

Name ____

Vocabulary • Suffixes *-ly, -ous*

- A **suffix** is a word part added to the end of a base word to change its meaning or the way it is used in a sentence.
- The suffix *-ly* means "in a manner that is" or "in a way that is."
- The suffix *-ous* means "full of."

Directions Read the following passage. Then answer the questions below.

Lin frequently watched the ducks gather in the pond on her grandfather's farm. Winter was coming on quickly, and she knew it was soon time for their migration south. Usually her dog Ace and the ducks tolerated each other pretty well. For some reason, one of the ducks had become aggressive with Ace. When Ace approached the flock, it would rush at Ace with its wings flapping wildly. Ace tried to be courageous, but the duck made him too nervous. Instead, Ace retreated and just watched the ducks in frustration. This continued for a week. It appeared that this duck could detect when Ace approached, and it would rush and flap and quack riotously. This game between Acc and the duck continued until the ducks finally began their migration south.

1. How does the suffix *-ly* change the meaning of the base word *quick* in the word *quickly?*

____

2. How does the suffix *-ous* change the meaning of the base word *courage* in the word *courageous?*

____

3. How does the suffix *-ous* change the meaning of the base word *nerve* in the word *nervous?*

____

4. The word *riotously* contains two suffixes. How is the base word *riot* changed by adding the two suffixes?

____

5. Think of another word that ends with either *-ly* or *-ous*. Use it in an original sentence that makes its meaning clear.

____

____

School + Home **Home Activity** Your child read a short passage and identified suffixes at the ends of words. Read a story with your child and identify the suffixes *-ly* and *-ous* at the ends of words in the story. Ask your child how the suffix changed the meaning of the word.

Card Catalog / Library Database

- A **card catalog** and **library database** provide information you need to find a book in the library. The card catalog has drawers with cards in them.
- A library database is the online version of a card catalog. Instead of cards, the database has files called *records*.
- The cards or records provide information about a book, including its **author, title, subject,** and its **call number.**
- You can search a catalog, online or in cards, by author, title, or subject.

Directions Read the starting search screen for a library database shown below. Then answer the questions that follow.

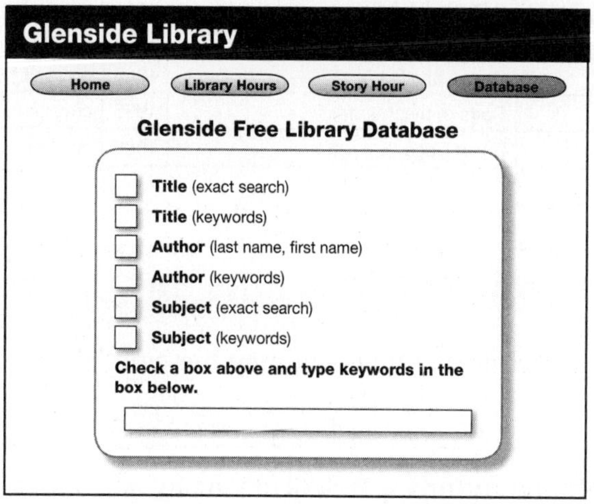

1. Which box would you check to find a book about dogs? Which keyword would you type?

____

2. Which box would you check to find the novel titled *My Life in Dog Years?* Which keywords would you type?

____

3. Which box would you check to find a book by Pamela S. Turner? Which keywords would you type?

____

____

4. Which box would you check to find a book with *dogs* in its title? Which keyword would you type?

____

5. Which box would you check to find a book about the caring for puppies? Which keywords would you type?

____

Name ____________________

Directions Look at the search results from a library database. Then answer the questions below.

Glenside Library

Home | Library Hours | Story Hour | Database

Glenside Free Library Database

Search results for **Title** containing **dogs**

8 records found

Results page **1** of 1

Number	Title	Year	Status
1	Dogs	1985	on shelf
2	The Dog and the Serpent	1996	on shelf
3	Dogs Can't Count	1992	checked out
4	A Guide to Dogs	1977	on shelf
5	A Dog's Journey	1996	reserved
6	Statue of a Dog	1966	on shelf
7	Dogs of the World	1996	checked out
8	Show Dogs	1988	on shelf

6. These results are from a search for a title containing the word *dogs.* How can you tell?

____

7. How many records were found for this search? How many are shown on this page?

____

8. If you wanted to check out *Dogs of the World* today, would you be able to? How do you know?

____

9. Which book is reserved? What do you think it means for a book to be reserved?

____

10. Why does *Hachiko* not appear on this list?

____

Home Activity Your child learned about using a library database. Go to the library or go to an online library database with your child. Then search a topic you are both interested in.

Name ______________________________

Plural or Possessive

Proofread a Journal Entry Read this journal entry. Circle five words that are spelled incorrectly. Write them correctly on the lines. Find a sentence with a punctuation error. Write it correctly on the line.

Dear Journal,

My nieces moved a month ago, and I still miss them? Suddenly we live in two different countries'. Sometimes we talk on the phone, but ours conversations are so long that they become to expensive. We write so much that if we had secretaries' they'd be busy all the time. I probably will always miss my niece's.

Spelling Words

country's
countries'
countries
its
ours
theirs
hers
library's
libraries'
libraries
niece's
nieces'
nieces
crow's
crows
witness's
witnesses'
witnesses
secretary's
secretaries'

Frequently Misspelled Words

too
probably

1. ______________ 2. ______________

3. ______________ 4. ______________

5. ______________

6. ____

____

Plural or Possessive For each sentence, decide if the missing word is plural or possessive. Circle the correct word and write it on the line.

7. That ___ beak looks very sharp. 7. ______________

crow's crows

8. My ___ all have curly hair. 8. ______________

niece's nieces

9. Almost all ___ have computers these days. 9. ______________

libraries' libraries

10. The ___ all agreed on what happened. 10. ______________

witnesses' witnesses

School + Home **Home Activity** Your child identified misspelled words. Ask your child to think of and say sentences that contain list words.

Name ______________________________

Common and Proper Nouns

Directions Read the passage. Then read each question. Circle the letter of the correct answer.

The American Sewing Machine

(1) Elias Howe was the inventor of the first American sewing machine. (2) Inventor Howe was born in spencer, massachusetts in July 1819. (3) When he lost his factory job, he moved to Boston, where he found work in a machine shop and began to work on a sewing machine that could stitch 250 stitches a minute. (4) It took eight years until Howe was ready to demonstrate his machine. (5) By then, Mr. Isaac Singer was hard at work on what became the famous singer sewing machine. (6) Howe earned close to two million dollars from his invention. (7) During the civil war he donated part of his wealth to buy uniforms for the Union army.

1 What change, if any, should be made in sentence 1?

A Change *Elias Howe* to **elias howe**
B Change *inventor* to **Inventor**
C Change *American* to **american**
D Make no change

2 What change, if any, should be made in sentence 2?

A Change *spencer, massachusetts* to *Spencer, Massachusetts,*
B Change *July* to **july**
C Change *Inventor* to **inventor**
D Make no change

3 What change, if any, should be made in sentence 3?

A Change *machine shop* to **Machine Shop**
B Change *Boston* to **boston**
C Change *sewing machine* to **Sewing Machine**
D Make no change

4 What change, if any, should be made in sentence 5?

A Change the period to an exclamation point
B Change *Mr.* to **mr.**
C Change *singer sewing machine* to **Singer Sewing Machine**
D Make no change

5 What change, if any, should be made in sentence 7?

A Change *Union army* to **union army**
B Change *civil war* to **Civil War**
C Change *wealth* to **Wealth**
D Make no change

School + Home **Home Activity** Your child prepared for taking tests on common and proper nouns. With your child, find four examples each of common and proper nouns in a newspaper or magazine article.

Adding *-ed* and *-ing*

Spelling Words				
answered	answering	traveled	traveling	chopped
chopping	qualified	qualifying	panicked	panicking
interfered	interfering	omitted	omitting	magnified
magnifying	patrolled	patrolling	skied	skiing

Antonyms Write the list word ending in *-ed* that has the opposite or nearly the opposite meaning.

1. included 1. ______________
2. asked 2. ______________
3. snowboarded 3. ______________
4. unsuitable 4. ______________
5. minimized 5. ______________

Synonyms Write the list word ending in *-ed* that has the same or nearly the same meaning.

6. divided 6. ______________
7. frightened 7. ______________
8. meddled 8. ______________
9. went on vacation 9. ______________
10. monitored 10. ______________

Word Clues Write the list word that fits each clue.

11. what a person is doing down a snowy mountain 11. ______________
12. what students are doing when they respond 12. ______________
13. what a police officer is doing around a community 13. ______________
14. what a chef is doing to the onions 14. ______________
15. what people are doing when they intrude 15. ______________
16. what people are doing when they fly overseas 16. ______________
17. what a microscope is doing to a cell 17. ______________
18. what people are doing when they leave out information 18. ______________
19. what an athlete is doing at the Olympic trials 19. ______________
20. what people are doing when they have anxiety 20. ______________

School + Home **Home Activity** Your child has learned to spell words with *-ed* and *-ing*. To practice at home, name three verbs that describe weekend activities. Ask your child to spell each word with an *-ed* ending and with an *-ing* ending.

Name ______________________________

Four Kinds of Sentences

Directions Write *D* if the sentence is declarative. Write *IN* if the sentence is interrogative. Write *IM* if the sentence is imperative. Write *E* if the sentence is exclamatory.

1. The barking dog saved the family from the fire. ____

2. My, that's a beautiful parrot! ____

3. Have the dogs gone to obedience school? ____

4. Hang the leash near the back door. ____

Directions Put a period, a question mark, or an exclamation mark at the end of each sentence to show what kind it is.

5. Hold on to that dog's leash ____

6. How smart your pet pig is ____

7. Have you seen my ant farm ____

8. The cat should not eat leftovers ____

Directions: Write an example of each kind of sentence. Don't forget the proper capitalization and end mark.

9. (declarative) ______________________________

____

10. (interrogative) ______________________________

____

11. (imperative) ______________________________

____

12. (exclamatory) ______________________________

____

13. (exclamatory with an interjection) ______________________________

____

School + Home **Home Activity** Your child reviewed the four kinds of sentences. With your child, listen to an interview on TV. Have your child identify the kinds of sentences the people use in their conversation.

Name ______________________________

Short Vowels

Spelling Words

damage	gentle	injury	palace	cottage
honesty	mustard	legend	clumsy	message
modify	ruffle	glimpse	strict	dungeon
fender	fantastic	dignity	property	cannon

Analogies Write the word that completes each comparison.

1. Repair is to fix as change is to ______________.
2. Movie is to television show as formal letter is to ______________.
3. Bicycle is to handlebars as car is to ______________.
4. Red is to ketchup as yellow is to ______________.
5. Sandpaper is to harsh as cotton is to ______________.
6. Smart is to intelligent as stern is to ______________.

Scramble Unscramble the list words and write them on the lines.

7. maedag 7. ______________
8. ycmlsu 8. ______________
9. rjyuni 9. ______________
10. tafacisnt 10. ______________
11. nonanc 11. ______________
12. goneund 12. ______________
13. aealcp 13. ______________
14. euflfr 14. ______________

Hidden Words Each of these small words can be found inside one of the list words. Write the list word that contains the small words.

15. tag 15. ______________
16. leg 16. ______________
17. one 17. ______________
18. rope 18. ______________
19. dig 19. ______________
20. limp 20. ______________

School + Home **Home Activity** Your child has learned to spell words with short vowels. Find words with short vowel sounds in a magazine or newspaper and ask your child to spell them.

Subjects and Predicates

Directions Draw a line between the complete subject and the complete predicate in each sentence.

1. Teresa's parents have formed a service organization for the community.
2. Many people in our neighborhood are joining the organization.
3. The group will provide help to older people in the community.
4. Each member has a special talent.
5. Mrs. Gallo can fix leaky plumbing.

Directions Write *F* after fragments. Write *R* after run-ons. Write *S* after complete sentences.

6. Can put on a new roof. ______
7. Mr. Larkin is repairing his next-door neighbor's driveway he is pouring cement. ______
8. Neighborhood children will shovel snow in the winter. ______
9. Some women drive senior citizens to their doctors' appointments. ______
10. The Meadowbrook Service Club. ______

Directions: Add a subject or a predicate to each fragment to make a complete sentence. Write the sentence. Underline the simple subject and simple predicate.

11. A good neighbor ________ .

____

12. ________ will be working together.

____

13. ________ will benefit from the help.

____

14. A rundown house on our block ________ .

____

School + Home

Home Activity Your child reviewed subjects and predicates. Ask your child to prepare a definition and an example for each of these terms: *simple subject, complete subject, simple predicate, complete predicate, fragment,* and *run-on.*

Name ______________________________

Vowel Sounds with *r*

Spelling Words				
porch	servant	shore	disturb	market
margin	worth	purchase	kernel	perhaps
ignore	concern	attorney	barge	detergent
corridor	ornament	artistic	particle	nervous

Classifying Write the list word that belongs in each group.

1. beach, tide, sand, ________ 1. ____________
2. bleach, suds, soap, ________ 2. ____________
3. butler, maid, cook, ________ 3. ____________
4. buy, pay for, shop, ________ 4. ____________
5. maybe, possibly, conceivably, ________ 5. ____________
6. entrance, hall, foyer, ________ 6. ____________
7. groceries, cart, shop, ________ 7. ____________
8. interest, attention, consideration, ________ 8. ____________
9. boat, ship, raft, ________ 9. ____________
10. balcony, steps, deck, ________ 10. ____________
11. decoration, accessory, trinket, ________ 11. ____________
12. bit, speck, atom, ________ 12. ____________

Word Scramble Riddle Unscramble each list word and then write the numbered letters on the lines below to answer the riddle.

Riddle: What kinds of clothes do attorneys wear?

13. ohtwr ___ ___ ___ ___ ___ (3)
14. trcisita ___ ___ ___ ___ ___ ___ ___ ___ (8)
15. eknlre ___ ___ ___ ___ ___ ___ (1)
16. nmiagr ___ ___ ___ ___ ___ ___ (2)
17. veusnro ___ ___ ___ ___ ___ ___ ___ (5)
18. geiron ___ ___ ___ ___ ___ ___ (6)
19. tdibrus ___ ___ ___ ___ ___ ___ ___ (4)
20. oyeatrtn ___ ___ ___ ___ ___ ___ ___ ___ (7)

___ ___ ___ ___ ___ ___ ___ ___
1 2 3 4 5 6 7 8

School + Home

Home Activity Your child has learned to spell words with vowels combined with the letter *r*. Ask your child to give an example of a word with each vowel and *r* combination and spell it.

Name ______________________________

Independent and Dependent Clauses

Directions Write *IC* if the group of underlined words is an independent clause and *DC* if it is a dependent clause.

1. ________ Since my best friend lives next door, we get to see each other every day.
2. ________ Because New Jersey is close to New York City, people often commute to New York to work.
3. ________ After I thought about them all day, the tamales tasted delicious.
4. ________ When the lights went out, Martina climbed the stairs in the dark.
5. ________ Gabriel's grandmother liked to sing when she couldn't sleep.

Directions Match each dependent clause with an independent clause to make a complete sentence.

6. ________ Although the alarm sounded, A. Kate stayed with her aunt.
7. ________ Before they became friends, B. no one left the room.
8. ________ Whenever it rained, C. he was still hungry.
9. ________ While her parents were away, D. our basement flooded.
10. ________ After Jose ate lunch, E. Ann and Lee rarely spoke.

Directions: Add a dependent clause to enhance each sentence. Write the new sentence on the line.

11. She helped her mother prepare fried bananas. ______________________________

____

12. The dog barked and whimpered all night. ______________________________

____

13. Spanish songs made her homesick. ______________________________

____

14. The family of four lived in a downtown apartment. ______________________________

____

15. The stray cat could end up in a shelter. ______________________________

____

School + Home **Home Activity** Your child reviewed independent and dependent clauses. Have your child pick out three examples of sentences with independent and dependent clauses in a magazine article.

Difficult Spellings

Spelling Words				
fierce	weird	piece	perceive	perfume
preserve	soldier	model	multiple	fuel
briefcase	retrieve	deceit	perception	vegetable
preferable	rectangle	bushel	pinnacle	preliminary

Word Search Circle ten hidden list words. Words are down, across, and diagonal. Write the word on the line.

A	B	Q	P	S	S	P	M	P	L
B	P	I	E	C	E	E	O	E	I
R	U	O	R	F	N	R	D	R	S
I	I	S	F	O	U	C	E	F	O
E	E	F	H	I	R	E	L	U	L
F	R	I	N	E	N	P	L	M	D
C	P	E	R	C	L	T	E	E	I
A	E	R	I	E	R	I	I	R	E
S	R	C	O	E	L	O	F	N	R
E	R	E	C	T	A	N	G	L	E

1. ____________________ 2. ____________________

3. ____________________ 4. ____________________

5. ____________________ 6. ____________________

7. ____________________ 8. ____________________

9. ____________________ 10. ____________________

Synonyms Write the list word that has the same or nearly the same meaning.

11. favorable ____________________ 12. strange ____________________

13. before ____________________ 14. notice ____________________

15. highest point ____________________ 16. many ____________________

17. get back ____________________ 18. dishonesty ____________________

19. produce ____________________ 20. maintain ____________________

School + Home **Home Activity** Your child wrote words with difficult spellings. Have your child choose a word and tell a word that is the opposite or nearly the opposite of the list word.

Name ______________________________

Compound and Complex Sentences

Directions Identify each sentence as *simple, compound, complex,* or *compound-complex.*

1. The chameleon scurried up the tree and disappeared into a hole.

____

2. Before he knew it, dinner was ready, and everyone was waiting for him.

____

3. Tropical rain forests are valuable, but they are disappearing rapidly.

____

Directions Complete each compound sentence with the conjunction *and, but,* or *or.*

4. We could hear the waterfall in the distance, ________ it sounded very loud.

5. I stumbled over a tree root, ________ I didn't lose my balance.

6. Don't lose sight of the group, ________ you may get lost.

7. The toucan's bill is very large, ________ it is not heavy.

Directions Underline the dependent clause in each complex sentence.

8. I will leave for the campsite at six unless I hear from you.

9. After he stalked his prey, the jaguar sat and waited.

10. Whenever the forest ranger called the campers on his cell phone, he got a busy signal.

11. Toucans are hard to overlook in the rain forest because they have brightly colored feathers.

12. Although he left for Brazil on Tuesday, he did not arrive until Thursday.

School + Home **Home Activity** Your child reviewed complex and compound sentences. Give your child a simple sentence, such as *Our dinner is ready*. Ask your child to make the sentence into a compound sentence and then into a complex sentence.

Name ______________________________

Plural or Possessive

Spelling Words

country's	countries'	countries	its	ours
theirs	hers	library's	libraries'	libraries
niece's	nieces'	nieces	crow's	crows
witness's	witnesses'	witnesses	secretary's	secretaries'

Word Meaning Write the list word that matches each definition.

1. belonging to one girl — **1.** ____________
2. more than one niece — **2.** ____________
3. more than one library — **3.** ____________
4. belonging to more than one country — **4.** ____________
5. belonging to one thing — **5.** ____________
6. belonging to more than one secretary — **6.** ____________
7. belonging to one crow — **7.** ____________
8. more than one witness — **8.** ____________
9. belonging to one witness — **9.** ____________
10. belonging to us — **10.** ____________

Proofread Write the underlined list word correctly on the line.

11. Her nieces' dress will fit me perfectly. — **11.** ____________
12. All the witness testimonies helped the attorney. — **12.** ____________
13. The country leader agrees with the laws. — **13.** ____________
14. Our libraries teen collection is the best I have ever seen. — **14.** ____________
15. I couldn't believe the idea was their's. — **15.** ____________
16. My three nieces performance will open the show. — **16.** ____________
17. The park has many crows in the trees. — **17.** ____________
18. The sizes of the library book collections were amazing. — **18.** ____________
19. When I list all the country I visited, I have a long list. — **19.** ____________
20. The secretarys organization was important to his boss. — **20.** ____________

School + Home

Home Activity Your child has learned to spell plural and possessive words. Have your child choose a list word and use it in a sentence. Then have him or her spell the word.

Name ______________________________

Common and Proper Nouns

Directions Write *P* if the underlined noun is a proper noun. Write *C* if it is a common noun.

1. My mom walked me to the station. ______
2. The locomotive was frighteningly loud. ______
3. Dr. Ueno got the dog as a puppy. ______
4. Hachiko always sniffed for morsels. ______
5. Do you live near Shibuya Station? ______
6. Hachiko sat patiently, waiting. ______

Directions Underline the proper nouns and circle the common nouns.

7. The boy first saw the dog at a Tokyo station.
8. Kentaro often brought the dog a little treat.
9. Father took the train to his job at the university.
10. In summer, warm breezes rustle the leaves.
11. Mother prepared extra food to give to Hachiko.
12. Ms. Turner writes stories on her computer.
13. In April, the trees are full of flowers.
14. Dr. Ueno worked with the father of Kentaro.
15. The gardener of Dr. Ueno saw Hachiko every night.

Directions Replace the common nouns in ( ) with proper nouns. Be sure to use appropriate capitalization.

16. My (relative) ____________________ has never been to (continent) ____________________.
17. (title) ____________________ Arthur Chin was born in (country) ____________________.
18. Luke's friend (name) ____________________ works for (company) ____________________.
19. (school) ____________________ is closed on (date) ____________________.
20. (city) ____________________ is in (state) ____________________.

School + Home

Home Activity Your child reviewed common nouns and proper nouns. With your child, find three common nouns and three proper nouns in a printed advertisement.

Name ______________________________

Notes for a Personal Narrative

Directions Fill in the graphic organizer with information about the event or experience that you plan to write about.

Summary

What happened? ______________________________

When? ______________________________

Where? ______________________________

Who was there? ______________________________

Details

Beginning

Middle

End

Name ______________________________

Words That Tell About *You*

A writer can use vivid words to show how the narrator and other characters in a story look, act, and feel. A writer can also use dialogue to reveal their thoughts and feelings. *Dialogue* refers to the words a character speaks. Readers can learn a lot about a character by looking at what the character says.

Directions Read each character's dialogue. Tell what the dialogue reveals about that character.

1. Kwan said, "Oh, no! My alarm didn't go off! I can't find my shoes! Where's my backpack? Is that the bus already? Out of my way!"

____

____

2. Trey said, "My piano recital is this afternoon. I'm playing one of my favorite sonatas. I've been practicing it for an hour every day for weeks."

____

____

3. Anita said, "*Space Raiders IV* opens on Friday. I plan to be the first one in line! I bet it will be even better than *S.R. I–III,* and those movies were incredible!"

____

____

Directions Write several lines of dialogue for each person in your personal narrative. Use the dialogue to reveal something about that person's character, personality, or state of mind.

Name: ______________________________

Dialogue: "______________________________

______________________________."

Name: ______________________________

Dialogue: "______________________________

______________________________."

Name ______________________________

Combining Sentences

- When you write, you can combine two short, choppy simple sentences to make compound or complex sentences. The sentences you combine must be related in some way.
- To make a compound sentence, combine the two sentences using the word *and, but,* or *or*.
- To make a complex sentence, combine the two sentences using a word such as *if, because, after, before, since,* or *when*.

Directions Choose one of the words in parentheses to combine each pair of sentences. Remember to punctuate the new compound or complex sentence correctly.

1. I go outside to play. The day is clear and sunny. (but, when)

____

____

2. The pond is a good place. I like the big elm tree too. (if, and)

____

____

3. Don't climb up too high. You might slip and fall. (or, after)

____

____

4. The sun was hot. My hands were wet with sweat. (because, or)

____

____

5. The crutches were hard to use. I figured out how to do it. (but, before)

____

____

Name ______________________________

Peer and Teacher Conferencing
Personal Narrative

Directions Read your partner's narrative. Refer to the Revising Checklist as you write your comments or questions. Offer compliments as well as revision suggestions. Then take turns talking about each other's draft. Give your partner your notes. After you and your teacher talk about your narrative, add your teacher's comments to the notes.

Revising Checklist

Focus/Ideas

- ☐ Is the personal narrative focused on one specific event?
- ☐ Are there enough details about that event?

Organization

- ☐ Does the narrative have a clear beginning, middle, and end?
- ☐ Is there a strong opening sentence that grabs readers' attentions?

Voice

- ☐ Is the narrative interesting and lively?
- ☐ Do vivid words show how the narrator and other characters look, act, and feel?

Word Choice

- ☐ Do vivid adjectives and strong verbs make descriptions livelier and more interesting?

Sentences

- ☐ Could any related, choppy simple sentences be combined to make smoother-sounding compound or complex sentences?

Things I Thought Were Good ______________________________

____

____

Things I Thought Could Be Improved ______________________________

____

____

Teacher's Comments ______________________________

____

____

Name ______________________________

Main Idea and Details

- The **topic** is what a paragraph or article is about.
- The **main idea** is the most important idea about the topic.
- **Details** are pieces of information that explain or support the main idea.

Directions Read the following passage. Then complete the diagram with the topic, the main idea, and details from the passage.

The North Star has been and still is an important tool for travelers. Before navigational instruments were developed, many sailors used the North Star to navigate. Measuring angles between themselves and the star allows people to determine their location at sea. Hikers and other outdoor enthusiasts still use the North Star to find their way in the wilderness. The North Star is easy to see if you know where to look in the sky. It is quite bright and is the last star in the tail of the Little Dipper.

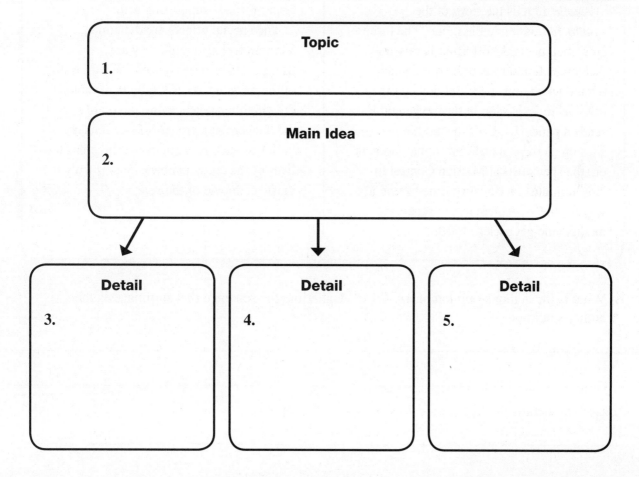

Topic

1.

Main Idea

2.

Detail

3.

Detail

4.

Detail

5.

School + Home

Home Activity Your child identified the main idea and details of a nonfiction passage. Work with your child to identify the main idea and details of each paragraph in an article about stars or planets.

Name ____________________

Writing • Movie Review

Key Features of a Movie Review

- gives an opinion of a movie
- includes a plot summary without revealing the ending
- shares the writer's thoughts and opinions

Apollo 13, Movie of the Year

Apollo 13 grabs you and won't let go. Nominated for nine Oscars, *Apollo 13* deserves credit as one of the best movies of the year for its remarkable acting, ingenious special effects, and thrilling suspense.

Apollo 13 tells the story of the *Apollo 13* mission to the moon. The three crew members take off after dismissing the connection between the mission and the unlucky number 13. But during the mission, an explosion in the oxygen tank sends a panel flying off the module, causing an oxygen leak. From that moment on, the specialists at Mission Control in Houston must race against time to find a way for the crew members to repair the module and get back to Earth.

The acting in *Apollo 13* is first-rate. Standout performances include Tom Hanks as astronaut Jim Lovell and Ed Harris as Flight Director Gene Kranz. Hanks portrays Lovell as tough but sensitive, and Harris was nominated for an Oscar for best-supporting actor.

The special effects are dynamite. Viewers feel as though they are transported to outer space. The explosion of the oxygen tank is totally believable, drawing the audience into the reality of the danger the astronauts face. Tension builds as each new challenge threatens the lives of the crewmembers. This is truly the must-see movie of the year.

1. What is the author's opinion of *Apollo 13*? Underline the sentence that summarizes the author's opinion.

____

____

2. List two details that the author uses to support this opinion.

____

____

3. Circle the paragraph that presents a summary of the plot.

Name ______________________________

Vocabulary

Directions Choose the word from the box that best matches each definition. Write the word on the line.

Check the Words You Know

___ astronomers
___ collapse
___ collide
___ compact
___ galaxy
___ particles

______________ **1.** firmly packed together

______________ **2.** to cave in

______________ **3.** to hit or strike violently together

______________ **4.** extremely small units of matter

______________ **5.** scientists who study the sun, moon, planets, stars, etc.

Directions Choose the word from the box that best matches each clue. Write the word on the line.

______________ **6.** You might use this word to describe something packed together.

______________ **7.** You might use this word to describe what two cars do in an accident.

______________ **8.** You might use this word to describe what a folding chair does.

______________ **9.** You might use this word to describe the Milky Way.

______________ **10.** You might use this word to describe specks of dust.

Write a Newspaper Article

On a separate sheet of paper, write a newspaper article about the discovery of a new planet. Use as many of the vocabulary words as you can.

School + Home **Home Activity** Your child identified and used vocabulary words from *The Universe*. Make up a story with your child about outer space. Use as many of the vocabulary words as you can.

Name ______________________________

Regular and Irregular Plural Nouns

Plural nouns name more than one person, place, or thing.

- Most plural nouns are formed by adding *-s*.
  swing/swings   animal/animals   boy/boys
- Add *-es* to nouns ending in *ch, sh, x, z, s,* and *ss*.
  fox/foxes   bush/bushes   church/churches   address/addresses
- If a noun ends in a consonant and *y*, change *y* to *i* and add *-es*.
  blueberry/blueberries   pony/ponies   penny/pennies
- Some nouns have **irregular plural** forms. They change spelling.
  man/men   tooth/teeth   child/children   foot/feet
- For most nouns that end in *f* or *fe*, change *f* to *v* and add *-es*.
  half/halves   wolf/wolves   thief/thieves   shelf/shelves
- Some nouns have the same singular and plural forms.
  salmon   trout   sheep   moose   deer
- For compound nouns, make only the important word plural.
  mothers-in-law   commanders-in-chief
- When a noun ends in a vowel and *o*, add *-s*: *video/videos*, *radio/radios*.
- Check a dictionary for plurals of nouns ending in a consonant and *o*: *photo/photos*, *potato/potatoes*, *tomato/tomatoes*, *hero/heroes*.

Directions Write the plural form of the noun in parentheses.

1. They tuned their ____________________ (radio) to the shuttle liftoff.
2. How many ____________________ (mystery) does our universe hold?
3. My brother likes to read about space ____________________ (hero).
4. Casey had model rockets on all of his ____________________ (shelf).
5. Space telescopes are able to transmit amazing ____________________ (image).
6. Ian packed his astronomy books in ____________________ (box).
7. Mrs. Peck divided the class into ____________________ (half).
8. All of the ____________________ (chairman) met at the space summit.
9. Alan has seen three space shuttle ____________________ (launch).
10. Ellen searched three ____________________ (library) for books on quasars.

School + Home

Home Activity Your child learned about regular and irregular plural nouns. With your child, look at labels on food products. Ask him or her to identify regular and irregular plural nouns.

Multisyllabic Words I

Spelling Words				
possibility	linear	ridiculous	artificial	calculator
competitive	curiosity	organization	individual	encyclopedia
peony	tarantula	correspondent	cauliflower	optimistic
enthusiastic	sophisticated	satisfactory	irritable	simultaneously

Finish the Sentences Use a list word to finish each sentence. Write the word on the line.

1. The network news ___ reported about the big forest fire. 1. ______________
2. I'm feeling ___ today because I didn't get enough sleep. 2. ______________
3. One of my favorite vegetables is ___. 3. ______________
4. I'm scared of spiders, so I'm sure a ___ would terrify me. 4. ______________
5. I like to use my ___ to multiply large numbers. 5. ______________
6. That was the silliest, most ___ movie I've ever seen. 6. ______________
7. The problem with some ___ flavors is that they taste bitter. 7. ______________
8. Pessimistic is the opposite of ___. 8. ______________
9. A ___ plant has pink, red, or white flowers. 9. ______________
10. My mom belongs to a charitable ___. 10. ______________
11. Everyone in town is ___ about our team winning the championship. 11. ______________
12. It is not recommended to watch television and do your homework ___. 12. ______________
13. Your grades are ___, but you could do better. 13. ______________
14. That fellow is dressed like a ___ gentleman. 14. ______________
15. I used an ___ to learn about the Roman Empire. 15. ______________
16. My taking the test early is a ___. 16. ______________
17. Our football team is very ___. 17. ______________
18. I bought ___ servings of applesauce. 18. ______________
19. The graph shows ___ growth. 19. ______________
20. The kitten gets into trouble because of her ___. 20. ______________

School + Home **Home Activity** Your child used list words to finish sentences. Select two or three words from the list and ask your child how to count the syllables in those words.

Name ________________________________

Word Web

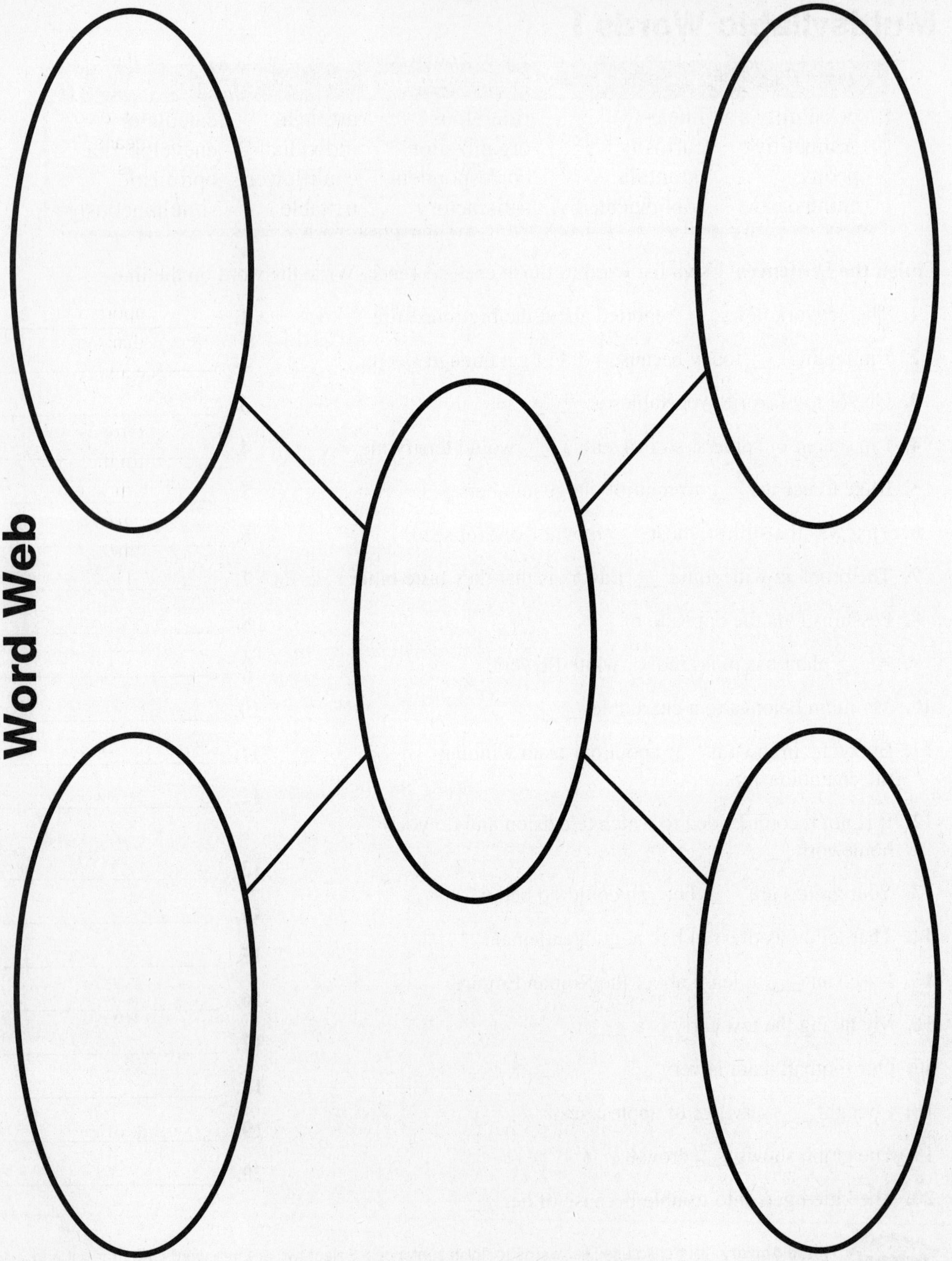

Name______________________________

Vocabulary • Greek and Latin Roots

- Many words in English are based on **Greek** and **Latin roots.** Sometimes you can use these roots to figure out the meaning of an unfamiliar word.
- The Greek root *astro-* means "star." The Greek root *geo-* means "earth." The Greek root *-ology* means "the study of." The Greek word *nautes* means "sailor." The Latin word *spiritus* means "soul, courage, vigor." The Latin root *-mit* means "send." The Latin prefix *trans-* means "across, over."

Directions Read the following passage. Then answer the questions below.

Until astronauts can safely visit Mars, we are able to familiarize ourselves with "the red planet" from images sent to Earth by satellites and from the Mars exploration rovers, *Spirit* and *Opportunity*.

The two rovers are clever robots that function like geologists on the surface of Mars. As the rovers move over Mars's surface, they take pictures and transmit them back to Earth. The pictures are of hills and valleys, rocks and boulders, and even particles of sand. An important discovery made by the rovers is that Mars probably had water on its surface a very long time ago.

It won't be long before the two rovers wear out. There is no way to return them to Earth to be fixed. Even though they won't last forever, *Spirit* and *Opportunity* have helped us know more about the galaxy beyond our own planet.

1. What can you tell about the meaning of *astronaut* from its Greek roots?

____

2. How do you think the definition of *spiritus* relates to the rover named *Spirit*?

____

3. What do the Latin prefix and root in *transmit* tell you about the word's meaning?

____

____

4. Based on the meanings of the Greek roots of the word, what do you think the Mars rovers do to function as *geologists*?

____

5. Write as many words as you can think of that use the root *astro-*. If you cannot think of any words by yourself, use the dictionary for help.

____

School + Home **Home Activity** Your child identified and used Greek and Latin roots to understand new words in a passage. Work with your child to identify unfamiliar words in an article by examining their Greek or Latin roots.

Name ______________________________

Skim and Scan

- To **scan** is to move one's eyes quickly down the page, seeking specific words and phrases. Scanning is used to find out if a resource will answer a reader's questions. Once a reader has scanned a document, he or she might go back and skim it.
- To **skim** a document is to read the first and last paragraphs as well as using headings, summaries, and other organizers as you move down the page. Skimming is used to quickly identify the main idea. You might also read the first sentence of each paragraph.

Directions Scan the phone book entries. Then answer the questions below.

ICE & ICE CUBES

Ken's Locker
2001 S. Maplewood Dr. 555-9001

Mack's Ice of Homewood
319 E. Harvey Ave. 555-0902

ICE SKATING RINKS

See Skating Rinks and Parks

ILLUSTRATORS

See Artists, Commercial

IMPORTERS

Safari Imports
938 W. River Dr. 555-3434

INCOME TAX PREPARATION

See Accountants, Certified Public; Accountants, Public; Tax Preparation Services

IN-HOME CARE SERVICES

See Home Health Care and Services

1. What do you need to do if you want to find an illustrator?

____

2. What do you have to do to find the number and address of the nearest ice skating rink?

____

3. Where can you buy ice on Harvey Ave.?

____

____

4. Where would you go if you wanted to buy a gift imported from another country?

____

5. Can you find the phone number for a Certified Public Accountant on this page? Where would you look?

____

____

Name ______________________________

Directions Skim the passage by reading the headings and the first sentence of each paragraph. Then answer the questions below.

MERCURY

Mercury is the second smallest of the planets. It is not much larger than our moon. It even looks like our moon. At night Mercury can only be seen for a brief time before sunrise and after sunset. Because it is so close to the sun, its temperatures soar to more than 800 degrees Fahrenheit.

Mercury has many craters like our moon. It has a huge basin called the *Caloris Basin.* It was formed when a meteorite crashed into it billions of years ago.

VENUS

Venus is similar in size to Earth. It is very bright and is seen as a morning star and an evening star. Venus is so bright because it is covered with clouds that reflect the sunlight very well.

Venus comes closer to Earth than any other planet. Its atmosphere is very different than Earth's.

6. Which two planets is this passage about? How can you tell?

____

____

7. Will this passage help you answer questions about Pluto? Why or why not?

____

____

8. Will this passage help you answer questions about Earth? Explain.

____

____

9. If you were looking for information about craters, would this passage help? Explain.

____

____

10. If you needed to find information to compare the sizes of Venus and Mercury, would this passage help you? Explain.

____

School + Home **Home Activity** Your child learned about scanning and skimming to help find a main idea or information. Look at a newspaper or magazine with your child and have him or her skim it to find the main idea. Then ask your child to scan it for a particular piece of information.

Name ____________________

Multisyllabic Words I

Proofread an Article Circle six spelling errors in this article. Write the words correctly. Then find a run-on sentence. Write it correctly.

Blueberries

A few indivijual studies show that blueberries are rich in antioxidants. These chemicals suggest the possability of preventing heart attacks, they may improve your eyesight, prevent brain impairment, and improve memory. If you want to be optemistic about your health, become enthuseastic about beutiful blueberry recipes. And remember, try not to use artaficial ingredients when you cook.

1. ____________ 2. ____________
3. ____________ 4. ____________
5. ____________ 6. ____________
7. ____________________________________

Spelling Words
possibility
linear
ridiculous
artificial
calculator
competitive
curiosity
organization
individual
encyclopedia
peony
tarantula
correspondent
cauliflower
optimistic
enthusiastic
sophisticated
satisfactory
irritable
simultaneously

Proofread Words Circle the word that is spelled correctly. Write it.

8. peony	peonie	8.	____________
9. lineare	linear	9.	____________
10. ridikulous	ridiculous	10.	____________
11. tarantula	taranteula	11.	____________
12. cauliflour	cauliflower	12.	____________
13. calculater	calculator	13.	____________
14. competitive	competive	14.	____________
15. cureosity	curiosity	15.	____________

Frequently Misspelled Words

business
beautiful

School + Home

Home Activity Your child identified misspelled words. Ask your child to think of a word from the list with five syllables, spell it, and use that word in a sentence.

Regular and Irregular Plural Nouns

Directions Read the passage. Then read each question. Circle the letter of the correct answer.

Best Birthday Presents

(1) The new toy store in town features many exciting products for children. (2) Before their birthday partys, many parents give their children time to write wish lists. (3) Lots of children consider their hobbies. (4) Do they love to collect different stuffed animals? (5) If so, the jungle monkies, fluffy sheep, and unusual donkeys get a lot of interest. (6) Some of the stuffed animals can walk, but they require batteries. (7) Many older children ask for videos and DVDs. (8) Their new favorites include funny movies about ten moose that live in Montana and an animated film about swordfish.

1 How many plural nouns are in sentence 1?

A 0
B 1
C 2
D 3

2 What change, if any, should be made in sentence 2?

A Change ***partys*** to **parties**
B Change ***parents*** to **parentes**
C Change ***lists*** to **lists'**
D Make no change

3 In sentence 3, *hobbies* is which type of noun?

A Collective
B Regular plural
C Irregular plural
D Proper

4 What change, if any, should be made in sentence 5?

A Change ***donkeys*** to **donkies**
B Change ***monkies*** to **monkeys**
C Change ***sheep*** to **sheeps**
D Make no change

5 What are the irregular plural nouns in this paragraph?

A products, parents, lists, hobbies
B lots, videos, animals, donkeys
C batteries, movies, favorites, moose
D children, sheep, moose, swordfish

School + Home **Home Activity** Your child prepared for taking tests on regular and irregular plural nouns. Have your child make flash cards with singular and plural forms of nouns on opposite sides. Use the cards to help him or her learn plural forms.

Name ______________________________

Main Idea and Details

- The **topic** is what a piece of writing is all about. It can usually be stated in one or two words.
- The **main idea** is the most important idea about the topic.
- **Details** are pieces of information that explain or support the main idea.

Directions Read the following passage. Then complete the diagram below.

Pompeii: An Underground City

The eruption of Mount Vesuvius in A.D. 79 left the entire Italian city of Pompeii buried in volcanic mud for about 1,700 years. Archaeologists discovered the city only a few hundred years ago. Because the citizens of Pompeii were unprepared, thousands died and were buried under about thirty feet of volcanic material. Archaeologists have slowly uncovered houses, public baths, and other structures, including several amphitheaters, large stadiums where residents gathered to see spectacles such as plays and gladiator fights. The relics of Pompeii give us a glimpse into what life was like more than 2,000 years ago during the first century.

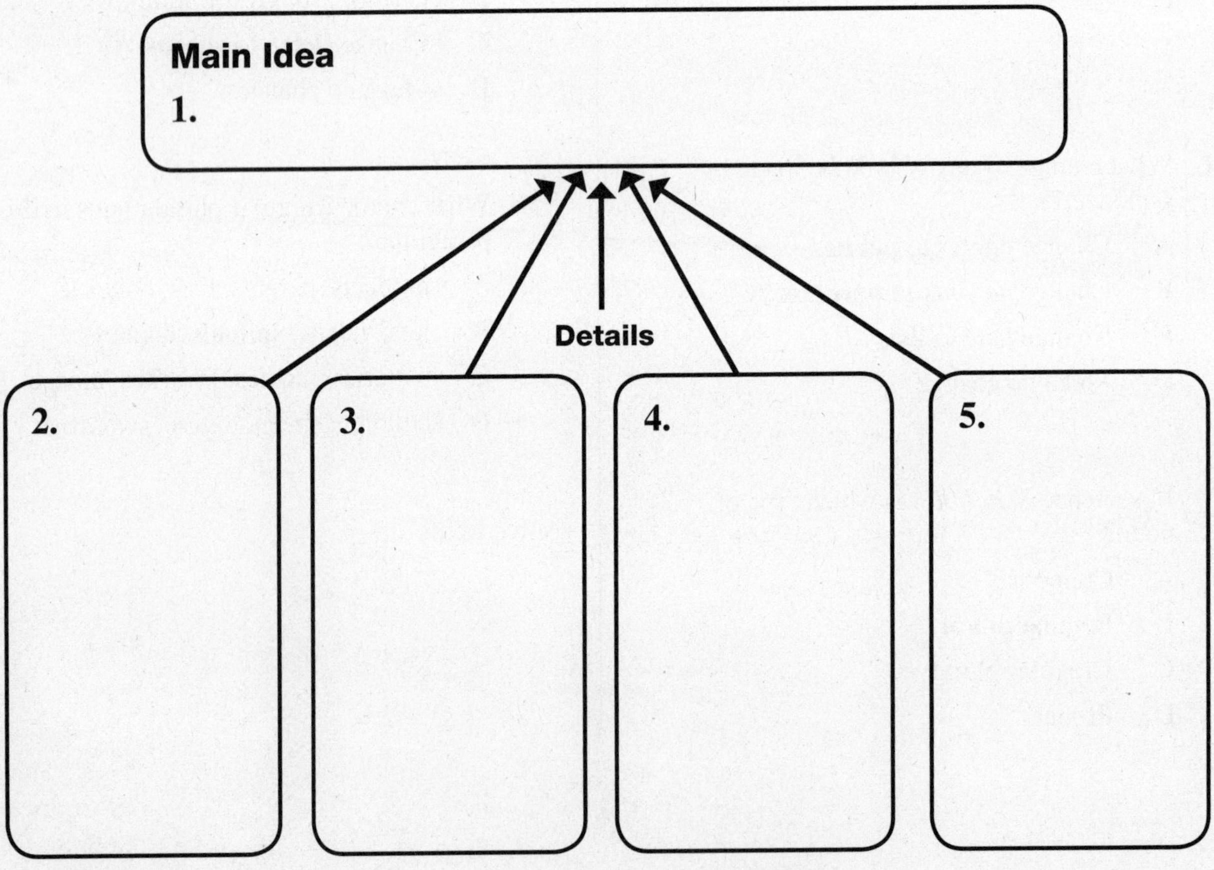

Home Activity Your child read a short passage and identified its main idea and supporting details. Work with your child to identify the main idea and supporting details of individual paragraphs in a magazine article or encyclopedia article.

Name ____________________

Writing • Mystery

Key Features of a Mystery

- has a plot that revolves around unexplained events
- may have elements of suspense or terror
- has signs or clues that help reveal the mystery

The Puzzle Box

The dusty wooden box sat in front of the fireplace. Although it looked worthless, Alexis and Federico knew that if the legend was true, it contained a great treasure.

They both jumped when they heard the knock on the door. It was Mr. Livingston, standing in the pouring rain. "Lovely evening," he said. "I understand you found an unusual box—one that can't be opened. Why call me?"

"You've researched the legend for years," Federico said. "If the box can be opened, I'm hoping that you know how." Alexis was not pleased with Federico's decision to call Livingston. He was known for being greedy and untrustworthy; if the box contained riches, he would want more than his share.

Livingston's eyes beamed in the firelight as he reached for the box. He ran his thin, gaunt hand over it and slid out a panel. He continued, sliding out thirteen panels in all and when the last panel slid out, the top flew open.

"It's empty!" Alexis mumbled in disbelief. Federico remained silent.

Livingston grabbed his umbrella, and headed back out into the stormy night. "I guess this legend is just that," he said, "a legend."

Alone again, Federico smiled at Alexis and pulled up the box's false bottom revealing the treasure. "I guess Livingston hadn't heard the part of the legend of the Emerald Necklace of Isis that describes the box's secret compartment. I just needed someone to open the box!"

1. What mystery are Federico and Alexis trying to solve in the story?

____

____

2. What clue is given that Federico knows about the secret compartment in the box?

____

____

____

Name ______________________________

Vocabulary

Directions Choose the word from the box that best matches each definition. Write the word on the line.

Check the Words You Know

- ___approximately
- ___divine
- ___excavated
- ___mechanical
- ___pottery
- ___restore
- ___superstitious
- ___terra cotta
- ___watchfully

______________ **1.** uncovered, unearthed, or dug out

______________ **2.** to bring back to its original condition by rebuilding or fixing

______________ **3.** in an observant manner; alertly

______________ **4.** supremely great or holy; god-like

______________ **5.** characterized by having unreasonable beliefs

Directions Choose the word from the box that best completes each sentence. Write the word on the line.

6. People have been using clay to make ______________ for thousands of years.

7. The pottery wheel was invented ______________ 5,000 years ago.

8. ______________ can be used to make walls and structural supports, as well as pots and sculptures.

9. Early ______________ pottery wheels were operated with a foot pedal.

10. Artisans work to ______________ ancient relics.

Write a Newspaper Article

On a separate sheet of paper, write a short newspaper article describing a piece of pottery discovered by archaeologists. Use as many vocabulary words as you can.

School + Home

Home Activity Your child identified and used vocabulary words from *The Emperor's Silent Army.* Read a newspaper, magazine, or encyclopedia article about an archaeological dig. Work with your child to identify words with suffixes and use word structure to determine their meanings.

Possessive Nouns

A **possessive noun** shows ownership. A **singular possessive noun** shows that one person, place, or thing has or owns something. A **plural possessive noun** shows that more than one person, place, or thing has or owns something.

- To make a singular noun show possession, add an apostrophe (') and *-s*.
  an emperor's robe   Sis's hat
- To make a plural noun that ends in *-s* show possession, add an apostrophe (').
  many emperors' robe   the Jonses' house
- To make a plural noun that does not end in *-s* show possession, add an apostrophe (') and *-s*.
  the men's tools   many sheep's wool

Directions Write each noun as a possessive noun. Write *S* if the possessive noun is singular. Write *P* if the possessive noun is plural.

1. parents ____________ ____
2. photo ____________ ____
3. child ____________ ____
4. Miss Meyer ____________ ____
5. stores ____________ ____
6. country ____________ ____
7. James ____________ ____
8. teeth ____________ ____

Directions Add an apostrophe (') or an apostrophe (') and *-s* to make the underlined nouns possessive. Write the possessive noun on the line.

9. <u>Qin Shi Huang</u> army was enormous. ____________
10. The <u>emperor</u> death was kept a secret. ____________
11. The <u>soldiers</u> uniforms were copied exactly. ____________
12. Each <u>horse</u> tail was braided. ____________
13. The <u>headquarters</u> area is in Pit 3. ____________
14. All the <u>people</u> expressions look real. ____________

School + Home **Home Activity** Your child learned about possessive nouns. Together read a newspaper or magazine article. Have your child find and circle three singular and three plural possessive nouns in the article.

Name ______________________________

Latin Roots I

Spelling Words				
suspend	pendant	conductor	novel	productive
numeral	reserve	numerous	preserve	pending
pendulum	deduction	novelty	numerator	reservoir
conservatory	appendix	impending	induct	innovative

Missing Words Write two list words to complete each sentence correctly.

You must **(1)** ____ the **(2)** ____ from the mechanism of the grandfather clock.

1. ____________________ **2.** ____________________

This **(3)** ___ new device is quite a **(4)** ___.

3. ____________________ **4.** ____________________

The book's **(5)** ___ contains **(6)** ___ important facts.

5. ____________________ **6.** ____________________

The **(7)** ___ vote will decide if they **(8)** ___ the player into the Hall of Fame.

7. ____________________ **8.** ____________________

I plan to **(9)** ___ tickets for the **(10)** ___ concert.

9. ____________________ **10.** ____________________

The garden **(11)** ___ is next to the water **(12)** ___ near the park.

11. ____________________ **12.** ____________________

Analogies Write list words to complete the analogies.

13. Shirt is to collar as necklace is to ___. **13.** ____________________

14. Band is to leader as orchestra is to ___. **14.** ____________________

15. Buy is to purchase as number is to ___. **15.** ____________________

16. Useless is to futile as effective is to ___. **16.** ____________________

17. Waste is to discard as save is to ___. **17.** ____________________

18. Bottom is to denominator as top is to ___. **18.** ____________________

19. Song is to CD as chapter is to ___. **19.** ____________________

20. Addition is to increase as subtraction is to ___. **20.** ____________________

School + Home **Home Activity** Your child wrote words with Latin roots. Say a word from the list and ask your child to identify and define the Latin root.

Plot Structure Diagram

Title ____

Characters

Setting

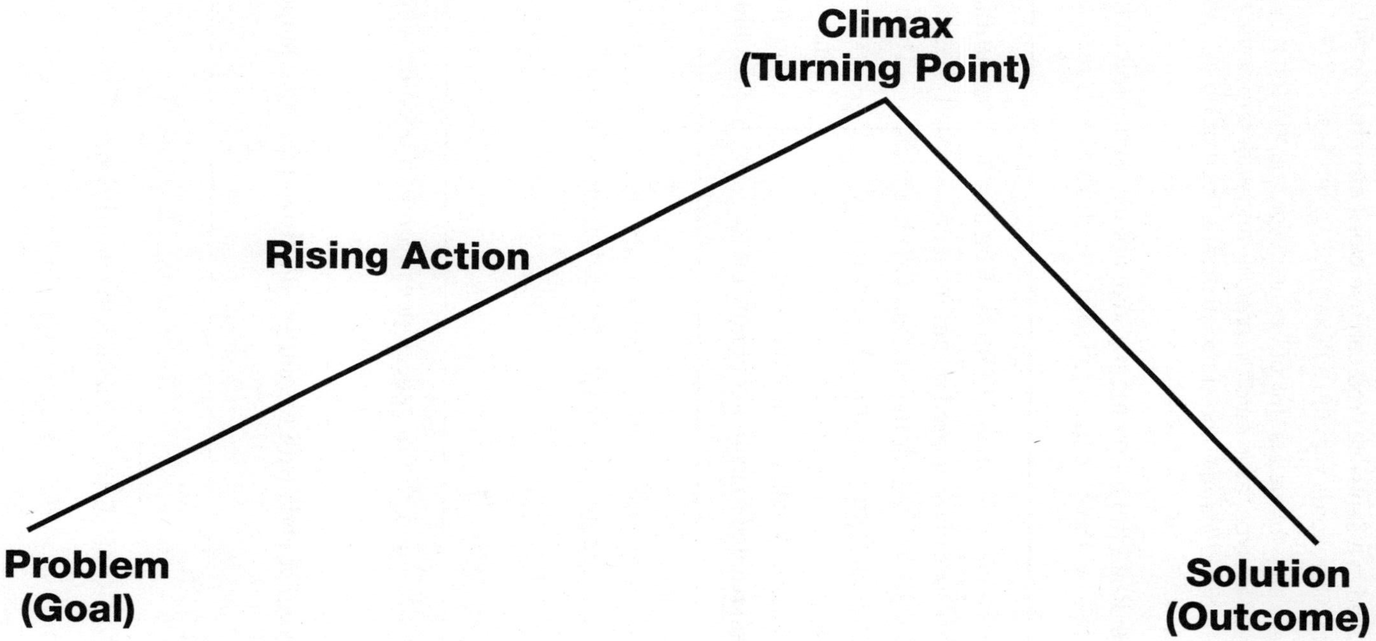

Name ______________________________

Vocabulary • Suffixes *-ful, -ly, -al*

- A **suffix** is a word part added to the end of a base word to change its meaning or the way it is used in a sentence. You can use **word structure** to help you figure out the meanings of unfamiliar words with the suffixes *-ful, -ly,* and *-al.*
- The suffix *-ful* means "full of," as in *delightful;* the suffix *-ly* is added to adjectives to make adverbs, as in *careful/carefully,* and added to some nouns to make adjectives, as in *friend/friendly;* the suffix *-al* means "pertaining to," as in *natural.*

Directions Read the following passage about a school field trip to a museum. Then answer the questions below. Pay attention to word structure as you read.

The guards stood watchfully as Kim and Sasha's class entered the art museum. They were headed for the Ancient Greek and Roman Pottery exhibit. As they passed through the mechanical turnstile, they could barely contain their excitement.

Kim wanted to learn about how the artifacts were excavated. Sasha wanted to learn about how the pieces were restored. Their art teacher, Miss Hayes, patiently explained everything they wanted to know and more. They spent approximately three hours at the museum, and Kim and Sasha could have spent three more!

1. *Watchfully* has two suffixes. What is the first suffix added to the base word *watch?* How does this suffix change the part of speech used in the sentence?

____

____

2. What word and part of speech does *watchful* become when you add the suffix *-ly?*

____

3. *Mechanical* ends with the suffix *-al.* How does *-al* change the meaning of the base word?

____

____

4. How does the suffix *-ly* change the word *patient?*

____

5. Does the suffix *-ly* added to *approximate* change the part of speech in the same way it does with the word *patient?* Explain.

____

School + Home

Home Activity Your child read a short passage and identified suffixes *-al, -ly,* and *-ful.* Read a story or article with your child, and ask him or her to point out words that have these suffixes. Ask how the suffixes change the words.

Name________________________________

Note Taking

- **Note taking** can help you when you are gathering information for a report. It can also help you focus your reading and memorize information.
- Recording key words and notes in a chart like the one below is a helpful strategy. When taking notes, paraphrase by putting the information into your own words. Use short sentences or phrases. Synthesize, or combine, information so you include only important details.

Directions Read the following passage. As you read, add to the notes in the chart below.

The first emperor of China, Qin Shi Huang, ruled for only 36 years, yet he left behind a cultural legacy that includes two ancient wonders: an army of life-sized terra cotta soldiers and the Great Wall of China. These two feats of craftsmanship and engineering share more in common than you might think. Both were designed to protect the emperor. Both are considered wonders of the ancient world. And, both were paid for in the thousands, possibly millions, of human lives of the workers who died or were killed in the process of sculpting or building.

Built and rebuilt between the fifth century B.C. and the sixteenth century, the Great Wall of China is actually a series of connected walls. When the emperor unified China in 221 B.C., he had the walls of individual warring states united along the northern border. The four-thousand-mile-long Great Wall was designed to defend China from nomadic invaders from the North.

Excavation of the terra cotta warriors began about thirty years ago and continues today. Archaeologists believe there are about 7,500 in total: each life-sized with individual facial features and expressions. The warriors were created to protect the emperor, not during his life, but after he died, and were placed in a massive underground tomb.

Both the Great Wall and the terra cotta army were created on a monumental scale to protect one man. Emperor Qin Shi Huang, however, died at the age of forty-nine. Although they may not serve their original purpose, the Great Wall of China and the terra cotta warriors have taken on lives of their own, attracting thousands of visitors to China each year, and offering us a glimpse into the first empire of China.

Key Words	Notes
Qin Shi Huang	first emperor of China; left behind Great Wall of China and an army of terra cotta soldiers; **1.**
Great Wall of China	**2.**
terra cotta warriors	**3.**

Name ______________________________

Directions Answer the questions using the article and your notes.

4. Summarize the information in the first paragraph in a single sentence.

____

____

____

5. Paraphrase the first sentence of the second paragraph of the article.

____

____

6. What is another way you could organize your notes from this article?

____

7. How would organizing your notes this way help you understand the article?

____

____

8. Why is writing down key words a good way to organize your notes?

____

____

9. Why should you write down only important ideas when taking notes?

____

____

10. How can taking notes help you study for a test?

____

____

School + Home **Home Activity** Your child learned how to take notes using a key words and notes graphic organizer. Read an article or story with your child. Help your child determine important key words and summarize or paraphrase the important information in note form.

Name ____________________

Graphic Sources

- **Graphic sources,** such as charts, diagrams, and time lines, show information visually.
- As you read, connect information in a graphic source to information in the text to strengthen your understanding.

Directions Study the time line below about the Pueblo people. Then answer the questions.

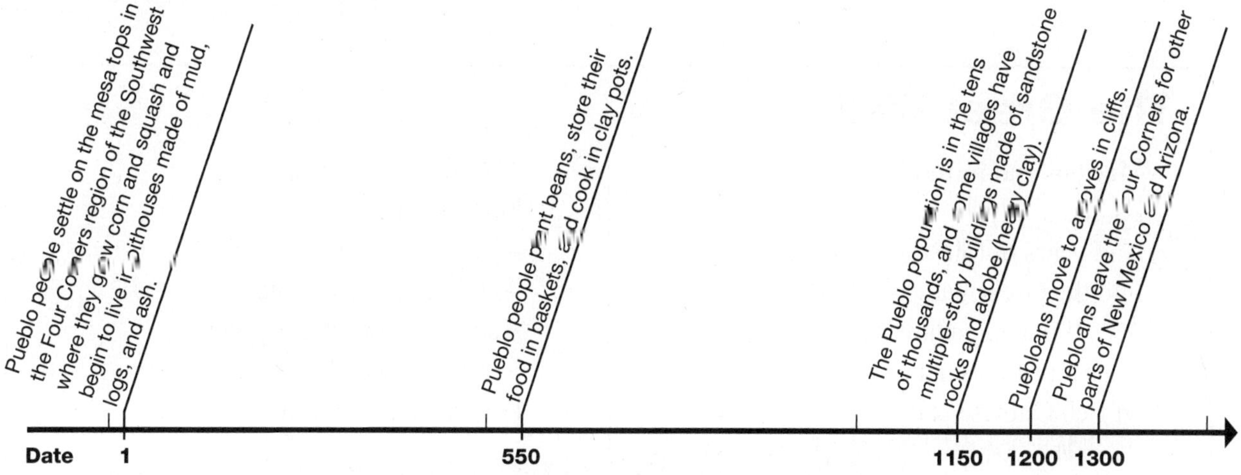

Pueblo People in the Four Corners (region where Colorado, New Mexico, Utah, and Arizona borders meet)

1. What information is shown on this time line? Would you find information about the Pueblo people in Texas? Why or why not?

____

____

2. For about how many years did the Puebloans live in alcoves?

____

3. How many years passed between the first pithouses and the use of clay pots for cooking?

____

4. What is one reason the Puebloans might have moved their homes from the mesas to the alcoves in the cliffs?

____

5. Why do you think the last entry is at 1300?

____

____

School + Home **Home Activity** Your child used a time line to learn information visually. Look in an encyclopedia for an article about an invention. Look at any graphic sources that accompany the article and discuss how the graphic sources help you understand the article.

Writing • Poem

Key Features of a Poem

- words arranged in lines, or groups of lines called stanzas
- lines have rhythm
- words may rhyme

The Great Wall

Millions and millions
Poured sweat, hours,
And years of toil
Into the Great Wall—
A wall that stretches
Over four thousand miles
Of rich Chinese soil.

Brick by brick,
Layer by layer,
The wall was built slowly,
Its beauty and
Strength a testament
To young and old,
Rich and lowly.

The wall was built to
Stand strong
Against harsh, summer sun
And bitter, winter cold,
And still stands strong as a
Symbol of wonder
For you and everyone.

1. Reread the poem. What kinds of emotions does the poem express about the Great Wall of China?

____

____

2. Circle words and phrases that express these emotions.

Name ______________________________

Vocabulary

Directions Choose the word from the box that best matches each definition. Write the word on the line.

Check the Words You Know

___alcoves
___decades
___obsidian
___prehistoric
___pueblo
___trowels

______________________ **1.** from a time before recorded history

______________________ **2.** periods of ten years

______________________ **3.** a hard, dark, glassy rock that is formed when lava cools

______________________ **4.** recesses or large, hollow spaces in walls

______________________ **5.** a Native American village consisting of houses built of adobe and stone, usually with flat roofs and often several stories high

Directions Choose the word from the box that best completes each sentence. Write the word on the line.

6. Archaeologists use ______________________ to dig through rock and dirt to unearth artifacts.

7. In ancient times, people used ______________________ to make sharp knives and weapons.

8. Natural weathering and erosion of the sides of mountains

created ______________________ that the Pueblo people used as homes.

9. The woolly mammoth is a ______________________ animal that is now extinct.

10. Some archaeological sites may take ______________________ to excavate.

Write a Journal Entry

On a separate sheet of paper write a journal entry you might make after a long day of working at an archaeological dig. Use as many vocabulary words as you can.

School + Home

Home Activity Your child identified and used vocabulary words from *Stones, Bones, and Petroglyphs.* Read an article with your child about a recent archaeological discovery. Ask him or her to point out unknown words. Help your child guess their definitions, and then check the meanings using a dictionary or glossary.

Name ____

Action and Linking Verbs

A **verb** is the main word in the predicate of a sentence. The verb tells what the subject of the sentence is or does. An **action verb** tells what the subject does. A **linking verb** links, or joins, the subject with a word or words in the predicate that tell what the subject is or is like. Linking verbs are forms of *be*, such as *am, is, are, was,* and *were*. *Become, seem, appear, feel, taste, smell,* and *look* can be linking verbs.

Action Verbs Grandma scrubs the wooden floor. We pump water.

Linking Verbs The bread smells wonderful. He is hungry.

- A **predicate nominative** is a noun or pronoun that follows a linking verb and identifies or explains the subject: *Sarah's brother was the leader on his team.*

Directions Write *A* if the underlined word is an action verb. Write *L* if the underlined word is a linking verb. Write *PN* if the underlined word is a predicate nominative.

1. The Colorado canyons are deep. ______
2. The students climbed to the top. ______
3. Sarah and Ken are educators. ______
4. Pueblo people lived all over. ______
5. Everyone was patient with the visitors. ______

Directions Underline each action verb. Circle each linking verb.

6. They saw many potsherds on the ground.
7. The day was hot and smelled of dust.
8. The Puebloans turned cliffs into homes.
9. Amanda felt it is still a big mystery.
10. Bill felt the walls of the kiva with his hands.
11. Archaeology is really about understanding people.
12. The students worked steadily until sunset.
13. They said that Mesa Verda was like a time machine.
14. The cliff dwellings seemed amazing to the students.

School + Home

Home Activity Your child learned about action and linking verbs. Describe what a family member looks like and does. Say the sentences slowly and have your child identify the action and linking verbs you use.

Final Syllable Patterns

Spelling Words				
ancestor	hospital	grumble	sponsor	superior
escalator	encounter	shoulder	skeleton	forbidden
appetizer	identical	abandon	governor	endeavor
outspoken	durable	lengthen	cinnamon	interior

Antonyms Write the list words that have opposite meanings.

1. exterior **1.** ____________

2. shorten **2.** ____________

3. descendant **3.** ____________

4. flimsy **4.** ____________

5. different **5.** ____________

6. allowed **6.** ____________

7. inferior **7.** ____________

8. shy **8.** ____________

Word Meaning Write a list word that matches each definition.

9. to leave behind **9.** ____________

10. to attempt **10.** ____________

11. a place for medical treatment **11.** ____________

12. a spice **12.** ____________

13. a snack before a meal **13.** ____________

14. the body's framework **14.** ____________

15. to meet **15.** ____________

16. the joint above the arm **16.** ____________

17. leader of a state **17.** ____________

18. a moving stairway **18.** ____________

19. to complain **19.** ____________

20. to support or be responsible for **20.** ____________

School + Home

Home Activity Your child wrote words with final syllable patterns. Say words from the list and ask your child to spell them correctly.

Idea Web

Name____

Vocabulary • Unknown Words

- A **dictionary** is a book that alphabetically lists words and their meanings.
- A **glossary** is a short dictionary at the back of a book. It provides definitions of some of the words used in the book.

Directions Read the following passage about petroglyphs. Then answer the questions below.

Petroglyphs are images carved into rocks. Prehistoric people probably used bones or antlers to create this ancient art. They also may have used hard stones, such as obsidian, to cut into softer materials, such as sandstone. Along the San Juan River in Utah, there is a two-hundred-foot-long panel of petroglyphs carved into the side of the cliff where the Pueblo people once lived in alcoves.

The Puebloans lived in these cliff dwellings for several decades and left behind a legacy of images that continue to intrigue scholars and tourists alike.

1. Find *prehistoric* in a glossary or dictionary. What part of speech is it?

____

2. Find *obsidian* in a glossary or dictionary. What does it mean?

____

3. Find the word *Pueblo* in a glossary or dictionary. How does this definition add to your understanding of the passage?

____

____

____

4. Use a glossary or dictionary to look up the definition of *alcoves*. Which words in the definition could replace the word *alcoves* in this passage?

____

5. Find *decades* in a glossary or dictionary. Which meaning fits this passage?

____

School + Home

Home Activity Your child used a glossary or dictionary to understand new words in a passage. Work with your child to identify unknown words in an article or story. Look up these words in a dictionary. Go over the pronunciations, parts of speech, and meanings of these words with your child. See how many new words your child can learn.

Name ______________________________

Graphic Organizer

- **Graphic organizers** are story maps, semantic maps, pictorial maps, webs, graphs, frames, charts, time lines, and other devices that help you view and construct relationships among events, concepts, and words.

Directions Read the paragraph below. Then complete the graphic organizer with the steps in the process you read about in the paragraph.

The ancient Pueblo people made coil pots out of clay. You can make a coil pot too! First, knead a chunk of clay so it has no air bubbles. Next, take a piece of the kneaded clay and shape it into a small, round, flat patty to form the base of the pot. Then, take a handful of the clay and roll it between your hands or on a flat surface to form a long, thin coil. When the coil is smooth and even, lay it along the top outer edge of the base, pressing and smoothing the inside of the coil to the base until it is firmly attached. Continue making and adding coils of clay, pressing each coil onto the coil beneath, until your pot is the desired height. Let your clay pot slowly dry to prevent cracking.

How to Make a Coil Pot

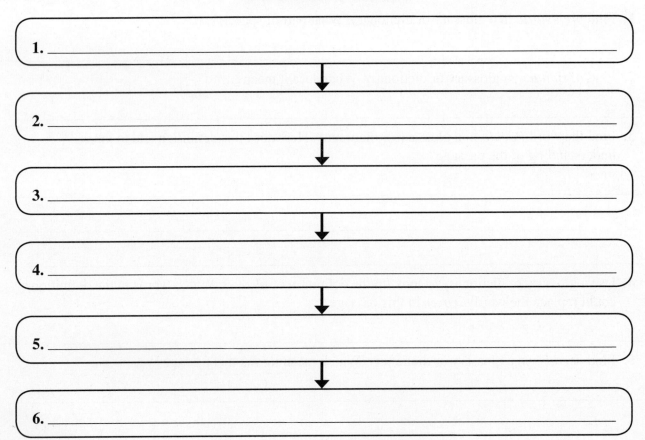

1. ______________________________

2. ______________________________

3. ______________________________

4. ______________________________

5. ______________________________

6. ______________________________

Name____

Directions Imagine you will teach a friend how to do a new activity, such as playing a board game or jumping rope. Think of a simple activity you enjoy. Then fill in the graphic organizer with the title of the activity and four key steps you would use to teach the activity.

____

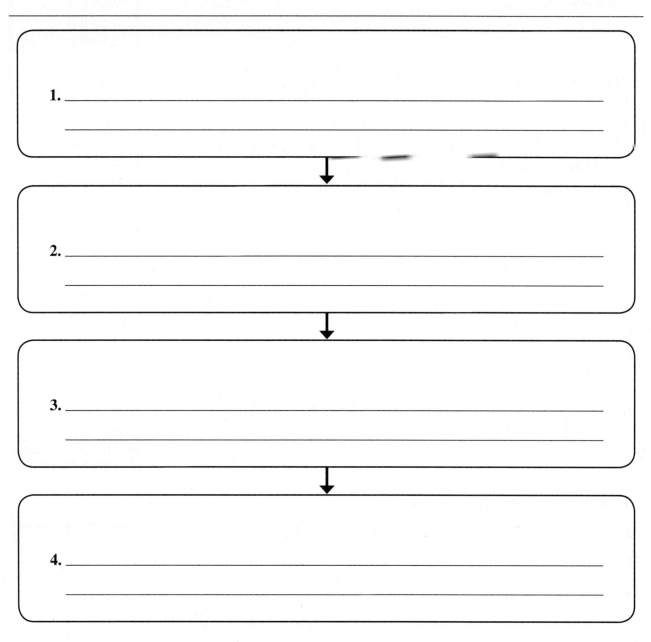

1. ____

↓

2. ____

↓

3. ____

↓

4. ____

School + Home

Home Activity Your child completed a graphic organizer to organize and understand information. Discuss with your child how to make his or her favorite food. Then, to help him or her visualize the information, create a graphic organizer together that shows the steps in the process of making the food.

Name ______________________________

Final Syllable Patterns

Proofread an Article Circle six misspelled words in the article. Write the words correctly. Find a sentence with a capitalization error. Write it correctly.

My Grandfather

My grandfather is my most famous ancester. He was the guvernor of our state. He led the state government to abandun many bad policies. He was also the sponser of important legislation. He was an outspokan representative of hard-working people and worked to provide funding to build a new hospitel. no matter how hard the work, he was always willing to shoulder the burden.

ancestor
hospital
grumble
sponsor
superior
escalator
encounter
shoulder
skeleton
forbidden

appetizer
identical
abandon
governor
endeavor
outspoken
durable
lengthen
cinnamon
interior

1. ____________ 2. ____________
3. ____________ 4. ____________
5. ____________ 6. ____________
7. ______________________________
____

Frequently Misspelled Word

again

Proofread Words Circle the word that is spelled correctly. Write it on the line.

8.	skeletun	skeleton	skeletin	8. ____________
9.	cinnamon	cinnamun	cinnamin	9. ____________
10.	forbiddin	forbiddan	forbidden	10. ____________
11.	appetizer	appetizur	appetizir	11. ____________
12.	superier	superiur	superior	12. ____________
13.	interior	interier	intearior	13. ____________
14.	outspoken	outspokin	outspokun	14. ____________
15.	derable	dirable	durable	15. ____________

School + Home **Home Activity** Your child identified misspelled words. Ask your child to spell the word *ancestor* and use it in a sentence.

Name ____________________

Action and Linking verbs

Directions Read the passage. Then read each question. Circle the letter of the correct answer.

Coming to America

(1) Travel to the New World was difficult in 1620. (2) England seemed much farther than it does now. (3) The *Mayflower* carried about 130 Pilgrims across the very dangerous Atlantic Ocean. (4) The trip required 66 days of stormy seas. (5) The Pilgrims came to the new land to find religious freedom and created a charter to start a new colony. (6) Myles Standish was one of the leaders on the ship. (7) He also became a leader of the new colony. (8) Standish succeeded in building peaceful relations with the natives. (9) The Pilgrims overcame many obstacles to survive in their new home.

1 Which word is the linking verb in sentence 1?

- **A** Travel
- **B** was
- **C** difficult
- **D** in

2 What type of verb is *seemed* in sentence 2?

- **A** Plural verb
- **B** Action verb
- **C** Linking verb
- **D** None of the above

3 What type of verb are *came* and *created* in sentence 5?

- **A** Action verbs
- **B** Linking verbs
- **C** Singular verbs
- **D** None of the above

4 Which word is the linking verb in sentence 7?

- **A** He
- **B** colony
- **C** leader
- **D** became

5 What type of verb is *overcame* in sentence 9?

- **A** Present tense
- **B** Action verb
- **C** Linking verb
- **D** None of the above

School + Home

Home Activity Your child prepared for taking tests on action and linking verbs. Have your child look through a magazine or newspaper article and circle linking verbs and underline action verbs.

Name____

Compare and Contrast

- When you **compare and contrast,** you tell how two or more things are alike and how they are different.
- Clue words such as *like, as,* and *similarly* can show similarities. Clue words such as *however* and *instead* can show differences.

Directions Read the following passage. Then complete the diagram below by giving details that compare and contrast the characteristics of Earth and its moon.

If you ever travel to the moon, you will experience low gravity. As you know, both Earth and its moon are spheres. Yet the moon, with a diameter of about 2,000 miles, is only one-quarter the size of Earth. As a result, the moon's gravity is much lower. In fact, it has only one-sixth of Earth's gravity. For that reason, walking on the moon is like bouncing on a mattress. In 1969, astronauts were delighted to learn how easily they could leap and bounce upon the lunar surface.

The difference in gravity also affects how much objects weigh. Objects on Earth weigh six times as much as they do on the moon. In other words, if a person weighs 120 pounds on Earth, he or she would weigh only 20 pounds on the moon!

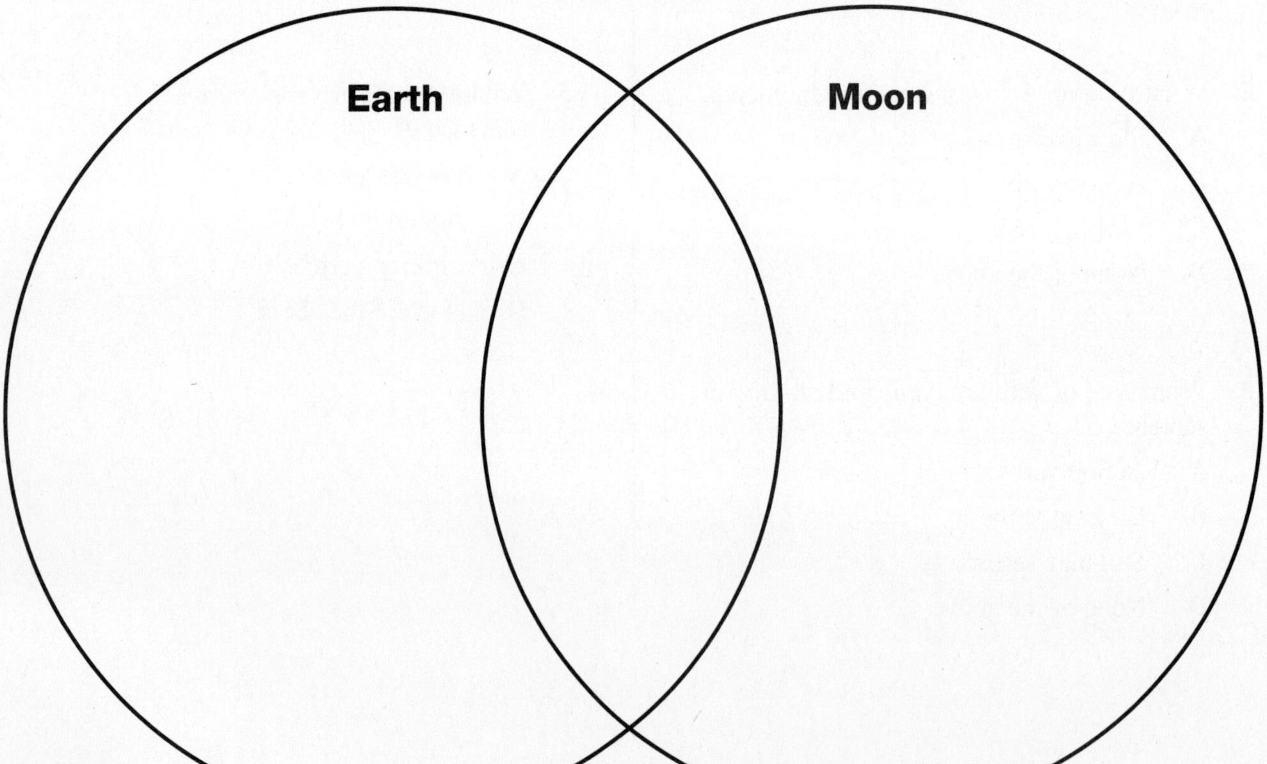

Home Activity Your child used details from a nonfiction passage to compare Earth and its moon. Work with your child to compare and contrast details of individual paragraphs in a magazine article about outer space. Challenge your child to ask questions to clarify points and check understanding.

Name ______________________________

Writing for Tests

Prompt: Imagine a middle school hundreds of years from now. Write a short fantasy story about what it would be like to be a student there.

Day 1 @ Orion

Jack3Bn was the last student to step down from the heli-bus. It was his first day at Orion Middle School and he was a little nervous. "Have a good day," said the robot driver as the solar-powered heli-bus prepared to lift off.

"How am I supposed to have a good day when I don't know anyone at this school?" Jack thought. Then he remembered what his mother had told him that morning as they'd IM'd from their heli-buses. "Day 1 = alwAz hardest. Nx week = U have > nu frenZ!!." He hoped his mother was right.

As Jack walked through the front door, a robotic voice droned, "Jack3Bn, you are late. Please proceed immediately to homeroom 118A." A map of the school flashed onto the wall and a laser light traced the way to get there.

The door to room 118A slid open automatically just as Jack arrived. He scanned the room, looking for a familiar face, as he took his assigned seat. Just as he expected, he recognized no one. "Please take out your laser pens and answer the following questions," the robot teacher snapped. Jack wished the programmers had given the robots more friendly voices.

"Oh, no," Jack said as he realized he had forgotten his laser pens. "Here," the student next to him whispered, placing an extra laser pen on Jack's floating desk.

"Thanks," Jack said as he picked up the pen and turned to see who had given it to him. The girl smiled shyly and then went back to her work. The heli-bus driver's words suddenly sounded in Jack's mind, their chirpy robot cheer taking him back to the sunny ride. Maybe it would be a good day after all.

1. How can you tell this story belongs to the fantasy genre?

____

____

____

____

2. Underline examples of story elements that are based on imagination.

3. Stories sometimes include flashbacks. Circle two flashbacks in the story.

Name____

Vocabulary

Directions Choose the word from the box that best matches each definition below. Write the word on the line.

Check the Words You Know

___combustion
___dingy
___negotiate
___traversed
___waft
___waning

______________________ **1.** going through its regular reduction in the amount of its visible portion

______________________ **2.** passed across, over, or through

______________________ **3.** act or process of burning

______________________ **4.** lacking brightness or freshness; dirty-looking

______________________ **5.** to talk over and arrange terms; confer; consult

Directions Choose the word from the box that best matches each clue below. Write the word on the line.

______________________ **6.** This occurs when something burns.

______________________ **7.** This might describe a dirty, dark room.

______________________ **8.** An example of this is a small breath of perfume.

______________________ **9.** This is what you do to make a bargain.

______________________ **10.** This happens to the moon as its visible bright side gradually faces away from Earth.

Write a Weather Report

On a separate sheet of paper, write a weather report you might make the day after an unusual weather event. Use as many vocabulary words as you can.

School + Home

Home Activity Your child identified and used vocabulary words from *Good-bye to the Moon*. Read a story or nonfiction article with your child. Have him or her point out unfamiliar words. Work together to figure out the meaning of each word by using other words that appear near it.

Subject-Verb Agreement

The subject and verb in a sentence must **agree**, or work together. A singular subject needs a singular verb. A plural subject needs a plural verb.

Use the following rules for verbs that tell about the present time.

- If the subject is a singular noun or *he, she,* or *it,* add *-s* or *-es* to most verbs.
  The star *shines*. The girl *looks* at the star. She *smiles*.
- If the subject is compound, a plural noun, or *I, you, we,* or *they,* do not add *-s* or *-es* to the verb.
  The stars *shine*. Sarah and Renee *look* at the stars. They *smile*.
- For the verb *be*, use *am* and *is* to agree with singular subjects and *are* to agree with plural subjects.
  I *am* a space traveler. The astronaut *is* leaving.
  The scientists *are* here. The pilots *are* on the plane.
- A **collective noun** names a group, such as *family, team,* and *class*. A collective noun is singular if it refers to a group acting as one: The class *is learning* about the universe. A collective noun is plural if it refers to members of the group acting individually: The class *are disagreeing* about the size of the Milky Way.

Directions Write *Yes* if the subject and the verb in the sentence agree. If they do not agree, write *No* and the correct form of the verb.

1. The science lessons intrigues the students. ____________
2. Space travelers realize the risks of lunar landings. ____________
3. Passengers sometimes waits in the cramped quarters for hours. ____________
4. Jordan is interested in space travel. ____________
5. Her eyes is red from the smog. ____________

Directions Underline the verb in ( ) that agrees with the subject.

6. Their heads (throbs, throb) from the enormous pressure.
7. Derek (are, is) ashamed of his torn jacket.
8. The stewardess (volunteers, volunteer) to get him a wheelchair.
9. Renee and Eric (marvels, marvel) at the Earth fashions.
10. The landscape (enthrall, enthralls) Sarah.

School + Home **Home Activity** Your child learned about subject-verb agreement. Underline several sentences in a newspaper or magazine article and ask your child to identify the subject and verb in each sentence and tell why they agree.

Name ________________________________

Schwa

Spelling Words				
different	sentence	American	brilliant	substitute
opinion	material	complete	jewelry	dramatic
instance	communicate	hesitate	elementary	vitamin
ingredients	invitation	discipline	lasagna	desperate

Missing Words Write the list word that finishes each sentence below.

1. Difficult times call for ___ measures. 1. ____________
2. My favorite Italian food is ___. 2. ____________
3. When speaking, it is important to ___ clearly. 3. ____________
4. Self-___ is important when you try to perfect a skill. 4. ____________
5. If you ___, you may lose an opportunity. 5. ____________
6. I received an ___ to a party. 6. ____________
7. There is an ___ school at the end of my street. 7. ____________
8. The ___ for the recipe are listed on the package. 8. ____________
9. I take ___ C every day. 9. ____________
10. The final scene of the play is very ___. 10. ____________
11. These two shades of red are very ___. 11. ____________
12. I'll get my mom a bracelet at the ___ store. 12. ____________
13. A paragraph needs a strong opening ___. 13. ____________
14. I will ___ my report tonight. 14. ____________

Word Meaning Write the list word that matches each definition.

15. example 15. ____________
16. belonging to or coming from the United States 16. ____________
17. fabric or cloth 17. ____________
18. intensely bright; highly intelligent 18. ____________
19. point of view 19. ____________
20. replacement 20. ____________

School + Home **Home Activity** Your child used list words to finish sentences. Say a word from the list and ask your child to spell it and define it.

Scoring Rubric: Fantasy

	4	3	2	1
Focus/Ideas	Clear, focused fantasy that addresses the prompt	Ideas are clear and focused; needs more supporting details	Writing is vague or misses the prompt	Missing fantasy genre elements or unintelligible
Organization	Strong beginning, middle, and end; well-organized paragraphs	Recognizable beginning, middle, and end	Plot events do not build to a climax or resolution	Plot events are random or unordered
Voice	Engaging and interesting narrator and character voices	Interesting character(s) but no narrator voice	Little drama or personality in the voice	No compelling voice
Word Choice	Vivid, precise language brings the story to life	Clear details, adequate language	Limited or redundant language	Vague, dull, or cliché language
Sentences	Excellent variety of sentences, natural rhythm	Correctly constructed sentences; some variety	Little variety; many awkward sentences	Choppy; many incomplete or run-on sentences
Conventions	Excellent control; few or no errors	Reasonable control; few distracting errors	Weak control with distracting errors	Many errors that prevent understanding

Name______________________________

Vocabulary • Unfamiliar Words

- When you are reading and see an unfamiliar word, you can use **context clues**, or words around the unfamiliar word, to figure out its meaning.
- Context clues include definitions, explanations, examples, and synonyms.

Directions Read the following passage about outer space. Then answer the questions below.

Gil was at the controls of the space shuttle, and he was under pressure because Governor Otis of the Moon and his son were on board. Suddenly, the smell of combustion reached him. A waft of a burnt odor was coming from the back of the craft. Gil inched his way to the dingy, dirty engine room to check the status. If necessary, he was prepared to consult with Mission Control to negotiate for emergency repairs. As he traversed, or crossed, the space shuttle to the food court, he saw the problem. A meal was burning in the service cell.

"How's everything going?" called the Governor.

"Just great!" Gil answered with a smile as he hurried back to the controls.

1. What does *combustion* mean? What clues help you to determine the meaning?

____

2. What is a *waft*? What clues help you to determine the meaning?

____

____

3. How do context clues help you determine the meaning of *dingy*?

____

____

4. What does *negotiate* mean as it is used in this text? How can you use context clues to determine this meaning?

____

____

5. What does *traversed* mean? What clues help you to determine the meaning?

____

____

School + Home

Home Activity Your child identified and used context clues to understand unfamiliar words in a passage. Work with your child to identify unfamiliar words in an article or fiction story. Have him or her find context clues to help clarify the meanings of the unfamiliar words.

Name ______________________________

Dictionary and Glossary

- A **dictionary** is a book of words and their meanings. Words are listed in alphabetical order, and each entry shows a word's spelling, syllable parts, pronunciation, and parts of speech. Many entry words contain more than one definition and more than one part of speech.
- A **glossary** is a short dictionary at the back of some books. It includes definitions of words used in the book. Often it tells the page number where the word can be found.
- Entry words in dictionaries and glossaries are usually printed in boldface. Using guide words can help you find entry words quickly. Pairs of guide words appear at the top of each page and show the page's first and last entry words.

Directions Use the following glossary entries to answer the questions below.

oppose to be against (page 289)
orbit to travel in an orbit or circle (page 231)
orbiter a person or object that travels in an orbit (page 231)
organism a living thing (page 38)

1. Under which pair of guide words—*operate* and *orient, oak* and *oral*, or *orchard* and *outer*—would you find the four glossary entries shown above?

____

2. In what order are these four entry words presented?

____

3. Which of these four words appears earliest in the main text? On what page does the word appear?

____

4. Why is only one definition listed for each entry word above?

____

____

5. To find out all possible parts of speech for the word *orbit*, what resource could you use?

____

____

School + Home

Name____

Directions Use this dictionary entry for *orbit* to answer the questions below.

> **or•bit** (ôr' bit) **n.** 1. eye socket; 2. the path of a heavenly body or spacecraft revolving around a heavenly body; 3. the scope of a person's activity; **v.** 1. to travel in an orbit or circle; 2. to put into motion in a circle in space SYN path, course [<Latin *orbita*, path <*orbis*, a circle]

6. How many definitions are listed in this entry?

____

____

7. Which parts of speech for *orbit* are listed? What is a synonym for *orbit?*

____

____

8. Which definition listed above best fits the meaning of *orbit* in the sentence, "Mars, Neptune, and Pluto orbit the sun"?

____

____

____

9. How many syllables does orbit have? Where do the syllables divide? Which syllable is accented?

____

____

____

10. What is the origin of the word *orbit*? How does this origin relate to the meaning of the word?

____

____

____

____

School + Home

Home Activity Your child learned about using dictionaries and glossaries as resources. Look at a dictionary together. Ask your child to locate several entries, using guide words. Discuss the elements of the entry, including pronunciation, word history, part(s) of speech, and definition.

Name ______________________________

Schwa

Proofread a List Circle six misspelled words in the list. Write the words correctly. Find a sentence with a capitalization error. Write it correctly.

How to Conserve Energy

There are many ways you can conserve Energy.
For instence:

- Install insulating matiriel and different, energy-efficient doors and windows.
- Plant trees to block the wind and to provide shade.
- Turn lights off when you don't need them, and use less briliant bulbs.
- Use less hot water, turn down the thermostat on your water heater, and insulate your water heater and pipes.
- Drive slower and keep your car properly maintained.
- If you can, substatute public transportation for driving a car.
- Disipline yourself to recycle, and don't hesatate to reuse anything you can.

different
sentence
American
brilliant
substitute
opinion
material
complete
jewelry
dramatic

instance
communicate
hesitate
elementary
vitamin
ingredients
invitation
discipline
lasagna
desperate

Frequently Misspelled Word

outside

1. ______________ 2. ______________
3. ______________ 4. ______________
5. ______________ 6. ______________
7. ____

____

Proofread Words Circle the word that is spelled correctly. Write it.

8.	discipline	disipline	discplane	8. ______________
9.	jewelery	jewelry	jewlry	9. ______________
10.	hezitate	hesutate	hesitate	10. ______________
11.	lasana	lasanya	lasagna	11. ______________
12.	opinion	opinyun	opineon	12. ______________

School + Home **Home Activity** Your child identified misspelled words. Read list words your child did not write on this page and have your child spell them.

Name ______________________________

Subject-Verb Agreement

Directions Read the passage. Then read each question. Circle the letter of the correct answer.

Tomatoes Galore

(1) My grandfather have a green thumb. (2) He and my grandmother grow every type of vegetable. (3) The whole family enjoy the rewards of their backyard summer garden. (4) The beautiful round and red tomatoes are their best product. (5) They is plentiful in the summer garden, too many for us to use. (6) We have cooking contests to see who makes the best pasta sauce with their fresh tomatoes. (7) Last summer my mother, father, brother, and I was winners of the family contest! (8) We will still have sauce next summer when Grandma and Grandpa have a new crop of fresh tomatoes.

1 What change, if any, should be made in sentence 1?

- **A** Change ***have*** to **has**
- **B** Change ***My*** to **our**
- **C** Add *-s* to ***grandfather***
- **D** Make no change

2 What change, if any, should be made in sentence 3?

- **A** Change ***family*** to **families**
- **B** Delete *-s* from ***rewards***
- **C** Change ***enjoy*** to **enjoys**
- **D** Make no change

3 How would you describe the subject in sentence 4?

- **A** Plural noun
- **B** Singular noun
- **C** Collective noun
- **D** None of the above

4 What is true about sentence 5?

- **A** The subject is singular.
- **B** The verb is an action verb.
- **C** The subject and verb agree.
- **D** None of the above

5 What change, if any, should be made in sentence 7?

- **A** Delete *-s* from ***winners***
- **B** Change ***was*** to **were**
- **C** Change ***I*** to **me**
- **D** Make no change

School + Home **Home Activity** Your child prepared for taking tests on subject-verb agreement. Ask your child to read aloud and correct sentences 2 and 8.

Name ____________________

Graphic Sources

- **Graphic sources** are used to show information visually. Maps, charts, graphs, pictures, and schedules are some examples of graphic sources.

Directions Study the following graphic source. Then answer the questions below.

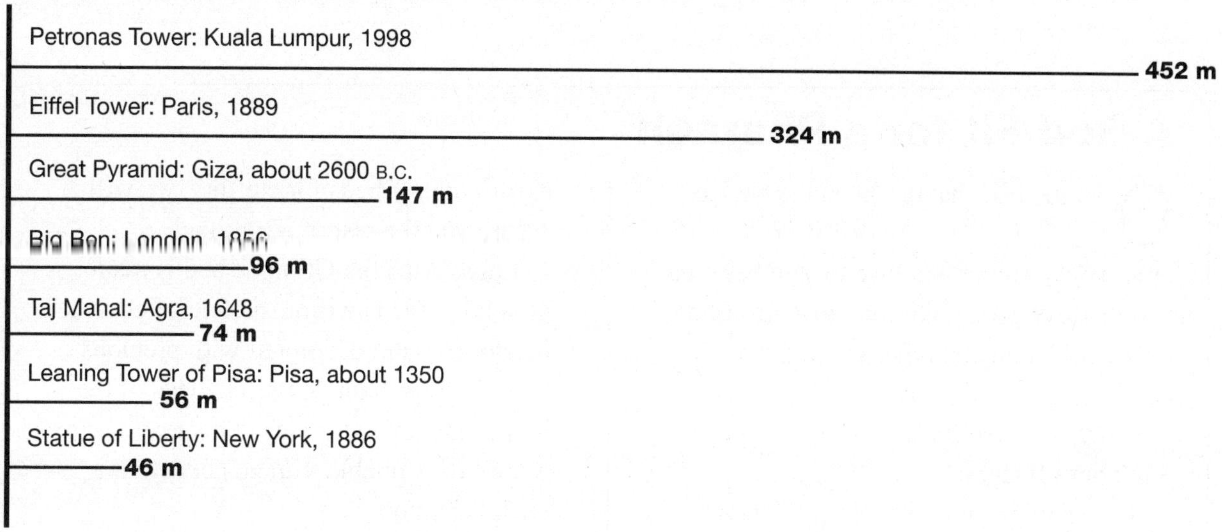

1. Which is the tallest of these famous structures? Which is the oldest?

____

2. Which is the second tallest? the third?

____

____

3. The Great Pyramid in Egypt was the world's tallest structure for 4,000 years. How tall is the Great Pyramid?

____

4. How does the Great Pyramid compare with the Statue of Liberty and Big Ben? Be specific.

____

____

5. Write a one-sentence summary of what this graphic source shows.

____

____

School + Home **Home Activity** Your child used a graphic source to answer questions. Work together to identify the purpose of a graphic source in a magazine. Challenge your child to answer questions based on the graphic source.

Name ______________________________

Writing • Advertisement

Key Features of an Advertisement

- makes a claim about a product and develops an argument to persuade people to buy it
- supports the claim with clear reasons, relevant evidence, and descriptive language
- provides a concluding statement that summarizes the advertisement's argument

A Bed Fit for a Pharaoh

Own the bed that has been the choice of pharaohs for dynasty after dynasty! Wouldn't you love to slumber on a bed made of pure gold, like the ones used by Tutankhaten and other pharaohs of our beloved Egypt? Well, now you can! They are now available for a short time from **All That Glitters.**

The pharaohs not only sleep on their golden beds every day of their lives, but they also make sure that the beds are placed in burial chambers so the deceased ruler can sleep in luxury for all eternity. Although we cannot guarantee these extraordinary beds for eternity, we will assure you the rest of a lifetime!

Each "All That Glitters" bed is made of solid gold. The exquisitely crafted headboards are decorated with precious ivory and brilliant gems. The legs of the bed frame are extra long. This feature allows for valuable storage needed in a burial chamber.

If you order a Pharaoh-size or the Queen-size "All That Glitters" bed by the end of the month, we will include a set of linen sheets absolutely free!

1. What is the author's purpose?

____

____

2. The author used paragraphs to organize this advertisement. Write the main idea of each paragraph.

____

____

____

____

Vocabulary

Directions Choose the word from the box that best matches each definition below. Write the word on the line.

________________ **1.** more than enough; very plentiful

________________ **2.** living forever; never dying

________________ **3.** moved backward

________________ **4.** ruled

________________ **5.** all time; time without beginning or ending

Check the Words You Know

- ___abundant
- ___artifacts
- ___decrees
- ___eternity
- ___immortal
- ___receded
- ___reigned

Directions Choose the word from the box that best matches each clue. Write the word on the line.

________________ **6.** This is the longest possible period of time.

________________ **7.** This is what kings and pharaohs did.

________________ **8.** This describes gods rather than people.

________________ **9.** These are made by kings or other authorities.

________________ **10.** Tools, art, and weapons from a past civilization are examples of this.

Write a Narrative

On a separate sheet of paper write a narrative about a ruler from ancient times. Use as many vocabulary words as you can.

School + Home **Home Activity** Your child identified and used vocabulary words from *Egypt*. Read a story or nonfiction article about Egypt together. Point out unfamiliar words concerning details about the country and its people. Use the context to try to figure out what the words mean.

Past, Present, and Future Tenses

The **tense** of a verb shows when something happens. Verbs in the **present tense** show action that happens now. Most present tense singular verbs end with *-s*. Most present tense plural verbs do not end with *-s*.

Callie keeps her makeup in little jars. They keep the makeup fresh.

Verbs in the **past tense** show action that has already happened. Most verbs in the past tense end in *-ed*.

She brushed on two coats of mascara.

Verbs in the **future tense** show action that will happen. Add *will* (or *shall*) to most verbs to show the future tense.

Heat will make mascara run.

- Some regular verbs change spelling when *-ed* is added. For verbs ending in *e*, drop the *e* and add *-ed*: *loved, hoped*. For verbs ending in a consonant and *y*, change the *y* to *i*, and add *-ed*: *cried, married*.
- For most one-syllable verbs that end in one vowel followed by one consonant, double the consonant and add *-ed*: *hopped, grabbed*.
- Irregular verbs change spelling to form the past tense: *are/were, break/broke, bring/brought, build/built, buy/bought, do/did, find/found, go/went, have/had, is/was, keep/kept, make/made, ring/rang, sit/sat, see/saw, take/took, teach/taught, tell/told, wear/wore, write/wrote*.

Directions Identify the tense of each underlined verb. Write *present, past,* or *future*.

1. Hieroglyphics tell us about ancient Egypt. ____________
2. Archaeologists will search for artifacts. ____________
3. Ramses II is a well-known pharaoh. ____________
4. Pharaohs built huge statues. ____________
5. Egypt was a major world power in 1500 B.C. ____________

Directions Write the correct present, past, and future tense of each verb.

Verb	**Present**	**Past**	**Future**
6. find	I ____________.	I ____________.	I ____________.
7. sit	She ____________.	She ____________.	She ____________.
8. carry	We ____________.	We ____________.	We ____________.

School + Home

Home Activity Your child learned about past, present, and future tenses. Have your child write three sentences about Egypt using a present tense verb, a past tense verb, and a future tense verb and identifying each.

Name ______________________________

Suffixes *-ian, -ant, -ent, -ist*

Spelling Words				
musician	politician	novelist	scientist	historian
tenant	student	patient	resident	comedian
vegetarian	soloist	specialist	motorist	merchant
participant	occupant	custodian	descendant	chemist

Word Clues Write the list word that identifies the speaker of each statement below.

1. "I believe this chemical compound will lead to a cure." 1. ____________
2. "I believe a healthy diet is one that does not include meat." 2. ____________
3. "I love driving to work." 3. ____________
4. "I clean up at night after everyone else has gone home." 4. ____________
5. "I sell a wide variety of things in my shop." 5. ____________
6. "My new apartment is much bigger than the last one." 6. ____________
7. "I think my new jokes are the best ever." 7. ____________
8. "I practice on my instrument an hour every day." 8. ____________
9. "I have to stay in the hospital one more day." 9. ____________
10. "I believe I can win this election." 10. ____________
11. "School starts next week." 11. ____________
12. "I have been working on this book for two years." 12. ____________

Word Meanings Write a list word that matches each definition.

13. a person born of a certain family or group 13. ____________
14. a person who writes about history 14. ____________
15. a person who sings or plays an instrument alone 15. ____________
16. a person who has expert knowledge of some branch of science 16. ____________
17. a person who lives in a certain area 17. ____________
18. a person who is an expert in a particular subject 18. ____________
19. a person who takes up a certain space 19. ____________
20. a person who joins in on an activity 20. ____________

School + Home **Home Activity** Your child spelled words with *-ian, -ant, -ent,* and *-ist*. Say a word from the list and ask your child to define what that person does.

Outline

Title ______________________

I. ______________________

A. ______________________

1. ______________________

2. ______________________

3. ______________________

B. ______________________

1. ______________________

2. ______________________

II. ______________________

A. ______________________

B. ______________________

III. ______________________

Name ____________________

Vocabulary • Greek and Latin Roots

- When you are reading and see an unfamiliar word, check to see if you recognize any **Greek** or **Latin roots**. These can help you figure out the word's meaning.
- Latin roots include *ars* for "skill, knowledge," *factum* for "made," *cedere* for "to go away," *abundare* for "abound," *regnare* for "to rule," and *mortis* for "death."

Directions Read the following passage. Then answer the questions below.

When the flood waters receded, the archaeologists started to dig along the Nile River. Their efforts were richly rewarded. They found abundant artifacts from an ancient civilization. Much of the jewelry and artwork dated back to the time when pharaohs reigned over the lands. The pharaohs' tombs contained gifts pharaohs had made to the gods in an attempt to become immortal and live for eternity.

1. How does knowing the Latin root *cedere* help you to determine the meaning of *receded?*

____

____

2. Which Latin root do you think *abundant* comes from? How does this root help you to determine the meaning?

____

____

3. How does the meaning of *artifacts* combine the meanings of two roots, *ars* and *factum?*

____

____

4. How would using Latin roots help you determine the meaning of the word *reigned?*

____

____

5. *Immortal* combines the prefix *im-*, meaning "not," with the Latin root *mortis*. How can this word structure help you to determine the meaning of the word?

____

____

School + Home

Home Activity Your child identified and used Latin roots to understand new words of a passage. Work with your child to identify unfamiliar words of an article. Then see if he or she recognizes any Latin roots that can help in understanding the new words. Confirm the meanings with your child.

Name____

Reference Book

A **reference book** is a kind of **manual.** A manual usually contains instructions for immediate use or for reference. It usually has a table of contents, an index, sections, illustrations, and explanations.

Directions Use this excerpt from a grammar reference book to answer the questions.

Simple Tenses
Verbs have three simple tenses: present, past, and future.

Present tense of a verb is the same as the name of the verb.

try jump use

Past tense for regular verbs is formed by adding *-d* or *-ed.* (Sometimes the spelling changes.)

tried jumped used

Future tense is formed by placing *will* or *shall* before the present tense verb.

will try shall jump will use

Irregular Verbs
Irregular verbs do not follow the usual pattern for past tense. These are some examples of irregular verbs:

bring/brought	sing/sang
write/wrote	eat/ate

Learn irregular verbs. You can also find verb forms for irregular verbs in a dictionary. These are common irregular verbs:

begin	fall	know	see
break	go	lie	speak
come	have	ride	take
drink	hide	ring	throw

1. Which sections of the grammar reference book are shown here?

____

2. What might you look up in the index to find this information?

____

3. What does this manual tell you about how to form the past tense of a regular verb?

____

4. If you wanted to know what irregular verbs were, what could you learn from this manual? What are four examples of irregular verbs?

____

____

5. Would a grammar reference book be a good source to find information about how to study for English tests? Explain.

____

____

Name____

Directions Use this excerpt from a manual to answer the questions.

How to Read Hieroglyphics

Hieroglyphics is the ancient Egyptian system of writing. You can learn to read hieroglyphics yourself.

Sometimes hieroglyphic writing is supposed to be read from left to right, and sometimes it's supposed to be read from right to left. You can always tell which way to read a set of hieroglyphics because the animal and people symbols face toward the beginning.

In hieroglyphics, some symbols are picture symbols and others are sound symbols. These are the four types of symbols you'll find:

1. Alphabet signs — Each symbol represents a sound. Some Egyptian signs such as *th* and *kh* differ from English sounds.

2. Syllable signs — These represent combinations of consonant sounds.

3. Word pictures —These are pictures used as the signs for objects.

4. Determiners — These give the reader clues to how a sign is being used.

Consult the charts in this manual for alphabet signs, syllable signs, word pictures, and determiners. If you put sounds and pictures together, you'll have a good idea of how to read hieroglyphics.

6. Which section of the manual is shown here? What would you look up in the index to find this information?

____

____

7. Which way should you read hieroglyphics—left to right or right to left?

____

____

8. Which hieroglyphic signs are pictures of what they represent?

____

9. Which hieroglyphic signs represent a single sound?

____

10. Summarize the instructions in this manual section.

____

____

School + Home **Home Activity** Your child learned about using grammar reference books and manuals as resources. Look at a grammar reference book together. Ask your child to locate information and examples of the following: *possessives, clauses,* and *pronouns.*

Name ______________________________

Suffixes *-ian, -ant, -ent, -ist*

Proofread a Scene Circle six spelling errors in this scene from a play. Write the words correctly. Find a sentence with a punctuation error. Write it correctly on the line.

Food Festival

Beth: I think the studant Heritage Food Festival will be fun.

Luke: I'm glad to, be a particapent. I enjoy tasting diffrent foods.

Kathleen: Beth, your family's from Louisiana, right?

Beth: Yes. I'm a descendant of Cajun people.

Luke: So what are you bringing to the food festival?

Beth: A pot of gumbo. It's a soup made with chicken, rice, okra, and lots of other stuff. You practically have to be a chemust to make it, but my mom is a real specialist.

Kathleen: What are you bringing, Luke?

Luke: My grandfather was a residant of Mexico, so I'm bringing tamales and refried beans.

Kathleen: My mother's a vegeterien, so we're making a vegetable lasagna.

musician
politician
novelist
scientist
historian
tenant
student
patient
resident
comedian
vegetarian
soloist
specialist
motorist
merchant
participant
occupant
custodian
descendant
chemist

Frequently Misspelled Words

different
except

1. ______________ 2. ______________
3. ______________ 4. ______________
5. ______________ 6. ______________
7. ____

Proofread Words Circle the word that is spelled correctly. Write it.

8.	soloist	soloest	8. ______________
9.	occupent	occupant	9. ______________
10.	scientist	sciuntist	10. ______________
11.	custodian	custodien	11. ______________
12.	merchent	merchant	12. ______________

School + Home

Home Activity Your child identified misspelled words with the suffixes *-ian, -ant, -ent,* and *-ist*. Ask your child to explain the difference between words with similar meanings, such as *chemist* and *scientist*, and *musician* and *soloist*.

Name ______________________________

Past, Present, and Future Tenses

Directions Read the passage. Then read each question. Circle the letter of the correct answer.

The New Nutrition

(1) Birthday cupcakes are not okay. (2) Neither is soda. (3) Students _____ pizza from the menu. (4) Potato chips will not be on the menu unless they are baked. (5) Schools _____ more new nutrition guidelines. (6) In the past, students bought jelly beans and other types of candy in school vending machines. (7) The new guidelines prohibit these snacks. (8) As these guidelines take hold, many students _____ how much better they feel when they eat less junk food.

1 What is the verb tense in sentence 1?

A Past
B Present
C Future
D There is no verb.

2 Which future tense form of *enjoy* best completes sentence 3?

A will enjoy
B have enjoyed
C enjoy
D Make no change

3 Which future tense form of *follow* best completes sentence 5?

A follow
B followed
C will follow
D are following

4 What is the verb tense in sentence 6?

A Future
B Past
C Present
D There is no verb.

5 Which form of the verb best completes sentence 8?

A learned
B learn
C learning
D will learn

School + Home **Home Activity** Your child prepared for taking tests on past, present, and future tenses. List *take, make, build,* and *are* on paper. Have your child write the past and future tenses for each verb.

Name ____________________

Multisyllabic Words I

Spelling Words				
possibility	linear	ridiculous	artificial	calculator
competitive	curiosity	organization	individual	encyclopedia
peony	tarantula	correspondent	cauliflower	optimistic
enthusiastic	sophisticated	satisfactory	irritable	simultaneously

Synonyms Write the list word that has the same or nearly the same meaning.

1. large spider — 1. ____________
2. chance — 2. ____________
3. eager for — 3. ____________
4. at the same time — 4. ____________
5. wants to win — 5. ____________

Antonyms Write the list word that has the opposite or nearly the opposite meaning.

6. disinterest — 6. ____________
7. unrefined — 7. ____________
8. inadequate — 8. ____________
9. cheerful — 9. ____________
10. genuine — 10. ____________

Word Groups Write the list word that fits into each group.

11. rose, tulip, daisy, _____ — 11. ____________
12. dictionary, thesaurus, atlas, _____ — 12. ____________
13. broccoli, carrot, lettuce, _____ — 13. ____________
14. ruler, protractor, compass, _____ — 14. ____________
15. journalist, reporter, writer, _____ — 15. ____________
16. one, single, only, _____ — 16. ____________
17. neat, order, plan, _____ — 17. ____________
18. absurd, silly, outrageous, _____ — 18. ____________
19. cheerful, positive, hopeful, _____ — 19. ____________
20. line, straight, even, _____ — 20. ____________

School + Home

Home Activity Your child has learned to spell multisyllabic words. Have your child look for words in magazines or books that have 3, 4, and 5 syllables.

Name ____

Regular and Irregular Plural Nouns

Directions Write the plural form of the noun.

1. shoe ____________________

2. wrist ____________________

3. knife ____________________

4. strawberry ____________________

5. fox ____________________

6. wife

7. wish ____________________

8. father-in-law ____________________

9. zoo ____________________

10. potato ____________________

Directions Circle the correct plural form of the nouns in parentheses.

11. One of my (wishes/wish's) is to be an astronaut.

12. A group of (ladys/ladies) from Iowa toured the space center.

13. Fifteen (childs/children) rode a bus to space camp.

14. Alex builds model space (shuttles/shuttle's).

15. Three (deer/deers) ate by moonlight.

16. The day of the moon landing was the best day of their (lifes/lives).

17. The telescope stood two (foots/feet) from the ground.

18. Audrey has a collection of Jupiter (photos/photoes).

19. My brother doesn't appreciate the (mysterys/mysteries) of the universe.

20. Neither of my (sister-in-laws/sisters-in-law) could locate the North Star.

School + Home **Home Activity** Your child reviewed regular and irregular plural nouns. Ask your child to list things you have in your kitchen and write the plural form for each noun.

Name________________________

Latin Roots I

Spelling Words				
suspend	pendant	conductor	novel	productive
numeral	reserve	numerous	preserve	pending
pendulum	deduction	novelty	numerator	reservoir
conservatory	appendix	impending	induct	innovative

Word Clues Write the list word that fits each clue.

1. This is part of a necklace. 1. ____________
2. This is a longer piece of literature. 2. ____________
3. This is a word that expresses a number. 3. ____________
4. This is extra information at the end of a book. 4. ____________
5. This describes something new and original. 5. ____________
6. This is something that is about to happen. 6. ____________
7. This is the person who directs an orchestra or choir. 7. ____________
8. This is when you save something for future use. 8. ____________
9. This is to maintain something in its original condition. 9. ____________
10. This is another word for "many." 10. ____________

Scramble Unscramble the list words and write them on the lines.

11. topveiducr 11. ____________
12. nedutdioc 12. ____________
13. stororyvcnea 13. ____________
14. rnueatmor 14. ____________
15. eerrovrsi 15. ____________
16. dsespnu 16. ____________
17. ncudit 17. ____________
18. gdnenip 18. ____________
19. dpneumul 19. ____________
20. lnteyov 20. ____________

School + Home **Home Activity** Your child has learned to spell words with Latin roots. Name a Latin root (*duct, pend, nov, serv, numer*) and have your child spell a word with that root.

Possessive Nouns

Directions Write each noun as a possessive noun. Write *S* if the possessive noun is singular. Write *P* if the possessive noun is plural.

1. statues ______________ ______
2. emperor ______________ ______
3. tomb ______________ ______
4. warriors ______________ ______
5. chariot ______________ ______

Directions Circle the correct possessive noun in ( ) to complete each sentence.

6. The terra cotta discoveries are the three (farmer's, farmers') claim to fame.
7. The (men's, mens') discovery of a giant head surprised everyone.
8. Had you heard about (China's, Chinas') new attraction?
9. The class watched a video about the six (archaeologist's, archaeologists') findings.
10. Would you want to be one of the (potter's, potters') assistants?

Directions Write each sentence. Change the underlined phrase to show possession.

11. The <u>diaries of the tourists</u> recorded their adventures.

____

12. The <u>red hue of the rocks</u> looked eerie at night.

____

13. A group of travelers filled <u>the buses of the school.</u>

____

14. The <u>faces of the figures</u> were clearly visible.

____

15. The <u>events of the day</u> excited the tourists.

____

School + Home **Home Activity** Your child reviewed possessive nouns. Point to single and multiple objects in your home and have your child say and spell the possessive forms of the names.

Name ____________________

Final Syllable Patterns

Spelling Words				
ancestor	hospital	grumble	sponsor	superior
escalator	encounter	shoulder	skeleton	forbidden
appetizer	identical	abandon	governor	endeavor
outspoken	durable	lengthen	cinnamon	interior

Classifying Write the list word that belongs in each group.

1. arm, elbow, _____ **1.** ____________
2. senator, mayor, _____ **2.** ____________
3. reliable, strong, _____ **3.** ____________
4. elevator, stairs, _____ **4.** ____________
5. direct, unreserved, _____ **5.** ____________
6. entrée, dessert, _____ **6.** ____________
7. body, bones, _____ **7.** ____________
8. forebear, family member, _____ **8.** ____________
9. same, alike, _____ **9.** ____________
10. banned, off-limits, _____ **10.** ____________

Word Search Circle ten list words hidden in the puzzle. Words are found down and across. Then write the words.

R	I	E	N	C	O	U	N	T	E	R
S	H	D	O	I	E	R	P	E	I	G
U	O	L	E	N	G	T	H	E	N	R
P	S	P	O	N	S	O	R	N	T	U
E	P	I	T	A	L	E	N	N	E	M
R	I	O	A	M	B	L	E	A	R	B
I	T	R	L	O	U	N	T	M	I	L
O	A	B	A	N	D	O	N	O	O	E
R	L	E	N	D	E	A	V	O	R	Z

11. ____________
12. ____________
13. ____________
14. ____________
15. ____________
16. ____________
17. ____________
18. ____________
19. ____________
20. ____________

School + Home **Home Activity** Your child has learned to write words with final syllable patterns. Ask your child to choose a word group and explain why the list word belongs in that group.

Name ______________________________

Action and Linking Verbs

Directions Write *A* if the underlined verb is an action verb. Write *L* if the underlined verb is a linking verb. Write *PN* if the underlined word is a predicate nominative.

1. The linens smelled fresh. ______

2. Who mowed the lawn? ______

3. Cook the green beans for 15 minutes. ______

4. I am tired of waking up at dawn. ______

5. Matthew became captain of the team. ______

6. Which apples taste sweetest? ______

7. Emily is the best cook. ______

8. The workers sliced the potatoes. ______

Directions Circle *A* if the verb is an action verb. Circle *L* if it is a linking verb.

9. The kids took water with them.	A	L
10. The artifacts seemed old and fragile.	A	L
11. Some kids ground corn.	A	L
12. The hike was hot and tiring.	A	L
13. The ranger spoke quietly to the group.	A	L
14. Sara made a clay bowl.	A	L
15. Bill's face looked mischievous.	A	L
16. The group climbed ladders that day.	A	L
17. Balcony House seemed dangerous.	A	L
18. The kids felt strange going inside it.	A	L
19. Why did the ancient Puebloans leave?	A	L
20. It is a big mystery.	A	L

Home Activity Your child reviewed action and linking verbs. Have your child make a chart with the headings *Action* and *Linking*, scan a page of a favorite book, and see how many action and linking verbs he or she can find to write on the chart.

Name ______________________________

Schwa

Spelling Words				
different	sentence	American	brilliant	substitute
opinion	material	complete	jewelry	dramatic
instance	communicate	hesitate	elementary	vitamin
ingredients	invitation	discipline	lasagna	desperate

Synonyms Write the list word that has the same or nearly the same meaning.

1. alternative 1. ______________
2. total 2. ______________
3. pause 3. ______________
4. smart 4. ______________
5. proposal 5. ______________

Antonyms Write the list word that has the opposite or nearly the opposite meaning.

6. alike 6. ______________
7. fact 7. ______________
8. unimpressive 8. ______________
9. hopeful 9. ______________
10. lack of control 10. ______________

Word Groups Write the list word that fits in each group.

11. Italian, British, _____ 11. ______________
12. nutrient, supplement, _____ 12. ______________
13. example, situation, _____ 13. ______________
14. fabric, cloth, _____ 14. ______________
15. subject, verb, _____ 15. ______________
16. simple, basic, _____ 16. ______________
17. parts, contents, _____ 17. ______________
18. bracelet, ring, _____ 18. ______________
19. pasta, sauce, _____ 19. ______________
20. talk, gesture, _____ 20. ______________

School + Home

Home Activity Your child has learned to spell words with schwa. Have your child choose a list word from the top two activities and think of two words that would fit in the same group as it. Repeat with other list words.

Name ______________________________

Subject-Verb Agreement

Directions Underline the verb in ( ) that agrees with the subject.

1. The astronomers at the observatory (study, studies) the stars at night.
2. Dr. Fields (struggle, struggles) with his paperwork.
3. The Waterman family (are, is) going away for six months.
4. Both Lynn and Gene (feels, feel) cold all the time.
5. The hydroponic gardens on the moon (supply, supplies) the residents with oxygen.
6. A layer of dust and rocks (forms, form) on the floors.
7. The magnetrain (speed, speeds) over the Earth's surface.
8. The spaceships (arrives, arrive) at the destination.
9. The trip to the planets (includes, include) a wonderful view of the sun.
10. Derek and Renee (bring, brings) only two suitcases on the trip.

Directions Write a complete sentence using the correct noun as subject and the verb.

11. (airplanes, airplane) flies

____

12. Ben and Brad (watches, watch)

____

13. dogs (howls, howl)

____

14. stars (shine, shines)

____

15. two pilots (fly, flies)

____

School + Home **Home Activity** Your child reviewed subject-verb agreement. Say singular and plural subjects, such as *the house, the houses, my shoes,* and *my shoe,* and have your child use the subjects in sentences with verbs that agree.

Name ______________________________

Suffixes *-ian, -ant, -ent, -ist*

Spelling Words

musician	politician	novelist	scientist	historian
tenant	student	patient	resident	comedian
vegetarian	soloist	specialist	motorist	merchant
participant	occupant	custodian	descendant	chemist

Classifying Write the list word that tells the kind of person that would use the item or items.

1. vegetables, tofu — 1. ____________
2. vehicle, gasoline — 2. ____________
3. textbooks, notebooks — 3. ____________
4. primary sources, encyclopedias — 4. ____________
5. speeches, campaigns — 5. ____________
6. money, goods — 6. ____________
7. mop, tools — 7. ____________
8. medicine, insurance — 8. ____________
9. jokes, microphone — 9. ____________
10. guitar, keyboard — 10. ____________

Word Choice Circle the correct list word. Write it on the line.

11. We need to find a (participant, resident) to join the race. — 11. ____________
12. She considered herself a (tenant, soloist), not a group act. — 12. ____________
13. I am a (descendant, specialist) of an American hero. — 13. ____________
14. They needed one more (occupant, scientist) to fill the space. — 14. ____________
15. The landlord advertised for a quiet (novelist, tenant). — 15. ____________
16. She majored in chemistry to become a (resident, chemist). — 16. ____________
17. The (novelist, specialist) hopes to finish her book this week. — 17. ____________
18. I know she has been a (specialist, resident) of five towns. — 18. ____________
19. The lab is a second home for a (descendant, scientist). — 19. ____________
20. A (student, specialist) is an expert of a certain subject. — 20. ____________

School + Home

Home Activity Your child has learned to spell words that end with *-ian, -ant, -ent,* and *-ist.* Choose a list word and pretend to be that type of person. Say things that type of person would say. Have your child say the list word you are pretending to be and spell it.

Name ______________________________

Past, Present, and Future Tenses

Directions Identify the tense of each underlined verb. Write *present, past,* or *future.*

1. Egypt is in Africa. ______________
2. Pharaohs lived in luxury. ______________
3. The Moore family will visit Egypt. ______________
4. They will find other Egyptian artifacts. ______________
5. Thirty-one dynasties reigned in Egypt. ______________
6. Memphis, Thebes, and Cairo were capitals of Egypt. ______________
7. The Great Pyramid covers thirteen acres. ______________
8. Some blocks in the Great Pyramid weigh fifteen tons. ______________

Directions Rewrite each sentence twice. First, change the underlined verb to past tense. Then change it to future tense.

9. Burial chambers tell us about ancient Egypt.

   Past: ______________________________

   Future: ______________________________

10. Egyptians carry possessions to the chambers.

    Past: ______________________________

    Future: ______________________________

11. They use a stone coffin called a sarcophagus.

    Past: ______________________________

    Future: ______________________________

12. Archaeologists find burial chambers in other cultures.

    Past: ______________________________

    Future: ______________________________

School + Home **Home Activity** Your child reviewed past, present, and future tenses. Ask your child to look through a magazine article and find examples of past, present, and future tense verbs.

Name ___________________________

How-to Chart

Directions Fill in the graphic organizer with information about your project.

Explain Task ___________________________

Materials ___________________________

Introduction ___________________________

Steps ___________________________

Conclusion ___________________________

Name ____________________

Time-Order Words

Directions Rewrite each sentence to make the sequence of the steps clearer. Use more than one sentence. Use time-order words such as *first, next, then, last,* and *finally*.

1. Cole took everything off his bed, got clean sheets out of the closet, and made up the bed with pillows and a cover after he put the sheets on the bed.

2. When going down a slide you must climb the ladder, sit down at the top and slide down, making sure your feet land on the ground.

3. After Sylvia decided to make pancakes, she heated the griddle, added ingredients, mixed, poured the batter, and flipped the pancakes until they were fully cooked.

Name ______________________________

Using Strong Verbs

Strong verbs can express your ideas accurately and vividly.

Not Vivid I could tell her mood by the way she walked along.

Vivid I could tell her mood by the way she trudged along.

Directions Choose the verb in ( ) that gives a more vivid picture. Write the sentence.

1. Alma (ran, sprinted) toward the finish line.

____

2. Fireworks (exploded, went off) in the distance.

____

3. Thunder (rumbled, sounded) before the rain began.

____

4. Did you (scrape, hurt) your knee on the sidewalk?

____

5. Lemonade (fell, trickled) down Sara's chin.

____

6. Ms. Welk has (stalked, gone) out of the meeting.

____

Directions Describe an animal moving or doing something. Use strong verbs such as *pounce, prowl, wiggle, scamper, lunge, gobble, yelp,* or your own strong verbs.

____

____

____

Name ______________________________

Editing

Directions Edit these sentences. Look for errors in spelling, grammar, and mechanics. Use proofreading marks to show the corrections.

Proofreading Marks	
Delete (Take out)	⌐
Add	^
Spelling	⬭
Uppercase letter	≡
Lowercase letter	/

1. First, open the battery cover and insert to AA batteries in the compartment, matching the digram inside.
2. After the batteries is installed, the clocks display lights up and beeps once.
3. The clock automaticly starts searching for the radio signal and the T icon starts flashing.
4. After the signal was detected and the time and calender are set, the T icon will stop flashing.
5. You can press the Z button to show different North american time zones (Pacific, mountain, Central and Eastern).
6. To set the alarm, press and hold the S button for three second until the digits starts flashing.
7. use the Up and Down arrows to selected the desired hour and minutes press the S button again.
8. When the alarm is activated a B icon appear on the display.

Now you'll edit the draft of your how-to report. Then you'll use your revised and edited draft to make a final copy of your report. Finally, you'll share your written work with your audience.

Name ________________________________

Sequence

- **Sequence** is the order in which things happen. Clue words such as *next, then,* and *yesterday* help to indicate the sequence in which events occur.
- Some events in a story happen simultaneously, or at the same time. Clue words such as *meanwhile* and *at the same time* signal simultaneous events.

Directions Read the following passage. Then complete the diagram below.

Janie and Finn walked down the campground road to get some fresh water. It was getting dark, but Janie remembered the way to the water pump—a left at the fork in the road and then a right. When they got there, Janie pumped the cool water while Finn held the bucket. Then Finn started to splash Janie with the water. Janie was furious, and yelled at him to put the bucket down and let her get the water. Janie refilled the bucket. Meanwhile, Finn ran away. Janie called his name, but there was no response. She raced back to the campground to tell her mother that Finn was lost, all the while worried about him. To her surprise, Finn had already made it back and was sitting quietly by the fire.

End

4. ________________________________

3. ________________________________

2. ________________________________

1. ________________________________

Beginning

5. What did you visualize Janie's face to look like at the end of the story?

____

School + Home **Home Activity** Your child identified the sequence of events in a story. Discuss a time when someone or something got lost. Together, identify the sequence of events in the memory.

Writing for Tests

Prompt: Think about your favorite animal and what makes it special. Write a speech about a type of animal and why you think people should learn more about it.

Scorpion . . . Feared or Famed?

Scorpions are one of the oldest and most fascinating animals on Earth, and we can help them stay that way. Around the world people are destroying their habitats. If people learn more about these unusual creatures, maybe they'll learn how to conserve resources and survive hardships like the scorpion does.

Fans who like to observe scorpions in nature must be adventurous and patient. Scorpions are nocturnal (active at night) and hide under stones, bark, and other things during daylight. Scorpions glow under ultraviolet light, so scorpion researchers use ultraviolet lights to find the animals at night when they are active.

Scorpions often live in habitats near humans, where insects can be more plentiful. A scorpion's favorite foods are yummy insects, spiders, small lizards, snakes, and mice. However, many animals eat scorpions too—birds, shrews, meat-eating grasshopper mice, and bats. Scorpions can actually slow down their metabolism, making it possible for them to survive on eating 1 insect a year!

Another amazing thing about scorpions is that they are able to regulate the amount of venom they use. They release more venom into larger prey and use less for smaller animals. They conserve the venom as much as possible since it may be needed some day to save their life!

You already know that scorpions cause pain with their venom-filled sting, but did you know that only about 40 of the thousands of species of scorpions are deadly to humans? Scorpions have amazing abilities that are interesting to scientists. You have to decide whether you are fan or foe of the scorpion.

1. Circle the thesis statement. What makes it a thesis?

____

____

____

2. Put a box around the topic sentence in each paragraph. Then underline supporting details in that paragraph.

3. Sentence variety gets attention. Draw brackets around three *different types* of sentences. Label their type (declarative, interrogative, imperative, or exclamatory).

Name ____

Vocabulary

Directions Choose the word from the box that best matches each definition. Write the word on the line.

Check the Words You Know
___hatchet
___ignite
___painstaking
___quill
___registered
___smoldered
___stiffened

____________________ **1.** to set on fire

____________________ **2.** to have been made or become rigid

____________________ **3.** a stiff, sharp hair or spine

____________________ **4.** extremely careful

____________________ **5.** burned and smoked without flame

Directions Choose the word from the box that best matches each clue. Write the letters of the word on the blanks. The boxed letters spell out one of the words from this selection.

6. ___ ___ ___ ___ ___ ___ [ ] ___ ___
[e]
[g]
7. ___ ___ [ ] ___ ___
[s]
8. ___ ___ [ ] ___ ___ ___ ___
[e]
[r]
9. ___ ___ ___ ___ ___ [ ]
[d]

6. This happens to a match after it is blown out.
7. This is a porcupine's defense.
8. You might use this to chop wood.
9. You use a match to do this to a pile of wood.
10. The mystery word is: ____________________

Write a News Report

On a separate sheet of paper, write a news report about a sixth-grade student who managed to survive after being marooned on a deserted island. Use as many vocabulary words as you can.

Home Activity Your child identified and used vocabulary words from *Hatchet*. Together, create a crossword puzzle and clues with the words in the selection.

Name ______________________________

Principal Parts of Regular Verbs

A verb's tenses are made from four basic forms. These basic forms are called the verb's **principal parts.**

Present	**Present Participle**	**Past**	**Past Participle**
watch	(am, is, are) watching	watched	(has, have, had) watched
carry	(am, is, are) carrying	carried	(has, have, had) carried

A **regular verb** forms its past and past participle by adding *-ed* or *-d* to the present form.

- The present and the past forms can be used by themselves as verbs.
- The present participle and the past participle are always used with a helping verb.

Remember, when a verb ends with a consonant and *y*, change the *y* to *i* before adding *-ed: cried.* When a one-syllable verb ends with a vowel and a consonant, double the consonant before adding *-ed: hopped.*

Directions Write *present, present participle, past,* or *past participle* to identify the principal part of the underlined verb.

1. The bobcat <u>limped</u> away into the trees. ____________________
2. Sparks from the rock <u>are raining</u> down on the cave floor. ____________________
3. She <u>places</u> more wood on the fire. ____________________
4. The darkness <u>has filled</u> him with fear. ____________________
5. He <u>scrapes</u> bark from the tree with his hatchet. ____________________
6. The plane <u>slammed</u> into the forest. ____________________
7. Mosquitoes <u>are swarming</u> around Brian's head. ____________________

Directions Underline the verb in each sentence. Write *present, present participle, past,* or *past participle* to identify the principal part used to form the verb.

8. Alex is hiking along the path with his two brothers. ____________________
9. His grandfather owned a twin engine plane. ____________________
10. Steve and Mike are wiping the grease from the engine. ____________________
11. The snakes have slithered away from the fire. ____________________
12. Jane picks the roots from the ground. ____________________

School + Home **Home Activity** Your child learned about principal parts of regular verbs. Have your child describe activities in your home using present participle forms of verbs: *My sisters are playing outside. Mom is reading the mail.*

Name ______________________________

Unusual Spellings

Spelling Words				
crescent	language	vehicle	exhibit	examine
Michigan	parachute	unique	conquer	rhyme
penguin	exertion	exotic	brochure	symptom
antique	exhausted	heirloom	rhinoceros	bureau

Missing Words Write the list word that best completes each statement.

1. My socks are in the middle drawer of the ___. 1. ____________
2. If you went to Antarctica, you might see a baby ___. 2. ____________
3. The movie about an African safari showed a charging ___. 3. ____________
4. It can take days to recover from the ___ of running in a marathon. 4. ____________
5. I can't bear to part with this precious family ___. 5. ____________
6. The tropical garden has many ___ plants. 6. ____________
7. The movers were ___ after moving all the furniture. 7. ____________
8. The pictures in this ___ make the hotel look luxurious. 8. ____________
9. That ___ shop was filled with beautiful treasures from the past. 9. ____________
10. Your cough could be a ___ of the flu. 10. ____________
11. I can make words ___ all the time. 11. ____________
12. The ___ moon looks beautiful tonight. 12. ____________
13. The Roman Empire was able to ___ much of the ancient world. 13. ____________
14. I would like to learn to speak the Japanese ___. 14. ____________
15. That special type of pine tree is ___ to this area. 15. ____________

Analogies Write a list word to finish each analogy.

16. Car is to ___ as house is to building. 16. ____________
17. Life vest is to sink as ___ is to fall. 17. ____________
18. Hide is to conceal as show is to ___. 18. ____________
19. ___ is to state as Japan is to nation. 19. ____________
20. Inspect is to ___ as hunt is to search. 20. ____________

School + Home **Home Activity** Your child wrote words with unusual spellings. Say a word from the list and ask your child to define it and spell it.

Scoring Rubric: Speech

	4	3	2	1
Focus/Ideas	Clear, focused thesis statement addresses the prompt	Thesis is clear or focused, may be too broad or too narrow	Thesis is vague or misses the prompt	Thesis statement missing or unintelligible
Organization	Strong topic sentences and many supporting details	Most details support topic sentence of paragraph and central thesis	Some topic sentences and some supporting details	Few details support thesis; few topic sentences
Voice	Sincere and interested	Mostly sincere and interested	Voice at times uninterested	Writer without feeling or interest
Word Choice	Most details are unique and vivid	Many details are unique or vivid	Some details are unique or vivid	Most details are vague or cliché
Sentences	Uses short and long sentences, of varying types	Some variety in sentence type and length	Variety only in sentence type or length	Sentences all of one type or length
Conventions	Excellent control; few or no errors	Good control; few errors	Little control; many errors	Many serious errors

Name ____________________

Vocabulary • Word Endings *-ed, -ing*

- An **ending** is a letter or letters added to the end of a base word. For example, the ending *-ed* can be added to verbs to show past action, and the ending *-ing* can be added to verbs to show ongoing or current action.
- Sometimes the *-ed* or *-ing* form of the verb is used as an adjective.

Directions Read the following passage. Then answer the questions below.

Joseph took his hatchet with him into the thick forest. He had to find the plant before the skin on his palm stiffened and became crusty. Moments before he had been walking past his fading campfire, which had smoldered for a half-hour. He had tripped and landed hands-first in the still-hot embers. When it finally registered with Joseph that his right palm was badly burned, he cried out in pain. He knew the only cure for the burn was a special plant that grew deep in the forest. It was a painstaking task to locate this single plant in so much vegetation, but he had no choice. The pain was now throbbing in his palm. It was unbearable. Finally, Joseph saw the long stems of the plant among some bushes in front of him.

1. What is the base word in *stiffened*? What does it mean?

____

2. What is the ending in the word *smoldered*? What does the word mean?

____

3. Is there a word ending in *painstaking*? Why or why not?

____

4. *Registered* is in what tense? Rewrite the sentence using the *-ing* ending instead of *-ed* for *registered.*

____

____

5. Write a word that can change from a verb to an adjective when the ending *-ing* is added. Use the word in a sentence.

____

____

School + Home **Home Activity** Your child identified word endings to determine the meanings of words. While reading an article with your child, have your child underline word endings. Use the endings to help your child define the words.

Poster/Announcement

- An **announcement** makes something known to the public.
- A **poster** is a type of announcement that gives specific facts about an event. It should answer the questions *Who? What? When? Where?* and *Why?*

Directions Read the poster below.

If you were stranded on a deserted island, would you know how to survive? We would!

On Friday, February 5, at the Yukon Memorial Library, the Survival Enthusiasts of Tri-City are hosting their annual *Be Smart: Learn All There Is to Know About Survival* seminar. Eight mini-sessions will teach you how to prepare yourself for just about anything.

The chart below gives you just a sampling of what is in store for you at the seminar.

Name	Description	Time	Location
Survival Kits	Learn what items everyone must have in order to make a survival kit for almost any circumstance. Make your own survival kit during the session.	**8:00 A.M.– 8:45 A.M.**	Hendricks Room
Natural Disasters Awareness	Have you ever witnessed a hurricane, tornado, or earthquake? If you haven't, then come to this session to learn what you need to do to prepare yourself for these natural disasters.	**9:00 A.M.– 10:00 A.M.**	Conference Room B

If you're interested in joining us for a hands-on look at how to survive just about any situation, please **call us at 555-2000** to get more information or to request the registration form. You may send the form directly to the *Survival Enthusiasts of Tri-City, P.O. Box 580, Yukon, Minnesota, 55509*, with your check made out to the organization for the seminar fee of $150. The price of the seminar includes the mini-sessions, a survival kit, lunch, and your very own *Learn How to Survive* packet. The **deadline for registration** is **January 20**. Hope to see you there!

Name ________________________________

Directions Use the poster to answer the following questions.

1. What event is this poster announcing?

____

2. Where is this event being held?

____

3. When is it too late to register for the event?

____

4. What will you learn about in Conference Room B at 9 A.M.?

____

____

5. How does this poster try to get your attention?

____

____

6. How would you get more information about the event?

____

7. Where would you post this poster if you were part of the organization putting on the event?

____

____

8. Why do you think the poster tells you what is included in the registration price?

____

____

9. What kind of people might be interested in this event?

____

____

10. What might you add to this poster to make it more appealing?

____

____

School + Home **Home Activity** Your child learned about posters and announcements. Have your child create a small announcement or poster that describes an upcoming event in your family (such as a birthday party, special dinner, or gathering).

Name ______________________________

Unusual Spellings

Proofread a Report Circle six spelling errors in the report. Write the words correctly. Find a sentence with a punctuation error. Write it correctly.

Spelling Words
crescent
language
vehicle
exhibit
examine
Michigan
parachute
unique
conquer
rhyme
penguin
exertion
exotic
brochure
symptom
antique
exhausted
heirloom
rhinoceros
bureau

Antique Hunting

I'm completely exausted after all the antikue hunting, we did today. Everything we saw was interesting and unikue. We took time to examen many family heirlooms, an old TV, even a farm vehikle from the 1930s that still worked! One shop had a beautiful bureau that I almost bought and an exotic oriental rug Another offered a brochure that told us how to hunt for antiques using the Internet.

1. ______________ 2. ______________

3. ______________ 4. ______________

5. ______________ 6. ______________

7. ____

____

Proofread Words Circle the word that is spelled correctly. Write it on the line.

8.	crescent	cresant	crecent	8. ______________
9.	langwige	language	laneguge	9. ______________
10.	exibit	exhibit	exhibet	10. ______________
11.	conquer	concur	conqer	11. ______________
12.	rhyme	ryme	rihm	12. ______________
13.	exotic	exzotic	exatic	13. ______________
14.	penqwin	pengin	penguin	14. ______________
15.	symptom	simptom	symtom	15. ______________
16.	burro	bureau	burea	16. ______________

Frequently Misspelled Words
TV
Christmas

School + Home **Home Activity** Your child identified misspelled words with unusual spellings. Ask your child to spell and use list words in sentences.

Principal Parts of Regular Verbs

Directions Read the passage. Then read each question. Circle the letter of the correct answer.

Abraham Lincoln's War

(1) The American people elected Abraham Lincoln president of the United States at a time of great national conflict. (2) The Southern slave states had planned to withdraw from the country. (3) This issue divided the American people. (4) Lincoln (believe) that his most important job was to preserve the Union. (5) Scholars have stated that he tried to prevent the Civil War, but he pursued victory for the North by choosing the best generals. (6) For years, Americans consistently (rank) Lincoln as one of the greatest American presidents because he saved the Union.

1 What is the present form of the underlined verb in sentence 1?

- **A** is electing
- **B** elect
- **C** am electing
- **D** are electing

2 What term identifies the principal part of the underlined verb in sentence 2?

- **A** Past
- **B** Present
- **C** Present participle
- **D** Past participle

3 Which form of the verb in parentheses best completes sentence 4?

- **A** believes
- **B** believed
- **C** has believed
- **D** had believed

4 What terms identify the principal parts of the two underlined verbs in sentence 5?

- **A** Present/Past
- **B** Past participle/Past
- **C** Present participle/Past
- **D** Present participle/Past participle

5 Which form of the verb in parentheses best completes sentence 6?

- **A** has ranked
- **B** have ranked
- **C** is ranking
- **D** are ranking

School + Home **Home Activity** Your child prepared for taking tests on principal parts of regular verbs. Ask your child to write four regular verbs that tell about things he or she can do (*play, kick, skate, dance*) and then write the four principal parts for each verb.

Name____

Generalize

- Sometimes authors **generalize**, or make a broad statement or rule that applies to many examples. Often, clue words such as *most, all, sometimes, always, usually, generally, seldom,* and *never* help to identify generalizations.
- Generalizations supported by facts and logic are called valid generalizations. Faulty generalizations are not always supported by facts.
- Generalizations should always be supported with facts.

Directions Read the following passage. Then complete the diagram below.

Robert was a talented actor. When he was young, neighbors came to see him put on plays with his siblings in the backyard. As Robert grew older, he wanted to become a professional actor. At the time, African Americans were rarely given roles. Robert knew his goal would be hard to reach, but he was determined to do it.

First, Robert moved from his town to a big city where there were more opportunities. He tried out for all kinds of roles, but he was never offered a part. Often it was clear to Robert that he was a better actor than the people who were given parts. Several times he asked directors to explain their choices, but it never changed the outcome. Robert waited for the next audition and tried again. It was difficult to stay confident and to avoid feeling bitter, but he was determined to meet that challenge.

Robert began to hear stories about African American actors finding work in theaters in Europe. Robert decided to make the big move across the sea. Nothing was going to stop him.

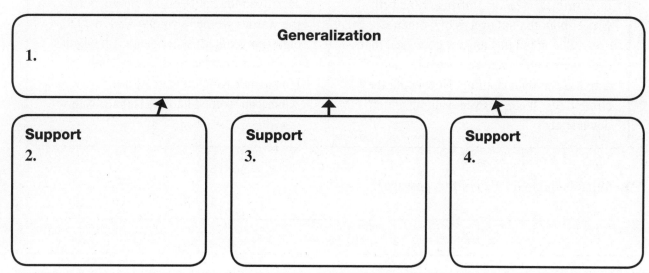

Generalization

1.

Support

2.

Support

3.

Support

4.

5. What is one question you generated while completing the diagram?

____

School + Home **Home Activity** Your child made a generalization and supported it with details. Read a story together. Make a generalization about a character based on details from the story.

Name ______________________________________

Writing • Biography

Key Features of a Biography

- tells the story of someone else's life
- may include the subject's entire life or only a part of the subject's life
- written in the third person

Elizabeth's Bloomers

You've probably heard of Elizabeth Cady Stanton. She was a leader of the fight for women's right to vote. Did you know that she also fought for other freedoms for women as well? One such battle was for the freedom of dress. In the years of Elizabeth's life from 1815 to 1902, women had very few rights. In 1852, Elizabeth and other reformers took to wearing bloomers instead of long dresses. The reaction was dramatic.

At that time, American women wore long dresses that were pulled in painfully at the waist and weighed many pounds. In *History of Woman Suffrage*, Elizabeth wrote about the unfairness of women's dress. She noted that anyone could see that even young girls were restricted in their activities by such clothing. How could they climb trees, skate, or even walk up and down stairs?

Elizabeth's solution seems simple now, but in her day it was shocking. She began wearing balloon-like trousers or "bloomers" under a wide, knee-length skirt. Wearing bloomers as she spoke out for women's rights and against slavery, Elizabeth struck a blow for common sense. But the crowds and the press grew ugly. Elizabeth's bloomers had become a symbol of all that threatened life as they knew it. Her message faced a storm of protests against her costume.

Elizabeth Cady Stanton braved those protests for two years. Finally, she sacrificed the battle of the bloomers for the war for women's rights. And in 1920, eighteen years after her death, Elizabeth's war was won. Congress passed the Nineteenth Amendment. At last, American women had the right to vote.

1. What is the main idea of this passage?

____

____

2. List a few facts that support the main idea.

____

____

____

Name ____________________________________

Vocabulary

Directions Choose the word from the box that best matches each definition. Write the word on the line.

Check the Words You Know

- ___application
- ___dramatic
- ___enraged
- ___formal
- ___momentous
- ___opera
- ___prejudice
- ___privileged
- ___recital

____________________ **1.** unreasonable dislike of an idea or group of people

____________________ **2.** according to set customs or rules

____________________ **3.** having some special rights, advantage, or favor

____________________ **4.** a request for employment, a loan, etc.

____________________ **5.** very important

____________________ **6.** a musical entertainment, given usually by one performer

Directions Choose the word from the box that best matches each clue. Write the letters in the crossword puzzle.

Down

7. made very angry or furious

8. This is a play in which the words are sung instead of spoken.

Across

9. A violinist or pianist might give one of these performances.

10. like a drama; of or about plays

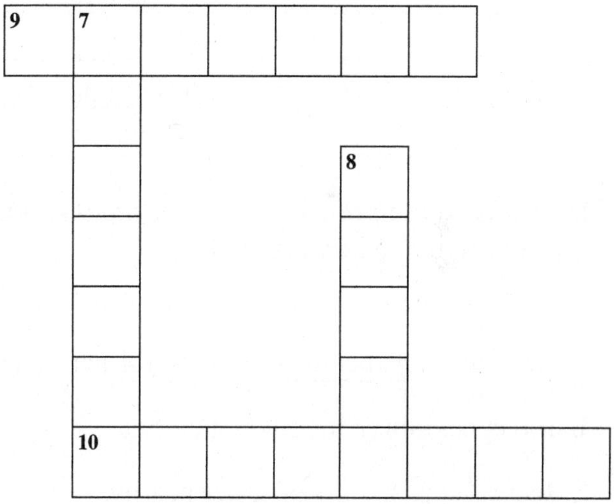

Write a Review

Imagine you are a music reviewer for the local newspaper. On a separate sheet of paper, write a review of a recital or concert. Use as many vocabulary words as you can.

School + Home **Home Activity** Your child identified and used vocabulary words from *When Marian Sang*. Together, create a crossword puzzle with the vocabulary words from this selection.

Name ______________________________

Principal Parts of Irregular Verbs

Usually you add *-ed* to a verb to form the past and past participle. **Irregular verbs** do not follow this rule. Instead of having *-ed* forms, irregular verbs usually change to other words.

Present Tense	Benny writes a pop song.
Present Participle	He is writing a pop song.
Past Tense	Benny wrote several pop songs.
Past Participle	He has written pop songs for several years.

Present Tense	Present Participle	Past Tense	Past Participle
begin	(am, is, are) beginning	began	(*has, have, had*) begun
bring	(am, is, are) bringing	brought	(*has, have, had*) brought
buy	(am, is, are) buying	bought	(*has, have, had*) bought
come	(am, is, are) coming	came	(*has, have, had*) come
feel	(am, is, are) feeling	felt	(*has, have, had*) felt
grow	(am, is, are) growing	grew	(*has, have, had*) grown
keep	(am, is, are) keeping	kept	(*has, have, had*) kept
see	(am, is, are) seeing	saw	(*has, have, had*) seen
sing	(am, is, are) singing	sang	(*has, have, had*) sung
take	(am, is, are) taking	took	(*has, have, had*) taken
tell	(am, is, are) telling	told	(*has, have, had*) told
write	(am, is, are) writing	wrote	(*has, have, had*) written

Directions Write *present, present participle, past,* or *past participle* to identify the principal part used to form the underlined verb.

1. Marian began music school at eighteen. ______________________
2. Her family had come to Europe for her concert. ______________________
3. Joe is beginning his singing career. ______________________
4. Jenny keeps a glass of water nearby. ______________________

Directions Underline the form of the verb in ( ) that correctly completes each sentence.

5. Dana (feeled, felt) faint after singing in the warm hall.
6. Tom (had written, writed) a letter to his favorite folk singer.
7. Charlie (buyed, bought) a ticket and went to the musical.
8. Cathy (has began, began) her voice lessons.

School + Home **Home Activity** Your child learned about principal parts of irregular verbs. Together look through a newspaper or magazine. Have your child find three irregular verbs and identify which principal part of each verb is being used.

Name ______________________________

Multisyllabic Words 2

Spelling Words				
international	prehistoric	untrustworthy	constellation	honorary
disagreement	preparation	Philadelphia	promotional	constitution
unbreakable	biodegradable	coordination	compassionate	impossibility
entirety	executive	companionship	unthinkable	predicament

Missing Words Write a list word to complete each statement.

1. Choosing between the two equally talented singers presents quite a ___.
2. Mom buys plastic drinking cups because they are
3. I never dreamed that such an ___ event could actually happen.
4. I use ___ laundry detergent because it's good for the environment.
5. My dog gives me love and ___.
6. It takes a lot of ___ to be a juggler.
7. My mother is a junior ___ of a large corporation.
8. The nurse who cared for me was efficient and ___.
9. I have completed the assignment in its ___.
10. The sun's setting in the north is an ___.
11. The United States has a written ___.
12. The ___ conference was attended by people from many countries.
13. The electronics store is offering a free vacation as a ___ gimmick.
14. I often wonder what life was like in ___ times.
15. ___ is home to the famous Liberty Bell.

Definitions Write a list word to match each definition.

16. readiness
17. dishonest
18. argument
19. group of many stars
20. degree given as a reward for accomplishments

1. ____________
2. ____________
3. ____________
4. ____________
5. ____________
6. ____________
7. ____________
8. ____________
9. ____________
10. ____________
11. ____________
12. ____________
13. ____________
14. ____________
15. ____________
16. ____________
17. ____________
18. ____________
19. ____________
20. ____________

School + Home **Home Activity** Your child wrote multisyllabic words. Spell the first two syllables of a list word. Challenge your child to guess the word and spell the remaining syllables.

Name ____________________

Time Line

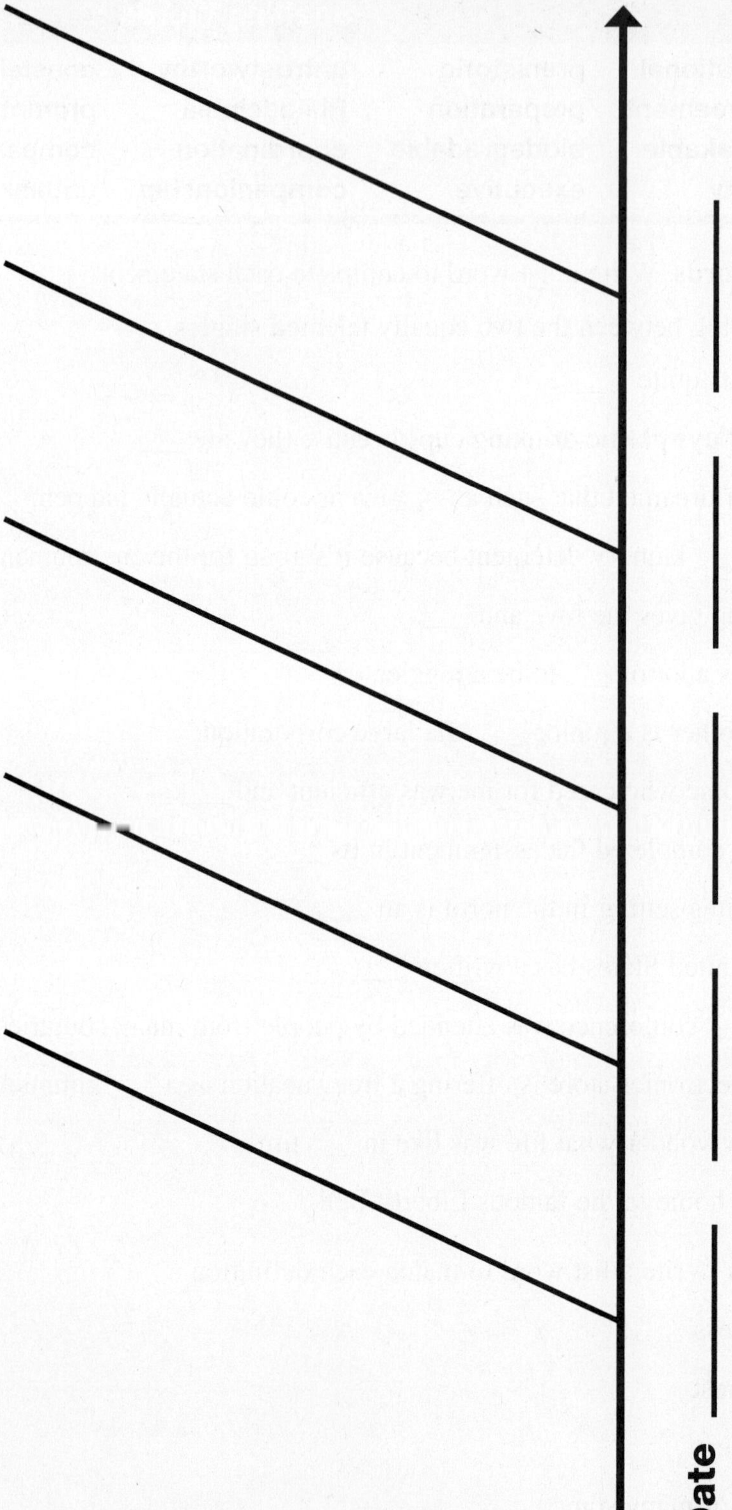

Name______________________________

Vocabulary • Suffixes *-ic, -ous, -ation*

- A **suffix** is a word part added to the end of a base word to change its meaning or the way it is used in a sentence.
- The suffix *-ic* means "pertaining to or associated with," as in *artistic*. The suffix *-ous* means "full of," as in *poisonous*. The suffix *-ation* means "the state of being," as in *frustration*. You can use suffixes to figure out the meanings of words.

Directions Read the following passage. Then answer the questions below.

Autumn desperately wanted to be in an opera. She had attended a few with her mom, and she loved the way the singers' voices resonated throughout the grand theaters. The downtown opera house was offering a summer camp for young singers, so Autumn found the application online and printed it out.

She was a little worried, because she had no formal singing experience. Autumn did have dramatic experience, though. She was in all the school plays, and she even took acting classes on the side.

When the application was complete, Autumn sent it in. All she could do now was dream about how joyous she would feel singing such beautiful music on an opera stage. How momentous that day would be!

1. What is the suffix in *application*? What does the word mean?

____

2. How does the suffix change the meaning of the base word in *dramatic*?

____

____

3. Define the word *joyous* in terms of its suffix.

____

4. How can the suffix help you to figure out the meaning of *momentous*?

____

____

5. Describe a moment in your life that you would call *momentous*. Use the word in context.

____

____

School + Home **Home Activity** Your child identified suffixes in order to determine the meanings of words. Together, make a list of other words that use the suffixes *-ic*, *-ation*, and *-ous*. Have your child guess at their meanings based on their suffixes. Then use a dictionary to confirm the meanings.

Readers' Guide to Periodical Literature

- The ***Readers' Guide to Periodical Literature*** is a set of books that lists, alphabetically by author and subject, the articles that are published in more than 200 periodicals. Each entry provides an article's title, author, volume, pages, and date.
- Volumes of the *Readers' Guide* are indexed by time period. You can find a *Readers' Guide* in most libraries.

Directions Read the following page, which is similar to one you would find in the *Readers' Guide to Periodical Literature*. Then answer the questions on the next page.

Volume, April 2003–January 2004

AFRICAN AMERICANS

See also
Africa
Culture

Art

African American Art Expo. W. Carter. *American Artists* v73 p86–92 Jy '03

Artists to Watch 2004. K. Jackson. *African American Art* v36 p112–15 D '03

History

From Slavery to Congress [a look at African American history]. T. Weatherby. *Historical Happenings* v204 p21–8 Ap '03

We Shall Overcome [Civil Rights movement]. S. Barnes. *African Americans Today* v59 p60–7 My '03

Performing Arts

The Academy Finally Responds [Academy Awards given to African American actors]. P. Ames. *That Is Entertainment* v276 p9–15 Jy '03

The Fabulous Josephine Baker. O. Rather. *Appearing Nightly* v39 p90–101 Au '03

Jazz's Finest Players. E. Douglass. *Jazz Now* v73 p43–55 O '03

Revisiting the Career of Marian Anderson. *The Performers' Magazine* v75 p88–95 S '03

Politics

The African American Vote. R. Cooper. *Politics and You* v23 p65–8 O '03

African Americans in Congress. C. Johnson. *Washington Today* v54 p19–27 S '03

Name ______________________

1. What kinds of sources are listed in a *Readers' Guide*?

2. Why would it be useless to look in this volume for an article published in February 2004?

3. How are the articles arranged on this sample page?

4. What is the purpose of the note directing the reader to see also "Africa" and "Culture"?

5. When did K. Jackson's article appear in a magazine?

6. What article appeared in *Jazz Now*?

7. What is the purpose of the brackets after some of the articles' titles?

8. If you were researching Martin Luther King Jr., what magazines might you consult?

9. If you needed the latest information on a topic, how would you go about selecting a volume of the *Readers' Guide* to use?

10. How can using the *Readers' Guide* save you time when researching a subject?

School + Home **Home Activity** Your child answered questions about the *Readers' Guide to Periodical Literature*. Have him or her explain the different parts of a *Readers' Guide* page to you. Then plan a trip to the library to take a look at a real *Readers' Guide* in order to conduct research for an upcoming report.

Multisyllabic Words 2

Proofread a Biography Circle six spelling errors in the biography. Write the words correctly. Find a sentence with a wrong verb. Write it correctly.

Spelling Words

international, prehistoric, untrustworthy, constellation, honorary, disagreement, preparation, Philadelphia, promotional, constitution, unbreakable, biodegradable, coordination, compassionate, impossibility, entirety, executive, companionship, unthinkable, predicament

Helen Keller

Until she was nineteen months old, Helen Keller was a happy, healthy child. Then, in spite of her strong constatution, she developed a high fever that caused her to become deaf and blind.

Her parents find a teacher named Annie Sullivan to help Helen. Annie was compassionate but tough. She began by teaching Helen elementry manners. Then she taught Helen signs for the letters of the alphabet. When Helen had learned the alphabet in its entirity, Annie "spelled" words into Helen's hand.

Helen wrote a book called *The Story of My Life*. She became an inturnashional traveler, speaking to large groups of people. She received many honerary awards. Helen Keller was successful because of her unbrakeable spirit. She also owed a lot to Annie Sullivan.

Frequently Misspelled Words

elementary, usually

1. ____________ 2. ____________
3. ____________ 4. ____________
5. ____________ 6. ____________
7. ______________________________
____

Proofread Words Circle the word that is spelled correctly. Write it.

8. constelltion	constellation	8.	____________
9. coordination	cordination	9.	____________
10. Philadelphia	Philadelpha	10.	____________
11. biodegradble	biodegradable	11.	____________
12. executive	executiv	12.	____________

School + Home **Home Activity** Your child identified misspelled multisyllabic words. Ask your child to find the common syllable *tion* in four list words.

Name ____________________

Principal Parts of Irregular Verbs

Directions Read the passage. Then read each question. Circle the letter of the correct answer.

Early Writing

(1) The people who left their earliest writing for us did not have computers. (2) Thousands of years ago there was no paper, so humans thought about ways to record their observations on stone. (3) Anthropologists of the nineteenth century had seen early writing on the walls of caves. (4) More recently, historians have written about the first carving tools with sharp points like knives. (5) Artifacts have shown that bone and ivory were used to scratch markings on shells. (6) There is evidence of writing from the first pens made of reeds and using plant dyes. (7) What a long way we have come in the development of human writing!

1 What is the present form of the underlined verb in sentence 1?

A leave

B is leaving

C am leaving

D None of the above

2 What term identifies the principal part of the underlined verb in sentence 3?

A Past

B Present

C Present participle

D Past participle

3 What term identifies the principal parts of the underlined verbs in sentences 4 and 5?

A Present

B Present participle

C Past

D Past participle

4 Which present tense verb is found in this passage?

A was

B have come

C were used

D is

5 Which three past tense verbs are found in this passage?

A record, seen, used

B scratch, is, using

C left, was, thought

D None of the above

School + Home

Home Activity Your child prepared for taking tests on principal parts of irregular verbs. Help your child make flash cards for the principal parts of difficult irregular verbs such as *is, see, write,* and *come* by writing the present form on one side and the other forms on the other side. Quiz your child with the cards.

Name ______________________________

Sequence

- In both fiction and nonfiction, **sequence** is the order of events.
- The time of day and clue words such as *before* and *after* can help you determine the order in which things happen.

Directions Read the following passage. Then complete the diagram by writing the main events in sequence on the time line.

Raj was determined to learn all the swimming strokes in one summer. First he learned how to swim the front crawl. After two weeks, Raj had mastered the stroke. Next came the backstroke. Floating on his back was something Raj learned as a child, so this stroke came easy to him. The breaststroke, his next challenge, was even easier, and Raj barely had to practice it. Raj thought he'd have no problem mastering the last and final stroke, the butterfly. Immediately, though, Raj struggled with getting the timing of his arm and leg movements right. Somehow, he just couldn't seem to get it. His teacher told him to feel the rhythm and to relax. Raj was so busy trying to learn all the strokes that he had forgotten the main principle—to have fun!

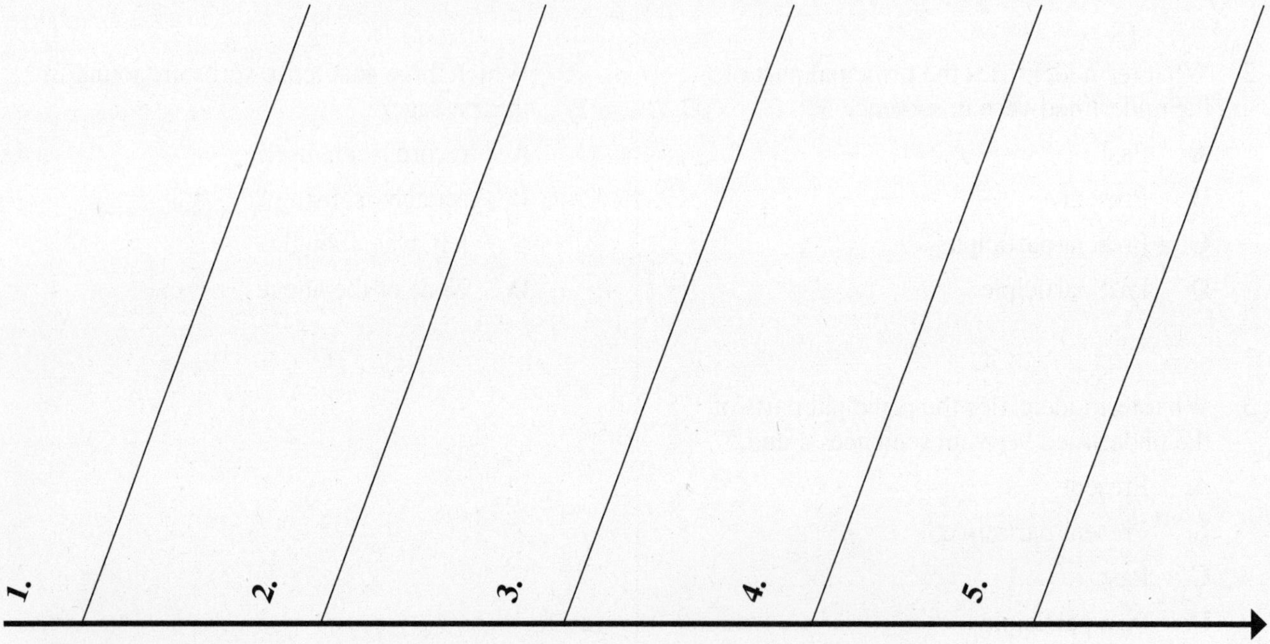

School + Home **Home Activity** Your child identified the sequence of events in a story. Together, discuss the sequence of events in a scene from a favorite movie or television program.

Name ________________________________

Writing • Autobiographical Sketch

Key Features of an Autobiographical Sketch

- describes a true event or events in a writer's life
- includes the writer's thoughts and feelings
- may be part of a longer autobiography
- uses first-person point of view

The Contest

I was eight years old when I decided to enter the library poetry contest. My best friend, Michelle, was entering too. I was so excited! Who wouldn't be? We had a month to get our poems ready—plenty of time. And, win or lose, all poetry would be displayed in the front window of the library.

All poems were supposed to be about winter. Michelle got started right away. I thought, "I need to spend some time just thinking about winter," so I waited. Michelle called. She had her poem done and wanted to know how I was doing. "Oh, fine," I said. Well, actually, it wasn't fine. I just didn't want anyone to know how little I had done.

Pretty soon, it was the night before our poems were due. "Don't worry," I told myself. "You can write. You'll be able to do it." I sat with the pencil in my hand, a blank paper before me, filling up with doodles. I couldn't think of a single idea. "Come on, come on, Susan, you can do this," I said to myself.

Oh, sure, I was able to write a few lame lines, but nothing I wanted displayed in a library. My mother kept coming in to check on me. Finally, she said, "That's it! Time for bed." I never did write an entry for that poetry contest. My friend Michelle did, and she won second prize. It was hard for me, because I had told the librarians, my friends, and my family that I was going to enter and win first prize. From that experience, I learned something important about writing. Plain and simple, good writing takes time!

1. Underline three different types of sentences in the story. Label the types.

2. What details in the opening paragraph grab the reader and draw you into the story?

____

____

3. Write three sentences telling the beginning, middle, and end of this story.

____

____

____

Name ____

Vocabulary

Directions Choose the word from the box that best matches each definition. Write the word on the line.

Check the Words You Know
___customary
___emphasized
___frantic
___stunned
___treaded

____________________ **1.** stressed; called attention to

____________________ **2.** dazed

____________________ **3.** kept the body straight in the water with the head above water by moving the arms and legs

____________________ **4.** usual; according to custom

____________________ **5.** very much excited

Directions Choose the word from the box that best completes each sentence. Write the word on the line shown to the left.

____________________ **6.** During the swimming test, he ______ water for three minutes.

____________________ **7.** The teacher ______ the importance of never swimming alone.

____________________ **8.** It was ______ to learn the crawl stroke before the butterfly stroke.

____________________ **9.** She was ______ by the size of the wave.

____________________ **10.** Try not to become ______ if caught in a riptide.

Write a Speech

Imagine that you are the head lifeguard at a beach. On a separate sheet of paper, write a speech to give to the other lifeguards before the summer swimming season begins. Your speech should remind the lifeguards of the importance of their jobs. Use as many vocabulary words as you can.

School + Home

Home Activity Your child identified and used vocabulary words from *Learning to Swim*. Together, write a story about a day at the beach. Include as many vocabulary words from the selection as possible.

Verbs, Objects, and Subject Complements

A **direct object** follows an action verb and tells who or what receives the action of the verb.
Meg gave a signal. (*Gave* is an action verb. *Signal* is a direct object.)

An **indirect object** follows an action verb and tells to whom or what the action of the verb is done.
Meg gave Luis a signal. (The indirect object *Luis* tells to whom Meg gave a signal. Note that an indirect object comes before the direct object.)

A **subject complement** follows a linking verb and tells who or what the subject is or is like.
Chidi seemed sad. (*Seemed* is a linking verb and *sad* is a subject complement that describes Chidi.)
Todd is the captain of the team. (*Is* is a linking verb, and *captain* is a subject complement that describes who Todd is.)

- A noun used as a subject complement is a predicate noun. An adjective used as a subject complement is a predicate adjective.

Directions Write the subject complement in each sentence.

1. The waves seemed rough. ____________________
2. The flutter kick is a strong kick used with the crawl. ____________________
3. The water felt cool in the July sun. ____________________
4. Ice cream tastes refreshing on a hot day at the beach. ____________________
5. Jill was happy about her progress. ____________________

Directions Circle direct objects and underline any indirect objects.

6. Ted visited his grandparents' village.
7. Barb handed Dex a dry towel.
8. Adam prefers soccer to aquatic sports.
9. My mother taught me rules for safe swimming.
10. Sylvia set a new record for her team.
11. Sandy gave her sisters matching blue swimsuits.
12. Anne practiced the breaststroke.

School + Home **Home Activity** Your child learned about verbs, objects, and subject complements. Have your child tell you what direct objects, indirect objects, and subject complements are and find two examples of each in the newspaper.

Name ______________________________

Using Just Enough Letters

Spelling Words				
nuclear	helicopter	anxious	appreciate	plastic
familiar	athletic	escape	apologize	Washington
pastime	exquisite	lantern	fulfill	souvenir
tragedy	sherbet	algebra	icicles	escort

Words in Context Write the list word that best completes each statement.

1. Thanks! I ___ your help. 1. ______________
2. Baseball is America's national ___. 2. ______________
3. Our company can ___ all your household needs. 3. ______________
4. The foul ball I caught will make a great ___. 4. ______________
5. The sun is shining, and the ___ are melting. 5. ______________
6. Will you ___ me to the class party? 6. ______________
7. The soccer players were very ___. 7. ______________
8. Get away from it all and ___ your daily grind. 8. ______________
9. The treaty limits the use of ___ weapons. 9. ______________
10. This new ___ wrap keeps leftovers fresh. 10. ______________

Word Groups Write a list word that fits into each group.

11. geometry, calculus, ___ 11. ______________
12. airplane, jet, ___ 12. ______________
13. ice cream, frozen yogurt, ___ 13. ______________
14. worried, nervous, ___ 14. ______________
15. disaster, crisis, ___ 15. ______________
16. well-known, usual, ___ 16. ______________
17. lamp, flashlight, ___ 17. ______________
18. California, Oregon, ___ 18. ______________
19. beautiful, marvelous, ___ 19. ______________
20. make amends, express regret, ___ 20. ______________

School + Home **Home Activity** Your child wrote words that are often mispronounced or misspelled. Ask your child to choose a word group from the second activity and explain why the list word fits into the group.

Name ______________________________

Story Sequence Chart

Title ______________________________

Beginning

↓

Middle

↓

End

Name ____________________

Vocabulary • Synonyms

- **Synonyms** are words that have the same or similar meanings.
- When you read, you may come across a word you don't know. Look for synonyms as clues to the unknown word's meaning.

Directions Read the following passage. Then answer the questions below.

It was customary that all lifeguards must pass a test before being hired to work at the beach. Ally was aware of this usual procedure, so she made sure to prepare for the test well ahead of time. Every day, she practiced swimming against a current in the lake, and she treaded water for several minutes at a time. Ally reminded herself not to get too frantic, or excited, during the test. In that case, of course, she wouldn't be able to concentrate. All her life, her swimming teachers emphasized, or stressed, that lifeguards need to stay calm in all situations. Ally was stunned when she first heard this. She was also astonished at how serious this summer job really was.

1. What synonym for the word *customary* appears in the passage?

____

2. What does the word *frantic* mean in this passage? How do you know?

____

____

3. What is the meaning of *emphasized*? How can you tell?

____

____

4. What synonym for *stunned* is included in the passage? Name a second synonym for *stunned*.

____

5. Another synonym for *customary* is *traditional*. Explain why this word is not an appropriate synonym for *customary* as it is used in this passage.

____

____

School + Home

Home Activity Your child identified synonyms using context clues. Together, read an article in a magazine or newspaper. Have your child choose a few unfamiliar words from the article and look up synonyms for them in a thesaurus. Together, rewrite the sentences by adding the synonyms in order to help clarify the meanings of the unfamiliar words.

Name ______________________________

Study Strategies

- Use **study strategies** to help you save time and avoid reading irrelevant information. You can make a KWL table, a two-column comparison table, or you can follow the steps of SQP3R.
- CD-ROM resources can help you gather information on a particular topic. You might use a CD-ROM dictionary, encyclopedia, or a topic-related CD-ROM. You can use search CD-ROMs to find specific information or click on underlined links to find related information.

Directions Use the following study strategies to answer the questions below.

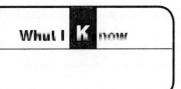

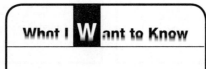

Topic ______________________________

What I Know	What I Want to Know	What I Learned

SQP3R

- **Survey** the text.
- Formulate **questions** about it.
- **Predict** what the text will be about.
- **Read** the text.
- **Recite** what you have learned.
- **Review** what you have learned.

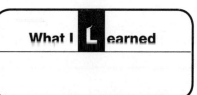

Details About "A"	Details About "B"

1. In the comparison table, what would you write in the two columns?

____

2. How do you think reciting what you have learned might help you?

____

3. For what reason is it helpful to write down what you already know about a topic?

____

____

4. What do you do when you survey a text?

____

____

5. Which strategy do you find most helpful? Explain.

____

____

Name ______________________________

Directions Use the two CD-ROM sample screens to answer the following questions.

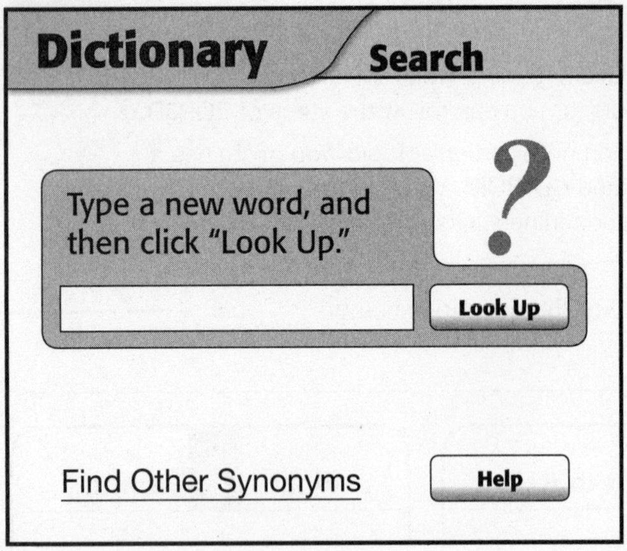

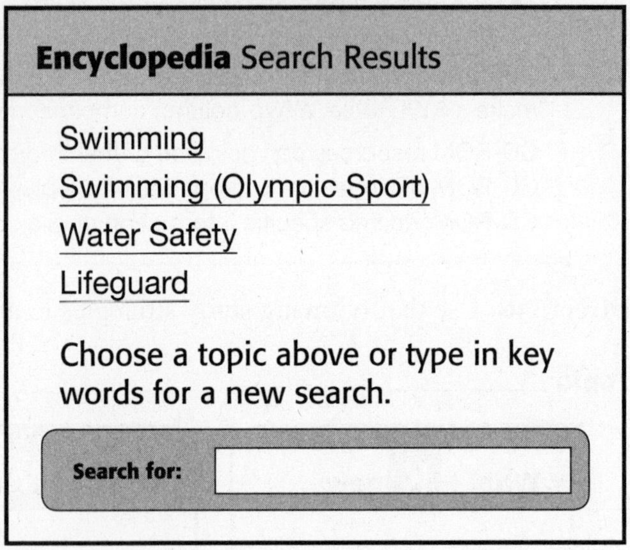

6. How would you use one of the above media sources to make a two-column table to compare *riptides* and *ebb tides*?

____

____

7. Imagine you are researching *Swimming (Olympic Sport)* and using a KWL chart to organize your information. Write a sentence you might put in the K column.

____

____

8. Imagine you are researching *Swimming (Olympic Sport)* and using a KWL chart to organize your information. Write a question you might put in the W column.

____

____

9. When you go to the Encyclopedia Search Results for *Swimming (Olympic Sport)* and find text for this topic, if you are using SQP3R, what are your next two steps?

____

____

10. When using SQP3R, after you predict what the text will be about, what should you do?

____

____

School + Home **Home Activity** Your child learned about several study strategies. Choose a nonfiction article to read together. Have your child apply one of the study strategies to the reading. Work through the article together, using the study strategy. Then discuss how the strategy helped with understanding the topic.

Using Just Enough Letters

Proofread Safety Tips Circle six spelling errors in the list of safety tips. Write the words correctly. Write the last sentence, using correct punctuation.

Earthquake Safety Tips

Become familiur with these rules. They may help you avoid trajedy:

- Remain calm.
- If you are indoors, get under a desk or table, or stand in a doorway. Stay away from windows, shelves, and heavy equipment.
- If you are outdoors, quickly move away from buildings, utility poles, overhead wires, and other structures. Avoid downed power or utility lines, wich may have electricity flowing through them.
- If you are in an automobile, stop in an open area away from power lines and trees. Stay in the vehicle for shelter. Do not try to exscape.
- Do not use a lanturn, torches, lighter, or open flame.
- Do not get anxshus. Do not panic?

Spelling Words

nuclear
helicopter
anxious
appreciate
plastic
familiar
athletic
escape
apologize
Washington

pastime
exquisite
lantern
fulfill
souvenir
tragedy
sherbet
algebra
icicles
escort

1. ____________ 2. ____________
3. ____________ 4. ____________
5. ____________ 6. ____________
7. ______________________________

Frequently Misspelled Words

doesn't
which

Proofread Words Circle the word that is spelled correctly. Write it on the line.

8.	helacopter	helicopter	8. ____________
9.	athletic	athaletic	9. ____________
10.	fulfill	fullfill	10. ____________
11.	sherbet	sherbert	11. ____________
12.	nucular	nuclear	12. ____________

School + Home **Home Activity** Your child identified misspelled words. Have your child circle letters or letter combinations in the list words that could cause spelling problems.

Name ______________________________

Verbs, Objects, and Subject Complements

Directions Read the passage. Then read each question. Circle the letter of the correct answer.

Oncoming Storm

(1) The lake was surprisingly <u>tranquil</u> on this beautiful day. (2) The sailors raised their sails and tried to catch some wind. (3) Some sailors even started the engines on their boats because the waters were too calm. (4) No one expected the storm. (5) Suddenly, however, our dog seemed jittery. (6) Moe became nervous and began to bark loudly. (7) We gave him a few <u>biscuits</u>, but he wanted us to know that he was worried. (8) We tied up the *Goodfella* just as the skies opened. (9) No one ran faster to our cabin than Moe!

1 Which describes the underlined word in sentence 1?

- **A** Direct object
- **B** Indirect object
- **C** Subject complement
- **D** None of the above

2 Which word is the direct object in sentence 2?

- **A** sailors
- **B** sails
- **C** raised
- **D** None of the above

3 Which words are the direct object and the subject complement of sentence 3?

- **A** engines, calm
- **B** sailors, waters
- **C** even started, on their boats
- **D** None of the above

4 Which describes the underlined word in sentence 7?

- **A** Direct object
- **B** Indirect object
- **C** Subject complement
- **D** None of the above

5 Which sentence in this paragraph has an indirect object?

- **A** Sentence 4
- **B** Sentence 5
- **C** Sentence 6
- **D** Sentence 7

School + Home

Home Activity Your child prepared for taking tests on verbs, objects, and subject complements. Read a favorite story with your child. Ask him or her to find direct objects, indirect objects, and subject complements in the story.

Name ____________________

Generalize

- A **generalization** is a broad statement or rule that applies to many examples.
- Valid generalizations are supported by examples, facts, or good logic. Invalid generalizations are not supported.

Directions Read the following passage. Then complete the diagram below by making a generalization about Jung and supporting it with examples.

After Jung lost her grandmother's brooch, she wasn't sure what to do. She feared telling her grandmother the truth because it would break her heart. So, Jung took all of her savings and went downtown to see if she could find a similar brooch to replace the lost one. She found one with beautiful emerald stones, but it was too expensive. She found another one that she could afford, but it paled in comparison to the original.

Jung decided to tell her grandmother the truth. She crept up the stairs to her grandmother's room and softly knocked on the door. When her grandmother answered it, she was wearing the brooch! Jung told her what had happened anyway. Her grandmother was pleased that Jung had been honest and allowed Jung to borrow the brooch again. Jung realized it's always best to tell the truth.

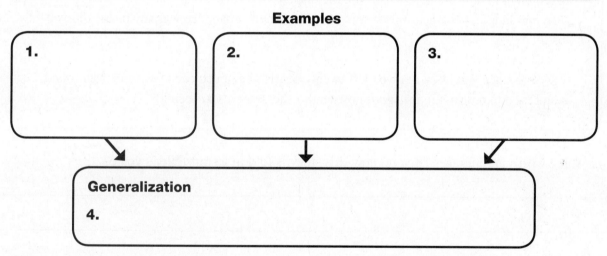

Examples

1.

2.

3.

Generalization

4.

5. Make a prediction about whether or not Jung will lose the brooch the next time.

____

____

____

School + Home **Home Activity** Your child made a generalization based on examples in a story. Have your child make a generalization about his or her personality or behavior. Discuss examples from your child's life that would support this generalization.

Writing • Folk Tale

Key Features of a Folk Tale

- is a traditional narrative story
- may contain a lesson
- may have been passed down for generations or originate from a particular culture

A Tale from China

Long ago, in a village in China, lived a poor young girl named Mei. Every day Mei gathered berries to sell at the market so she could buy food.

One day, Mei started for home when she saw a blue silk pouch lying on the ground. She opened it and found twelve beautiful shiny pearls. She knew that someone must have lost it. So, she decided to sit down and wait for the owner to appear.

Mei noticed a woman searching for something. "Did you lose this pouch?" Mei asked.

"Yes, I did," the woman answered. She grabbed the pouch, opened it, and counted out the pearls. "There are only twelve pearls in this pouch. I had twenty pearls. You must have stolen the rest."

Mei protested, but the woman continued to scream accusations. Finally, the merchants urged them to have Judge Cheng settle the dispute.

When Judge Cheng heard their story, he asked the woman, "How many pearls did you lose?"

"Twenty," she answered.

"Well, since you insist that you lost twenty pearls, the pouch can't be yours. Mei found it and tried to return it to its rightful owner. So she deserves to keep it."

1. What words and phrases let you know this story is told in a storyteller's voice?

____

____

____

____

2. What do you think is the moral, or lesson, of this tale?

____

____

____

____

Vocabulary

Directions Draw a line to connect each word on the left with its definition on the right.

1. repay	in great pain or sorrow
2. distressed	to do something in return
3. fulfill	got off a horse
4. dismounted	to grow or develop well
5. flourish	to perform or carry out a duty

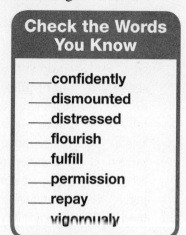

Check the Words You Know

- ___confidently
- ___dismounted
- ___distressed
- ___flourish
- ___fulfill
- ___permission
- ___repay
- ___vigorously

Directions Circle the word that has the same or nearly the same meaning as the first word in each group.

6. permission	consent	disagreement	response
7. repay	cheat	keep	refund
8. confidently	with certainty	unsurely	timidly
9. vigorously	weakly	strongly	sadly
10. flourish	decrease	thrive	decline

Write a Friendly Letter

Imagine you are asking for someone's permission to do something or to borrow something. On a separate sheet of paper, write a friendly letter to this person. Use as many vocabulary words as you can.

School + Home **Home Activity** Your child identified and used vocabulary words from *Juan Verdades*. Together, write a creative tall tale using all the vocabulary words from this selection.

Name ______________________________

Troublesome Verbs

Some pairs of verbs are **troublesome verbs** because they look alike or have similar meanings.

Verb	Meaning	Present	Past	Past Participle
sit	sit down	sit	sat	*(has, have, had)* sat
set	put or place	set	set	*(has, have, had)* set
lie	rest or recline	lie	lay	*(has, have, had)* lain
lay	put or place	lay	laid	*(has, have, had)* laid
rise	get or move up	rise	rose	*(has, have, had)* risen
raise	lift something up	raise	raised	*(has, have, had)* raised
let	allow or permit	let	let	*(has, have, had)* let
leave	go away	leave	left	*(has, have, had)* left
lend	give use of	lend	lent	*(has, have, had)* lent
borrow	get from someone	borrow	borrowed	*(has, have, had)* borrowed
teach	show how	teach	taught	*(has, have, had)* taught
learn	find out	learn	learned	*(has, have, had)* learned

Directions Underline the correct verb in each sentence.

1. She had (raised, risen) the window in the kitchen.
2. Don Arturo has (laid, lain) awake many nights.
3. Araceli (taught, learned) her friend Juan a good lesson.
4. (Sit, Set) the silverware on the table.
5. The wealthy rancheros have (sat, set) in the village plaza.

Directions Complete each sentence with the correct verb from the list above.

6. Will you ________________ me some money until next Tuesday?
7. Yesterday, Juan ________________ his house and went to the fields.
8. The men in the village ________________ from their chairs when it was time to go home.
9. Yesterday, Ms. Cortez ________________ us the Spanish word for *apple*.
10. ________________ me go out to the orchard to pick fruit from the trees.

School + Home

Home Activity Your child learned about troublesome verbs. Have your child choose pairs of verbs from the list on this page, use them correctly in sentences, and explain how he or she knew which verb to use.

Name____________________

Vocabulary • Prefixes *re-, dis-*

- A **prefix** is added to the beginning of a base word and changes the base word's meaning.
- The prefix *re-* means "again" or "back"; the prefix *dis-* means "to remove" or "the opposite of."

Directions Read the following passage. Then answer the questions below.

Pete dismounted from Shadow's saddle and led his beloved horse toward the stable. He was distressed. Shadow was clearly too sick to run in the race next week. He knew he would never fulfill his dream of winning the Crescent City Classic now. When Pete entered the stable, he found Tyler, the stable's owner, waiting for him. "Pete," said Tyler, "I want you to enter the Classic with Dale."

"Dale?" Pete shook his head, recalling the last time he had seen Dale race. "But he's the fastest horse here! Why me?"

"I can say confidently that you and Dale will work well with each other," Tyler said. "I think it's a great match."

"But ... how will I ever repay you?"

"Do your best at the Classic and that will be more than enough."

1. How does the prefix change the meaning of the base word in *dismounted*?

____

____

2. What is the prefix in *recalling*? What does the word mean?

____

3. Can you apply the rules of prefixes with finding the meaning of the word *distressed*? Why or why not?

____

____

4. For what does Pete want to *repay* Tyler?

____

5. What is the meaning of *dishonor*? Give an example of how Pete could dishonor his agreement with Tyler.

____

____

Home Activity Your child identified prefixes to help determine the meanings of words. Make a two-column chart on a piece of paper. In the first column, write the prefixes *dis-* and *re-*. In the second column, write as many base words as the two of you can think of that would make sense when added to these prefixes.

Name ______________________

Outline

- An **outline** is a plan that shows how a story, article, report, or other text is organized. You can use an outline to better understand how a text is organized or as a way to organize your own thoughts before you write something of your own.
- Outlines contain a title, heads, subheads, and details.

Directions Study the following outline. Then answer the questions below.

My Two Best Friends

I. Luis
   A. Personality
      1. funny
      2. trustworthy
      3. intelligent
   B. Why we are friends
      1. We're lab partners in science class.
      2. We play on the soccer team together.
      3. He's an older brother to me.

II. Mandy
   A. Personality
      1. serious
      2. athletic
      3. understanding
   B. Why we are friends
      1. We walk to school together.
      2. We have Spanish and math classes together.
      3. We think the same way about the world.

1. What might be the purpose of this outline?

____

____

2. What are the two topics?

____

3. What is similar about why the author is friends with Luis and Mandy?

____

4. What is one major difference between the personalities of Luis and Mandy?

____

5. Why do you think it is important to have about the same number of subtopics under each topic?

____

____

Directions Read the following essay. Then fill in the missing sections of the outline below.

Ellen and I met when we were two years old. She and I were in day care together. I remember playing in the sandbox with Ellen, and I know we had a lot of fun. Later on, we attended the same elementary school and junior high.

Ellen is always cheerful and friendly. On my birthday, she baked me a cake and made a card for me. I am friends with Ellen because I know that I can tell her anything, and she won't laugh at me. It is nice to have a friend like that.

Lionel just moved to town this year. I remember on the first day of school, he was wearing a Tigers jersey. I was wearing one too. When we saw each other in math class, we both started cracking up about it. I invited Lionel over to my house to watch the Tigers game one Saturday afternoon, and after that we have never missed a game.

Lionel is intelligent and fun to hang out with. We can talk about sports, school, or just about anything. He wants to be an archaeologist when he grows up, and his stories about ancient civilizations are always interesting.

Friends

6. I. ______________________________

A. How we know each other

1. day care when we were two

7. 2. ______________________________

B. Personality

1. cheerful

8. 2. ______________________________

3. good listener

II. Lionel

A. How we know each other

1. math class

2. watch all the Tigers games

9. B. ______________________________

1. intelligent

2. fun to hang out with

10. 3. ______________________________

School + Home **Home Activity** Your child learned how to use an outline. Have your child pretend he or she is going to write an essay comparing two family members. Have your child make an outline of information about his or her subjects in preparation for writing the essay.

Name ______________________

Compound Words

Proofread an Article Circle five misspelled words in the article. Write them correctly. Then circle the verb that is used incorrectly. Write the sentence correctly.

Field Trip

Last winter our class take a fieldtrip to a museum. Snow flakes fell gently around us as we watched a worker apply a coat of white wash to a fence nearby. Suddenly the weather changed and a thunder storm began. We moved inside to the theater. I pushed my friend up the wheel chair ramp. Once inside we saw a show about the solar system that made the planets look like different-sized pinholes and the sun one giant polka dot on the ceiling of the dark room. All in all, it was an interesting day.

1. ____________ **2.** ____________

3. ____________ **4.** ____________

5. ____________

6. ______________________________

____

Spelling Words

- field trip
- someone
- snowflakes
- polka dot
- roller coaster
- solar system
- thunderstorm
- leftovers
- cell phone
- whitewash
- lightning rod
- myself
- life jacket
- bulldozer
- masterpiece
- area code
- cliffhanger
- wheelchair
- hour hand
- rain forest

Frequently Misspelled Words

- a lot
- basketball

Proofread Words Circle the word that is spelled correctly. Write it on the line.

7. rain forest	rainforest	**7.**	____________
8. my self	myself	**8.**	____________
9. hour hand	hourhand	**9.**	____________
10. someone	some one	**10.**	____________
11. left overs	leftovers	**11.**	____________
12. life jacket	lifejacket	**12.**	____________
13. bull dozer	bulldozer	**13.**	____________
14. masterpiece	master piece	**14.**	____________

Home Activity Your child identified misspelled compound words. Have your child spell all the open (two-word) compound words, saying the word *space* to indicate where the first word ends and the second begins.

Troublesome Verbs

Directions Read the passage. Then read each question. Circle the letter of the correct answer.

The New Car

(1) A shiny new car (sit) in our driveway. (2) My father cannot wait to take us for a ride in his first convertible. (3) The keys lay on the kitchen counter. (4) "Come with me," he says to my mother and me. (5) He (set) his briefcase on the back seat. (6) I happily (leave) my homework on the table so I can go with them. (7) "You can sit in the front seat," he tells Mom proudly. (8) We leaved quietly so that we will not wake my grandmother. (9) Suddenly we hear, "I'm not going to lie here while you have all the fun." (10) In five minutes, Grandma leaves the house with us, and we are traveling down Main Street, the wind whistling through our hair.

1 Which form of the verb in parentheses best completes sentence 1?

A sets
B sits
C have sat
D has set

2 What change, if any, should be made in sentence 3?

A Change *lay* to **lie**
B Change *lay* to **laid**
C Change *lay* to **laying**
D Make no change

3 Which form of the verb in parentheses best completes sentence 5?

A sit
B sits
C sets
D set

4 Which form of the verb in parentheses best completes sentence 6?

A leave
B leaved
C lie
D layed

5 What change, if any, should be made in sentence 8?

A Change ***leaved*** to **left**
B Change ***leaved*** to **let**
C Change ***leaved*** to **leave**
D Make no change

School + Home **Home Activity** Your child prepared for taking tests on troublesome verbs. Ask your child to look through a newspaper article and find three sentences in which troublesome verbs are used correctly.

Name

Draw Conclusions

- When you **draw conclusions,** you form opinions or make decisions about what you have read.
- Your conclusions should be reasonable and make sense. They should be based on details and facts from the reading and your own experiences.

Directions Read the following passage. Then complete the diagram with facts or details from the passage and a reasonable conclusion.

After searching the living room, Max and Paulo ran to the bedroom. They looked under the bed, but there was no mouse there. They looked in the closet, but the mouse wasn't there either. Both boys frowned, and Max began to sweat. How were they going to finish their project in time if they couldn't find the mouse?

Frantic, Paulo raced to the bathroom, but there was no mouse in sight. Max flew to the kitchen. He opened all the cabinets and every drawer. He even looked in the refrigerator. Paulo came into the kitchen, and together the boys slumped to the floor, discouraged. Where *was* that mouse?

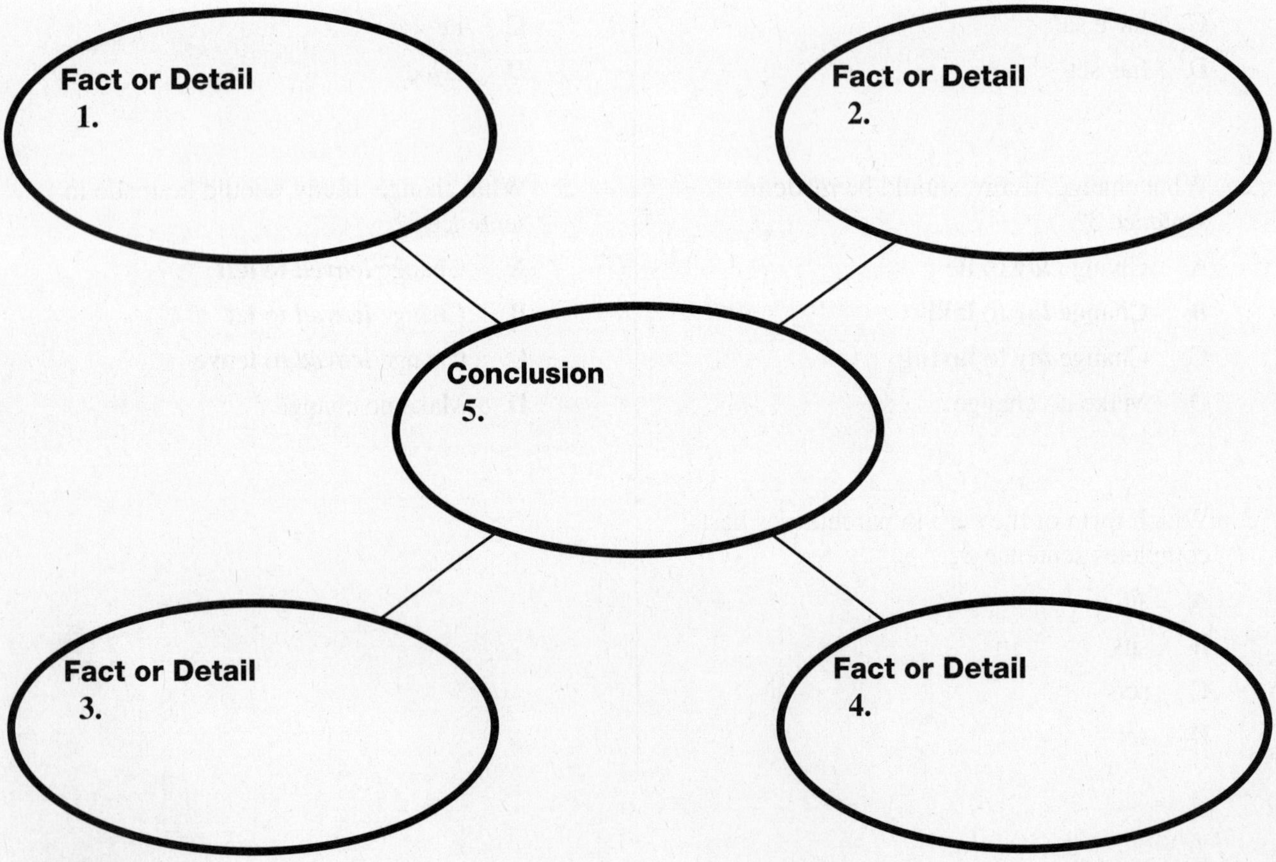

Home Activity Your child drew a conclusion from facts or details in a reading passage. Tell your child a short story about an event that happened in your life. Have him or her single out two or three facts or details from the story and form a conclusion from them.

Name ____________________

Writing • Personal Narrative

Key Features of a Personal Narrative

- describes an experience or event in the writer's life
- is written in the first person
- reveals the writer's thoughts and feelings about the experience
- uses vivid description

Beach Blanket Blunder

Have you ever had a day that you wish you could forget? Mine was a steamy day last summer when I went to the beach with three friends. After depositing our bags and spreading our sunny yellow blanket across a square of sand, we raced for the water.

My friends and I crashed into the foaming waves and instantly began yelping in pain. The icy water felt like thousands of sharp little needles.

My friends darted back to the blanket almost immediately. After a minute, however, I began to enjoy the water's refreshing chill. I paddled around for a while before deciding to warm up. I stepped out of the surf and spotted the yellow blanket where my friends napped peacefully. I plopped down next to them and closed my eyes.

"Umm, Lisa?" I opened my eyes to find my three friends peering down at me with amused expressions. There were also three people lying beside me, but they were wide-awake now.

I had fallen asleep on the wrong blanket! I sprang to my feet and apologized while my friends erupted into uncontrollable giggles. Then I sprinted to the water and plunged in. But even that frigid water couldn't cool my embarrassment!

1. Who is the narrator of this story?

____

2. Circle at least two vivid adjectives in each paragraph.

Name ______________________________

Vocabulary

Directions Choose the word from the box that best matches each definition. Write the word on the line shown to the left.

Check the Words You Know

- ___pawn
- ___reception
- ___remote
- ___resume
- ___rummage
- ___rustling
- ___simultaneous

____________________ **1.** moving, working, or acting with energy or speed

____________________ **2.** quality of a sound or picture reproduced in a receiver

____________________ **3.** happening at the same time

____________________ **4.** begin again; go on

____________________ **5.** one of the sixteen pieces of lowest value in the game of chess

Directions Choose the word from the box that best completes each sentence. Write the word on the line.

6. Arthur used a ____________________ control to fly his airplane.

7. I had to ____________________ through the drawer to find a spoon.

8. Sarah began ____________________ around in her hurry to clean the kitchen.

9. Kevin moved his ____________________ during the game of chess.

10. I want to ____________________ playing our game after I answer the phone.

Write a Scene from a Play

On a separate sheet of paper, write a short scene from a play about a boy who has lost something important. Use as many vocabulary words as you can.

School + Home **Home Activity** Your child identified and used vocabulary words from *Morning Traffic*. Make up a story with your child. Take turns adding sentences that contain one vocabulary word each.

Prepositions

A **preposition** shows a relationship between a noun or pronoun and another word in the sentence, such as a verb, adjective, or other noun. A **prepositional phrase** begins with a **preposition** and usually ends with a noun or pronoun. The noun or pronoun is called the **object of the preposition.**

Luke lived above the pharmacy. ← Prepositional Phrase

↑ Preposition ↑ Object of the Preposition

Here are some prepositions: *about, above, across, after, against, along, among, around, as, at, before, behind, below, beneath, beside, between, beyond, by, down, during, except, for, from, in, inside, into, near, of, off, on, onto, out, outside, over, past, since, through, throughout, to, toward, under, underneath, until, up, upon, with, within, without.*

- Like an adjective, a prepositional phrase can modify a noun or pronoun.
  She wrote to her brother at medical school.
- Like an adverb, a prepositional phrase can modify a verb.
  The neighbors gathered around the toy airplane.

Directions Circle the preposition and underline the object of the preposition in each prepositional phrase.

1. Joanna could barely see the pawns in the dim light.
2. David had basic questions about the chess game.
3. The play's action unfolds inside the apartment.
4. Sadly, one of the adults lost something valuable.
5. The flower guy rushed toward the refrigerator.

Directions Underline the prepositional phrase in each sentence. Write *Adjective* if the prepositional phrase acts as an adjective. Write *Adverb* if it acts as an adverb.

6. David's mother came home after work. ________________
7. Gil put David on his shoulders. ________________
8. Everyone looked for the missing ticket. ________________
9. The flower guy found the ticket to the concert. ________________

School + Home **Home Activity** Your child learned about prepositions. Have your child scan a paragraph from a newspaper article and underline each preposition and circle each object of the preposition.

Name ______________________________

Homophones

Spelling Words				
heel	heal	symbol	cymbal	herd
heard	patients	patience	capitol	capital
straight	strait	aisle	isle	stationery
stationary	sheer	shear	bread	bred

Words in Context Write the list word that completes each sentence.

1. They bake fresh ___ at the bakery every day. 1. ______
2. When I need to draw a ___ line, I use a ruler. 2. ______
3. Always use a ___ letter to begin a sentence. 3. ______
4. These new shoes are giving me a blister on my ___. 4. ______
5. I will ___ off several branches from the bush. 5. ______
6. The bride looked beautiful walking down the ___. 6. ______
7. The drummer ended the song with a loud crash from the ___. 7. ______
8. Amy wrote a letter to her friend on her new ___. 8. ______
9. I ___ a new song that I really like. 9. ______
10. I don't have the ___ for this boring chore. 10. ______

Word Meanings Write a list word that fits each definition.

11. to restore to health 11. ______
12. a building in which a state legislature meets 12. ______
13. a narrow passage of water 13. ______
14. raised or grew 14. ______
15. something that stands for or represents something else 15. ______
16. very thin or transparent 16. ______
17. a group of animals 17. ______
18. remaining in one place 18. ______
19. people under medical care 19. ______
20. a small piece of land surrounded by water 20. ______

School + Home **Home Activity** Your child wrote homophones. Spell one word of the homophone pair, and ask your child to spell the other word.

Name ____________________

Story Sequence Chart

Title ____________________

Beginning

↓

Middle

↓

End

Name ____________________

Vocabulary • Antonyms

- An **antonym** is a word that has an opposite meaning of another word.
- Look for words that may indicate opposites (*unlike, however, but, not*).
- A thesaurus is a book that lists words and their antonyms and synonyms.

Directions Read the following passage. Then answer the questions below. Look for antonyms as you read.

Mariela walked into the kitchen to find her disheveled brother Alec searching through his backpack in a frantic way. She tried to get him to calm down, but he wouldn't listen. He explained that he had lost his keys and would be tardy for work if he didn't find them. Mariela optimistically suggested that they split up and search the rooms simultaneously. But Alec stubbornly wanted to search each room separately. Mariela began searching through a cabinet, but Alec soon stopped her. He had found his car keys in a tennis shoe. He thanked her for her help and rushed out the door to his car.

1. What word in the passage is an antonym for *frantic?* What does *frantic* mean?

____

2. What word in the passage is an antonym for *simultaneously*? What does *simultaneously* mean?

____

Directions Use a thesaurus to find antonyms for the following words.

3. disheveled ____________________

4. tardy ____________________

5. optimistically ____________________

6. stubbornly ____________________

School + Home

Home Activity Your child read a short passage and identified antonyms, words that have the opposite meaning, to understand the meanings of unfamiliar words. Help your child select some unfamiliar words in a newspaper article. Encourage your child to figure out the meanings of unfamiliar words using antonyms.

Name________________________________

Print Sources/Media

- Libraries contain many sources of information. You can use a library database or a card catalog to identify and locate these materials. In both cases, you can search for materials by author, title, or subject.
- **Print sources** include encyclopedias, newspapers, magazines, dictionaries, and other reference books, including the *Readers' Guide to Periodical Literature.*

Directions Study the following examples of reference sources.

Newspaper Article

Local Science Fair Winner Overcomes Obstacles

by Tiffany Gibson

This week, Javier Ramirez proved he is able to overcome obstacles and find success. Javier is a local middle school student who was severely injured in a car accident last year. Undeterred, Javier has not allowed his injuries to stop him from doing what he loves. For the past seven years, he has participated in the school district's science fair. This year, however, his parents and teachers warned him that he might not be able to participate due to the many hours he must spend in physical therapy learning to walk again. But Javier did not let his injuries or the time crunch keep him from participating. He and his partner created a solar car that won a first place ribbon at the fair. Javier has proven that obstacles can be overcome with hard work and determination.

Encyclopedia Entry

George Washington Carver (1864–1943) was a scientist, botanist, teacher, and inventor. He overcame many obstacles and worked hard to obtain an education. Carver taught farmers in Alabama to grow sweet potatoes and peanuts. He also experimented with these foods, making soap, paint, and gasoline products from them. George Washington Carver's work helped farmers in Alabama and throughout the United States. (See also: *agriculture, sweet potatoes, peanuts, Alabama, inventor, scientist*)

Card Catalog Entry

OBSTACLES—BIOGRAPHY

The Story of George Washington Carver / Eva Moore. New York: Scholastic Inc., 1971.

Biography of a scientist who overcame obstacles.

1. Obstacles—Biography. 2. Obstacles—Scientists. 3. History—Men

Magazine Article

Overcoming Obstacles

by Elizabeth Jones

Everyone has obstacles in their lives. Obstacles are things that make it hard for us to do what we want. Some obstacles are small. You might want to go to a movie, but you have to clean your room first. Other obstacles are larger. For example, your father lost his job so you can't pay for the sports equipment you need for basketball. No matter how small or large an obstacle is, it is important to try to find a solution. When we work to overcome obstacles we learn how to solve problems. But how can we overcome obstacles? What is the best way to approach them and . . .

Name ______________________________

Directions Imagine you are writing a report about people who have overcome obstacles. Use the samples of print resources on the preceding page and your prior knowledge to answer the questions below.

1. Which of the four entries would you use to begin your report?

____

2. Which of these resources provides information about people who have overcome obstacles in a local community?

____

3. What is a good strategy to find the information you need in the print encyclopedia?

____

____

4. How could magazine articles enrich your report?

____

____

5. Does the encyclopedia entry shown relate to your report?

____

6. What is the topic of the newspaper article?

____

7. What would you use to find appropriate books for your research in a library?

____

8. What topics would you look for in the card catalog?

____

____

9. List the advantages and disadvantages of using newspapers and encyclopedias.

____

____

10. Why is it a good idea to use a variety of sources when possible?

____

____

School + Home

Home Activity Your child learned how to use print sources to write a report. Discuss what print sources are available in your home. Decide which sources your child might use for a future report, and make a plan to visit your local library to become familiar with its sources as well.

Name ______________________________

Homophones

Proofread an Article Circle six misspelled words in the article below. Write them correctly. Find a sentence with a missing punctuation mark. Write the sentence correctly.

> Shearing Sheep
>
> I recently saw a film about sheepherders on a small aisle across a narrow straight from New Zealand. The sheep are bread to have very thick wool Once a year the sheepherders sheer the sheep to get the wool. It takes a lot of patients to hold the sheep stationery as the work is being done. It's hard work, but the sheep are not hurt, and their wool soon grows back.

1. ______________ 2. ______________

3. ______________ 4. ______________

5. ______________ 6. ______________

7. ____

____

Spelling Words

heel
heal
symbol
cymbal
herd
heard
patients
patience
capitol
capital
straight
strait
aisle
isle
stationery
stationary
sheer
shear
bread
bred

Missing Letters Figure out which letters are missing. Then write the list word on the line.

8. _ a p _ t a l — 8. ______________
9. h _ a _ — 9. ______________
10. b r _ _ d — 10. ______________
11. s y _ _ _ l — 11. ______________
12. c _ m b _ l — 12. ______________
13. a _ s _e — 13. ______________
14. s t a _ _ _n e r_ — 14. ______________
15. s t r _ _ _ _ t — 15. ______________
16. p _ t _ _ n t s — 16. ______________

Frequently Misspelled Words

their
there
they're

School + Home **Home Activity** Your child identified misspelled homophones. Give clues and have your child guess and spell the correct homophone.

Prepositions

Directions Read the passage. Then read each question. Circle the letter of the correct answer.

Our Neighborhood Emergency Room

(1) St. Bartholomew is the hospital down the street and around the corner. (2) We always considered it our insurance policy. (3) It is there for emergencies. (4) When I slipped ______ the ice, I went ______ the clinic ______ an X-ray. (5) Two nights ago we were really glad that St. Bartholomew was in our neighborhood. (6) My dad had a high temperature in the middle of the night, so we took him to the emergency room. (7) Doctors did some tests and released him from the hospital. (8) He went home with an antibiotic. (9) It was a miracle cure! (10) His fever was gone ______ 24 hours.

1 Sentence 1 has how many prepositions?

A 0
B 1
C 2
D 3

2 Which three prepositions best complete sentence 4?

A on/to/for
B in/with/on
C over/between/into
D up/through/by

3 What change, if any, should be made in sentence 5?

A Change ***in*** to **until**
B Change ***in*** to **over**
C Change ***in*** to **by**
D Make no change

4 Sentence 6 has how many prepositions?

A 0
B 1
C 2
D 3

5 Which preposition best completes sentence 10?

A beyond
B within
C through
D about

Home Activity Your child prepared for taking tests on prepositions. Read aloud sentences from a favorite book. Pause after each sentence and ask your child to identify any prepositional phrases in the sentence.

Name ______________________________

Unusual Spellings

Spelling Words				
crescent	language	vehicle	exhibit	examine
Michigan	parachute	unique	conquer	rhyme
penguin	exertion	exotic	brochure	symptom
antique	exhausted	heirloom	rhinoceros	bureau

Crossword Puzzle Use the clues to find the list words. Write each letter in a box.

Across

1. the words we speak and write
3. what a skydiver uses
7. one of a kind
8. a moon can have this shape
9. car or truck

Down

2. old object
3. black-and-white bird
4. sound the same
5. look at closely
6. not native

Word Groups Write the list word that fits in each group.

11. booklet, handout, flyer, ________ 11. ______________
12. heritage, inherit, legacy, ________ 12. ______________
13. display, show, model, ________ 13. ______________
14. sign, indicator, evidence, ________ 14. ______________
15. elephant, giraffe, lion, ________ 15. ______________
16. hard work, effort, sweat, ________ 16. ______________
17. desk, dresser, drawers, ________ 17. ______________
18. Illinois, Wisconsin, Indiana, ________ 18. ______________
19. win, defeat, overcome, ________ 19. ______________
20. tired, drained, worn-out, ________ 20. ______________

School + Home **Home Activity** Your child has learned to spell words with unusual spellings. Take turns choosing a list word and discussing the unusual way it is spelled.

Name ________________________________

Principal Parts of Regular Verbs

Directions Write *present, present participle, past,* or *past participle* to identify the principal part of the underlined verb.

1. The children are picking wild strawberries. ____________________
2. The shelter protects Rosa from the rain. ____________________
3. Dan sharpened his hatchet with a file. ____________________
4. Carrie had hoped the matches were dry. ____________________
5. The sun is moving toward the west. ____________________
6. Jenny waves to us from the plane. ____________________
7. Brian wondered if he would ever be found. ____________________
8. Tara jumped every time she heard a noise. ____________________
9. Bobby had covered the radio with a tarp. ____________________
10. Jake ripped the paper into shreds. ____________________

Directions Complete each sentence with the principal part of the given verb as indicated in ( ).

11. Hungry and tired, Will ____________________ the root from the ground. (pull/past tense)
12. Chelsea and Ron ____________________ the batteries in the flashlight before they set out. (change/past participle with *had*)
13. Kira ____________________ strips of bark and small twigs. (gather/present participle with *is*)
14. She ____________________ the bark from the trees. (peel/present)
15. The rescuers did not know how much Brian ____________________. (suffer/past participle with *had*)

School + Home **Home Activity** Your child reviewed principal parts of regular verbs. Have your child find a sentence in a favorite book that contains a regular verb. Ask your child to rewrite the sentence using another principal part of the verb. Continue with other sentences.

Name ______________________

Multisyllabic Words 2

Spelling Words				
international	prehistoric	untrustworthy	constellation	honorary
disagreement	preparation	Philadelphia	promotional	constitution
unbreakable	biodegradable	coordination	compassionate	impossibility
entirety	executive	companionship	unthinkable	predicament

Synonyms Write the list word that has the same or nearly the same meaning.

1. dishonest — 1. ______________
2. foundation — 2. ______________
3. ancient — 3. ______________
4. indestructible — 4. ______________
5. can use together — 5. ______________
6. unlikelihood — 6. ______________
7. problem — 7. ______________
8. beyond belief — 8. ______________
9. sympathetic — 9. ______________
10. dispute — 10. ______________

Separate the Syllables Draw lines to separate the syllables in each list word. Write each word.

11. c o n s t e l l a t i o n — 11. ______________
12. P h i l a d e l p h i a — 12. ______________
13. b i o d e g r a d a b l e — 13. ______________
14. i n t e r n a t i o n a l — 14. ______________
15. h o n o r a r y — 15. ______________
16. c o n s t i t u t i o n — 16. ______________
17. e x e c u t i v e — 17. ______________
18. p r o m o t i o n a l — 18. ______________
19. c o m p a n i o n s h i p — 19. ______________
20. e n t i r e t y — 20. ______________

School + Home

Home Activity Your child has learned to spell multisyllabic words. Say each word and have your child count the number of syllables.

Principal Parts of Irregular Verbs

Directions Write *present, present participle, past,* or *past participle* to identify the principal part used to form the underlined verb.

1. Marian felt nervous in front of the audience of 75,000 people. ____________
2. Mrs. Anderson feels proud of her daughter. ____________
3. Esther is beginning a new role. ____________
4. She often sings with her eyes closed. ____________
5. The quartet had chosen an old Civil War song. ____________
6. Marian told about her love of singing. ____________
7. She has taken her pain and turned it into beautiful music. ____________

Directions Underline the form of the verb in ( ) that correctly completes each sentence.

8. Mother and Father (are speaking, have spoke) with Mr. Boghetti about Marian's future.
9. She (had become, had became) a symbol for her people.
10. Fans (writing, wrote) letters protesting the sponsor's decision.
11. The Russian audience (gave, gived) the opera singer a standing ovation.
12. Kelsey (has keeped, keeps) in touch with her mother in America.
13. People all over the world (heard/is hearing) Marian sing.
14. Marian (had sang/sang) in many different countries.
15. She (knowed/had known) she would sing in Russia.

School + Home **Home Activity** Your child reviewed principal parts of irregular verbs. Have your child listen to a dialogue between two people and write some irregular verbs that are used. Have your child use the list to make a chart and fill in the other principal parts of each verb.

Name ______________________________

Using Just Enough Letters

Spelling Words				
nuclear	helicopter	anxious	appreciate	plastic
familiar	athletic	escape	apologize	Washington
pastime	exquisite	lantern	fulfill	souvenir
tragedy	sherbet	algebra	icicles	escort

Word Meanings Write the list word that fits each definition.

1. well-known, common 1. ____________
2. portable lamp 2. ____________
3. a frozen dessert 3. ____________
4. to say you are sorry 4. ____________
5. a memento or keepsake 5. ____________
6. a sad or terrible event 6. ____________
7. troubled or worried 7. ____________
8. to satisfy a requirement 8. ____________
9. to be thankful for something or someone 9. ____________
10. an aircraft without wings 10. ____________
11. to get away 11. ____________
12. very lovely 12. ____________
13. amusement, recreation 13. ____________
14. hanging sticks of ice 14. ____________

Scramble Unscramble each word below to form a list word. Write the word.

15. htnoasgiwn 15. ____________
16. gblreaa 16. ____________
17. tciahlte 17. ____________
18. csetro 18. ____________
19. ruencal 19. ____________
20. tpsicla 20. ____________

School + Home **Home Activity** Your child has learned to spell words that are often mispronounced or misspelled. Ask your child to choose a list word and use it in a sentence. Then ask him or her to spell the word.

Name ___________________________________

Verbs, Objects, and Subject Complements

Directions Write the subject complement in each sentence.

1. The sea air smelled clean. ______________

2. Larry is a strong swimmer. ______________

3. Max was calm in the strong current. ______________

4. The girls looked sad when they lost the race. ______________

5. Laura became a good swimming teacher. ______________

Directions Circle direct objects and underline any indirect objects.

6. Paul bent his knees so he could kick.

7. Mother told me a story about the ocean.

8. The Festival of Stars celebrates a meeting between two characters.

9. Write your wishes on colored paper.

10. The teacher offered Cindy some tips about breathing.

11. She added distance by weaving back and forth in the water.

12. Waves pounded the shore at high tide.

13. Show her the stroke so she can see what to do.

14. Dan won a gold medal in the Olympics.

15. I showed my gym teacher my frog kick.

16. I asked her questions about the Olympic winners.

17. Mira gave me articles from an old newspaper.

18. I have set goals for the future.

School + Home **Home Activity** Your child reviewed verbs, objects, and subject complements. Have your child look through a magazine and find three subject complements and three direct objects.

Name ______________________

Compound Words

Spelling Words				
field trip	someone	snowflakes	polka dot	roller coaster
solar system	thunderstorm	leftovers	cell phone	whitewash
lightning rod	myself	life jacket	bulldozer	masterpiece
area code	cliffhanger	wheelchair	hour hand	rain forest

Word Meanings Write the list word that fits each definition.

1. event in a story or movie that prolongs suspense 1. ______________
2. a portable telephone 2. ______________
3. the short hand of a clock 3. ______________
4. a tractor that pushes rocks and earth 4. ______________
5. rain with thunder and lightning 5. ______________
6. lighten walls or wood 6. ______________
7. the sun, planets, and things that revolve around them 7. ______________
8. somebody 8. ______________
9. round spot repeated to form a pattern 9. ______________
10. a dense forest that gets a lot of rain 10. ______________

Drawing Conclusions Write the list word that answers each question.

11. What do you wear in the water for safety? 11. ______________
12. How can you refer to yourself? 12. ______________
13. What is the uneaten food after a meal? 13. ______________
14. What are the first three numbers of a phone number? 14. ______________
15. What fall from the sky in the winter? 15. ______________
16. What can you use if you can't walk? 16. ______________
17. What is a kind of ride at an amusement park? 17. ______________
18. What can you use to prevent damage from lightning? 18. ______________
19. What is a person's greatest piece of work? 19. ______________
20. What is an outing with your class away from school? 20. ______________

School + Home **Home Activity** Your child has learned to spell compound words. Read each list word to your child. Have your child tell if the compound word is one word or two words.

Name ______________________________

Troublesome Verbs

Directions Write the letter of the definition of the underlined verb.

______ **1.** Juan left the orchard.	**A** gave use of
______ **2.** Set the basket on the ground.	**B** lifted up
______ **3.** He raised his arms and stretched.	**C** was seated
______ **4.** She lent a dress to her cousin.	**D** went away from
______ **5.** Teresa sat on the lawn.	**E** place or put

Directions Write the form of the underlined verb indicated in ( ).

6. Juan and Araceli sit together at the table and drank coffee. (past) ______________

7. The men had rise to their feet and saluted the flag. (past participle) ______________

8. The girls lie in lawn chairs near the orchard. (present) ______________

9. Don Ignatio let Juan have the ranch because he told the truth. (past) ______________

10. The gardener has set out tulip bulbs. (past participle) ______________

Directions Underline the correct verb in each sentence.

11. He had (laid, lain) the tools on the sidewalk.

12. Señora Arturo (borrowed, lent) a needle and thread from her hostess.

13. Don't (lend, borrow) your valuable belongings to anyone.

14. Juan (taught, learned) his children an important lesson.

15. The children have (taught, learned) how to speak English.

School + Home

Home Activity Your child reviewed troublesome verbs. Have your child write several sentences about what he or she does in the morning using at least three troublesome verbs.

Name ______________________________

Homophones

Spelling Words				
heel	heal	symbol	cymbal	herd
heard	patients	patience	capitol	capital
straight	strait	aisle	isle	stationery
stationary	sheer	shear	bread	bred

Synonyms Write the list word that has the same or nearly the same meaning.

1. listened — 1. ______________
2. island — 2. ______________
3. representation — 3. ______________
4. to recover from — 4. ______________
5. motionless — 5. ______________

Antonyms Write the list word that has the opposite or nearly the opposite meaning.

6. intolerance — 6. ______________
7. thick — 7. ______________
8. curved — 8. ______________
9. doctors — 9. ______________
10. lowercase — 10. ______________

Classifying Write the list word that belongs in each group.

11. waterway, narrow channel, connector, ______ — 11. ______________
12. letters, notes, cards, ______ — 12. ______________
13. drums, guitar, keyboard, ______ — 13. ______________
14. biscuit, roll, loaf, ______ — 14. ______________
15. lane, path, passageway, ______ — 15. ______________
16. official building, state, Congress, ______ — 16. ______________
17. toe, arch, foot, ______ — 17. ______________
18. group, crowd, pack, ______ — 18. ______________
19. cut, crop, trim, ______ — 19. ______________
20. produced, developed, brought up, ______ — 20. ______________

School + Home **Home Activity** Your child has learned about homophones. Ask your child to find some of the list words in a newspaper or magazine. Then ask your child to use the words in sentences.

Name ____________________

Prepositions

Directions Circle the preposition and underline the object of the preposition in each prepositional phrase.

1. David put the empty milk carton into the refrigerator.
2. She stood over the table and examined the chess pieces.
3. People even looked under the couch.
4. Gil keeps looking around for good reception.
5. Karen took a deep breath and stepped inside the apartment.
6. The flower guy saved Gabe from a disaster.
7. The concert was scheduled for the evening of their anniversary.
8. An alarm sounded in Gabe's mind about the misplaced ticket.

Directions Underline the prepositional phrase in each sentence. Write *Adjective* if the prepositional phrase acts as an adjective. Write *Adverb* if it acts as an adverb.

9. All the people in the living room were preoccupied. ____________
10. No one expected the noise level to drop below zero. ____________
11. The neighbors from upstairs brought their plane. ____________
12. They flew it above the chessboard. ____________

Directions Add a prepositional phrase to each sentence. Write the new sentence.

13. We saw Gil standing.

____

14. David quietly asked Gil.

____

15. The delivery guy is waiting.

____

School + Home

Home Activity Your child reviewed prepositions. Have your child create a way to remember prepositions. *The plane flies **through** the cloud, **around** the cloud, **near** the cloud, **below** the cloud, **into** the cloud, **under** the cloud, etc.*

Name ____________________

Venn Diagram

Directions Fill in the Venn diagram with similarities and differences about the two people or characters you are comparing and contrasting.

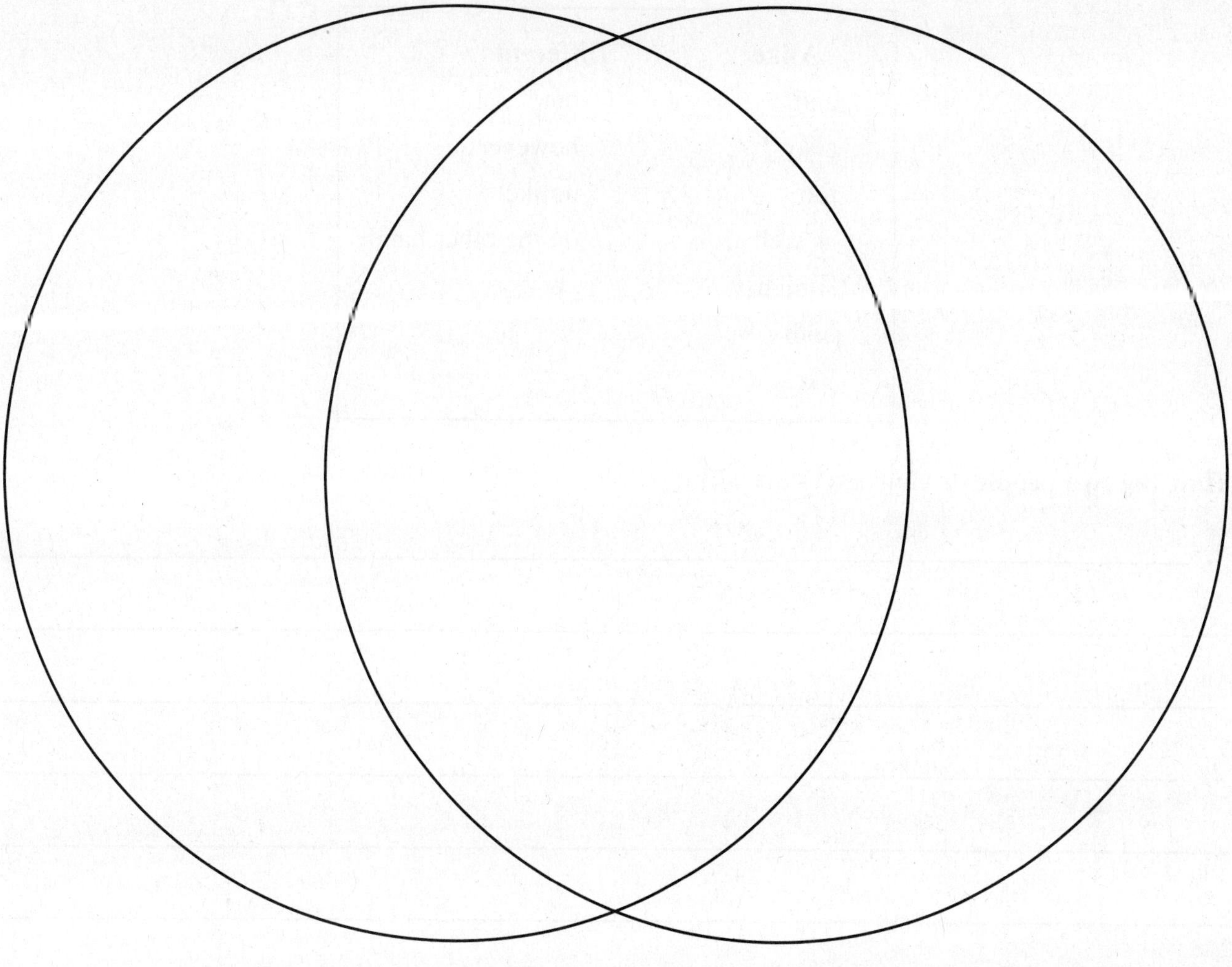

Name ____________________________________

Words That Compare and Contrast

Directions The box shows words that help compare and contrast. Write two sentences that tell how the two people or characters you chose are alike. Write two sentences that tell how they are different. Use words from the box in your sentences.

Alike	Different
and	but
also	however
too	unlike
as well	on the other hand
similarly	yet
both	
like	

How the two people or characters are alike

1. ____________________________________

____

____

2. ____________________________________

____

____

How the two people or characters are different

3. ____________________________________

____

____

4. ____________________________________

____

____

Name ______________________________

Adding Prepositional Phrases

Add information to sentences by adding prepositional phrases. This will help make the sentences more specific.

General The child won first place.

Improved The child <u>in the blue shorts</u> won first place <u>in the race</u>.

Directions Add one or more prepositional phrases to each sentence to make it more specific. Write the new sentence and underline each prepositional phrase.

1. The boy made a fire.

____

____

2. The singer impressed her audience.

____

____

3. The girl swam quickly.

____

____

4. The foreman could not tell a lie.

____

____

5. The boy wanted to play chess.

____

____

Name ______________________________

Peer and Teacher Conferencing Compare-and-Contrast Essay

Directions Read your partner's essay. Refer to the Revising Checklist as you write your comments or questions. Offer compliments as well as revision suggestions. Then take turns talking about each other's draft. Give your partner your notes. After you and your teacher talk about your essay, add your teacher's comments to the notes.

Revising Checklist

Focus/Ideas

☐ Is the compare-and-contrast essay focused and informative?

☐ Do all sentences tell about similarities and differences?

Organization

☐ Are the similarities and differences organized logically?

☐ Are words that compare and contrast used to signal the similarities and differences?

Voice

☐ Is the essay lively and engaging?

Word Choice

☐ Are specific words used to describe the similarities and differences?

Sentences

☐ Are sentences well developed with prepositional phrases that provide additional information?

Things I Thought Were Good ______________________________

____

Things I Thought Could Be Improved ______________________________

____

Teacher's Comments ______________________________

____

Name ____________________________________

Cause and Effect

- A **cause** is what makes something happen. An **effect** is something that happens as a result of a cause. To find a cause, ask yourself, "Why did this happen?" To find an effect, ask yourself, "What happened?"
- Clue words such as *because, so,* and *due to* can help you spot cause-and-effect relationships.

Directions Read the following passage. Then complete the graphic organizer.

The northern lights are beautiful lights that dance in the northern sky at night. They are most visible in the northern states. They occur due to large explosions on the sun. The explosions release particles that travel through space and are attracted to Earth's magnetic poles. Because of a collision between these particles and Earth's atmosphere, light particles are released. These particles are what form the northern lights.

Cause		Effect
What makes something happen 1.	→	**What happened** 2.
What makes something happen 3.	→	**What happened** 4.

5. Write a one-sentence summary of this passage.

____

____

School + Home **Home Activity** Your child identified causes and effects in a passage about the northern lights. Read another article about the northern lights with your child and discuss the cause of the different colors of the northern lights.

Name ______________________

Writing • Narrative Poem

Key Features of a Narrative Poem

- tells a story through poetry
- has lines with rhythm or rhyme
- may appeal to reader's emotions

A Day at the Beach

It was too windy to go to the beach,
but we did.
Waves were like tall ships out of our reach.

It was too hot to sit on the sand,
but we did.
We were mummies in towels but still got tanned.

Mom said it was dark but we begged her to stay,
and we did.
It was she who promised another day,
and we who shouted "hooray" and "yay!"

1. What verse tells the beginning of the story?

____

2. Name a metaphor and a simile used in the poem.

____

____

3. What are two rhyming words used in the poem?

____

____

Name____

Vocabulary

Directions Choose the word from the box that best matches each definition. Write the word on the line.

Check the Words You Know
___conquer
___destiny
___expedition
___insulated
___isolation
___navigator
___provisions
___verify

______________________ **1.** to overcome; get the better of

______________________ **2.** to prove to be true

______________________ **3.** what becomes of something or someone

______________________ **4.** person in charge of finding the position and course of a ship or aircraft

______________________ **5.** a supply of food and drinks

Directions Choose the word from the box that best matches each clue. Write the word on the line.

______________________ **6.** This is a journey taken for a special purpose.

______________________ **7.** This is done to keep something from losing heat by wrapping it with special material.

______________________ **8.** This is a state of being separate from the rest of the group.

______________________ **9.** A witness is often called to do this to a person's statement in a trial.

______________________ **10.** This is what you try to do to your enemy in a war.

Write a Description

Imagine you have just explored the North Pole. On a separate sheet of paper, write a description of your trip there. Use as many vocabulary words as you can.

School + Home **Home Activity** Your child identified and used vocabulary words from *Into the Ice.* Write a poem together about exploring. Use the vocabulary words from the selection.

Name ______________________________

Subject and Object Pronouns

A personal pronoun used as the subject of a sentence is called a **subject pronoun**.
She planned an archaeological dig. He and I heard the details.

A personal pronoun used as a direct object, indirect object, or object of a preposition is called an **object pronoun**.
The sea captain took us for a ride. He told him and me stories.

- Subject pronouns are *I, you, he, she, it, we,* and *they*.
- Object pronouns are *me, you, him, her, it, us,* and *them*.
- Remember to use the correct pronoun form with a compound subject or object pronoun.
- Subject pronouns replace the nouns they represent. Do not use a subject pronoun with the noun it represents.
  No: Carrie she studied oceanography.
  Yes: Carrie studied oceanography.

Directions Circle the pronoun in ( ) that completes each sentence correctly.

1. (I, Me) am fascinated by maritime exploration.
2. (Them, They) believed the sea captain was a good navigator.
3. Robert and (he, him) read about the first people to reach the North Pole.
4. (We, Us) studied relics and artifacts.
5. Bill and (me, I) studied the habitat of the penguin.
6. David and (she, her) have always wanted to visit Alaska.
7. Mr. Douglas taught me and (her, she) about Arctic explorers.
8. The class put the fossils back in the case after students studied (they, them).
9. Teddy Roosevelt supported Admiral Peary and often wrote to (he, him).
10. She took (us, we) on a field trip.
11. I helped Sara and (they, them) with the science project.
12. My sister told you and (me, I) stories about her visit to Alaska.

School + Home **Home Activity** Your child learned about subject and object pronouns. Have your child show you subject and object pronouns in something he or she has written.

Name ____________________

Greek Word Parts

Spelling Words				
hydrant	chronic	archive	synonym	antonym
democracy	hydrogen	aristocrat	dehydrated	chronicle
hydroplane	chronology	archaic	homonym	synchronize
hydraulic	archaeology	anarchy	hydroelectric	bureaucracy

Word Meanings Write a list word that fits each definition.

1. production of electricity by water power — 1. ____________
2. an arrangement in order of occurrence — 2. ____________
3. an historical account — 3. ____________
4. a word that has the same spelling but different meaning than another word — 4. ____________
5. absence of government and law — 5. ____________
6. to skim over the water — 6. ____________
7. water or moisture taken from — 7. ____________
8. lasting a long time — 8. ____________
9. a system of government by groups of officials — 9. ____________
10. no longer in general use — 10. ____________

Words in Context Write the list word that finishes each statement below.

11. Let's ___ our watches before we begin. — 11. ____________
12. The European ___ lived in a mansion on the hill. — 12. ____________
13. I've been going through the family ___ to learn about my ancestors. — 13. ____________
14. Water is made of molecules of oxygen and ___. — 14. ____________
15. We studied ancient Greece in my ___ class. — 15. ____________
16. *Almost* is a ___ for *nearly*. — 16. ____________
17. The United States government is an example of a ___. — 17. ____________
18. *Near* is an ___ for *far*. — 18. ____________
19. My new car's ___ brakes work very well. — 19. ____________
20. The fireman attached the hose to the fire ___. — 20. ____________

School + Home **Home Activity** Your child matched words with statements and definitions. Ask your child to pick a list word from exercises 11-20 and define it.

Name ______________________________

Word Web

Name ______________________________

Vocabulary • Unfamiliar Words

- When you are reading and see an unfamiliar word, use context clues, or words around the unfamiliar word, to figure out its meaning.
- Context clues include definitions, explanations, and synonyms (words that have the same or nearly the same meanings as other words).

Directions Read the following passage. Then answer the questions below.

Jared was preparing for their expedition. He was very excited about this journey. He packed their provisions: plenty of water and multigrain bars. He put their water in an insulated jug so it would stay cold. Tonight, his older brother would verify their route with their father, making sure it was the safest one possible. Tomorrow, Jared and his brother would leave early on their fishing trip. His brother would be the navigator of their fishing boat because he knew the best fishing spots. Jared felt it was their destiny to catch enough fish for their dinner.

1. What does *expedition* mean? What clues help you to determine its meaning?

____

____

2. Give examples of *provisions* mentioned in the passage. What is another example of a *provision*?

____

3. What does *verify* mean? What clues help you to determine its meaning?

____

____

4. What does *navigator* mean? Why is Jared's brother the *navigator*?

____

____

5. Rewrite the sentence with the word *destiny* in it so that it contains a context clue.

____

____

School + Home

Home Activity Your child identified and used context clues to understand new words in a passage. Work with your child to identify unfamiliar words in an article using context clues. Have your child come up with original context clues that could be added to the article to help the reader understand the unfamiliar words.

Name ____________________

Diagram/Scale Drawing

- A **diagram** is a drawing, usually with parts that are labeled. A diagram shows how something is put together, how an object's parts relate to one another, or how something works. Sometimes a diagram must be looked at in a certain order—left to right, top to bottom, or bottom to top. Diagrams often have text that explains how different parts in a diagram work.
- A **scale drawing** is a diagram that uses a mathematical scale, such as *1 inch on the drawing equals 1 foot in real life.*

Directions Use this diagram to answer the questions below.

A Home Weather Station

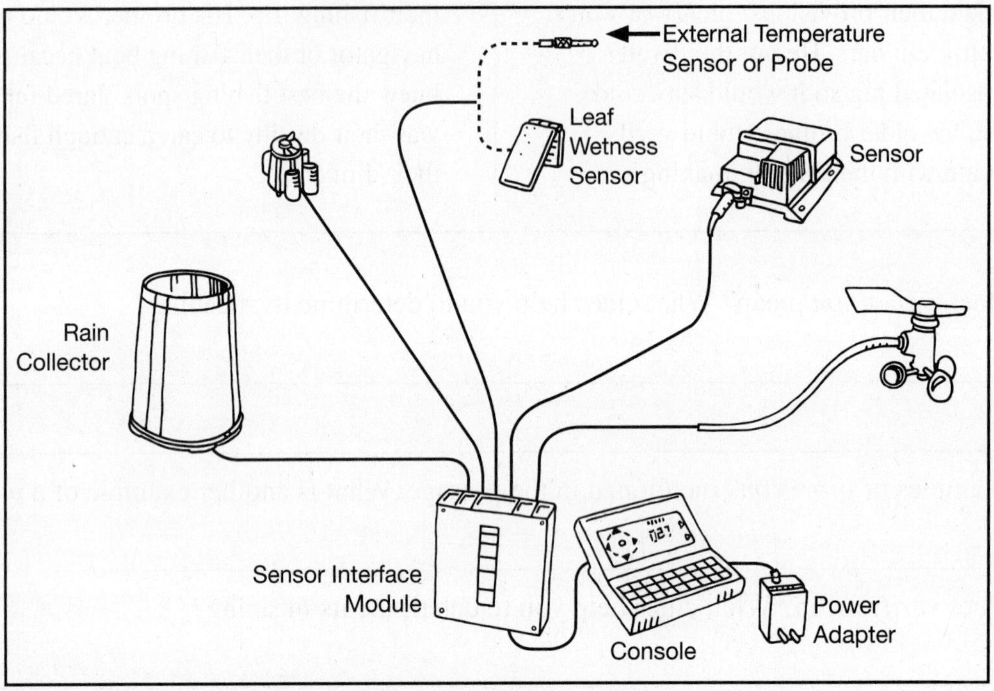

1. What part would you plug into an electrical outlet?

____

2. What part is placed outside to read the temperature?

____

3. What part is placed outside to determine the amount of rainfall?

____

4. What seems to be missing from this diagram?

____

5. What kind of information would you expect to see accompanying this diagram?

____

____

Name ________________________________

Directions Use this diagram of a thunderstorm to answer the questions below.

The diagram below is a cross-section of a thunderstorm moving from right to left. Warm, moist air fuels updrafts. As the air rises, it cools and falls as rain in downdrafts.

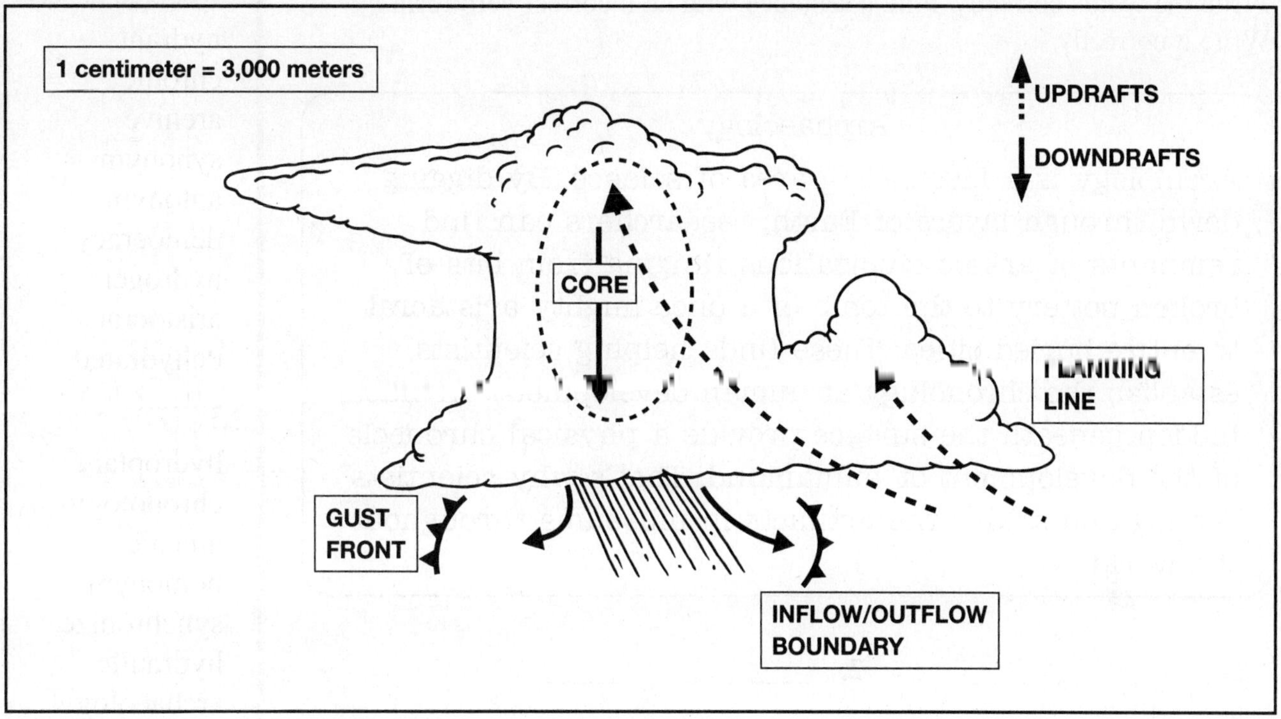

6. What do the dotted arrows of the diagram show?

____

7. What do the solid arrows show?

____

8. Where does the rain form in the thunderstorm cloud?

____

9. If the thunderstorm cloud is five centimeters tall on the diagram, what is its actual height?

____

____

10. How are diagrams helpful to readers?

____

____

School + Home **Home Activity** Your child learned about using diagrams as resources. Find a scale drawing on the Internet or in a reference book. Have your child explain to you the actual measurements of the item in the scale drawing.

Name ______________________________

Greek Word Parts

Proofread an Article Circle six misspelled words in the article below. Write the words correctly. Find a sentence with an incorrect verb form. Write it correctly.

Archaeology

Archiology is a fascinating area of science. By digging down through layers of Earth, researchers can find remnants of arkaic civilizations ranging from bits of broken pottery to the tomb of a once mighty aristacrat to entire buried cities. These finds helping scientists establish the chronolugy of human development. Artifacts hidden beneath the surface provide a physical chronecle of the development of humankind. That's why scientists catalog and arkive the artifacts in museums throughout the world.

1. ____________ 2. ____________

3. ____________ 4. ____________

5. ____________ 6. ____________

7. ______________________________

____

Spelling Words

hydrant
chronic
archive
synonym
antonym
democracy
hydrogen
aristocrat
dehydrated
chronicle
hydroplane
chronology
archaic
homonym
synchronize
hydraulic
archaeology
anarchy
hydroelectric
bureaucracy

Frequently Misspelled Words

were
they

Proofread Words Circle the word that is spelled correctly. Write it on the line.

8.	hydroplane	hidroplane	8. ____________
9.	chronology	cronology	9. ____________
10.	arcaic	archaic	10. ____________
11.	homanym	homonym	11. ____________
12.	synchronize	syncronize	12. ____________
13.	hidraulic	hydraulic	13. ____________
14.	archaeology	arceaology	14. ____________
15.	anarchy	anarky	15. ____________

School + Home

Home Activity Your child identified misspelled words. Ask your child to think of a word from the list with five syllables, spell it, and use that word in a sentence.

Name ______________________________

Subject and Object Pronouns

Directions Read the passage. Then read each question. Circle the letter of the correct answer.

The Bakery Tour

(1) We wrote a letter to Mr. Samuels to thank _____ for the bakery tour. (2) The letter said that he helped us with our project. (3) Marie and _____ enjoyed meeting his bakers. (4) We especially liked watching them put the rows of breads into the oven. (5) Marie's brother Luis asked her and _____ about the bakery. (6) We told him about our tour. (7) Our friends and _____ would like to visit the bakery again.

1 Which pronoun best completes sentence 1?

A he
B him
C her
D they

2 Which pair describes the two underlined words in sentence 2?

A Subject pronoun/object pronoun
B Subject pronoun/subject pronoun
C Object pronoun/object pronoun
D None of the above

3 Which is the correct pronoun/type of pronoun for sentence 3?

A they/object pronoun
B me/object pronoun
C I/subject pronoun
D them/object pronoun

4 Which is the correct pronoun/type of pronoun for sentence 5?

A I/subject pronoun
B they/subject pronoun
C us/subject pronoun
D me/object pronoun

5 Which pronoun best completes sentence 7?

A us
B we
C them
D him

School + Home **Home Activity** Your child prepared for taking tests on subject and object pronouns. With your child, read a magazine article. Have your child circle subject pronouns and underline object pronouns on one page in the article.

Author's Purpose

- The **author's purpose** is the reason or reasons the author has for writing. Authors may write to persuade, inform, express ideas or feelings, or entertain.
- As you preview a selection, predict the author's purpose. After reading, ask if the author met his or her purpose.

Directions Read the following passage. Then complete the graphic organizer.

During the 1960s and 1970s, polar bears were a threatened species, so a landmark agreement was reached to stop sport hunting of the bears. However, a bigger threat to the polar bear today is global warming. The warmest temperatures in four centuries have reduced the ice cover over the Arctic waters. If there is more open water, younger bears may not be able to swim far enough to reach solid ice for their food. Warmer springs also lead to more rainfall, which can cause bears' dens to collapse. These conditions lead to lower fitness and reproduction.

Before Reading

What is the author's purpose?

1.

During Reading

What are three clues to the author's purpose?

2.

3.

4.

After Reading

Was the purpose met? How?

5.

School + Home **Home Activity** Your child identified the author's purpose of a nonfiction passage. Work with your child to identify the author's purpose in a magazine or newspaper article. Ask your child to identify some clues that revealed the author's purpose.

Writing for Tests

Prompt: If everyday objects could talk, what might they say? Write an imaginative story in which a household object comes to life.

A Voice in the Night

Brady was in a panic. "What am I going to do," he wondered. "My short story is due tomorrow, it's 8:00 o'clock at night, and I can't think of anything to write. This writer's block is terrible! Maybe if I sit down in front of the computer, I'll get inspired." Brady carried his snack into his bedroom and set his milk down next to his computer.

"Well, it's about time! It sure took you long enough!"

Brady jumped, sending the cookies on his plate flying into the air. He glanced around his room, but there was no one to be seen.

"Who's here?" he whispered nervously. "Who's talking to me?"

"It's me. Right here." Brady looked down at the computer on his desk.

"Yes! Yes! I'm talking to you. I've been waiting all night. First, you called Jamal and talked for half an hour. Then you had to go get a snack." The computer's tone was clearly disapproving.

The computer continued, "Now, let's get started on this story. We should have begun an hour ago."

"*We* should have begun?" repeated Brady. He could hardly believe his computer was talking. He was even more surprised that he was responding! "What do you mean by *We*?" he asked.

"You don't think you can do this without me?" the computer cried. "I correct your spelling mistakes. I suggest synonyms for words you want to replace. And if you want to talk about some of your ideas for this story, I'm sure I can help you conquer your writer's block. Hey, would you mind moving that glass of milk away from my keys? It's a little too close for comfort."

"Sure," said Brady, as he sat down to write.

1. Who are the main characters in this story? What element of the story could not happen in real life?

___

___

2. What is the conflict in the story? Underline the sentences that express the conflict.

___

___

___

3. Place brackets around the resolution of the story.

Name____

Vocabulary

Directions Choose the word from the box that best matches each definition. Write the word on the line.

Check the Words You Know
___captive
___companionship
___existence
___ordeal
___primitive
___sanctuaries
___stimulating

________________________ **1.** very simple

________________________ **2.** kept in confinement

________________________ **3.** a severe test or experience

________________________ **4.** places of refuge or protection

________________________ **5.** friendly feeling among companions

Directions Choose the word from the box that best completes each sentence. Write the word on the line shown on the left.

________________________ **6.** Margaret really enjoyed the ___ among her friends.

________________________ **7.** Karl did not believe in the ___ of ghosts.

________________________ **8.** She joined the Film Club so she could meet people who liked ___ conversations about movies.

________________________ **9.** The class survived the ___ of taking the hardest test they had ever had.

________________________ **10.** The science class went to visit several wildlife ___.

Write a Newspaper Article

On a separate sheet of paper, write a newspaper article about a person who is trying to save an endangered animal. Use as many vocabulary words as you can.

School + Home **Home Activity** Your child identified and used vocabulary words from *The Chimpanzees I Love.* Read a story or nonfiction article with your child. Have him or her point out unfamiliar words. Use a dictionary to look up the unfamiliar words.

Name ______________________________

Pronouns and Antecedents

A **pronoun** takes the place of a noun or nouns. An **antecedent**, or referent, is the noun or nouns to which the pronoun refers. A pronoun and its antecedent must agree in number and gender.

Before you use a pronoun, ask yourself whether the antecedent is singular or plural. If the antecedent is singular, decide whether it is masculine, feminine, or neuter. Then choose a pronoun that agrees. In the following sentences, the antecedents are underlined once; the pronouns are underlined twice.

Jay and I walked to the zoo, and we saw the new exhibit.
Jay called Carla to pick him up from the zoo.

Directions Circle the pronoun that refers to the underlined antecedent.

1. Infant chimps are cute and cuddly, but eventually (they, it) become more difficult.
2. Faustino's mother tried to comfort (him, them).
3. (We, They) humans must learn to respect the animal kingdom.
4. The African forest is perfect for chimps because (they, it) is full of life.
5. The chimp was caught in a snare, but (he, you) was able to break free.
6. I convinced Tim that (it, he) should come to the zoo with me.
7. Jane Goodall founded the Gombe Stream Research Center, where (she, they) studied chimps.
8. Chimps sometimes make a tool and use (them, it).

Directions Write the pronoun that completes each sentence. Underline the antecedent to which the pronoun refers.

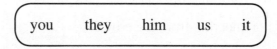

you   they   him   us   it

9. Hunters kill the animals so ______________ can sell the meat in the big town.
10. The "bush-meat trade" will be hard to stop because ______________ is a big money-making operation.
11. Dr. John wanted JoJo to walk to ______________.
12. Alexander and I sat next to Fax, and she played with ______________.

School + Home **Home Activity** Your child learned about pronouns and antecedents. Have your child find examples of singular or plural antecedents in a favorite book.

Prefixes *dis-*, *de-*, *out-*, *un-*

Spelling Words				
discontent	decline	outward	dispatch	unwavering
destruction	disintegrate	outstanding	uncommon	outburst
outrageous	defensive	unappetizing	disillusioned	disarray
unconscious	outskirts	unfasten	disenchanted	decompose

Word Meanings Write a list word that fits each definition.

1. to rot or decay 1. ___
2. unconventional, fantastic 2. ___
3. free from enchantment 3. ___
4. serving to defend or protect 4. ___
5. to make loose 5. ___
6. food that is not attractive or desirable 6. ___
7. edges of a town 7. ___
8. free from illusions 8. ___
9. having lost consciousness 9. ___
10. not in order, untidy 10. ___
11. lack of contentment 11. ___
12. not common or ordinary 12. ___
13. not wavering or hesitant 13. ___

Words in Context Write the list word that finishes each statement below.

14. His speech caused an ___ of cheering from the crowd. 14. ___
15. The snowstorm caused a ___ in sales at most stores. 15. ___
16. The new windows opened ___ from the house. 16. ___
17. I received an award for being an ___ student. 17. ___
18. I will ___ my assistant to get the tools we need. 18. ___
19. The rain caused the newspaper on the porch to ___. 19. ___
20. The hurricane caused terrible ___ in coastal areas. 20. ___

School + Home **Home Activity** Your child matched words with statements and definitions. Ask your child to pick a list word from Exercises 1-13 and use it in a sentence.

Name ______________________

Scoring Rubric: Story

	4	3	2	1
Focus/Ideas	Focus on a single conflict; shows great sense of imagination	Focus mainly on single conflict; shows imagination	Somewhat scattered focus; shows limited imagination	Rambling narrative; lacks imagination
Organization	Strong beginning, middle, end; appropriate order words	Coherent beginning, middle, end; some order words	Recognizable beginning, middle, end; few order words	Lacks beginning, middle, end; no order words
Voice	Engaging and unique voice	Pleasant voice but not compelling or unique	No clear, original voice	Uninvolved or indifferent
Word Choice	Vivid; creates humor or tension	Some vivid details that convey mood or description	Few vivid words; little emotional connection	No attempt to use vivid words
Sentences	Clear sentences; variety of sentences	Mostly clear sentences with some variety	Some sentences unclear; little or no variety	Incoherent sentences, or short, choppy sentences
Conventions	Few errors; pronouns and antecedents agree	Several minor errors; some pronoun-antecedent errors	Frequent errors; little clarity in use of pronouns	Many errors that seriously detract from writing

Vocabulary • Dictionary/Glossary

- **Dictionaries** and **glossaries** provide alphabetical lists of words and their meanings.
- Sometimes looking at the words around an unfamiliar word can't help you figure out the word's meaning. If this happens, use a dictionary or glossary to find the meaning.

Directions Read the following passage. Then answer the questions below.

Mary found the little bird on the ground after it had fallen from its nest. It survived the ordeal of the fall, but now needed someone to take care of it. Mary took it home and made a primitive shelter out of a shoe box. She called a bird sanctuary to ask what to do. They gave her feeding instructions and told her to keep the bird captive until it was strong enough to fly on its own. Mary enjoyed the bird's companionship for the two weeks she took care of it, but it was time to release the little bird to its wild existence.

1. Find the word *ordeal* in a dictionary or glossary. What does it mean?

____

2. Find the word *primitive* in a dictionary or glossary. Why is a shoe box a *primitive* nest?

____

____

3. Find the word *sanctuary* in a dictionary or glossary. What is the plural form of the word?

____

4. What does the word *captive* mean? Why would the bird experts want Mary to keep the bird captive until it could fly on its own?

____

____

5. What does the word *existence* mean? What is a wild existence?

____

____

School + Home **Home Activity** Your child used a dictionary or glossary to understand new words in a passage. Work with your child to identify unfamiliar words of an article. Then use a dictionary to look up the meanings of these unfamiliar words.

Name ______________________________

Electronic Media

- **Electronic media** includes online newspapers, magazines, encyclopedias, and other sources on the Internet.
- Noncomputer electronic media sources are audiotapes, videotapes, films, filmstrips, television, and radio.

Directions Use the following list of possible electronic media to answer the questions below.

- *The Rain Forest Project* (Public Television documentary about saving endangered species in the Brazilian rain forest)
- A Rain Forest of Flowers (Internet site developed by a 2nd-grade class about the flowers found in the rain forest)
- *Forest Voices* (CD of various rain forest animal sounds)
- "Rain Forest for the Future" (Taped interview with several rain forest experts about the future of the rain forest)
- *The Rain Forest Encyclopedia* (CD-ROM with general information about the flora and fauna of the rain forest)
- Natural Habitat (Internet site about endangered primates in the Brazilian rain forest)

1. Which source would be least helpful in writing a report on endangered animals in the rain forest? Why?

____

____

2. How would you find a video copy of *The Rain Forest Project*?

____

____

3. If you were doing an Internet search, what keywords would you type into the search engine to find the Web site Natural Habitat?

____

4. Which source would be most helpful if you needed sound effects for a class presentation about the rain forest?

____

5. Which source would you start with if you needed to decide on a subtopic for a report on the rain forest?

____

Name ______________________________

Directions Use the following Internet search results found on a search engine to answer the questions below.

Search Results

Rain Forest Monkeys
University of Brazil's official site for rain forest monkey information. Natural habitats, eating and sleeping habits, scientific studies.

The Eroding Environment
University of Brazil Professor Winston Soela's five-year study of the effect of the disappearing habitat on the spider monkey, its population, food and water sources, social habits.

Fight for the Rain Forest
Sao Paolo Endangered Species Protection Society site. Information about endangered species, monkeys, reptiles. Updates on preservation efforts, fundraising efforts, Brazilian government decision deadlines.

The Brazilian Rain Forest
Our trip to the Brazilian rain forest was fantastic! We saw monkeys, all kinds of insects. Photos.

6. What does the information below the underlined links tell you?

____

7. What key words might have been used to get these search results?

____

8. Which sites are university sites regarding rain forest monkeys?

____

9. Which site would be the least reliable if you were doing a report for school? Why?

____

____

10. Why might the *Fight for the Rain Forest* site be valuable if you wanted to help preserve endangered species?

____

School + Home

Home Activity Your child answered questions about electronic media. With your child, look around your house and see how many different types of electronic media you have on hand. Talk with him or her about how each of the various electronic media sources could be valuable in his or her studies.

Name ____

Prefixes *dis-*, *de-*, *out-*, *un-*

Proofread the Story Read the story below. Circle six misspelled words in the story. Write them correctly. Find a sentence fragment. Write it correctly.

Pete's New Pet

For Pete. today a day like no other. His parents had decided he was old enough to have a pet. They would go to the animal shelter and choose one.

At the shelter Pete was pleased becauze all the attendants were unwaviring in their kindness and knowledge. Pete wished he could take all the pets home.

Then he stopped before a cage with a tiny Chihuahua pup. When Pete unfastined the latch and took the little dog out of its cage, it ran around in an outragous outbirst of energy and joy. The little pup gently licked Pete's face. Pete thought this was an outstaning puppy.

The veterinarian examined the pup and gave it vaccinations. Then Pete's parents took him home, along with his new best friend.

Spelling Words

discontent
decline
outward
dispatch
unwavering
destruction
disintegrate
outstanding
uncommon
outburst

outrageous
defensive
unappetizing
disillusioned
disarray
unconscious
outskirts
unfasten
disenchanted
decompose

1. ________________ 2. ________________

3. ________________ 4. ________________

5. ________________ 6. ________________

7. ____

Frequently Misspelled Words

because
everything

Proofread Words Circle the word that is spelled correctly. Write it on the line.

8. destruction	distruction	8.	________________
9. outskirts	outskerts	9.	________________
10. unappetizing	unapetizing	10.	________________
11. unconscious	onconshious	11.	________________
12. diserray	disarray	12.	________________
13. disiluzioned	disillusioned	13.	________________
14. difensive	defensive	14.	________________
15. uncomon	uncommon	15.	________________

School + Home

Home Activity Your child identified misspelled words in a story. Have your child say words from the list and then spell them aloud.

Pronouns and Antecedents

Directions Read the passage. Then read each question. Circle the letter of the correct answer.

Basketball Gold Medal

(1) In 2008, my family and I were in Beijing to attend the Olympics, so we went to the men's basketball championship match. (2) The United States basketball team players could not win easily, so ______ played very skillfully. (3) The Spanish basketball squad tried hard to defend its 2006 gold medal. (4) When Spain's guard Ricky Rubio had six points and six rebounds, he became the youngest player to win an Olympic medal. (5) A Spanish woman watching the game said they could not be prouder of her team. (6) As the U.S. team won 118–107, the captain said that he and every player played 100 percent, and they knew it would be a historic match.

1 In sentence 1, which is the antecedent for the pronoun *we*?

- **A** Olympics
- **B** my family
- **C** my family and I
- **D** Beijing

2 Which pronoun best completes sentence 2?

- **A** them
- **B** they
- **C** we
- **D** you

3 In sentence 4, what is the relationship between the underlined words?

- **A** Pronoun-antecedent
- **B** Antecedent-pronoun
- **C** Pronoun-pronoun
- **D** Antecedent-antecedent

4 What change, if any, should be made in sentence 5?

- **A** Change ***they*** to **she**
- **B** Change ***said*** to **say**
- **C** Change ***they*** to **he**
- **D** Make no change

5 In sentence 6, what is the antecedent for the pronoun *they*?

- **A** historic match
- **B** he
- **C** player
- **D** he and every player

Home Activity Your child prepared for taking tests on pronouns and antecedents. Write a person's name, a noun, and a compound noun such as *Mom and Sam* on paper. Have your child write one sentence using the correct pronoun to refer to each antecedent you wrote.

Name________________________________

Cause and Effect

- A **cause** is what makes something happen. An **effect** is something that happens as a result of a cause. Sometimes several causes lead to one effect.
- Clue words and phrases such as *consequently, as a result,* and *therefore* can help you spot cause-and-effect relationships. Sometimes, though, there are no clue words.

Directions Read the following passage. Then complete the graphic organizer and answer the question below.

The tornado destroyed everything we had: our sod house, our windmill, and our barn. Even though the tornado touched down a mile away, the ferocious winds affected all the farms in the area. Also, this wasn't your ordinary tornado. According to witnesses, two funnel clouds came together to produce one strong force of nature. Pa still believed we could have avoided such a disastrous outcome, though. He said if we had had sturdier materials to build our home with, then maybe things would've been different. Because our house and the barn were made from the resources of the earth, they didn't stand a chance against the mighty tornado.

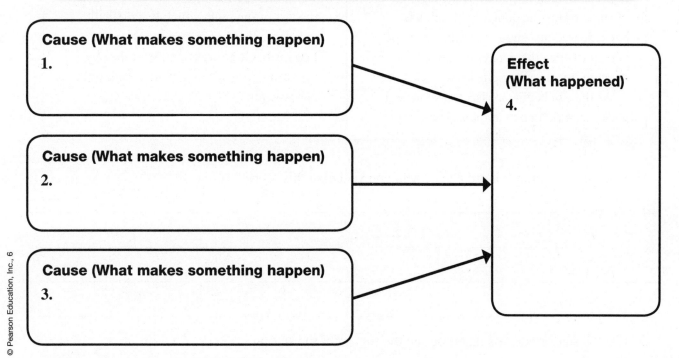

Cause (What makes something happen)
1.

Cause (What makes something happen)
2.

Cause (What makes something happen)
3.

Effect (What happened)
4.

5. What prior knowledge did you use to help you understand the passage?

____

____

School + Home

Home Activity Your child identified causes and effects in a passage while using prior knowledge to better understand its contents. Together, discuss the causes and effects of natural disasters in your area.

Name ____________________

Writing • Description

Key Features of Description

- may tell more about a person, place, object, or event
- uses specific language to help readers visualize a scene
- may be written with first- or third-person narration

A Home with a Heart

The old Victorian house sits on a hill, surrounded by great oak and pecan trees, their branches now bare and glazed with ice. The house itself seems frozen, with icicles hanging off the roof and drifts of snow engulfing the porch. On the porch, a wooden bench swing creaks in the wind.

Down the hill from the house, the barn looks small and forgotten. Huge piles of snow frame the doorway, which has been cleared just enough to allow a single person to open the door and squeeze through. Inside, a horse neighs.

As the sun begins to rise, the snow and icicles sparkle like diamonds. The air is quiet. Mourning doves huddled together on the tree branches fluff up like large down pillows, waiting for the sun to warm their frozen bodies. They are too chilled to coo or flap their wings.

Inside the house, the methodic ticking from the grandfather clock is the only sound. Across from the clock, on the far wall of the parlor, the wood stove finishes the last of the night's fuel. It is difficult to believe that in a few minutes, as the Logans begin to wake and start the day, this still house will come alive with light and warmth.

1. How did the author's word choice help you visualize this scene?

____

____

____

____

2. List the sensory details that describe the sounds of the setting.

____

____

____

____

Name ______________________________

Vocabulary

Directions Choose the word from the box that best matches each definition. Write the word on the line.

Check the Words You Know

- ___bondage
- ___commissioned
- ___earthen
- ___encounter
- ___homesteaders
- ___settlement

______________ **1.** to meet unexpectedly; meet in a battle

______________ **2.** group of buildings and the people living in them

______________ **3.** people who own and live on land granted by the government

______________ **4.** being held against your will

______________ **5.** made of the ground or soil

Directions Choose the word from the box that best matches each clue. Write the word on the line.

______________ **6.** This is what a town or city of today once was.

______________ **7.** A mud house could be described as this.

______________ **8.** This describes someone who holds the rank of second lieutenant or higher.

______________ **9.** Enslaved people experienced this condition.

______________ **10.** Two soldiers on opposite sides in a war might be involved in this.

Write a Friendly Letter

Imagine what it would be like living on the frontier. Write a friendly letter to someone back home about your experiences as a pioneer. Use as many vocabulary words as you can.

School + Home **Home Activity** Your child identified and used vocabulary words from *Black Frontiers*. With your child, write a story set back in the pioneer days. Use your family members as characters. Include as many vocabulary words from the selection as possible.

Name ______________________________

Possessive Pronouns

Pronouns that show ownership are called **possessive pronouns.** A possessive pronoun and its antecedent must agree in number and gender. Before you use a possessive pronoun, ask yourself whether the antecedent is singular or plural. If the antecedent is singular, decide whether it is masculine, feminine, or neutral. Then choose a pronoun that agrees.

Possessive Pronouns

My/mine, your/yours, his, her/hers, its, our/ours, their/theirs

- *My, your, her, our,* and *their* are always used with nouns.
  I did my report on the Exodusters.
- *Mine, yours, hers, ours,* and *theirs* stand alone.
  Which science project is yours?
- *His* and *its* can be used with nouns or can stand alone.
  His report discussed life on the frontier.
  The report on frontier life was his.
- Never use an apostrophe with a possessive pronoun.

Directions Underline the possessive pronoun in each sentence.

1. My history book tells the story of the Buffalo Soldiers.

2. Some black settlers moved to Nebraska and started their new lives.

3. Our country has a rich cultural heritage.

4. Does your family come from Louisiana?

5. Former slaves knew that, as sharecroppers, freedom would never be theirs.

6. As an American, the right to life, liberty, and the pursuit of happiness is mine.

7. The pioneer woman gathered buffalo chips for her cooking fire.

Directions Circle the pronoun in ( ) that completes each sentence.

8. John Lewis Solomon knew (their, his) rights.

9. The dog stayed in (our, its) warm bed on the floor.

10. For early black homesteaders, loneliness was part of (their, theirs) lives.

11. The woman worked to build (hers, her) home with mud walls.

School + Home **Home Activity** Your child learned about possessive pronouns. Make up or read a sentence with a possessive pronoun. Ask your child to identify the possessive pronoun.

Name ____________________

Words with *ci* and *ti*

Spelling Words				
precious	commercial	especially	ancient	gracious
position	question	suggestion	friction	lotion
potion	digestion	artificial	glacier	cautious
efficient	sensational	vicious	official	ration

Word Meanings Write a list word that fits each definition.

1. a drink or mixture of liquids — 1. ____________
2. a food allowance for one day — 2. ____________
3. the process of digesting food — 3. ____________
4. a person who holds an office — 4. ____________
5. imitation, unreal — 5. ____________
6. dangerously aggressive — 6. ____________
7. a large body of ice — 7. ____________
8. unexpectedly excellent or great — 8. ____________
9. careful — 9. ____________
10. without wasting time — 10. ____________

Words in Context Write the list word that finishes each statement below.

11. A diamond is a ___ stone. — 11. ____________
12. Use ___ to keep your skin soft and supple. — 12. ____________
13. The ___ was sixty seconds long. — 13. ____________
14. The ___ from the sandpaper makes the wood smooth. — 14. ____________
15. Your performance tonight was ___ great. — 15. ____________
16. I have a ___ for making your essay better. — 16. ____________
17. He enjoys learning about the history of ___ Greece. — 17. ____________
18. May I ask you a ___? — 18. ____________
19. The ___ host made his guests feel welcome. — 19. ____________
20. My favorite ___ when playing softball is third base. — 20. ____________

School + Home **Home Activity** Your child wrote words with *ci* and *ti*. Ask your child to pick a list word from Exercises 11–20 and define it.

Name ______________________________

Word Web

Name ____________________________________

Vocabulary • Unfamiliar Words

- When you are reading and see an unfamiliar word, you can use **context clues,** or the words around the unfamiliar word, to figure out its meaning.

Directions Read the following passage. Then answer the questions below.

Today I found out more about my family's history. I thought we had always lived in Kansas, but that wasn't the case. My ancestors were enslaved people in Alabama. When they were no longer held in bondage by white plantation owners, they decided to move as far away from the South as they could. They became homesteaders, moving to the open lands of the West that they bought from the government. My ancestors joined other African Americans who started their own settlement. Their community was a group of homes and buildings made out of earthen materials, such as sod, mud, and grass at first. I found it very strange that the towns and cities I know of today were once crude and small. I also found out that my great-great-great-uncle Thomas was a commissioned officer. I had no idea that my family's history was so interesting!

1. What is the definition of *bondage*? What context clue helps you figure out its meaning?

____

____

2. What context clue helps you figure out the definition of *homesteaders*?

____

3. How do you know a *settlement* is unlike the towns and cities of today?

____

4. What are some examples of *earthen* materials? What is another example not used in the passage?

____

5. The sentence containing the word *commissioned* does not have a context clue. Rewrite the sentence so that a context clue appears. (You may write it as more than one sentence.)

____

____

____

School + Home

Home Activity Your child identified the definitions of unfamiliar words by using context clues. Read a story or article together. Have your child underline or highlight the context clues that suggest the meanings of unfamiliar words.

Name ______________________________

Note Taking

- **Note taking** can help you when you are collecting information for a report. It can also help you keep track of information in a story and remember what you have read for a test.
- When you take notes, paraphrase, or put what you read into your own words. Synthesize, or combine, information so that you include only important details. Use key words, phrases, or short sentences.

Directions Read the following passage. Takes notes as you read on the lines to the right.

As a kid, I believed cowboys only existed in myths, legends, and movies. I wanted to think that people really roamed across the countryside and involved themselves in all kinds of adventures, but it just sounded like the stuff of bad novels to me. Then as I grew older, I began to do a little research into the subject, and, boy, were my eyes opened.

One of the cowboys I researched was Nat Love. Nat Love was born into slavery in 1854. He lived as an enslaved person until all such people were given their freedom in 1865. When he was 15, he decided he would try the cowboy life. He moved to Dodge City, in Kansas, where he found a job as a cowboy. Nat Love spent twenty years of his life driving cattle across the open lands of the country. He won a contest in 1876 for his cowboy skills (such as roping cattle, shooting, and riding a horse).

Eventually, Love decided to record his thoughts and stories about life as a cowboy in a book. The book was published as Love's autobiography in 1907. Books like these included the stories that I remember hearing as a child—the wild adventures of cowboys. Yet, experts believe many of Love's stories are tall tales and not very close to the truth. We may never know how exciting the cowboy life in the Old West really was, but we have the freedom of letting our imaginations run wild.

Notes

Name____

Directions Answer the questions below using the article and your notes.

1. Synthesize the information in the first paragraph and write it as a single sentence.

___

___

2. Paraphrase the first sentence in the third paragraph of the article.

___

3. How long was Nat Love's cowboy career?

___

4. What fact about Nat Love's childhood is most important to write down?

___

5. Why would writing your notes into a table or diagram help you understand the article?

___

6. What did Nat Love do in 1876 that led to his fame?

___

___

7. For what purpose would you want to take notes on the author's opinions of cowboy stories?

___

___

8. Why should you only write down important ideas when taking notes?

___

___

9. Is there only one way to take notes?

___

___

10. Name two ways taking notes can help you study for a test.

___

___

School + Home **Home Activity** Your child learned how to take notes, synthesize, and paraphrase information. Read an article or story with your child. Help your child experiment to find a method of note taking he or she is most comfortable with (traditional, chart, web, outline etc.).

Words with *ci* and *ti*

Proofread the Poem Circle six spelling errors in the poem. Write the words correctly. Find a line in the poem with an unnecessary capital letter. Write the line correctly.

Spelling Words

precious
commercial
especially
ancient
gracious
position
question
suggestion
friction
lotion
potion
digestion
artificial
glacier
cautious
efficient
sensational
vicious
official
ration

Grandfather Mountain

Wen I look at Grandfather Mountain I see
bears on the slopes and cautious white-tailed deer,
eagles and vicous panthers,
groundhogs and woodchucks,
a flock of wild turkeys and a red-tailed hawk,
blue Jays and squirrels.

The preshius fleeting bloom of spring,
the sensashional crimson hues of autumn,
in winter the glashier at the summit—
a lake of ice, rocky and wild.

When I look at Grandfather Mountain I see
that anciant mountain smiling down on me.

1. ____________ 2. ____________
3. ____________ 4. ____________
5. ____________ 6. ____________
7. ______________________________

Frequently Misspelled Words

especially
when

Proofread Words Circle the word that is spelled correctly. Write it.

8. preshius	precious	8.	____________
9. comercial	commercial	9.	____________
10. especially	espeshully	10.	____________
11. ancient	anshient	11.	____________
12. grashious	gracious	12.	____________
13. position	posishun	13.	____________
14. question	queschion	14.	____________
15. suggestion	sugeschiun	15.	____________

School + Home **Home Activity** Your child identified misspelled words. Say and spell the list words aloud for your child, making some spelling mistakes. Have your child tell if the word is spelled correctly and point out any errors you made.

Possessive Pronouns

Directions Read the passage. Then read each question. Circle the letter of the correct answer.

Hurricane Preparation

(1) The weather forecasts said that my town would be in the eye of the hurricane this evening. (2) Neighbors were preparing by restocking your pantries and filling our cars with gas. (3) Tension was in the air as we listened to our radios to check the storm's progress. (4) "My suggestion is that we have an emergency plan to leave town," Mother said. (5) She called ______ father and told him ______ plan. (6) "We will meet at your house," she yelled into her phone as the rain battered our shuttered windows. (7) As we drove away, we wondered if this neighborhood would still be ______ when we returned.

1 What change, if any, should be made in sentence 1?

- **A** Change ***my*** to **me**
- **B** Change ***my*** to **them**
- **C** Change ***would be*** to **had been**
- **D** Make no change

2 What changes, if any, should be made in sentence 2?

- **A** Delete ***were***
- **B** Change ***your*** to **their**/change ***our*** to **their**
- **C** Change ***Neighbors*** to **Them neighbors**
- **D** Make no change

3 Which possessive pronouns best complete sentence 5?

- **A** his, their
- **B** hers, your
- **C** our, her
- **D** their, your

4 How many possessive pronouns are in sentence 6?

- **A** 0
- **B** 1
- **C** 2
- **D** 3

5 Which possessive pronoun best completes sentence 7?

- **A** ours
- **B** its
- **C** theirs
- **D** his

School + Home **Home Activity** Your child prepared for taking tests on possessive pronouns. With your child, read a short article in the newspaper. Have your child circle any possessive pronouns he or she finds in the article.

Name ____________________

Draw Conclusions

- When you **draw conclusions**, you form reasonable opinions about what you have read.
- Use what you know about real life to help you draw conclusions.
- Be sure that there are enough facts or information in the text to support your conclusions.

Directions Read the following passage. Then complete the diagram and answer the question below.

I think in the future people will live on other planets in our solar system. They will have grown tired of the crowded cities on Earth and will manage a way to build smaller communities on other planets. Life will be slower on these planets. People won't feel like they have to compete with each other for space, jobs, and resources since the whole solar system will be opened up for their use. People will spend their days exploring the universe and learning about new life-forms instead of being consumed with day-to-day details.

Fact or Detail
1.

Fact or Detail
2.

Fact or Detail
3.

Conclusion
4.

5. How did you visualize the future described in the passage?

____

____

____

Home Activity Your child visualized the details in a passage to draw a conclusion about it. Look through books or magazines for a detailed illustration or photo. Have your child study the picture and draw a conclusion about what is going on in it.

Writing • Drama

Key Features of a Drama

- is written to be performed
- tells a story through character dialogue
- includes stage directions
- provides a character list and brief description of setting

Heroes on the High Seas

CHARACTERS: Lila and Carlos, kids at summer camp; Ben, their counselor; a radio announcer (offstage)

SETTING: (A sailboat off the coast of Miami, Florida. Distant clouds darken the sky.)

Lila (looking out to sea): Ben, I see some dark clouds, maybe thunderclouds, on the horizon.

Ben: Hmm . . . I'll check the radio. (Ben turns on the radio. As the static clears, they hear the voice of a radio announcer.)

Announcer (offstage): . . . for a special message. A thunderstorm off the coast of Florida is developing quickly, bringing strong winds and heavy rain.

Ben (turning off the radio): Okay, we need to be careful and stay calm. I'll take down the sails.

(Ben unties a rope, and as he releases it, the boom swings around and hits him on the head. He sits down heavily.)

Carlos: Ben, are you okay?

Ben (obviously in pain): Yeah, I'll be all right, but I don't think I can stand. Do you guys remember what to do when a storm approaches?

Lila: We can do this ourselves, no problem. First, we secure the boom and bring down the sail. Then we turn on the motor and check the compass to make sure we're headed in the right direction.

Carlos: I'll get an ice pack for your head, Ben. After a bump like that, you might feel sleepy, but do not go to sleep! I'll keep an eye on you just in case.

Ben (smiling despite his discomfort): Boy, I am in good hands with you two!

1. What is the setting of this drama?

____

2. What is the problem that the characters encounter?

____

____

Name ______________________________

Vocabulary

Directions Choose the word from the box that best matches each definition. Write the word on the line.

Check the Words You Know

- ___ego
- ___hatch
- ___intrepid
- ___propulsion
- ___silt
- ___submersible
- ___tentacles

______________ **1.** a vessel that travels underwater

______________ **2.** long flexible extensions on an animal

______________ **3.** force by which something is moved forward

______________ **4.** sand or soil carried by water

______________ **5.** an opening or a door

Directions Choose the word from the box that best completes each sentence. Write the word on the line.

6. Octopuses use their ______________ to catch food.

7. ______________ is carried in water and sinks to the bottom of rivers.

8. The crew opened the ______________ and went inside the submarine.

9. The ______________ crew stayed calm during the storm.

10. The captain's ______________ was so big that he took full credit for discovering the new species of squid.

Write a Scene from a Play

On a separate sheet of paper, write a short scene from a play about ocean explorers. Use as many vocabulary words as you can.

School + Home **Home Activity** Your child identified and used vocabulary words from *Deep-Sea Danger.* With your child, have a conversation about what it would be like to explore the ocean. Try to use the vocabulary words from the selection while conversing.

Name ____________________

Indefinite and Reflexive Pronouns

Indefinite pronouns may not refer to specific words. They do not always have definite antecedents: Someone needs to press her uniform.

Some common indefinite pronouns are listed below:

Singular Indefinite Pronouns
someone, somebody, anyone, anybody, everyone, everybody, something, no one, either, each

Plural Indefinite Pronouns
few, several, both, others, many, all, some

- Use singular verb forms with singular indefinite pronouns and plural verb forms with plural indefinite pronouns: Everyone here wants to pilot a submarine. Few do it well.

Reflexive pronouns reflect the action of the verb back upon the subject. Reflexive pronouns end in *-self* or *-selves*: The cadet wanted to see the underwater world herself.

Singular Reflexive Pronouns
himself, herself, myself
itself, yourself

Plural Reflexive Pronouns
ourselves, yourselves, themselves

- There are no such words as *hisself, theirself, theirselves,* or *ourself.*

Directions Underline the correct indefinite pronoun in ( ) to complete each sentence.

1. Does (few, anyone) see the horizon?
2. (Several, Everyone) believe that the planet is habitable.
3. (Many, No one) have volunteered to travel to the lowest depths.
4. If (others, somebody) pilots the submersible, Tom will go along.

Directions Write the correct reflexive pronoun to complete each sentence.

yourselves   myself   himself   ourselves

5. We may have to defend ____________________ against unexpected encounters.
6. I ____________________ will represent our scientific organization.
7. You cannot allow ____________________ to panic in any situation.
8. Tom blamed ____________________ for putting the crew in danger.

School + Home **Home Activity** Your child learned about indefinite and reflexive pronouns. Ask your child to circle three indefinite pronouns in a newspaper article and identify whether each is singular or plural.

Name ______________________________

Related Words I

Spelling Words				
poem	poetic	direct	direction	origin
original	combine	combination	repeat	repetition
critic	criticize	history	historic	academy
academic	inspire	inspiration	depart	departure

Missing Words Write two list words to finish each sentence.

If you don't know **(1)**___, you are likely to **(2)**___ it.

1. ______________ **2.** ______________

A thoughtful art **(3)**___ may **(4)**___ an artist to make changes in his or her work.

3. ______________ **4.** ______________

An art critic will sometimes **(5)**___ the **(6)**___ of colors an artist uses.

5. ______________ **6.** ______________

The train will **(7)**___ from its point of **(8)**___ at exactly noon.

7. ______________ **8.** ______________

Upon its **(9)**___, the train will head in a westerly **(10)**___.

9. ______________ **10.** ______________

I will **(11)**___ my chef to **(12)**___ the ingredients according to my recipe.

11. ______________ **12.** ______________

Definitions Write a list word that fits each definition.

13. new or previously unthought of **13.** ______________

14. having to do with poetry **14.** ______________

15. to do or occur again and again **15.** ______________

16. a written composition in verse **16.** ______________

17. having to do with history **17.** ______________

18. sudden insight or realization **18.** ______________

19. having to do with learning **19.** ______________

20. a place of learning **20.** ______________

School + Home **Home Activity** Your child used words in statements and matched words with definitions. Ask your child to pick three list words from Exercises 13–20, spell them, and use them in a sentence.

Outline

Title ____________________

A. ____________________

1. ____________________
2. ____________________
3. ____________________

B. ____________________

1. ____________________
2. ____________________
3. ____________________

C. ____________________

1. ____________________
2. ____________________
3. ____________________

Name____

Vocabulary • Multiple-Meaning Words

- When you are reading and see a word that has more than one meaning, you can use **context clues**, or words around the multiple-meaning word, to figure out its meaning.

Directions Read the following passage. Then answer the questions below.

Before we could start on the mission, we had to obtain a permit to land on the planet Apollo. The planet had recently been added to the Dangerous Zone by the Space Council. There was evidence that the environment of Apollo was dangerous to humans. Since we were on a special mission to extract molten lava for research purposes, we were granted permission.

It took a full day to gather the material into canisters and load it onto the space barge, the vehicle that would take us back to Earth. We had to refrain from bringing any other substance from Apollo onboard with us for fear of contamination. So when I noticed some planet Apollo dust on my elbow, I had to be quarantined immediately. I was not allowed to return to work until the foreign dust was contained and proven harmless.

1. What is the definition of *permit* in this passage? What is another definition of the word?

____

2. How do you know *barge* does not mean "to enter quickly" in the passage?

____

____

3. What is the definition of *refrain* as it is used in the passage? How do you know?

____

____

4. What is another meaning of *elbow*?

____

5. Use one of the multiple-meaning words in an original sentence. Make sure to include a context clue in the sentence, so that the intended meaning of the word is clear.

____

____

School + Home

Home Activity Your child identified the definitions of multiple-meaning words by using context clues. Make a list of words that have multiple meanings. Have your child pick a word from the list and draw an illustration of its meaning while you try to guess which word it is. Switch roles, and repeat the activity.

Follow and Clarify Directions

- **Following directions** involves doing or making something.
- **Clarifying directions** means writing clear directions for others to use.
- Directions usually are numbered. The numbers tell you the sequence of the steps. Read all directions before starting to act on the first direction given. Visualize the purpose or the end result of the directions while reading.

Directions Read the following set of directions.

How to Make a Papier-Mâché Planet

1. Gather the following items: all-purpose flour; water; balloon; old newspapers; large mixing bowl; measuring cups; mixing spoon; old newspapers; paintbrush.
2. In a large mixing bowl, combine three cups of water to one cup of flour. Stir together until you have a smooth mixture. (You may double or triple this recipe depending upon size and number of your papier-mâché planets.)
3. Cut the old newspapers into two-inch-wide strips. Cover designated work space with the rest of the newspaper.
4. Blow up your balloon to the desired size of your planet. Tie a knot at the bottom of it.
5. Place strips of paper into the mixing bowl. Use a paintbrush or your hands to wet the strips with the mixture. Place the strips of paper onto your balloon. Try to crisscross the strips of paper (or overlap them to form X's) as you add them to the balloon. Cover the entire balloon.
6. Allow the balloon to dry thoroughly before advancing on to the next step.
7. Gather the following items: clean paintbrush; paints of desired colors; paper towels; water; small bowl.
8. Choose the appropriate colors to paint your planet. You may want to consult an encyclopedia or another reference book with pictures or illustrations of the planets to get a good idea of what they look like. Paint your planet accordingly. Make sure to rinse your paintbrush in the small bowl of water between colors. Use the paper towels to wipe off your paintbrushes after painting.
9. Let the balloon dry completely. Cut a small slit into your papier-mâché surface. Insert a needle to pop the balloon. Pull the popped balloon out of the papier-mâché mold.
10. Display your planet for all to see and admire.

Name ______________________________

Directions Use the directions to answer the following questions.

1. If you were actually going to make a papier-mâché planet, what is the first thing you should do?

____

2. In what step do you blow up the balloon?

____

3. How could popping the balloon too early change your end result?

____

4. How could the directions in step 6 be clarified?

____

5. Why do you think the directions include two steps in which you gather materials?

____

____

6. How could the directions in step 3 be clarified?

____

____

7. Will this project always take the same amount of time to complete?

____

____

8. How does visualizing help you to follow directions?

____

____

9. Is there any way the steps in this process could be changed while getting the same final product?

____

____

10. Add a direction to the end of this set that explains how to display the papier-mâché planet.

____

____

School + Home

Home Activity Your child answered questions about a set of directions. Have your child write a set of directions to perform a task that he or she knows well. Help your child to write as clear and accurate directions as possible.

Name ______________________________

Related Words I

Proofread a Script Circle six spelling errors in the script. Write the words correctly. Find a sentence in the script with a punctuation error. Write it correctly.

Spelling Words

poem
poetic
direct
direction
origin
original
combine
combination
repeat
repetition
critic
criticize
history
historic
academy
academic
inspire
inspiration
depart
departure

Frequently Misspelled Words

always
myself

Time Out

(Nico is in his room, working on a school project Eric enters.)

Nico (sighing with frustration): I don't mean to critisize, but you're always tardy, Eric.

Eric (taking off his jacket): Yeah, I'm sorry. I just wanted to finish watching my favorite TV program.

Nico: If you repete this pattern, we'll never finish this histery project, or I'll end up doing most of the work myself. It's supposed to be a combenation of our work.

Eric (shrugging with resignation): I said I was sorry. It seems like time just flies by.

Nico: I know. But it's important that you be here on time. If we miss the deadline, we'll be the laughingstock of the acadimy. I'll let you borrow my watch until this project is finished if you promise me you'll be prompt from now on. Is that a deal?

Eric (breaking into a broad grin): Sure. I'll try to be more ackadimic.

Nico: Okay then. Now let's get to work.

1. ______________ 2. ______________

3. ______________ 4. ______________

5. ______________ 6. ______________

7. ____

Proofread Words Circle the word that is spelled correctly. Write it on the line.

8. origin	origen	**8.**	______________
9. origenul	original	**9.**	______________
10. cumbine	combine	**10.**	______________

Home Activity Your child identified misspelled words. Ask your child to identify the words that are most difficult for him or her to spell.

Indefinite and Reflexive Pronouns

Directions Read the passage. Then read each question. Circle the letter of the correct answer.

Vincent Van Gogh

(1) Vincent Van Gogh wanted to bring happiness to many through his paintings. (2) In his early years, he taught himself to draw and then spent long days painting with dull colors. (3) In his later years he effectively used color to express himself. (4) Someone suggested that he go to Paris where his brother Theo knew everyone. (5) Theo introduced Vincent to the greatest Impressionist painters. (6) These famous artists had a powerful effect on himself, and Van Gogh began to brighten the colors of his palette. (7) No one would say that *Starry, Starry Night* is a dull and dark painting. (8) His sunflower paintings are cheerful and became the favorites of everybody who knew his work. (9) Most recognize Vincent Van Gogh's paintings, and everyone can name a favorite.

1 What is the indefinite pronoun in sentence 1?

A through
B bring
C paintings
D many

2 Which describes the underlined word in sentence 2?

A Singular reflexive pronoun
B Singular indefinite pronoun
C Plural reflexive pronoun
D Plural indefinite pronoun

3 Which describes the two underlined words in sentence 4?

A Both are plural indefinite pronouns.
B Both are singular indefinite pronouns.
C Both are plural reflexive pronouns.
D Both are singular reflexive pronouns.

4 What change, if any, should be made to sentence 6?

A Remove the comma after ***himself***
B Change ***himself*** to **themselves**
C Change ***himself*** to **him**
D Make no change

5 Which sentence has two indefinite pronouns?

A sentence 7
B sentence 8
C sentence 9
D None of the above

School + Home **Home Activity** Your child prepared for taking tests on indefinite and reflexive pronouns. Ask your child to use the reflexive pronouns *myself, yourself, himself,* and *herself* in sentences and explain to whom they refer.

Author's Purpose

- The **author's purpose** is the reason or reasons the author has for writing.
- An author may write to persuade, to inform, to entertain, or to express ideas and feelings. An author may have more than one reason for writing.

Directions Read the following passage. Then complete the diagram.

One very cool invention is the refrigerator. Before refrigeration, it was difficult to store and ship fresh food. In the early twentieth century, food was kept cold with a block of ice in a cabinet called an "icebox." The cooling process used in today's refrigerators dates back to Michael Faraday's experiments in the eighteenth century with liquefying ammonia. The first refrigeration machine was designed in 1805 by the American inventor Oliver Evans. Other inventors improved on this device. The first commercial home refrigerator was sold in 1911 by General Electric. Today, homes all over the world have refrigerators.

Author's Purpose

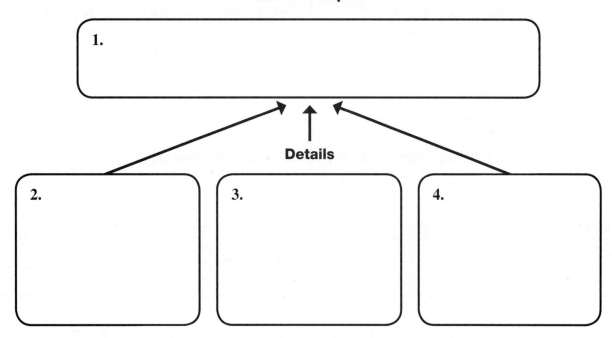

1.

Details

2.

3.

4.

5. How did the author's language or style help meet the purpose?

____

____

Home Activity Your child identified the author's purpose and cited details to support this analysis. Work with your child to identify the author's purpose and supporting details of individual paragraphs in a magazine article about an innovation. Challenge your child to set his or her reading pace to match the purpose of the article.

Name ______________________________

Writing • Summary

Key Features of a Summary

- tells what a selection is about
- includes the most important ideas and details
- leaves out unnecessary details

Dancing Wheels: A Summary

Dancing Wheels is the story of a dance troupe in Cleveland, Ohio, that includes both "stand-up" dancers and "sit-down" dancers who dance in wheelchairs.

The story begins by showing how dancers prepare for a performance and then tells how the troupe got started. Its founder, Mary Verdi-Fletcher, was born with a disease that weakened the lower half of her body. When she grew up, Mary formed The Dancing Wheels School and Company so that people with similar conditions could dance.

The book goes on to explain how dancers prepare for performances. It tells about workshops and rehearsals. Readers learn how the dancers work together. They also learn about some of the children in the dance troupe.

The last part of the book conveys what a Dancing Wheels performance is like. In words and pictures, it describes the show "The Sorcerer's Apprentices" and the reader learns what can happen when one person follows a dream.

1. What are some of the important details that are included in this summary?

____

____

____

____

____

2. Give an example of the kind of information that you wouldn't include in a summary about a dance performance.

____

____

____

Name________________________

Vocabulary

Directions Choose the word from the box that best matches each definition. Write the word on the line.

Check the Words You Know
___converts
___devise
___efficiency
___generated
___percentage
___proclaimed
___reproduce
___transmitted

____________ **1.** to invent

____________ **2.** allowance, figured by percent

____________ **3.** produced

____________ **4.** sent out signals by means of electromagnetic waves or by wire

____________ **5.** to make a copy of

Directions Choose the word from the box that best completes each sentence below. Write the word on the line shown to the left.

____________ **6.** The inventor ____ that he had a great invention.

____________ **7.** He claimed that his machine ____ food from one place to another, electronically.

____________ **8.** "It ____ food into electrical pulses," he declared.

____________ **9.** If it worked, it could result in more ____ by saving time.

____________ **10.** Although the idea ____ much interest, it turned out to be a fake.

Write a News Report

On a separate sheet of paper, write a news report you might make after observing a new invention. Use as many vocabulary words as you can.

School + Home **Home Activity** Your child identified and used vocabulary words from *Inventing the Future.* Have a conversation about useful inventions. Why are they useful? What do they do? Use the vocabulary words from the selection while conversing.

Using *Who* and *Whom*

The pronoun ***who*** is used as a subject.

Who planted the garden? (*Who* is the subject of the sentence.)
My sister is the only one who likes roses. (*Who* is the subject of the clause *who likes roses.*)

The pronoun ***whom*** is used as the object of a preposition, such as *to, for,* and *from*, and as a direct object. Very often, *whom* will be a direct object in questions.

To whom did you send the flowers? (*Whom* is the object of the preposition *to*.)
This is a man whom I admire. (*Whom* is the direct object of the verb *admire* in the clause *whom I admire*.)
Whom did you invite? (*Whom* is a direct object.)

You can check if *whom* should be used as a direct object. Change the word order so that the subject comes first. (*Whom* did you invite? You did invite *whom*?)

Directions Circle the pronoun in ( ) that correctly completes each sentence.

1. These are the inventors (who, whom) you should acknowledge.
2. Mr. Edison, (who, whom) was a fond father, nicknamed his children Dot and Dash.
3. Edison was the inventor (who, whom) wealthy investors supported.
4. The lab assistants were the ones (who, whom) built Edison's prototypes.
5. Edison worked with the assistants (who, whom) were best suited for the positions.
6. He is one of the people (who, whom) history honors as a brilliant inventor and scientist.
7. Give the data to the woman (who, whom) calls for it.
8. People (who, whom) own CD players can thank Edison for his inventions.

Directions Write *who* or *whom* to complete each sentence correctly.

9. Batchelor and Kruesi were two assistants to ______________ Edison entrusted his work.
10. Edison believed negative results were valuable to a scientist ______________ wanted to learn.
11. ______________ stole Edison's heart and married him?
12. To ______________ shall we award the patent for this clever invention?

School + Home **Home Activity** Your child learned about using *who* and *whom*. Have your child look through a magazine, point out the pronouns *who* and *whom*, and explain why each pronoun is used.

Word Endings *-ty*, *-ity*, *-tion*

Spelling Words				
electricity	equality	society	specialty	celebrity
recognition	description	reduction	tradition	loyalty
security	clarity	popularity	certainty	cruelty
subscription	reputation	intention	deception	penalty

Definitions Write a list word that fits each definition.

1. faithfulness to a cause, ideal, or custom 1. ____________
2. freedom from danger, fear, or anxiety 2. ____________
3. the passing of information and beliefs from one generation to the next 3. ____________
4. the quality of being clear 4. ____________
5. reduced in number or size 5. ____________
6. condition of being liked by most people 6. ____________
7. an account in words 7. ____________
8. condition of being free from doubt 8. ____________
9. condition of realizing someone or something is previously known 9. ____________
10. readiness to give pain to others 10. ____________

Words in Context Write a list word to finish each statement below.

11. It's time for me to renew my ___ to my local newspaper. 11. ____________
12. I can't believe I actually got an autograph from my favorite ___. 12. ____________
13. That company has a ___ for doing fine work. 13. ____________
14. I have many hobbies, but collecting baseball cards is my ___. 14. ____________
15. It was not my ___ to hurt your feelings. 15. ____________
16. I am glad that we live in a free and open ___. 16. ____________
17. I don't believe that you should live your life based on lies and ___. 17. ____________
18. The ___ of the two teams makes the game more interesting. 18. ____________
19. The ___ went off during that big storm last night. 19. ____________
20. I spent some time in the ___ box during today's hockey game. 20. ____________

School + Home **Home Activity** Your child spelled words that end in *-ty*, *-ity*, and *-tion*. Ask your child to choose five list words, say them, and then spell them.

Name ______________________________________

Main Idea Chart

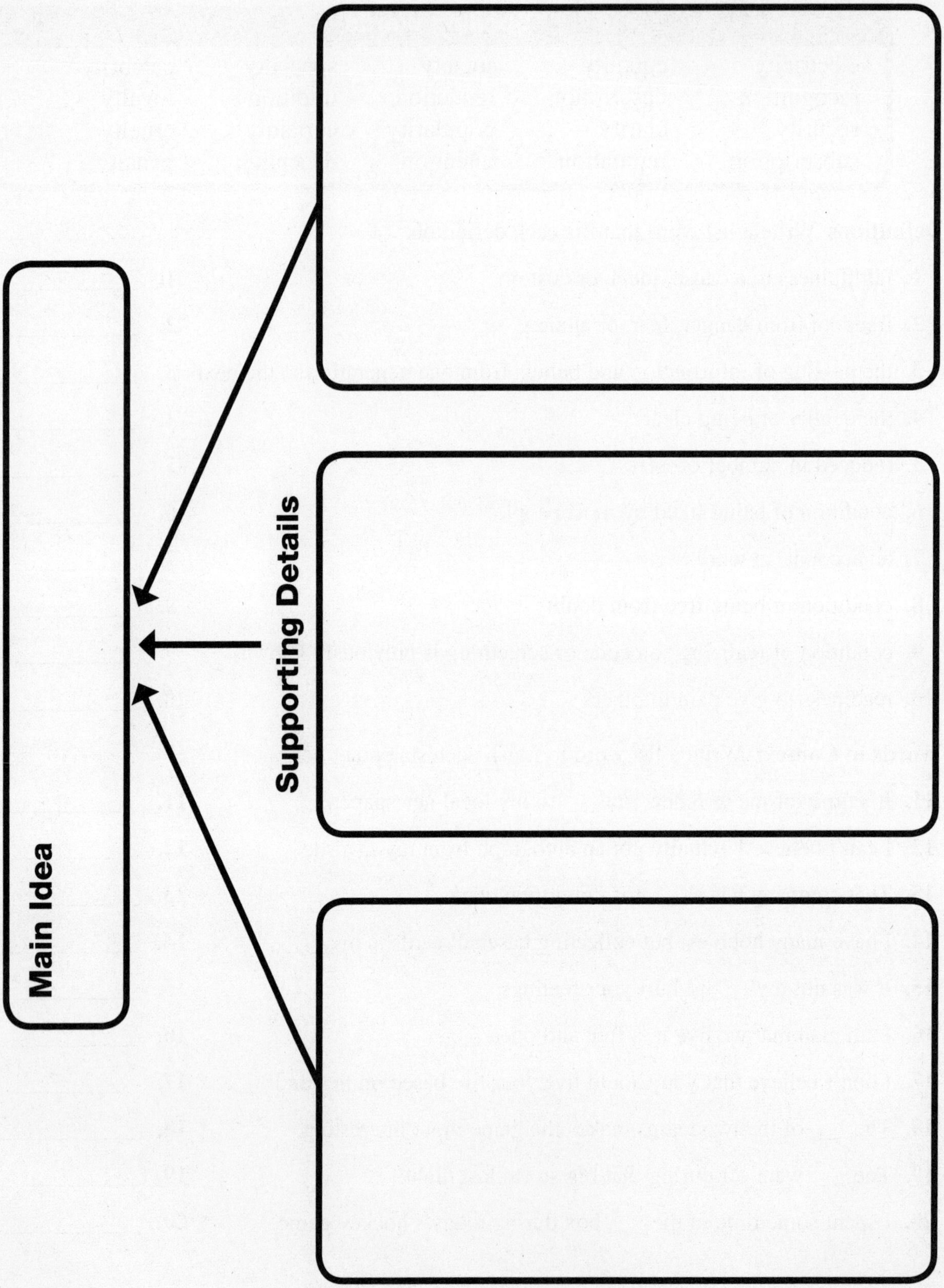

Name ____________________

Vocabulary • Prefixes *re-*, *pro-*, *trans-*

- If you see an unfamiliar word while you are reading, use word parts to figure out its meaning. **Prefixes** are word parts with their own meanings that are added to base words. They change the meanings of base words.
- The prefix *re-* means "again;" *pro-* means "before;" and *trans-* means "across."

Directions Read the following article. Then answer the questions below.

Who deserves to be recalled as the inventor of the telephone? The principle behind the telephone is that it converts sound waves to electrical impulses that are then transmitted through a wire to reproduce the sound. Although Alexander Graham Bell claimed to be the inventor of the telephone, a little-known inventor named Elisha Gray also devised a telephone. Both men raced to the patent office to apply for a patent, and Bell beat Gray by only hours. Alexander Graham Bell will always be remembered but not Elisha Gray. If Gray had arrived at the patent office a little bit earlier, he would be the famous one.

1. What does *transmitted* mean? How does the prefix contribute to the meaning?

____

____

2. How does the prefix in *reproduce* help you to determine the meaning of the word?

____

3. How would the prefix help you to determine the meaning of *proclaimed?*

____

4. What are two other words in the article that use the prefix *trans-*, *re-*, or *pro-*?

____

5. Write a sentence using one of the words from your answer to Question 4.

____

School + Home

Home Activity Your child identified and used prefixes to understand new words of a passage. Work with your child to identify unfamiliar words in another article. Then see if he or she can find prefixes to help with the understanding of the new words. Confirm the meanings with your child.

Name ______________________________________

Advertisements

- **Advertisements** are designed to sell a product or service. Usually advertisements have four elements: a headline, image, body copy, and signature.
- When you read advertisements, watch for persuasive language and loaded words that appeal to emotions. Also look for generalities that don't have any specific meaning, testimonials, and slogans.

Directions Use this advertisement to answer the questions below.

NEW! Have the music in you!

An exciting new invention lets you enjoy music all day long—even in the shower and as you sleep! No wires or headphones, just a tiny clip. For fabulous nonstop music. You have to hear it to believe it!

Music Magic. $49.95
at leading department stores

Love that music!

1. What is this advertisement selling?

____

2. Where are the four parts of this advertisement?

____

____

3. How do loaded words in the advertisement above appeal to emotions?

____

4. What is an example of a generality the advertisement contains? Explain.

____

____

5. What is the slogan in this advertisement? How does it appeal to the reader?

____

____

Name____

Directions Use this advertisement to answer the questions below.

Hello, Robot! Bye-Bye, Chores!

Teenage movie star Lindsay Cooper says, "I don't clean *my* room. Why should *you* clean yours?"

Have more time for fun! *Hello, Robot* will pick up, clean, dust, make your bed, and even prepare snacks. Let *Hello, Robot* do the work. Don't miss out! Get yours today!

Hello, Robot
Meet your fun machine!

6. Where are the four parts of this advertisement?

____

____

7. How is a testimonial used to persuade readers?

____

____

8. What loaded words does the advertisement use? How do they appeal to emotions?

____

____

9. What is an example of a generality the advertisement contains?

____

____

10. What is the slogan in this advertisement? How does it appeal to the reader?

____

____

School + Home **Home Activity** Your child learned about reading advertisements critically. Look at an advertisement together. Ask your child to explain what techniques are used to sell the product or service.

Word Endings *-ty, -ity, -tion*

Proofread an Article Circle six misspelled words in the article below. Write them correctly. Find a sentence with a misplaced adjective. Write it correctly.

Spelling Words

electricity
equality
society
specialty
celebrity
recognition
description
reduction
tradition
loyalty

security
clarity
popularity
certainty
cruelty
subscription
reputation
intention
deception
penalty

The Importance of Society

Humans are beings social. We all feel the need to belong to a social group. Within such a group, we come to value our reputashion and strive for recignition and populerity. Being members of society provides us with sicurity, and clarety about social tredition. And perhaps most important, being members of society prevents us from being alone.

1. ______________ 2. ______________

3. ______________ 4. ______________

5. ______________ 6. ______________

7. ______________________________

Proofread Words Circle the word that is spelled correctly. Write it on the line.

Frequently Misspelled Words

finally
really

8. electricity	electrisity	elecktricity	8. ______
9. penlty	penilty	penalty	9. ______
10. sosiety	society	socety	10. ______
11. certainty	curtainty	cirtainty	11. ______
12. cruelty	crulty	creulty	12. ______
13. subscribtion	subscription	subscripshun	13. ______
14. celebrty	cellebrity	celebrity	14. ______
15. intention	intenshun	intenshen	15. ______
16. specltly	specialty	specalty	16. ______
17. deseption	decepshun	deception	17. ______

School + Home **Home Activity** Your child identified misspelled words. Say a word from the list and have your child spell it aloud.

Name ____

Using *Who* and *Whom*

Directions Read the passage. Then read each question. Circle the letter of the correct answer.

Geography Bee

(1) "Who will enter this year's geography bee?" asked Ms. Graham. (2) "It's a contest for kids for ______ maps are a passion. (3) Are you one of those kids who loves maps?" (4) I knew a lot about the United States, and the family's atlas was my favorite book. (5) But <u>who</u> would help me learn about the African states? (6) My parents, who were born in South America, encouraged me. (7) They suggested that I find a buddy with <u>whom</u> I could study. (8) They named a friend who had entered the contest last year. (9) "I'm in," I said to Hector "but [illegible] go to the atlas this weekend?" (10) I was ready to prepare for the geography bee.

1 What change, if any, should be made in sentence 1?

- **A** Change ***year's*** to **years**
- **B** Change ***asked*** to **said**
- **C** Change ***Who*** to **Whom**
- **D** Make no change

2 Which pronoun best completes sentence 2?

- **A** who
- **B** us
- **C** whom
- **D** them

3 Which describes the underlined word in sentence 5?

- **A** Subject
- **B** Object of preposition
- **C** Direct object
- **D** None of the above

4 Which describes the underlined word in sentence 7?

- **A** Subject
- **B** Object of preposition
- **C** Direct object
- **D** None of the above

5 Which pronoun best completes sentence 9?

- **A** who
- **B** they
- **C** whom
- **D** them

School + Home **Home Activity** Your child prepared for taking tests on using *who* and *whom.* Have your child write a paragraph about friends. Ask him or her to use each pronoun *who* and *whom* at least once.

Name ____________________

Greek Word Parts

Spelling Words				
hydrant	chronic	archive	synonym	antonym
democracy	hydrogen	aristocrat	dehydrated	chronicle
hydroplane	chronology	archaic	homonym	synchronize
hydraulic	archaeology	anarchy	hydroelectric	bureaucracy

Word Groups Write a list word that fits into each group.

1. coordinate, match, coincide, _____ 1. ____________
2. nozzle, spout, valve, _____ 2. ____________
3. oxygen, carbon, helium, _____ 3. ____________
4. same, alike, similar, _____ 4. ____________
5. calendar, agenda, day planner, _____ 5. ____________
6. old, ancient, obsolete, _____ 6. ____________
7. dry, thirsty, drained, _____ 7. ____________
8. record, chronicle, excerpt, _____ 8. ____________
9. habitual, persistent, lingering, _____ 9. ____________
10. account, description, history, _____ 10. ____________

Word Search Find and circle ten list words in the word search. Words are across, down, diagonal, and backward. Write the words on the lines.

H	Y	D	R	O	E	L	E	C	T	R	I	C
Y	E	R	H	D	E	M	D	R	A	C	Y	I
D	B	R	Y	R	A	M	E	O	R	U	A	L
R	U	U	D	A	Y	A	M	L	C	A	R	U
E	R	P	R	N	A	N	O	T	O	L	C	A
C	E	T	O	E	N	A	C	G	T	I	H	R
A	U	M	P	O	A	A	R	Y	S	C	A	D
A	O	Y	L	Y	R	U	A	L	I	O	E	Y
H	L	N	A	D	C	A	C	E	R	A	O	H
O	O	L	N	R	H	R	Y	R	A	R	L	T
M	G	A	E	G	Y	C	N	A	A	A	O	Y
Y	Y	N	L	S	Y	N	A	C	Y	C	G	S
N	O	E	E	Y	Y	A	N	T	O	N	Y	M

11. ____________
12. ____________
13. ____________
14. ____________
15. ____________
16. ____________
17. ____________
18. ____________
19. ____________
20. ____________

Home Activity Your child has learned to spell words with Greek word parts. Ask your child to organize the list words into groups according to word parts and tell what the word parts mean.

Name ______________________________

Subject and Object Pronouns

Directions Circle the pronoun in each sentence. Write *SP* if it is a subject pronoun and *OP* if it is an object pronoun.

1. We felt bad that Admiral Peary's claims were disputed. ____________
2. The snow skis were bought for Ronny and me. ____________
3. Josephine Peary told them about the Arctic. ____________
4. He and the men hoped to reach the North Pole first. ____________
5. At last they spotted a ship on the horizon. ____________

Directions Circle the pronoun in ( ) that completes each sentence correctly.

6. Anna and (he, him) needed to do more research on Admiral Peary.
7. (They, Them) listed the obstacles an Arctic explorer might encounter.
8. (She, Her) was one of the few women who went on expeditions.
9. (We, Us) believe Admiral Peary was a great explorer.
10. Charles and (I, me) looked for a biography of Dr. Frederick A. Cook.
11. Peary quarreled with Cook and refused to allow (he, him) to publish a paper.
12. The curator gave Michael and (she, her) records on Peary's travels.
13. The compass pointed (he, him) in the right direction.
14. The tour was taken by Mr. Blades and (we, us).
15. My teacher gave Stacey and (I, me) an A on our Arctic Circle report.

School + Home **Home Activity** Your child reviewed subject and object pronouns. Ask your child to use subject and object pronouns in a letter he or she writes to a friend or family member.

Name ______________________________

Prefixes *dis-, de-, out-, un-*

Spelling Words

discontent	decline	outward	dispatch	unwavering
destruction	disintegrate	outstanding	uncommon	outburst
outrageous	defensive	unappetizing	disillusioned	disarray
unconscious	outskirts	unfasten	disenchanted	decompose

Synonyms Write the list word that has the same or nearly the same meaning.

1. exterior 1. ______________
2. consistent 2. ______________
3. edge 3. ______________
4. protective 4. ______________
5. drop 5. ______________
6. disorder 6. ______________

Antonyms Write the list word that has the opposite or nearly the opposite meaning.

7. satisfaction 7. ______________
8. regular 8. ______________
9. awake 9. ______________
10. construction 10. ______________
11. secure 11. ______________
12. average 12. ______________

Alphabetical Write the list word that fits in alphabetical order between the two words.

13. ourselves 13. ______________ outerwear
14. unable 14. ______________ unaware
15. disguise 15. ______________ disinfect
16. dislike 16. ______________ diversity
17. decode 17. ______________ decorate
18. disinclined 18. ______________ disk
19. outline 19. ______________ outside
20. discount 20. ______________ dish

School + Home

Home Activity Your child has learned to spell words with the prefixes *dis-*, *de-*, *out-*, and *un-*. Find three words with these prefixes in a newspaper or magazine. Ask your child to spell each word and name a word that means the opposite.

Name ________________________

Pronouns and Antecedents

Directions Circle the pronoun in each sentence and underline its antecedent.

1. Mrs. Taylor teaches about chimps because they are an endangered species.
2. Kent and James want to visit Africa so they can see chimps in a natural habitat.
3. The forest ranger just started working at the park, but he knows about the plants and animals.
4. Mike is driving to the wildlife shelter, and Carrie is following him.
5. Mrs. Taylor brought photos of Kenya and showed them during the presentation.
6. Scientists have tried to teach sign language to chimps, but Kaatu could not learn it.
7. One chimp tried to use a computer, but she failed.
8. Charlotte and Terry were hiding, but Tiki found them.
9. Emily was hoping Pete would go with her to the lecture.
10. Jesse and Owen's parents sat with them at the lecture.

Directions Write the pronoun that agrees with the antecedent. Underline the antecedent to which the pronoun refers.

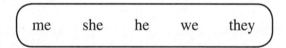

me	she	he	we	they

11. Jane Goodall gave a lecture; then ________________ answered questions.
12. As Jon listened attentively, ________________ took notes.
13. Laurel and Mike arrived later, so ________________ sat in the back of the hall.
14. I wanted Dr. Goodall to call on ________________.
15. ________________ students were responsible for refreshments.

School + Home **Home Activity** Your child reviewed pronouns and antecedents. Have your child find correct pronoun and antecedent usage in an ad or a catalog.

Name ______________________________

Words with *ci* and *ti*

Spelling Words

precious	commercial	especially	ancient	gracious
position	question	suggestion	friction	lotion
potion	digestion	artificial	glacier	cautious
efficient	sensational	vicious	official	ration

Classifying Write the list word that belongs in each group.

1. mixture, drink, brew, _____ 1. ________________
2. sentence, exclamation, phrase, _____ 2. ________________
3. administrator, director, mayor, _____ 3. ________________
4. mainly, in particular, notably, _____ 4. ________________
5. competent, effective, productive, _____ 5. ________________
6. careful, guarded, watchful, _____ 6. ________________
7. place, location, spot, _____ 7. ________________
8. cruel, wicked, mean, _____ 8. ________________
9. fake, imitation, manufactured, _____ 9. ________________
10. kind, considerate, well-mannered, _____ 10. ________________
11. noticeable, spectacular, remarkable, _____ 11. ________________
12. expensive, rare, valuable, _____ 12. ________________
13. erosion, rubbing, grinding, _____ 13. ________________

Analogy Write the list word that completes each analogy.

14. Print ad is to newspaper as _____ is to television show. 14. ________________
15. Tell is to demand as recommendation is to _____. 15. ________________
16. Air is to respiration as food is to _____. 16. ________________
17. Conditioner is to hair as _____ is to skin. 17. ________________
18. New is to modern as old is to _____. 18. ________________
19. Water is to lake as ice is to _____. 19. ________________
20. Book is to page as whole is to _____. 20. ________________

School + Home **Home Activity** Your child has learned to spell words with *ci* and *ti*. Ask your child to choose a word group from Exercises 1–13 and tell why the list word fits in that group.

Possessive Pronouns

Directions Underline the possessive pronoun in each sentence.

1. Our class is studying the plight of slaves after the Civil War.
2. Slaves read about Israelites who were delivered out of their bondage.
3. Nicodemus marked its legacy by becoming a National Historic Landmark.
4. Can you remember the date of Emancipation Day from your study of history?
5. Exodusters were named for their exodus, or departure, from the South.
6. The Army paid every black man in the cavalry thirteen dollars a month for his service.
7. Anne claimed that the idea to make soap from the yucca plant was hers.
8. We should respect our civil rights.
9. Mr. Singleton hoped two hundred families would settle in his community.
10. That book about African Americans is mine.

Directions Replace the underlined word or words with a possessive pronoun. Write the possessive pronoun.

11. African American athletes owe a great deal of African American athletes' success to athletes such as Satchel Paige. ________________
12. A pioneer woman worked hard making a home for a pioneer woman's family. ________________
13. The Exodusters left the Exodusters' homes in the South. ________________
14. The small animal made the small animal's bed inside the home in cold weather. ________________
15. Christine was happy that the story her teacher read aloud was Christine's. ________________

School + Home **Home Activity** Your child reviewed possessive pronouns. Ask your child to look at a story in a magazine or newspaper and provide the correct possessive pronouns for at least three proper nouns.

Name ______________________

Related Words I

Spelling Words				
poem	poetic	direct	direction	origin
original	combine	combination	repeat	repetition
critic	criticize	history	historic	academy
academic	inspire	inspiration	depart	departure

Crossword Puzzle Use the clues to find the list words. Write each letter in a box.

Across

2. starting point

5. imagery and figurative language

6. in the past

8. to leave

10. place for instruction

Down

1. type of literature

3. motivate

4. to the point

7. do over

9. unite

Synonyms Write the list word that means the same or nearly the same.

11. reviewer ______________

12. duplication ______________

13. influence ______________

14. scholarly ______________

15. noteworthy ______________

16. judge ______________

17. new ______________

18. route ______________

19. exit ______________

20. mixture ______________

School + Home **Home Activity** Your child has learned to spell and define related words. Ask your child to use two pairs of related words in sentences.

Name ____________________

Indefinite and Reflexive Pronouns

Directions Underline the correct word in ( ) to complete each sentence.

1. Everyone (thinks, think) the captain is strange because he talks to himself.
2. Many of the navigators (practices, practice) on the dive simulator.
3. Everybody (studies, study) the *Explorer's Safety Manual.*
4. The captain assures us that nothing (are, is) going to stop our journey.
5. Both of the boys (stumbles, stumble) onto the bridge.
6. (Several, One) of them have gone back to the academy for training.
7. The alarm is sounding because (many, something) is wrong!
8. (Both, Anyone) the Professor and Dale were on alert.
9. The giant squid approaches the submersible, but (few, nobody) panics.
10. (Everyone, Both) shows (their, his) best scientific manners.

Directions Write the correct reflexive pronoun from the box to complete each sentence.

yourself	myself	herself	themselves	ourselves

11. The First Officers designed the training program ____________________.
12. I am very interested in deep-sea travel ____________________.
13. We introduced ____________________ to Stan and Willie.
14. Do not leave ____________________ open to an accident.
15. Dale organized the group photo ____________________.

School + Home **Home Activity** Your child reviewed indefinite and reflexive pronouns. Have your child make up a slogan for a favorite product using one indefinite pronoun or one reflexive pronoun.

Name ______________________________

Word Endings *-ty, -ity, -tion*

Spelling Words

electricity	equality	society	specialty	celebrity
recognition	description	reduction	tradition	loyalty
security	clarity	popularity	certainty	cruelty
subscription	reputation	intention	deception	penalty

Word Groups Write the list word that belongs in each group.

1. decrease, diminishments, cutback, _____ 1. ____________
2. gas, water, cable, _____ 2. ____________
3. actor, musician, singer, _____ 3. ____________
4. dependability, reliability, devotion, _____ 4. ____________
5. fair, balance, even, _____ 5. ____________

Words in Context Write the missing list word to complete each phrase.

6. a holiday _____ 6. ____________
7. the _____ box 7. ____________
8. a magazine _____ 8. ____________
9. with absolute _____ 9. ____________
10. the chef's _____ 10. ____________

Word Search Circle the ten hidden words. Words are down, across, and diagonal. Write the word on the line.

R	D	E	S	C	R	I	P	T	I	O	N
E	E	C	S	E	C	U	R	I	T	Y	R
C	C	I	L	I	T	Y	E	O	L	T	E
O	E	N	T	A	I	S	S	N	A	S	P
G	P	T	I	C	R	T	C	E	R	O	U
N	T	E	O	T	R	I	R	P	I	C	T
I	I	N	N	L	T	U	T	C	T	I	A
T	O	T	C	E	P	T	E	Y	Y	E	T
I	N	I	C	L	A	T	Y	L	O	T	I
O	P	O	P	U	L	A	R	I	T	Y	O
N	Y	N	D	E	S	C	R	T	O	Y	N

11. ____________
12. ____________
13. ____________
14. ____________
15. ____________
16. ____________
17. ____________
18. ____________
19. ____________
20. ____________

Home Activity Your child has learned to spell words that end with *-ty, -ity,* and *-tion.* Have your child find an example of a word with each ending in a magazine or newspaper and then spell each word without looking.

Name ____________________

Using *Who* and *Whom*

Directions Circle the pronoun in ( ) that correctly completes each sentence.

1. Edison bragged about his "muckers" (who, whom) turned out inventions.
2. To (who, whom) did Edison give blueprints?
3. (Who, Whom) was known as the "Wizard of Menlo Park"?
4. Batchelor was the assistant (who, whom) posed in a photo taken with electric light.
5. (Who, Whom) did *Scientific American* interview about the phonograph?

Directions Write *who* or *whom* to complete each sentence correctly.

6. The inventor ____________________ improved the telephone also invented the phonograph.
7. Edison chose associates ____________________ he could trust.
8. The scientist to ____________________ Bill was assigned was a brilliant statistician.
9. ____________________ is responsible for inventing the television?
10. ____________________ was present when the telephone transmitted Edison's faint voice?
11. The neighbor ____________________ lives down the street is an inventor.
12. Edison spoke to Batchelor, with ____________________ he had worked for many years.
13. I work with scientists for ____________________ I have great respect.
14. Edison met a 16-year-old girl named Mary Stilwell ____________________ worked as a clerk.
15. At 23, Edison was a promising scientist ____________________ had a reputation as an electrical inventor.

School + Home **Home Activity** Your child reviewed using *who* and *whom*. Ask your child to say a sentence using *who* and another sentence using *whom* and to tell why these words are correctly used.

Name ________________________________

Story Chart

Directions Fill in the graphic organizer with information about your adventure story.

Title

Characters

Setting

Events
↓
↓
↓

Solution

Name ____________________

Good Beginnings

Directions Below are some different ways to begin a story. Write an opening sentence or sentences using each idea. You can use one of your beginnings in your adventure story.

Ask a Question (*Example:* Have you ever done something that you almost instantly regretted doing? That's how I felt when I accepted this job.)

____

____

____

Use a Sound Word or an Exclamation (*Example:* Watch out! The loose rocks slid out from under my feet, and I almost slipped over the edge.)

____

____

____

Set the Scene (*Example:* It was a bitterly cold December day. My surroundings looked more like an Arctic wasteland than a Midwestern suburb.)

____

____

____

Use Humor (*Example:* I looked ridiculous in the chicken costume. It was so big that the head covered most of my body, and I could barely walk.)

____

____

Use Foreshadowing (*Example:* I thought nothing would keep me from going to Antarctica. I guess I was wrong.)

____

____

Name ______________________________

Using *Who* and *Whom* to Add or Combine

You can use clauses beginning with *who* and *whom* to add specific details to sentences. You can also use these clauses to combine short, related sentences. Remember to use *who* as a subject in a clause and *whom* as a direct object or the object of a preposition.

General	I talked with the man.
Specific	I talked with the man who explored the South Pole.
Choppy	The man has written a book. I traveled with him.
Smooth	The man with whom I traveled has written a book.

Directions Combine each pair of sentences. Make the second sentence into a clause beginning with *who* or *whom* and add it to the first sentence. Write the new sentence.

1. Explorers began sailing around the world in the 1400s. They had a spirit of adventure.

____

____

2. The two women set out to explore the Grand Canyon. They were experienced hikers.

____

____

3. The man has traveled to many islands in the South Pacific. I admire him.

____

____

4. The divers have often viewed the ocean floor. We spoke with them.

____

____

5. The pilot has been around the world many times. She has been flying for 20 years.

____

____

Name ____________________

Editing

Directions Edit these sentences. Look for errors in spelling, grammar, and mechanics. Use proofreading marks to show the corrections.

Proofreading Marks	
Delete (Take out)	⌐
Add	^
Spelling	○
Uppercase letter	≡
Lowercase letter	/

1. Even though swimsuits and deep water was two of her least favrit things, Lila was determined to learn how to snorkel.

2. Snorkeling was suposed to be a wonderful way to view the Great barrier Reef off Australias northeast coast.

3. Leaving Port Douglas the boat traveled 45 miles out into the Pacific ocean and docks at a small platform near the reef.

4. A crew member, whom was also the instructer, gave Lila snorkeling equipment and showed her how to use them.

5. He said, "if water gets into the tube, blow air through your mouth and force the water back out.

6. Breatheing deeply, Lila jumped into the water, bobbed up and down in the waves and then swimmed down toward the reef.

7. It was a amazing sight; the corals were many diffrent sizes, shapes, and colors, and so were the fish!

8. Lila dived again and again until she couldn't hardly move her legs but she was so happy that she didn't care.

Now you'll edit the draft of your adventure story. Then you'll use your revised and edited draft to make a final copy of your story. Finally, you'll share your written work with your audience.

Name____

Plot and Theme

- The **plot,** or story line, includes (1) a **problem** or **goal,** (2) **rising action,** as a character tries to solve the problem or meet the goal, (3) a **climax,** when the character meets the problem or goal head-on, and (4) a **resolution,** or outcome.
- The **theme** is the main idea or central meaning that the author wants you to learn.
- Sometimes a writer hints at an event that will happen later in the story. Such a hint is called **foreshadowing.** Sometimes a writer goes back in time to tell about an earlier event. The earlier event is called a **flashback.**

Directions Read the following passage. Then answer the questions below.

Carrie and Carlos wanted to buy their parents an anniversary present, but they didn't have any money. "How can we get enough money in two weeks?" Carlos moaned. Just then, Carrie remembered something. "You know, our band didn't have any money, and we needed new music. We had a car wash, and we earned enough money," she told Carlos. Carlos liked the idea. So Carrie made signs, and Carlos put them up. On the big day, Carrie and Carlos were ready. The car wash was a big success. Their parents loved their anniversary gift. They loved the car wash coupon, too!

1. What is the problem?

____

2. What is the climax, or turning point?

____

3. What is the resolution?

____

____

4. Underline the sentences that tell about Carrie's flashback.
5. What is a possible theme?

____

____

School + Home

Home Activity Your child read a short passage and identified the plot elements and theme. Work with your child to identify the problem, rising action, climax, and resolution in a short story that you read together. Then decide on a possible theme.

Name ____

Writing for Tests

Prompt: Think about a play or performance you have seen. Write a critical review, describing the performance and telling your opinion of it. Be sure to support your opinion with evidence, such as the effectiveness of key scenes and performers, the script, or the overall concept.

A Miracle of a Show

As I emerged from the theater into the bright daylight, I could not stop thinking about *The Miracle Worker.* Helen Keller never saw the sun, but she became a brilliant woman. The current production of *The Miracle Worker* at the Nettle St. Playhouse beautifully illustrates Helen Keller's early struggles and eventual breakthrough.

The play, written by William Gibson in the 1950s, tells the story of Helen Keller and her teacher, Annie Sullivan. By the time she was one-and-one-half years old, Helen had lost her eyesight and her hearing after suffering from a high fever. Helen's parents hired Annie Sullivan to handle Helen and attempt to teach her.

Actress Maria Walker captures the patience and persistence of Annie Sullivan, Helen's inspirational teacher. Walker convinced me that Miss Sullivan was truly a miracle worker. The young Helen Keller, played by Gabriela Sabatini, was a willful and difficult child, but Miss Sullivan managed to break through to her. Sabatini's temper tantrums show us the frustration that little Helen must have felt. Walker does a fine job as Annie Sullivan, who helped Helen break through the barriers of deafness and blindness and go on to lead a long and productive life.

Walker and Sabatini convey the tug-of-war that resulted in the breakthrough moment that occurs at the water pump. When Helen makes the connection between the water splashing from the pump and the word that Sullivan spells into her hand, Sabatini made me feel Helen's joy. Her face changed from sheer frustration to complete happiness. This is a wonderful production that succeeds in capturing the remarkable relationship of these two legendary women.

1. Why does the author begin the review with the remark about the bright daylight?

____

____

____

2. How does the author convince readers that the actresses do a convincing job?

____

____

____

Name ____

Vocabulary

Directions Choose the word from the box that best matches each definition. Write the word on the line.

Check the Words You Know

___accustomed
___decline
___former
___presence
___unaccompanied

____________________ **1.** process of losing strength or power

____________________ **2.** alone

____________________ **3.** usual, customary, used to

____________________ **4.** condition of being present in a place

____________________ **5.** earlier, past

Directions Choose the word from the box that best completes each sentence. Write the word on the line.

When Stan and Marie retired, Stan's health was in a state of **6.** ____________________.

They decided they needed a calmer life, **7.** ____________________ by the noise and activity of the big city. They also thought that the **8.** ____________________ of their grandchildren would make them happier. So they moved to a small town near where their son's family lived. Although they sometimes missed their **9.** ____________________ home, they quickly grew **10.** ____________________ to their new life. Stan and Marie felt better than they had for years.

Write a Journal Entry

On a separate sheet of paper write a journal entry about visiting your grandparents or some other older adults whom you know. Use words from the vocabulary list.

School + Home

Home Activity Your child identified and used vocabulary words from the story *The View from Saturday.* Read a story or nonfiction article with your child. Have your child point out unfamiliar words. Work together to figure out the meanings of unfamiliar words by using other words that appear near them.

Name ______________________________________

Contractions and Negatives

A **contraction** is a shortened form of two words. An **apostrophe** is used to show one or more letters that have been left out. Some contractions are made by combining pronouns and verbs: *I* + *will* = *I'll*. Other contractions are formed by joining a verb and *not* or *have*: *do* + *not* = *don't*; *should* + *have* = *should've*.

- *Won't* and *can't* are formed in special ways (*can* + *not* = *can't*; *will* + *not* = *won't*).

Negatives are words that mean "no" or "not": *no, not, never, none, nothing*. Contractions with *n't* are negatives too. To make a negative statement, always use only one negative word.

No He doesn't have no money.
Yes He doesn't have any money. *or* He has no money.

- Use positive words instead of negative ones in a sentence with *not*.

Negative	Positive	Negative	Positive
nobody	anybody, somebody	nothing	anything, something
no one	anyone, someone	nowhere	anywhere, somewhere
none	any, all, some	never	ever, always

Directions Write the letter of the two words used to form each contraction.

_____ **1.** couldn't   **A** I am

_____ **2.** would've   **B** would have

_____ **3.** they're   **C** could not

_____ **4.** I'm   **D** they are

Directions Write the contraction for each pair of words.

5. she + will = ______________________

6. did + not = ______________________

7. it + is = ______________________

8. will + not = ______________________

Directions Circle the word in ( ) that correctly completes each sentence.

9. No one has (never, ever) seen such a beautiful bride.

10. We couldn't find (nowhere, anywhere) to put all the gifts.

School + Home **Home Activity** Your child learned about contractions and negatives. Have your child find three contractions and three negatives in the newspaper comics and tell what words are used to form each contraction.

Name ______________________

Suffixes *-ate, -ive, -ship*

Spelling Words				
activate	negative	friendship	objective	representative
attractive	creative	membership	partnership	compassionate
fortunate	considerate	secretive	scholarship	restrictive
affectionate	cooperative	originate	township	relationship

Words in Context Write a list word to finish each statement below.

1. I have a good ___ with my neighbor. 1. ______________
2. I consider myself ___ to have such a good job. 2. ______________
3. Our village is in the western part of our ___. 3. ______________
4. The emergency room nurse was helpful and ___. 4. ______________
5. Many disagreements ___ from misunderstandings. 5. ______________
6. He was very ___ about the gifts he had bought. 6. ______________
7. Maintaining a community garden is a ___ effort. 7. ______________
8. My brother received a ___ to the best college in the state. 8. ______________
9. My new puppy is so ___ that she won't stop licking my face. 9. ______________
10. That artist's sculptures are very ___. 10. ______________

Word Meanings Write a list word that fits each meaning.

11. to make active 11. ______________
12. wishing to help those that suffer 12. ______________
13. the opposite of positive 13. ______________
14. the state of being a partner 14. ______________
15. condition of being friends 15. ______________
16. belonging to a group or organization 16. ______________
17. a purpose or goal 17. ______________
18. restricting; limiting 18. ______________
19. a typical example of a group or class 19. ______________
20. winning attention; pleasing 20. ______________

School + Home **Home Activity** Your child wrote words with suffixes *-ate, -ive,* and *-ship.* Ask your child to pick five list words, spell them, and use them in sentences.

Name ______________________

Scoring Rubric: Critical Review

	4	3	2	1
Focus/Ideas	Clear, focused review with well-supported opinions	Most ideas and opinions in review are clear and well-supported	Many ideas and opinions in review are unclear or unsupported	Review lacking clarity and focus
Organization	Organized logically, no gaps; strong central idea	Organized logically, few gaps; fairly strong central idea	Organization not clear; weak topic sentence	Lacking organization; topic sentence weak
Voice	Engaging; shows writer's opinion	Evident voice connecting with reader	Weak voice; opinion unclear	No identifiable voice
Word Choice	Vivid, precise word choice	Accurate word choice	Limited or repetitive word choice	Poor or limited word choice
Sentences	Varied sentences in logical progression	Not as much variety; mostly logical order	Too many similar sentences	Many sentence fragments and run-ons
Conventions	Excellent control; few or no errors	Good control; few errors	Little control; many errors	Many serious errors

Vocabulary • Antonyms

- An **antonym** is a word that means the opposite of another word.
- Look for clue words such as *unlike, no, but,* and *on the other hand* to identify antonyms.

Directions Read the following passage. Then answer the questions below.

My grandmother prefers lots of excitement, so she is disinclined to spend time alone. Unlike her current quiet life, her former life as a famous singer was thrilling. She still practices singing every day. However, her voice is deteriorating. It is not strong, the way it used to be. She's certainly not fragile, though. Her body may be frail, but her spirit is still robust.

I walked her to a doctor's appointment the other day. I was surprised at how excited everyone at the clinic was about my grandmother's presence. "We have missed your grandmother!" they exclaimed to me. "What a great singer!" Grandmother smiled and squeezed my hand.

1. Find the antonym in the passage for *disinclined.* How does this antonym help to define the word?

2. Find the antonym in the passage for *former.* How does this antonym help to define the word?

3. How does the antonym in the passage for *deteriorating* help to define the word?

4. How does the antonym in the passage for *robust* help to define the word?

5. Write a sentence or sentences using a word from the passage and its antonym.

School + Home **Home Activity** Your child read a short passage and identified and used antonyms to understand new words in a passage. Work with your child to identify unfamiliar words in an article. Ask your child to find antonyms and other context clues in the passage to help with understanding the new words.

Name ____________________

Schedule

- A **schedule** is a kind of table. The **rows** are a series of horizontal boxes, and the **columns** are a series of vertical boxes. These boxes are also called **cells.**
- Schedules show times, dates, and locations for airplanes, trains, buses, activities, and sporting events.

Directions Read the Alaska Cruise schedule for weeklong cruises between Whittier, Alaska, and Vancouver, British Columbia. Then answer the questions below.

DEPARTING	DAY	DATE	SHIP	COST
Whittier	Fri	7/08/11	*Ocean Dream*	$1,249
Vancouver	Fri	7/08/11	*Ocean Cloud*	$1,149
Whittier	Sun	7/10/11	*Ocean Whisper*	$949
Vancouver	Sun	7/10/11	*Ocean Breeze*	$849
Vancouver	Fri	7/15/11	*Ocean Dream*	$1,149
Whittier	Fri	7/15/11	*Ocean Cloud*	$1,249
Vancouver	Sun	7/17/11	*Ocean Whisper*	$849
Whittier	Sun	7/17/11	*Ocean Breeze*	$949

1. What information does this schedule tell about the Alaska cruises during ten days in July?

____

____

2. During this ten-day period, how many cruises depart from Vancouver? On what dates does the *Ocean Breeze* depart?

____

____

3. On which days of the week do cruises depart?

____

4. What is the name of the cruise ship that departs from Vancouver on July 17?

____

5. Which are the two most expensive cruises? What do they have in common?

____

____

Name ______________________________

Directions Use this activity schedule to answer the questions below.

FITNESS CENTER CLASSES							
Time	**Monday**	**Tuesday**	**Wednesday**	**Thursday**	**Friday**	**Saturday**	**Sunday**
6 A.M.	Run Club		Cardio		Cardio		Run Club
7 A.M.	Yoga	Strength	Yoga	Strength	Yoga		Yoga
8 A.M.	Tai Chi			Tai Chi		Yoga	
9 A.M.		Dance	Dance	Dance		Pilates	Yoga
11 A.M.	Cardio		Cardio		Cardio		
1 P.M.		Kickboxing		Kickboxing		Aerobics	Aerobics
3 P.M.	Water	Strength	Strength	Water	Strength		Strength
5 P.M.	Aerobics	Aerobics		Aerobics	Aerobics		Cardio
7 P.M.		Yoga	Cardio	Dance		Cardio	

6. What does this schedule show? How many classes does the fitness center offer each week?

____

____

7. On which days and at what times are aerobics classes offered? kickboxing?

____

____

8. What kinds of classes are offered on Saturday? What is offered at 8 A.M. on Saturday?

____

9. On which day are the most classes offered? at what times?

____

10. Explain how you would use this schedule to find what class is offered at a specific time on a specific day.

____

____

____

School + Home **Home Activity** Your child learned about reading schedules. Look at a train or bus schedule together. Ask your child to figure out departure and arrival times at a specific station or stop.

Name ______________________

Suffixes *-ate, -ive, -ship*

Proofread a Journal Entry Circle six spelling errors in the journal entry below. Write them correctly. Find a sentence in the journal with an incorrect pronoun. Write it correctly on the line.

Double Trouble

This is Cindy. Me live with my older sisters, Mindy and Lindy. They're identical twins. They think alike, have all the same little habits, and never say anything negetive about each other. They are very seecretive and even have their own language.

They like the same subjects at school. They're attractive and amazingly creative. They're both fortenate to get good grades all the time. They both hope to earn a scholership and go to the same collidge someday. There is only one way they are different. Mindy has a membership to a tennis club, while Lindy belongs to a swim club.

1. ______________ 2. ______________

3. ______________ 4. ______________

5. ______________ 6. ______________

7. ____

Spelling Words

- activate
- negative
- friendship
- objective
- representative
- attractive
- creative
- membership
- partnership
- compassionate
- fortunate
- considerate
- secretive
- scholarship
- restrictive
- affectionate
- cooperative
- originate
- township
- relationship

Frequently Misspelled Words

- until
- college

Proofread Words Circle the word that is spelled correctly. Write it on the line.

8.	friendship	freindship	8. ______________
9.	objektive	objective	9. ______________
10.	representetive	representative	10. ______________
11.	attractive	atractive	11. ______________
12.	creative	creatuve	12. ______________
13.	conciderat	considerate	13. ______________
14.	partnership	partnirship	14. ______________
15.	compashonate	compassionate	15. ______________

School + Home **Home Activity** Your child identified misspelled words. Ask your child to select a list word and use it in a sentence.

Contractions and Negatives

Directions Read the passage. Then read each question. Circle the letter of the correct answer.

The Old Oak Tree

(1) ________ ever looked forward to the day when the old oak tree ________ be standing. (2) The mayor announced that the 116-year-old tree was dying. (3) He'd have to remove the tree because nobody wanted it to fall and cause an accident. (4) The library director said he <u>would not</u> recognize the library without that oak and <u>he would</u> miss it. (5) Everybody ever walked by that tree without wanting to climb it. (6) They'd gathered its acorns for their fall crafts projects. (7) Once the tree was gone, we felt ________ lost a good friend.

1 Which pair of words best completes sentence 1?

- **A** No one/wouldn't
- **B** Everyone/couldn't
- **C** Everybody/wasn't
- **D** Nothing/hadn't

2 Which word in sentence 3 is a negative?

- **A** remove
- **B** nobody
- **C** fall
- **D** accident

3 Which pair of contractions could you make from the underlined words in sentence 4?

- **A** couldn't/he'll
- **B** can't/wouldn't
- **C** wouldn't/he'd
- **D** couldn't/wouldn't

4 What change, if any, should be made in sentence 5?

- **A** Change ***Everybody*** to *Nobody*
- **B** Change ***Everybody*** ever to *No one never*
- **C** Change ***Everybody*** to *Anyone*
- **D** Make no change

5 Which contraction best completes sentence 7?

- **A** they'd
- **B** he'd
- **C** we'd
- **D** I'd

School + Home **Home Activity** Your child prepared for taking tests on contractions and negatives. Read aloud three simple sentences from a magazine article one at a time. Ask your child to make each sentence negative.

Name ______________________________________

Fact and Opinion

- **Statements of opinion** are someone's beliefs or way of thinking about something. The statement *Cars are the best way to travel* is a statement of opinion.
- **Statements of fact** can be proved true or false. Statements of opinion cannot be proved, but can be shown to be valid or faulty. **Valid** statements of opinion are supported by facts or experts. **Faulty** statements are not supported by facts.

Directions Read the following passage and complete the diagram.

Everyone knows that Cesar Chavez was a major figure in American history. He was dedicated to an important struggle: the cause of migrant workers. His union drew attention to problems experienced by farm workers. A 1965 strike protested low wages for grape pickers, and a boycott of grapes started soon afterward. Chavez used marches and boycotts to protest unfair working conditions. In addition, he fasted to call attention to injustices. However, Chavez believed a protest should never become violent. At Cesar Chavez's funeral, President Bill Clinton spoke of him as "an authentic hero."

Statement of Opinion	Support	Valid or Faulty?
Everyone knows that Cesar Chavez was a major figure in American history.	1.	2.
However, Chavez believed a protest should never become violent.	3.	4.

5. Is the statement of opinion in the final sentence valid? Why do you think so?

____

____

____

____

School + Home

Home Activity Your child identified valid and faulty statements of opinion in a nonfiction passage. Work with your child to identify the facts and opinions in a magazine article about a social issue. Discuss how well supported the opinions are.

Writing • Letter to the Editor

Key Features of a Letter to the Editor

- is sent to the editor of a newspaper or magazine
- is written in response to a story, event, or issue
- usually aims to persuade others by supporting claims with clear reasons and relevant evidence
- establishes and maintains correct formal letter format

April 9, 2010

To the Editor:

I am writing to you about the dangerous landfill recently proposed by some members of our city council. The proposal is to use vacant land between the river and the railroad tracks on the west side of the city as a landfill site. If the proposal is approved, the consequences will be unpleasant for the surrounding neighborhoods and also harmful to our environment and our wildlife.

Since prevailing winds are westerly, and the proposed site is on the western edge of the city limits, the putrid smell from the landfill will blow across the city constantly. Our city home, of which we are proud, will be a less desirable location for residents and a less desirable destination for visitors. Fewer residents and visitors will translate into trouble for our businesses. Furthermore, because the proposed site is so close to the river, harmful pollutants will easily leach through the ground and into the river. The pollutants will make the water unlivable for fish, ducks, and other wildlife that are appreciated and treasured by residents and visitors alike.

For the reasons outlined above, I urge the city council to vote no on the proposed landfill location and to find a place that is better suited for it.

Sincerely,

Amy Rabideaux

1. List five persuasive adjectives in the letter.

____

____

2. Write two facts used by the author to support her opinion.

____

____

____

____

Vocabulary

Directions Choose the word from the box that best matches each clue. Write the word on the line.

Check the Words You Know
___access
___authority
___lush
___obstacle
___toll
___torment
___wilt

________________________ **1.** very great pain

________________________ **2.** something that prevents or stops progress

________________________ **3.** right to approach, enter, or use

________________________ **4.** to become limp and bend down; wither

________________________ **5.** power to enforce obedience

Directions Choose the word from the box that best completes each sentence. Write the word on the line shown to the left.

________________________ **6.** The fields of southern California are ____ with growing fruits and vegetables.

________________________ **7.** To harvest the crops, farm owners need ____ to a large supply of labor.

________________________ **8.** One ____ for farm owners is the difficulty of finding a large labor supply.

________________________ **9.** After many months, grueling farm labor can take a ____ on the workers.

________________________ **10.** They may not have the ____ to change their working conditions.

Write a Newspaper Article

On a separate sheet of paper, write a newspaper article about a civic event you observed. Be sure to tell why, when, where, and how it occurred. Use as many vocabulary words as you can.

School + Home

Home Activity Your child identified and used vocabulary words from *Harvesting Hope: The Story of Cesar Chavez*. Read a biography with your child. Have him or her point out unfamiliar words. Work together to try to figure out the meaning of each word by using other words that appear near it.

Name ______________________________

Adjectives and Articles

An **adjective** is a word that describes a noun or pronoun. It tells what kind, how many, or which one.

We stood in the crisp air. The girls were eager. (what kind)
Several people came. Four women worked. (how many)
What was that noise? These ideas are good. (which ones)

The words *a, an,* and *the* are special adjectives called **articles**. They appear before nouns and other adjectives. Use *a* before a word that begins with a consonant sound. Use *an* before a word that begins with a vowel sound. Use *the* before words beginning with any letter.

The boy grew up in a home in Arizona. An old friend called me.

A **proper adjective** is formed from a proper noun. Proper adjectives are capitalized.

They raised the Mexican flag.

Directions Underline the adjectives in the sentences once. Underline the articles twice.

1. Those eager supporters talked to leaders of the march.
2. A peaceful march was the goal.
3. Workers were welcomed into an inviting shelter.
4. A black eagle adorned the flag.
5. Tired workers hunched over the grapevines.
6. An irate landowner worried about that vineyard.
7. A ripe grape must be picked or it will rot.
8. Many people gathered at the ranch for friendly barbecues.

Directions Write *a, an,* or *the* to complete each sentence.

9. We planted ________________ interesting garden last year.
10. Maria picked ________________ artichoke from the garden.
11. He knew he was ________________ most stubborn boy in class.
12. Cesar Chavez did not believe he was ________________ strong fighter.
13. To help ________________ migrant workers, people boycotted certain crops.
14. Did you know that ________________ raisin comes from a grape?

School + Home **Home Activity** Your child learned about adjectives and articles. Have your child underline three sentences in the newspaper and then circle the articles and other adjectives in the sentences.

Name ____________________

Words from Many Cultures

Spelling Words				
ivory	cocoa	lilac	gorilla	pretzel
safari	kayak	crocodile	fiesta	dandelion
monsoon	slalom	amateur	boutique	suede
poncho	hammock	bungalow	sequin	burrito

Definitions Write a list word that fits each definition.

1. tortilla rolled around a seasoned filling — 1. ____________
2. seasonal wind that causes heavy rainfall when blowing from the southwest — 2. ____________
3. a small disc of shining metal used to decorate clothing — 3. ____________
4. to ski in a zigzag course — 4. ____________
5. a small one-story house — 5. ____________
6. a person who does things for fun rather than for money — 6. ____________
7. a hanging couch made of canvas or woven cords — 7. ____________
8. a small, fashionable shop — 8. ____________
9. a large piece of cloth with a hole for the head — 9. ____________
10. leather with a velvety surface — 10. ____________

Words in Context Write a list word to finish each sentence below.

11. Did you know you can use ___ leaves in salad? — 11. ____________
12. Tusks of elephants and walruses are made of ___. — 12. ____________
13. Another name for a party is a ___. — 13. ____________
14. Hot ___ hits the spot on a cold winter day. — 14. ____________
15. There are important differences between an alligator and a ___. — 15. ____________
16. A ___ is a type of flower. — 16. ____________
17. I rushed through the rapids without tipping my ___. — 17. ____________
18. The ___ is the largest primate in the zoo. — 18. ____________
19. My uncle brought back some great photos from his ___ in Africa. — 19. ____________
20. Some folks like chips, but I prefer a good ___. — 20. ____________

School + Home **Home Activity** Your child wrote words from many cultures. Ask your child to identify each food item in the list, spell the word, and use it in a sentence.

Name ______________________________

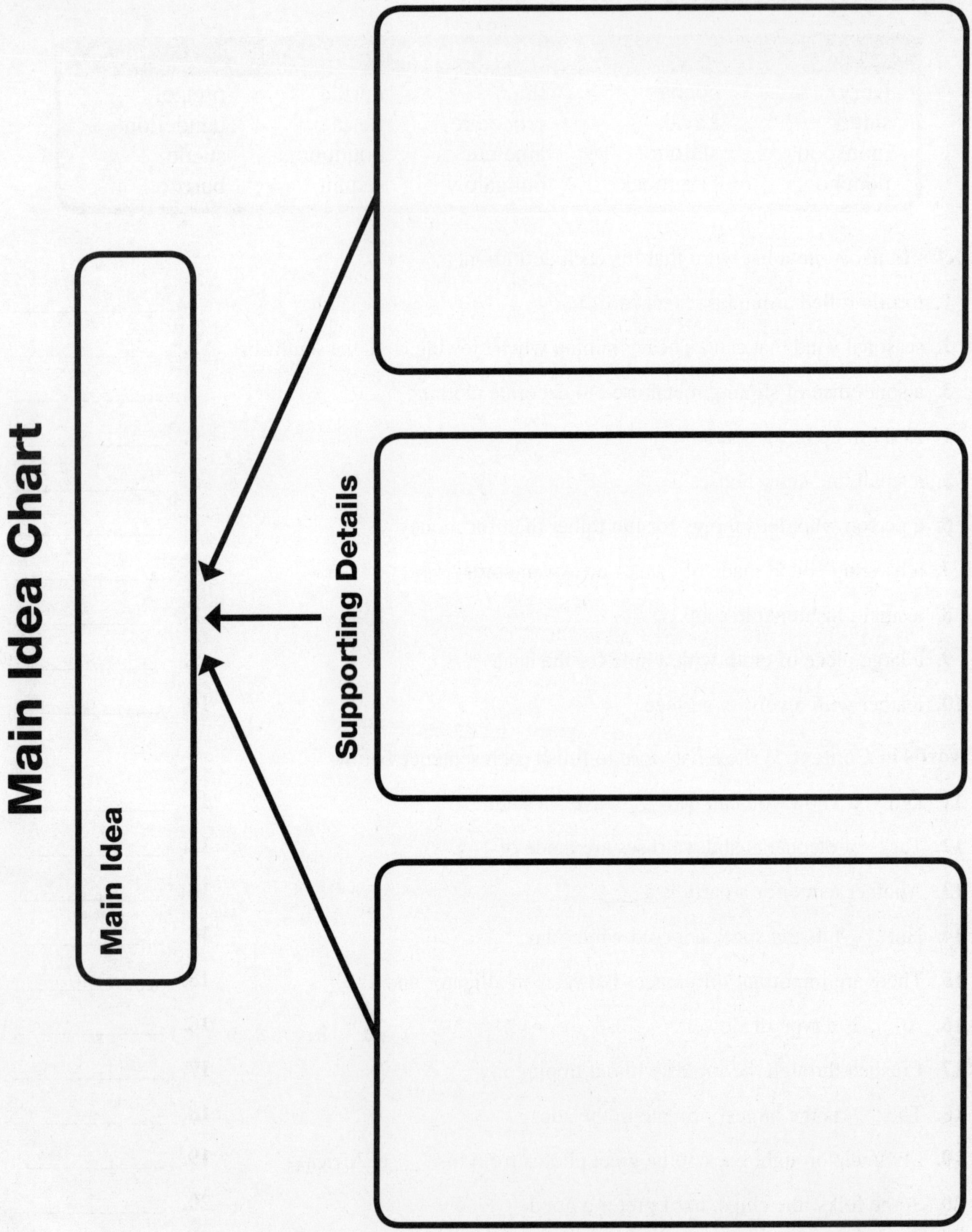

Name ____________________

Vocabulary • Homonyms

- **Homonyms** are words that sound the same but have different meanings.
- When you see a homonym in your reading, use context clues around the word to figure out its meaning. Decide which meaning makes sense in the sentence.

Directions Read the following passage. Then answer the questions below.

The signing of the Declaration of Independance was like the toll of a funeral bell for British control of the American colonies. The United States was founded on principles including the right to free speech and freedom of assembly. The U.S. Constitution guarantees access to these rights. The framers of the Constitution wanted to avoid any obstacle to expressing these rights. As a result, today citizens can take part in protest marches and access articles that are critical of the government. While resulting disagreements can take a toll, there are many advantages to giving authority to the people.

1. *Toll* can mean "to announce by sounding a bell" or "something paid, lost, or suffered." Which meaning of the homonym is used in the first sentence?

____

2. How do context clues help you determine the meaning of the homonym *toll* in the last sentence? What does it mean there?

____

____

3. *Access* can mean "to make information available" or "right to approach, enter, or use." What does it mean in the fifth sentence? What helps you to determine the meaning?

____

4. How does the meaning of *access* help determine the meaning of *obstacle* in the fourth sentence?

____

5. *Authority* can mean "power to enforce obedience," "person who has such power," or "an expert on some subject." What does *authority* mean in the last sentence? How can you use context clues to determine the meaning?

____

____

School + Home

Home Activity Your child identified and used context to understand homonyms and other new words in a passage. Challenge your child to find a homonym in an article. Then ask him or her to use context clues to help with the understanding of the homonym. Confirm the meanings with your child.

Name ______________________________

Newsletter

- A **newsletter** is a short publication containing news of interest to a particular group's members.
- Newsletters include news articles, features, and opinion pieces such as editorials. A news story, which has a headline and sometimes a byline giving the writer's name, tells who, what, when, where, why, and how something happened. Features, which are more informal, are written to inform in an entertaining way. Although news stories are intended to provide only facts, opinions can be expressed by leaving out certain facts.

Directions Use this article from a farmworkers' newsletter to answer the questions.

FARMWORKERS MARCH IN PROTEST

by Ana Ortega

More than 400 people marched through Davis County on March 11 in support of local mushroom farmworkers. Several film actors were among the group.

The march ended with a rally at Arojo Arena, where speakers demanded that local mushroom growers provide increased wages and benefits. "Immigrant workers deserve better treatment," a United Farm Workers spokesman told the crowd. Many workers carried signs or waved flags with the UFW emblem. Workers, who earn 80 cents per basket, are requesting a raise of 5 cents per basket. This would increase their wages to approximately $7.50 per hour.

Mushroom company officials did not comment.

"We need to give the farmworkers our support," said actor Tim Bond, a marcher.

1. Is the article a news story, feature, or editorial? Why?

____

2. How does the article answer these questions: Who? What? When? Where? Why?

____

____

3. What is the headline? the byline?

____

4. What is one fact presented in the article?

____

5. Explain if you think the article has been slanted by leaving out facts.

____

____

Name ______________________________

Directions This is another article from the farmworkers' newsletter about an event of interest to the group's members. Use it to answer the questions below.

JOIN THE CELEBRATION FOR CHAVEZ!

The week of April 21 to 28 has been named Cesar Chavez Week in Oxnard, California, and a special celebration on April 28 will cap off the festivities. Everyone should join in honoring the memory of Chavez, who did so much for the immigrant workers of California.

The day-long event will begin at 9 A.M. with a procession from Central Plaza to Chavez Park. Afterward, a ceremony will include speeches and songs. The mayor will give a memorable talk at 10 A.M., followed by a wonderful speech by a United Farm Workers representative. A Cesar Chavez scholarship will be presented. Dances, contests, songs, and theatrical performances will fill the day with fun.

This will be an event you will never forget. Be sure to attend—and bring your family.

6. What is the headline?

____

7. Is this article a news story, feature, or editorial? How do you know?

____

8. How does the article answer these questions: What? When? Where? Why? How?

____

____

9. What are two opinions given in the article?

____

____

10. Who is the audience for this newsletter? How is that audience reflected in the information this article contains?

____

____

School + Home

Home Activity Your child learned about reading newsletters and the types of articles they contain. With your child, look at a newsletter for an organization. Ask him or her to locate news stories, features, and editorials and point out the facts and opinions they contain.

Name ______________________________

Words from Many Cultures

Proofread a Letter Circle six misspelled words in the letter below. Write them correctly. Find a sentence with a mistake in capitalization. Write it correctly.

Dear Mark,

My family and I just got back from the greatest vacation ever—a real African safarie. there's a lot to tell you. We saw a crocadile, a gorila, and dozens of other wild animals. One night we slept in a small bungalow with no electricity. We each had our own hammuck and listened to the night sounds echoing throgh the jungle. We even took a kiyak trip down a remote river. Wait until you see the pictures!

See you soon,
David

1. ____________ 2. ____________
3. ____________ 4. ____________
5. ____________ 6. ____________
7. ______________________________

Spelling Words

ivory
cocoa
lilac
gorilla
pretzel
safari
kayak
crocodile
fiesta
dandelion
monsoon
slalom
amateur
boutique
suede
poncho
hammock
bungalow
sequin
burrito

Frequently Misspelled Words

through
there's

Proofread Words Circle the word that is spelled correctly. Write it on the line.

8.	ivery	ivory	8. ____________
9.	coco	cocoa	9. ____________
10.	lilac	lilack	10. ____________
11.	suede	seude	11. ____________
12.	pretzel	pretsel	12. ____________
13.	saphari	safari	13. ____________
14.	amiture	amateur	14. ____________
15.	poncho	ponchoe	15. ____________

School + Home

Home Activity Your child identified misspelled words. Ask your child to spell the word *crocodile* and use it in a sentence.

Adjectives and Articles

Directions Read the passage. Then read each question. Circle the letter of the correct answer.

Cesar Chavez

(1) In the 1960s, Cesar Chavez felt that farmworkers needed ________ working conditions and ________ pay. (2) He organized twelve marches to fight for the rights of the migrant workers. (3) He wanted lawmakers to vote for laws that would improve ________ lives of ________ farmworkers. (4) In addition to the marches, he planned ________ boycott of grapes and lettuce. (5) Many bitter and violent fights broke out between the police and the marchers. (6) When workers got contracts for better pay and safer working conditions, Chavez ended the boycotts. (7) Cesar Chavez received the Presidential Medal of Freedom for his untiring efforts.

1 Which adjectives best complete sentence 1?

- **A** poor/disappointing
- **B** better/higher
- **C** solid/surprising
- **D** disorganized/low

2 In sentence 2, the underlined word answers which questions about the workers?

- **A** What kind?
- **B** How many?
- **C** Which one?
- **D** How much?

3 Which article could be used in the two places in sentence 3?

- **A** a
- **B** an
- **C** the
- **D** None of the above

4 Which phrase best completes sentence 4?

- **A** the final
- **B** an angry
- **C** the hungry
- **D** a nationwide

5 In sentence 5, the underlined word answers which question about the workers?

- **A** What kind?
- **B** How many?
- **C** Which one?
- **D** How much?

School + Home **Home Activity** Your child prepared for taking tests on adjectives and articles. Ask your child to explain what articles and adjectives are and to point out examples of each in something he or she has written.

Name________________________________

Cause and Effect

- A **cause** is what makes something happen. An **effect** is something that happens as a result of a cause. Clue words such as *consequently, since, thus, as a result,* and *therefore* point to cause-and-effect relationships.
- When a cause is not directly stated, you must think about why something happened.

Directions Read the following myth from Polynesia. Then complete the diagram below.

Because he couldn't get enough done in a day, Maui the trickster wanted longer days. He set out to make the sun slow down. First, he made a lasso out of coconut fiber. But when he tied it to the sun, it burned. Then, he wove a rope out of his wife's long, sacred hair. At dawn, he tossed his noose and grabbed the sun. The sun pleaded to be released, but Maui wouldn't give in. As a result, the sun started losing more and more strength. Eventually, it couldn't race across the sky but could only crawl. Consequently, Maui gave humans more daylight.

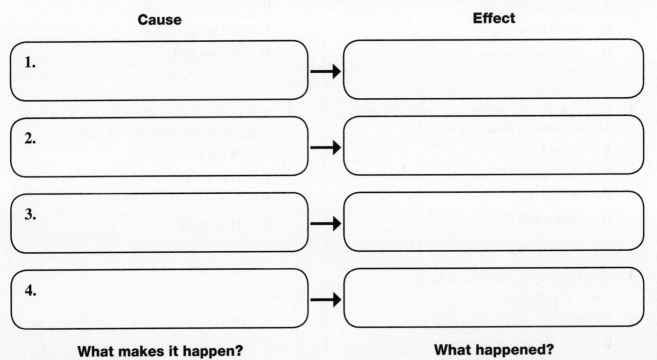

Cause		Effect
1.	→	
2.	→	
3.	→	
4.	→	
What makes it happen?		**What happened?**

5. Create a graphic organizer of your own to show another cause-and-effect relationship in the myth. Also show what you think the effect would have been if Maui had pulled the sun down to Earth.

Home Activity Your child identified cause-and-effect relationships expressed in a myth. Work with your child to identify the cause-and-effect relationships in a story. Challenge your child to consider "what if" questions about the story.

Writing • Tall Tale

Key Features of a Tall Tale

- may be based on real or fictional characters or events
- has larger-than-life characters
- includes exaggerated deeds or events

Slue-foot Sue

You may not have heard about Slue-foot Sue. She was a cowgirl who could ride as good as Pecos Bill, the greatest cowboy who ever lived. And that's where the story begins.

Bill and I were good friends back then, and we often headed down to the river to go fishing. One day we spotted a beautiful woman riding a giant catfish down the Rio Grande. And let me tell you, she was as sharp and quick as Bill in the saddle. There she was standing tall and holding on to that catfish with one hand. With the other hand, she swung her lasso at the clouds. Wow, what a sight! You should have seen the look on Bill's face.

That's when Bill told me he was going to ask her to marry him. And so he did. Slue-foot Sue had one condition. Bill had to prove his love for her by allowing Sue to ride Widowmaker, Bill's horse. Bill agreed, but Widowmaker was not happy. That horse wouldn't behave for anyone but Bill. So once Sue got on Widowmaker, the horse bucked and bucked, throwing Sue right up into the clouds. Sue kept hitting her head on the moon. She bounced and bounced for days because she was too stubborn to get off that horse. Bill finally took out his lasso and reeled her in. He just couldn't watch her bounce like that for one more day. They got married soon after that, and let me tell you that was one crazy wedding.

1. In what ways are the characters larger than life?

____

2. What exaggerated deeds or events take place?

____

3. Identify words and phrases that the writer uses that give this tall tale a lively tone.

____

____

Name____

Vocabulary

Directions Choose the word from the box that best matches each definition. Write the word on the line.

Check the Words You Know
___densest
___eaves
___expanse
___moisture
___ventured

______________________ **1.** slight wetness

______________________ **2.** most closely packed together

______________________ **3.** dared

______________________ **4.** open or unbroken stretch

______________________ **5.** the lower edges of a roof that extend over the side of a building

Directions Choose the word from the box that best matches each clue. Write the word on the line.

______________________ **6.** These protect a house from the rain.

______________________ **7.** This could be a desert or ocean.

______________________ **8.** Explorers and adventurers did this.

______________________ **9.** Dew is an example of this.

______________________ **10.** Compared to other areas of plant growth, a jungle is described as this.

Write a Myth

On a separate sheet of paper, write a myth to explain something in nature, such as how the oceans, jungles, or deserts came to be. Use as many vocabulary words as you can.

School + Home **Home Activity** Your child identified and used vocabulary words from *The River That Went to the Sky.* Read a story or myth with your child. Have him or her point out unfamiliar words. Work together to try to figure out the meaning of each word by using other words that appear near it.

Using *this, that, these,* and *those*

The adjectives *this, that, these,* and *those* are called **demonstrative adjectives**. They point out which one or which ones. *This* and *that* modify singular nouns. *These* and *those* modify plural nouns. *This* and *these* refer to things that are close by. *That* and *those* refer to things farther away.

This river is teeming with fish, but that one over the hill is not.
These animals look like those animals we saw by the road yesterday.

Do not use *here* or *there* after *this, that, these,* or *those*.

No: This here river runs fast. That there river is slow and quiet.
Yes: This river runs fast. That river is slow and quiet.

Do not use *them* in place of *these* or *those*.

No: Them animals are hiding in the trees.
Yes: Those animals are hiding in the trees.

Directions Underline the words in ( ) that complete the sentences correctly.

1. Tall grasses and willowy trees grow beside (these, this) flowing river.
2. (That, These) bushes and hedges guard the foothills of the great mountain.
3. A family of gazelles rests in (that, that there) patch of towering elephant grass.
4. The clouds remembered (this, those) peaceful times when they were a part of Earth.
5. (These, That) dense jungles are filled with huge trees and creeping vines.
6. The sun will take (this here, this) river up to the sky.
7. Will you go with me to (that, these) village near the foot of the great mountain?
8. (These, That) chimpanzees followed (those, that) gorillas into the jungle.
9. (This, These) river and (them, these) animals are part of a great African myth.
10. (Those, This) leopard is not as fast as (those, that) cheetahs.

Home Activity Your child learned about demonstrative adjectives. Ask your child to name the four demonstrative adjectives and use each one in a sentence.

Name ______________________________

Compound Words

Spelling Words				
old-fashioned	daydream	summertime	follow-up	knee-deep
foothills	nevertheless	self-control	themselves	baby-sit
make-believe	sunburn	bloodhound	fine-tune	great-grandmother
roller-skating	folklore	empty-handed	self-esteem	runner-up

Words in Context Write a list word to finish each statement below.

1. I can't go out tonight because I have to ___ my little sister. 1. ____________
2. My little sister likes to dress up and play ___. 2. ____________
3. She and her friends look at ___ in the mirror and laugh and giggle. 3. ____________
4. I stayed out in the sun too long and got a ___. 4. ____________
5. I was standing ___ in snow. 5. ____________
6. It takes a lot of ___ to sit and do homework. 6. ____________
7. We were late to the show, but we enjoyed it ___. 7. ____________
8. My report is almost done, but I still need to ___ it a bit. 8. ____________
9. My uncle lives in a cabin in the ___ of a big mountain range. 9. ____________
10. I found a picture of my ___ on her wedding day. 10. ____________

Word Meanings Write a list word that fits each definition.

11. a large, powerful dog with a good sense of smell 11. ____________
12. moving on shoes with wheels 12. ____________
13. any action designed to be a further effort 13. ____________
14. traditional customs, tales, or sayings 14. ____________
15. the time between spring and autumn 15. ____________
16. bringing or taking nothing of value 16. ____________
17. a pleasant creation of the imagination 17. ____________
18. confidence and satisfaction in oneself 18. ____________
19. characteristic of a past era 19. ____________
20. someone who comes in second 20. ____________

School + Home

Home Activity Your child wrote compound words. Ask your child to pick list words from Exercises 11-20, spell them, and use them in a sentence.

Name ___________________________

Outline

Title ___________________________

A. ___________________________

1. ___________________________
2. ___________________________
3. ___________________________

B. ___________________________

1. ___________________________
2. ___________________________
3. ___________________________

C. ___________________________

1. ___________________________
2. ___________________________
3. ___________________________

Name ________________________________

Vocabulary • Synonyms

- When you are reading and see an unfamiliar word, you can use **context clues,** or words around the unfamiliar word, to figure out its meaning.
- One kind of context clue is a **synonym,** a word that has nearly the same meaning as another word. Setting off a word with commas can indicate synonyms. Clue words like *such as* and *or* also signal synonyms.

Directions Read the following passage about the Sahara and answer the questions below. Look for context clues as you read.

The Sahara, in Africa, is a vast expanse, or stretch, of desert. All of it is very dry, but the Libyan part of the Sahara has the least moisture, such as rain or other water. If you ventured into the desert, you might ride a camel. Or, if you dared to go into the desert, you might look for an oasis. There you would see the densest population of people and animals; similarly, you would see the thickest groves of palms there. If you had a hut in the desert, sand cats and hedgehogs might gather in the shade of its eaves, or roof overhang. Now that you know about the Sahara, would you like to visit?

1. What is a synonym for *expanse*? What clue helps you to determine this?

____

2. What does *moisture* mean? What clues help you to determine the meaning?

____

____

3. How would you use context clues to determine the meaning of *ventured*?

____

____

4. What synonym is used for *densest*? How do you know it's a synonym?

____

5. What is the closest synonym for *eaves* in the context of the passage? What clues indicate a synonym?

____

School + Home **Home Activity** Your child identified and used synonyms as context clues to understand new words in a passage. Work with your child to identify unfamiliar words in an article. Then your child can find context clues to help with the understanding of the new words. Confirm the meanings with your child.

Chart or Table

- A **chart** or **table** usually is a box that contains words or numbers in rows and columns. Columns go down, and rows go across. These also are called cells. Most charts and tables have titles.

Directions Use this chart about Saharan animals to answer the questions below.

Animals of the Sahara

Animal	Type	Length	Food	Survival Features
Addax	Mammal	4 ft	Plants	Wide hooves help walk on sand
Caracal	Mammal	3 ft	Jerboas, birds, squirrels	Nocturnal, jumps well
Desert hedgehog	Mammal	3 ft	Insects, frogs, eggs	Extracts water from prey
Desert monitor	Reptile	5 ft	Fish, frogs, snakes, eggs	Withstands heat, burrows
Fennec fox	Mammal	16–17 in.	Rodents, lizards, insects	Withstands heat, burrows
Golden eagle	Bird	30 in.	Rabbits, rats, reptiles	Has mountain nest
Houbara bustard	Bird	2 ft	Insects, lizards, seeds	Extracts water from prey
Jerboa	Mammal	2–6 in.	Plants, seeds, insects	Recycles breath moisture; jumps
Sand cat	Mammal	15–16 in.	Rodents, birds, reptiles	Burrows, extracts water from prey
Striped hyena	Mammal	3–4 ft	Lizards, birds, mammals	Stays in den, nocturnal

1. What is the longest animal listed in the chart? the shortest?

____

2. What do the Houbara bustard, desert hedgehog, and sand cat have in common?

____

3. Which is bigger, the addax (a type of antelope) or the caracal (a large cat)?

____

4. What is the food of the golden eagle? the striped hyena?

____

____

5. What do the survival features tell you about the ways Saharan animals have adapted to stay alive in the desert?

____

____

____

Name________________________________

Directions Use this table about African lakes to answer the questions below.

Largest African Lakes				
African Lake	**Location**	**Area**	**Length**	**Maximum Depth**
Victoria	Tanzania-Uganda-Kenya	26,828 sq mi	200 mi	270 ft
Tanganyika	Tanzania-Congo-Burundi-Zambia	12,700 sq mi	470 mi	4,708 ft
Chad	Chad-Niger-Nigeria-Cameroon	550 sq mi	—	23 ft
Rudolf	Kenya-Ethiopia	2,473 sq mi	154 mi	240 ft
Albert	Uganda-Congo	2,046 sq mi	100 mi	180 ft
Kioga	Uganda	1,700 sq mi	50 mi	about 30 ft

6. What is the largest lake in Africa?

____

7. What lakes are wholly or partially located in Uganda?

____

____

8. What is the deepest lake in Africa? the longest?

____

9. What are the area, length, and depth of Lake Albert?

____

10. Explain how to find the area of a specific lake on the chart above.

____

____

____

____

____

____

____

School + Home

Home Activity Your child learned about using charts and tables as resources. Find a chart or table in an almanac. Ask your child to explain what it tells. Challenge your child to find specific information in the chart or table.

Compound Words

Proofread a Letter Circle six spelling errors in the letter. Write the words correctly. Find a line with an incorrect verb form. Write it correctly.

Dear Jenny,

My family take a summertime trip to my great-grandmother's house. She lives in the foothills of the Smoky Mountains. The drive was like a day-dream because it was so beautiful. We couldn't arrive emptyhanded so we shopped at an old-fashuned country store. It took selfcontrol not to buy many things.

When we arrived, my great-grandmother was kneedeep in the garden picking vegetables for dinner. That night we sat around the fireplace and talked about the folklor of the region. We had a very good time. Next time we visit I will be able to baby-sit a newborn lamb.

Sam

Spelling Words

old-fashioned
daydream
summertime
follow-up
knee-deep
foothills
nevertheless
self-control
themselves
baby-sit

make-believe
sunburn
bloodhound
fine-tune
great-grandmother
roller-skating
folklore
empty-handed
self-esteem
runner-up

1. ________________ 2. ________________

3. ________________ 4. ________________

5. ________________ 6. ________________

7. ______________________________________

____

Frequently Misspelled Words

themselves
something

Proofread Words Circle the word that is spelled correctly. Write it on the line.

8. make-believe makebelieve 8. ________________

9. sun-burn sunburn 9. ________________

10. blood-hound bloodhound 10. ________________

11. fine-tune finetune 11. ________________

12. great-grandmother greatgrandmother 12. ________________

School + Home

Home Activity Your child identified misspelled words. Read each list word to your child. Have your child tell if the compound word is written as one word or with a hyphen.

Name ___________________________________

Using *This*, *That*, *These*, and *Those*

Directions Read the passage. Then read each question. Circle the letter of the correct answer.

School Bullying

(1) <u>This</u> school has just begun a program to end bullying. (2) This here program will teach students who bully ways to be respectful of other students. (3) It will also help those students who are bullied know what to do in difficult situations. (4) The core of ________ program is a rule that encourages students to report bullying incidents. (5) Sometimes kids are afraid to report these bullying incidents. (6) Victims are worried that reporting will make it worse and that those there bullies will do more harm the next time. (7) ________ rule about reporting incidents also means that witnesses must report ________ incidents to their teachers or principals. (8) Teachers and principals must have a zero-tolerance policy against all bullying.

1 In sentence 1, the underlined word suggests what?

- **A** The author used to go to the school.
- **B** The author is in favor of an anti-bullying program.
- **C** The author is concerned about a school problem.
- **D** The author is part of the school.

2 What change, if any, should be made in sentence 2?

- **A** Change ***This here program*** to **This program**
- **B** Change ***ways to be*** to **way to be**
- **C** Change ***will teach*** to **has taught**
- **D** Make no change

3 Which adjective could be used to complete sentence 4?

- **A** these
- **B** this
- **C** those
- **D** that

4 What change, if any, should be made in sentence 6?

- **A** Change ***those*** to **this**
- **B** Change ***those*** to **these**
- **C** Change ***those there*** to **those**
- **D** Make no change

5 Which pair of. words best completes sentence 7?

- **A** That/this
- **B** This/these
- **C** Those/this
- **D** These/those

School + Home **Home Activity** Your child prepared for taking tests on the adjectives *this, that, these,* and *those.* Give your child singular and plural nouns, and have him or her name the two adjectives that can be correctly used with each noun.

Name________________________________

Main Idea and Details

- The **topic** is what a paragraph is about and can usually be stated in a word or two.
- To find the **main idea** of a paragraph, think about all of the important information the paragraph gives about the topic. The main idea is the most important of these. Sometimes it is stated directly, but sometimes it is not.
- **Details** tell more about the topic. They are less important pieces of information that support the main idea.

Directions Read the following passage. Complete the diagram below by telling the main idea of the paragraph. Then list supporting details that tell more about the main idea.

On January 24, 1848, gold was discovered at Sutter's Mill in California. What followed was a period of great turmoil and confusion. Settlers streamed in by wagon and by ship as the fever to make a fortune took hold. Very quickly, the population of San Francisco jumped from a few hundred to ten thousand.

However, at this time California was not a state and had no effective government. Consequently, there were few restrictions on the behavior of the people flooding the area. At Sutter's Mill, crops were destroyed and buildings were pulled down. Crime was everywhere. The California gold rush had begun!

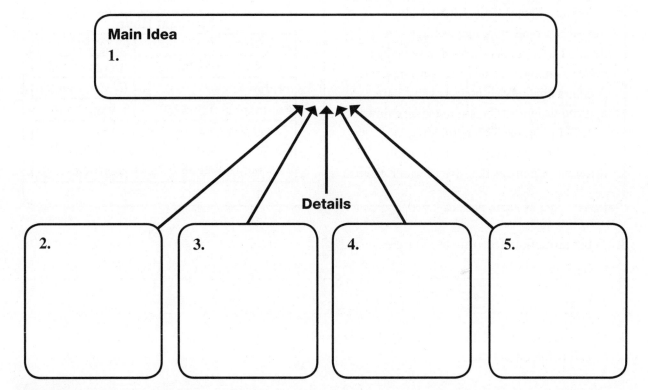

Main Idea

1.

Details

2.

3.

4.

5.

School + Home

Home Activity Your child identified the main idea and supporting details of a nonfiction passage. Work with your child to identify the main idea and supporting details of individual paragraphs in a magazine article about wild animals. Challenge your child to summarize the entire article.

Writing • Brochure

Key Features of a Brochure

- provides information about a specific place or thing
- is often written for special programs, events, exhibits, or tourist attractions
- provides important facts and details about the place or thing
- usually includes related illustrations, photographs, or charts

Water: From Puddles to Pipelines

All forms of life need water. From June 1–August 31, the City Museum invites you to experience "Water: From Puddles to Pipelines."

Water Cycle: Begin your tour with a 3-D video of the water cycle of the oceans. Then participate in an experiment illustrating how temperature affects ocean currents. Using a touch screen, discover how plants take part in the water cycle.

Water Works: This exhibit is about the ways people move and use water. A detailed scale model shows how aqueduct systems channeled water into ancient cities. A contrasting model shows how we have updated water distribution in modern times.

Life in Water: This exhibit begins with a video presentation of the many different organisms that live in water, from microscopic bacteria that multiply in the brown muck of small ponds to enormous blue whales that gracefully patrol the oceans. A large saltwater aquarium features tropical fish that dart in a neon rainbow.

And More! If you're ready to get wet, visitors can make dams, build fountains, or make fog and freezing rain! Are you ready to take the plunge?

Museum Hours	
Monday	CLOSED
Tuesday–Thursday	10 A.M.–5 P.M.
Friday	10 A.M.–6 P.M.
Saturday and Sunday	9 A.M.–7 P.M.
Ticket prices: Students and Seniors, $4.00; Adults, $7.50 Discounts available for large groups.	

1. What attraction does this brochure describe?

____

____

2. Circle the section of the brochure that gives important information about the hours and admission fees for this attraction.

Name ____

Vocabulary

Directions Choose the word from the box that best matches each definition. Write the word on the line.

Check the Words You Know

___characteristic
___corrode
___engulfed
___exploit
___extract
___hoard

____________________ **1.** swallowed up; overwhelmed

____________________ **2.** what is saved and stored away

____________________ **3.** to make use of

____________________ **4.** to wear or eat away gradually

____________________ **5.** to pull out or draw out

Directions Choose the word from the box that best completes each sentence. Write the word on the line.

6. Gold is valuable as a metal because it does not ____________________.

7. Many people are attracted by the ____________________ shininess of gold.

8. A wave of fortune seekers ____________________ the riverbed to search for gold.

9. New methods have been developed to ____________________ gold from the Earth.

10. Some people would enjoy having a ____________________ of gold because of its value.

Write a Business Letter

On a separate sheet of paper, write a letter to a science museum about how to find out more about precious metals. Your business letter should identify specific aspects of the topic that you wish to research further. Use as many vocabulary words as you can.

School + Home

Home Activity Your child identified and used vocabulary words from *Gold*. Together, read a story or nonfiction article. Ask your child to point out unfamiliar words. Work together to figure out the meaning of each word by using other words that appear near it.

Name ______________________________

Comparative and Superlative Adjectives

Comparative adjectives compare two people, places, things, or groups. Add *-er* to most short adjectives to make their comparative forms. Use *more* with longer adjectives. **Superlative adjectives** compare three or more people, places, things, or groups. Add *-est* to most short adjectives to make their superlative forms. Use *most* with longer adjectives.

Adjective	Comparative	Superlative
bright	brighter	brightest
expensive	more expensive	most expensive

Never use *more* or *most* with *-er* and *-est*.

No: more longer, most amazingest

Yes: longer, most amazing

When adding *-er* or *-est* to an adjective that ends in *e*, drop the *e: large, larger, largest*. If the adjective ends in *y*, change the *y* to *i: happy, happier, happiest*. If the adjective ends in a single consonant, double the consonant: *hot, hotter, hottest*.

Some adjectives have irregular comparative and superlative forms: *good, better, best; bad, worse, worst; much, more, most; little, less, least*.

Directions Write the comparative and superlative forms of each adjective.

Adjective	Comparative	Superlative
fine	1. ______________	2. ______________
easy	3. ______________	4. ______________
plentiful	5. ______________	6. ______________
sad	7. ______________	8. ______________
little	9. ______________	10. ______________
positive	11. ______________	12. ______________
brilliant	13. ______________	14. ______________

Directions Circle the correct form of the adjective to complete each sentence.

15. My sister's ring is (shinier, more shinier) than mine.

16. The diamond looked (spectacularer, more spectacular) than the sapphire.

17. John was the (most careful, carefullest) prospector of all the miners.

18. Can she make this gold leaf (more thin, thinner) than it is now?

School + Home **Home Activity** Your child learned about using comparative and superlative adjectives. Have your child scan a magazine article, select five adjectives, and tell the comparative and superlative forms of each adjective.

Name ____________________

Suffixes *-ism, -age, -ure*

Spelling Words

mileage	moisture	heroism	storage	passage
organism	journalism	failure	mixture	postage
luggage	departure	patriotism	optimism	acreage
percentage	enclosure	voltage	temperature	mannerism

Words in Context Write a list word that completes each sentence.

1. Another word for *dampness* is ___. 1. ____________
2. When you are running a fever, your ___ is high. 2. ____________
3. Someone with a lot of land owns a lot of ___. 3. ____________
4. If it's time for you to leave, it's time for your ___. 4. ____________
5. You need ___ to mail a letter. 5. ____________
6. If you have a lot of baggage, you have a lot of ___. 6. ____________
7. If something is not a success, it is a ___. 7. ____________
8. If you are brave, you are displaying ___. 8. ____________
9. If you drive a long distance in your car, you put on a lot of ___. 9. ____________
10. If you combine things, you make a ___. 10. ____________

Word Relationships Match each phrase with a list word. Write the list word.

11. way of acting 11. ____________
12. strength or electrical force 12. ____________
13. act of storing away 13. ____________
14. a way through 14. ____________
15. newspaper or broadcast news 15. ____________
16. positive attitude 16. ____________
17. part of each hundred 17. ____________
18. an enclosed area 18. ____________
19. love of country 19. ____________
20. living thing 20. ____________

School + Home

Home Activity Your child wrote words that ended in *-ism*, *-age*, and *-ure*. Ask your child to pick five words from the list, spell them, and use them in sentences.

Word Web

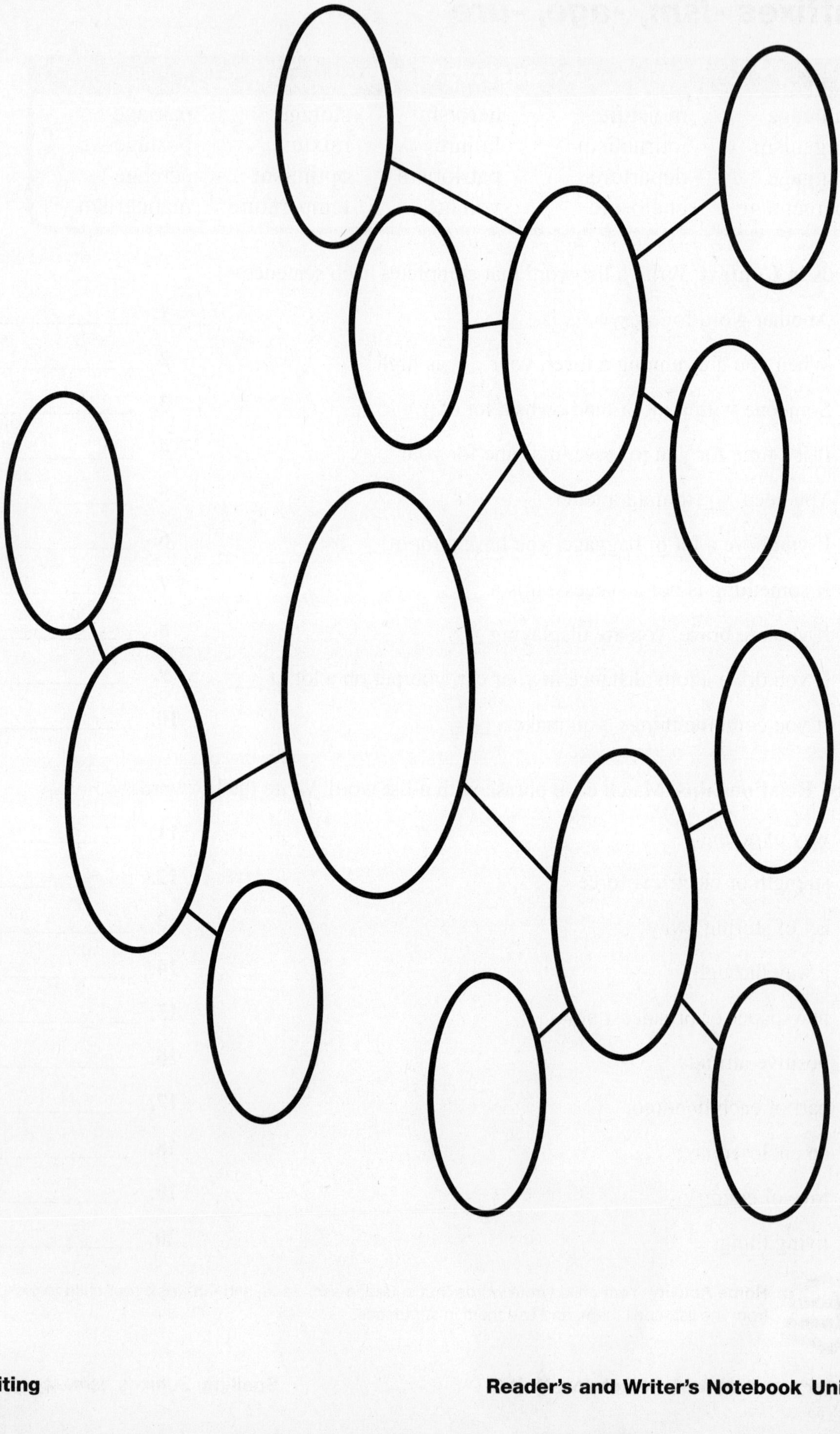

Vocabulary • Unfamiliar Words

- If you see an unfamiliar word as you read, use **context clues** to figure out the meaning of that word. Context clues are the words and sentences around an unfamiliar word.

Directions Read the following passage about gold mining. Then answer the questions below. Look for context clues as you read.

In 1848, thousands of hopeful people engulfed California, swarming into the state from around the world, to pan for gold. Today gold is mined in many countries, but South Africa is the world's largest source of this precious metal. Miners tunnel underground and use hydraulics and other advanced methods to extract, or pull out, gold from the Earth. Human beings exploit this natural treasure of the Earth, making use of it for various purposes. Some miners have been known to say that too much gold can corrode a person's soul, eating away at honesty and integrity. If you discovered gold, would you hoard it or give it away?

1. What does *exploit* mean? What clue helps you to determine the meaning?

2. What clues help you to determine the meaning of *engulfed*? What does this word mean?

3. Which words around the word *extract* give a clue to its meaning?

4. How do context clues help you determine the meaning of *corrode*?

5. What do you think *hydraulics* means? What clues help you decide on this meaning?

Home Activity Your child identified and used context clues to understand new words in a passage. As you read another nonfiction article with your child, have him or her identify unfamiliar words. Then work with your child to find context clues to help clarify the meanings of these words.

Name________________________________

Type Formats

Recognizing **type formats** helps you understand the structure and design of what you read.

- **Bullets** are used to list details or parts of a topic.
- **Boldface** is darker than regular type. It is used to set off titles, headings, and subheadings.
- **Underlining** and ***italics*** (slanted type) may signal important words or ideas.
- **Type size** can be varied to make titles and headings stand out.

Directions Read this article about panning for gold and answer the questions below.

PANNING FOR GOLD

The simplest method of mining gold is *panning.* All that is needed is a circular dish or pan and a water source.

A three-step process. Panning for gold involves these steps:

- Fill a dish with sand or gravel.
- Hold it under a stream of water.
- Rotate the pan at the same time.

The water swirls away the lighter parts of the sand and gravel. If there are gold particles, they will be left near the center of the pan.

Panning for gold today. Even though the Gold Rush was over long ago, prospectors still pan for gold. The western United States is known to hold gold. In addition, travelers can go on gold panning trips to many other countries.

1. What is the topic of this article? How do type formats help you determine the topic?

____

____

2. Within the text of the article, how can you recognize the article's main ideas?

____

3. What does the use of italics indicate in the first paragraph?

____

4. What do the bullets signal in the second paragraph?

____

5. How do type formats help you to understand this article?

____

____

____

Name____

Directions Read this portion of an encyclopedia entry about rocks. Then answer the questions below.

ROCKS. Under a layer of soil, the Earth is made of rock. Rocks tell the story of changes that have happened to the Earth over time. The study of rocks is called *geology*.

Rocks and Minerals. Rocks are made up of minerals. Anything that is not an animal or a vegetable is a mineral. Rocks are solid mineral deposits. Some examples of rocks are gold, silver, salt, and quartz. Nonsolids such as water and gas are considered minerals but not rocks.

Types of Rocks. There are three main groupings of rocks, based on the ways in which they were formed. They are as follows:

- <u>Sedimentary rocks</u>. These rocks were formed by layers of lake, river, or ocean deposits.
- <u>Igneous rocks</u>. These rocks were produced by heating and cooling. Lava is an example of igneous rock.
- <u>Metamorphic rocks</u>. These formerly igneous or sedimentary rocks were produced when heat and pressure changed their form.

Hardness of Rocks. Some rocks are harder than others. In 1822, Frederick Mohs developed a scale to rate the hardness of rocks. Talc has the lowest rating, and diamond has the highest.

6. What is the topic of this entry? How do you know?

____

7. How do type formats signal main ideas in the entry?

____

____

8. For what purpose are italics and underlining used in this article?

____

____

9. What do the bullets signal in the third paragraph?

____

____

10. In what ways do type formats help you to understand this encyclopedia entry?

____

____

School + Home

Home Activity Your child learned how recognizing type formats can help him or her understand the structure and ideas of a text. Together, look at a volume of an encyclopedia. Ask your child to explain the use of different typefaces. Challenge him or her to tell how the typefaces indicate topics, main ideas, details, and important terms.

Name ________________________________

Suffixes *-ism, -age, -ure*

Proofread a Brochure Circle six misspelled words in the brochure. Write the words correctly. Find a sentence with incorrect punctuation. Write it correctly.

What to Do on St. William Island

You will find sandy beaches, spectacular views, water sports, and great shopping. Whare? The island of St. William. St. William Island is a unique mixture of tropical island paradise and historic architecture. The high percentige of historic buildings will take you back in time. You'll marvel at the well-preserved old warehouses, public buildings, military structures, and churches in Port City. There are trolleys on the island that provide pasage to breathtaking views of the harbor and town. You won't need much lugage, because the temprature is always warm. Reserve your departere date today!

1. ____________ 2. ____________
3. ____________ 4. ____________
5. ____________ 6. ____________
7. ________________________________
____

Spelling Words

mileage
moisture
heroism
storage
passage
organism
journalism
failure
mixture
postage
luggage
departure
patriotism
optimism
acreage
percentage
enclosure
voltage
temperature
mannerism

Frequently Misspelled Words

where
off

Proofread Words Circle the word that is spelled correctly. Write it on the line.

8.	patriotism	patriotizm	8. ____________
9.	optimizum	optimism	9. ____________
10.	acrage	acreage	10. ____________
11.	percentage	percenteage	11. ____________
12.	enclosure	enclosere	12. ____________
13.	voltage	voltege	13. ____________
14.	tempureture	temperature	14. ____________
15.	mannerism	mannerizm	15. ____________

School + Home **Home Activity** Your child identified misspelled words with suffixes *-ism*, *-age*, and *-ure*. Ask your child to say and spell all list words that end with *-ism*.

Name ____________________ **Gold**

Comparative and Superlative Adjectives

Directions Read the passage. Then read each question. Circle the letter of the correct answer.

Have You Hugged a Robot Lately?

(1) Robots have become even more incredible in recent years. (2) The newest robots demonstrate that we can get rid of some of the ________ jobs in our daily lives. (3) New domestic robots, for example, have become skillful at sweeping floors or carrying a glass of milk. (4) In industry, robots are doing tasks with ________ accuracy at ________ cost than humans. (5) The smallest robots are some of the most interesting. (6) The Chinese have manufactured one of the cutest robotic boats. (7) It is the size of a postage stamp, yet it is among the strongest boats ever built. (8) From Japan comes a one-meter-tall robot that opens refrigerator doors and lifts heavy boxes with the most astonished look in his eyes. (9) Soon we'll be able to direct a robot to prepare our (enjoyable) meal.

1 Which superlative adjective best completes sentence 2?

- **A** cheapest
- **B** dullest
- **C** most interesting
- **D** most exciting

2 What change, if any, should be made in sentence 3?

- **A** Change ***skillful*** to **more skillful**
- **B** Change ***skillful*** to **least skillful**
- **C** Change ***skillful*** to **skill**
- **D** Make no change

3 Which pair of adjectives best completes sentence 4?

- **A** most major/highest
- **B** exact/minimal
- **C** more/least
- **D** greater/lower

4 Which comparative adjectives could replace the superlative adjectives in sentence 5?

- **A** happier/sadder
- **B** smaller/more interesting
- **C** tallest/fastest
- **D** oldest/funniest

5 Sentence 9 could best be replaced with which sentence?

- **A** Soon we'll be able to direct a robot to prepare our more enjoyable meal.
- **B** Soon we'll be able to direct a robot to prepare our less enjoyable meal.
- **C** Soon we'll be able to direct a robot to prepare our most enjoyable meal.
- **D** Soon we'll be able to direct a robot to prepare our least enjoyable meal.

School + Home **Home Activity** Your child prepared for taking tests on comparative and superlative adjectives. Ask your child to explain when to use the comparative form of an adjective and when to use the superlative form of an adjective.

Name ______________________________

Sequence

- **Sequence** refers to the order of events or the steps in a process.
- Dates, times, and clue words such as *first, finally, meanwhile,* and *then* can help you determine the order of events.
- Sometimes a text will present events out of order. In this case, you can read on, review, or reread the text in order to learn the correct sequence of events.

Directions Read the following passage. Then complete the diagram and answer the question below.

Today, millions of people around the world celebrate Earth Day. But that was not always the case. In 1962, Gaylord Nelson wanted to let people know that the environment was in trouble. He tried to get President Kennedy to make the environment a public issue. Nelson was unsuccessful, but he kept at it for several years. Finally, Earth Day was launched on April 22, 1970. That day, 20 million Americans gathered wherever they could in support of a healthy environment. In 1990, about 200 million people in 141 countries celebrated Earth Day and supported efforts such as recycling. Ten years later, in 2000, people in 184 countries showed their concern about planet Earth. Nelson died in 2005, but Earth Day lives on throughout the world.

First Event	Second Event	Third Event	Fourth Event
1.	2.	3.	4.

5. How were you able to determine the order of events in this passage?

____

____

School + Home **Home Activity** Your child read a short passage and identified the sequence of events. Work with your child to write down the events from a historical passage on note cards. Scramble the note cards, and then have your child put them in the correct order.

Name ______________________________

Writing • Cause-and-Effect Essay

Key Features of a Cause-and-Effect Essay

- includes a central idea in the topic sentence
- gives reasons and explanations for an event or situation
- identifies causes and effects
- often includes clue words such as *because, since, so that, therefore,* and *reason*

Litter: Uglier Than You Realize

Litter can ruin the landscape, but it also has effects that last much longer. Even small items such as cigarette butts and plastic bags have a huge impact on the environment.

Cigarettes contain poisonous chemicals such as arsenic and lead. When a cigarette butt is carelessly tossed aside as litter, it begins to break down and release those chemicals into the ground and water.

Once the chemicals from cigarette butts pollute a body of water, they can cause the plants and animals living there to sicken or die. Some animals eat discarded cigarette butts, which can become stuck in their digestive systems or deliver toxic amounts of chemicals.

Like cigarette butts, the plastic bags you get at the grocery store cause great harm to the environment. Since most people in the United States do not reuse plastic bags, close to 100 billion plastic bags end up on roadsides and in landfills and waterways each year. Plastic bags often land in bodies of water, where they are a danger to birds and marine animals. Many thousands of these creatures die each year because they eat the bags or become tangled in them.

People searching for ways to protect the environment are considering the effects of litter more seriously. We can all do our part by recycling and disposing of trash properly.

1. What is the topic sentence of this essay?

____

2. List the two causes described in this essay. Then underline details that describe the effects.

____

3. What clue words do you see in this essay?

____

Vocabulary

Directions Choose the word from the box that best matches each definition. Write the word on the line.

Check the Words You Know

- ___consequences
- ___emissions
- ___ferocious
- ___forecasters
- ___incubator
- ___sustainable
- ___turbines

____________________ **1.** people who make predictions

____________________ **2.** smoke or gases sent into the air

____________________ **3.** extremely fierce

____________________ **4.** able to support itself

____________________ **5.** the results of actions

Directions Choose the word from the box that best completes each sentence. Write the word on the line.

____________________ **6.** Engineers are looking at using wind _____ to generate electricity.

____________________ **7.** A house that uses solar panels to heat water is partly _____ .

____________________ **8.** The lab was used like an _____ to "hatch" scientists' ideas.

____________________ **9.** During the storm, a _____ wind tore the roof off the supermarket.

____________________ **10.** Weather _____ predict severe thunderstorms for the weekend.

Write a Story

On a separate sheet of paper, write a story about a character who survives a very severe storm. Use as many vocabulary words as you can.

School + Home **Home Activity** Your child identified and used vocabulary words from *Greensburg Goes Green.* With your child, read a story or article about a weather-related event. Have your child point out any vocabulary words he or she sees in the story.

Name ______________________________

Adverbs

An **adverb** tells *how, when,* or *where* something happens. An adverb may appear before or after the verb it modifies or between the parts of a verb phrase.

He sleepily watched the stars. (how)
She will soon go on a journey. (when)
The luggage was piled everywhere. (where)

Adverbs such as *too, very, quite, really, so, nearly,* and *almost* can modify adjectives as well as other adverbs.

I was too early. We left very quickly.

Comparative adverbs compare two actions. Add *-er* to many adverbs to make them comparative. **Superlative adverbs** compare three or more actions. Add *-est* to many adverbs to make them superlative. If an adverb ends in *-ly*, use *more* or *most* instead of *-er* or *-est.*

soon	sooner	soonest
carefully	more carefully	most carefully

Some adverbs do not follow the rules for comparative and superlative forms: *well, better, best; badly, worse, worst; much, more, most.*

Directions Underline the adverb or adverbs in each sentence.

1. The sun was shining very brightly in Greensburg on May 4, 2007.
2. Farmers working outside discussed the coming storm.
3. Parents decided now to change after-school plans.
4. The downtown quickly became almost empty.
5. Tornado sirens sounded much longer than usual.
6. They stopped suddenly, when the power station was hit.
7. Eventually, the new media center will be built there.
8. Greensburg is steadily rebuilding itself "green."

Directions Circle the word in ( ) that completes the sentence correctly.

9. Tornados happen (most often, oftenest) in Tornado Alley.
10. Town leaders searched (most seriously, most serious) for new ideas.
11. The Greensburg plan is the (better, best) of all possibilities.
12. Town residents (more proudly, proudly) show visitors around.

School + Home **Home Activity** Your child learned about adverbs. Give your child three verbs, such as *run, play,* and *swim,* and have your child make up a sentence using each verb and adding an adverb to modify the verb.

Prefixes *bi-, tri-, uni-, re-, semi-*

Spelling Words

bisect	triangle	universal	semicircle	biceps
bilingual	tricycle	university	semifinal	uniform
bifocals	reunion	unison	semicolon	unicorn
semiprivate	triplicate	semisweet	semiannual	biplane

Word Meanings Write a list word that matches each description.

1. an airplane with two wings on each side — 1. ______________
2. a legendary creature with one horn — 2. ______________
3. a pedaled vehicle with three wheels — 3. ______________
4. a geometric figure with three angles — 4. ______________
5. a large college — 5. ______________
6. one of what a member of a special group wears — 6. ______________
7. half of a circle — 7. ______________
8. not entirely private — 8. ______________
9. lenses with two different focal lengths — 9. ______________

Matching Statements Match a list word with a statement. Write the list word on the line.

10. Grammar Teacher: "Use a ___ to show a separation that is not as complete as a period but more so than a comma." — 10. ______________
11. Math Teacher: "When you draw a line through the midpoint of another line, you ___ it." — 11. ______________
12. Choir Director: "It's almost time for our ___ concert." — 12. ______________
13. Cooking Instructor: "Now add a packet of ___ chocolate." — 13. ______________
14. Party Organizer: "I'm putting together our class ___." — 14. ______________
15. Football Coach: "It's important that we win this ___ game." — 15. ______________
16. Language Teacher: "When you finish my class you will be ___." — 16. ______________
17. Office Worker: "I must fill out these forms in ___." — 17. ______________
18. Fitness Instructor: "Today we will work on our ___." — 18. ______________
19. Science Teacher: "The rules of motion are ___." — 19. ______________
20. Cheerleading Coach: "You must make these moves in ___." — 20. ______________

School + Home **Home Activity** Your child wrote words with prefixes *bi-*, *tri-*, *uni-*, *re-*, and *semi-*. Ask your child to pick a list word and use it in a sentence.

Name ______________________________

Cause-and-Effect Chart

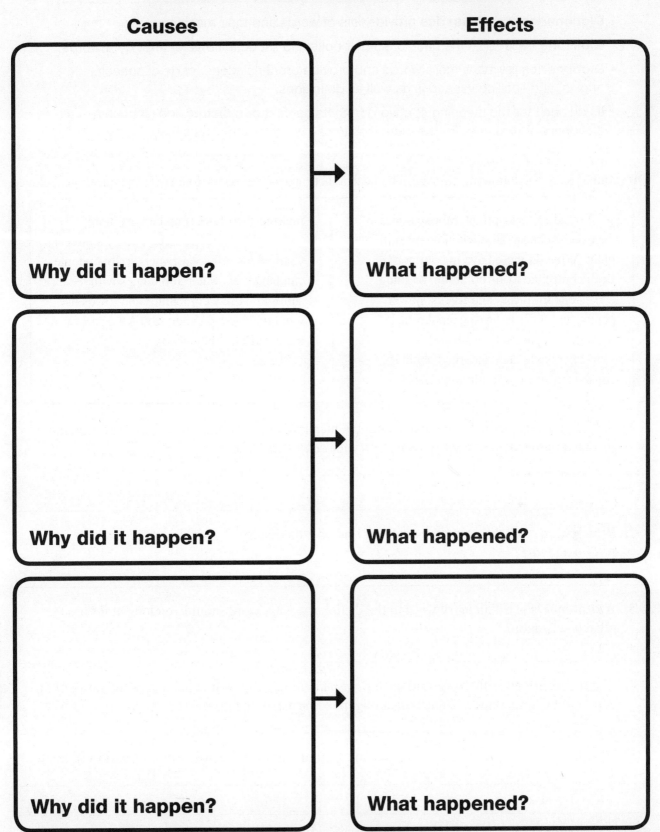

Causes		Effects
Why did it happen?	→	What happened?
Why did it happen?	→	What happened?
Why did it happen?	→	What happened?

Vocabulary • Unknown Words

- **Dictionaries** and **glossaries** provide lists of words and their meanings.
- **Glossaries** appear at the back of some books and list definitions for important words.
- **Dictionaries** list many more words and provide pronunciations, parts of speech, origins, and spelling variations as well as definitions.
- If you can't tell the meaning of a word from its context or structure, look it up in a dictionary or glossary. Try the meanings to see which one makes sense.

Directions Read the following passage. Then use a dictionary or glossary to answer the questions below.

Cars idle at a stoplight. Smoke pours out of the smokestack of a power plant. What do these have in common? Both contribute to air pollution, or smog. Emissions from cars and trucks, power plants, and other industrial smokestacks make the air unhealthy to breathe.

Many people are concerned about the consequences of air pollution. They are making their homes and towns more sustainable by using clean energy sources. Companies sell solar panels so that people can heat their water and homes with sunlight. A few companies and towns use wind turbines to generate at least part of the electricity they need.

1. Which context clues help you understand the meaning of *emissions*? What other information is included in the dictionary or glossary entry for *emissions*?

____

____

2. Which word from the passage would you find on a dictionary page with the guide words *turban* and *turf*?

____

3. If *sustainable* is not an entry word in the dictionary, what word should you look at for a related definition?

____

4. The dictionary gives these definitions for *consequences*: "things that happen as the result of an action" and "importance." Which meaning makes sense in the passage?

____

5. Which word comes from a word that means "spinning top" or "whirlwind"? How do you know?

____

____

School + Home **Home Activity** Your child read a short passage and used a dictionary or glossary to understand unfamiliar words. Work with your child to identify unfamiliar words in an article. Ask your child if he or she can understand the words using context clues. If not, then look up the meanings in a glossary or dictionary.

Name____

Encyclopedia

- **Encyclopedias** give general information about many subjects.
- An **entry** is an article. An **entry word** begins each entry by telling the subject. A **key word** will help you locate information in an encyclopedia.
- **Cross-references** help you find more information about the topic. **Visuals** help explain information too.
- **Electronic encyclopedias** may be quicker to use than printed volumes and may also contain more images and even sound.

Directions Read these entries about wind power from two different encyclopedias.

Entry from a print encyclopedia:

WIND POWER Wind power is a clean source of energy that occurs when humans use the wind to generate electricity.

Wind. Wind is the motion of air caused by the uneven heating of Earth's surface by the sun. Land heats up and cools off more quickly than water. The lighter warm air rises up, and the cooler, heavier air moves in to take its place.

Uses of Wind Energy. Over time, humans learned to capture the energy from the wind. Ancient Egyptians used wind to sail their boats on the Nile. Later, people built windmills to grind their grains. The first windmills were built in Persia (Iran). Eventually, the Dutch improved the design and are still well-known for their windmills. As late as the 1920s, windmills provided electricity to rural areas of the United States.

Wind Power Plants. A wind power plant, or wind farm, is created when multiple turbines are placed together in order to produce electricity. More than half the states in the United States produce some energy from wind power. The states that produce the most energy from wind are Texas, Oklahoma, Iowa, Minnesota, and California. Less than 1% of the energy used in the United States comes from wind power.

See also *alternative energy sources, turbines, windmills.*

Entry from an electronic encyclopedia:

Wind Power

Wind power is a clean, alternative energy source that can be used to produce electricity.

Humans have used wind energy for thousands of years. Usage progressed from sailing boats in ancient Egypt to grinding wheat and grains in Persia (Iran) to producing electricity (US).

Wind power plants, also called wind farms, are groups of many turbines placed together to generate electricity. They are usually found in wide-open spaces with a wind speed of at least 14 mph.

At least half the states in the United States produce some energy from wind power. However, only 0.4% of the energy used in the United States comes from wind power.

There are problems to solve before wind power can be a major source of electricity. Too much wind can damage the turbines. Too little wind does not provide enough power. Some people believe that tall wind turbines are dangerous for birds, which could fly into the blades. Finally, it is expensive to develop and build new technologies.

Name ______________________________

Directions Use the encyclopedia entries to answer the following questions.

1. The twenty-six volumes of a printed encyclopedia are organized alphabetically. What letter would be on the volume of the printed encyclopedia for this entry? Why?

____

2. Would the entry for Wind Power appear before or after the entry for Wind Energy? Explain.

____

3. You find entries in an electronic encyclopedia by searching for key words. Other than *wind power,* what key words might you use to locate this entry?

____

4. What illustrations or graphics do you think you would find in both entries?

____

____

5. Would an encyclopedia be a good reference for finding information on specific wind farms? Why or why not?

____

6. What cross-ıeferences are included in the print version? How can you tell?

____

7. What cross-references does the onlineion contain? How can you tell?

____

____

8. What do you learn from these entries about wind power plants?

____

____

9. In what way do the facts differ in the two articles?

____

____

10. Compare and contrast the format and organization of the two versions.

____

____

School + Home **Home Activity** Your child learned about using encyclopedias as resources. With your child, look at both a printed volume of an encyclopedia and an online encyclopedia. Ask your child to locate several entries using key words that you suggest.

Name ______________________________

Prefixes *bi-, tri-, uni-, re-, semi-*

Proofread an Article Circle five misspelled words. Write them correctly. Find a sentence with incorrect capitalization. Write it correctly on the line.

> My class met to talk about our semifinal exams. We are preparing to go to a University in the fall. We sat in a semycircle so we could talk to each other. Our teacher remembered his bifocels so he could read the agenda. We made a unaversal decision to study together one night each week until the end of the semester. We agreed to have a semianual reunyon during our college years. In unison we wished each other luck.

1. ______________ 2. ______________

3. ______________ 4. ______________

5. ______________

6. ____

Proofread Words Circle the word that is spelled correctly. Write it on the line.

7.	bisect	bisekt	**7.** ______________
8.	biseps	biceps	**8.** ______________
9.	bilingual	billingul	**9.** ______________
10.	tricycle	trisycle	**10.** ______________
11.	triangul	triangle	**11.** ______________
12.	semicolon	semecolon	**12.** ______________
13.	unison	uneson	**13.** ______________
14.	triplecate	triplicate	**14.** ______________
15.	univecity	university	**15.** ______________
16.	unicorn	unicorne	**16.** ______________
17.	uneform	uniform	**17.** ______________
18.	univecity	university	**18.** ______________

Spelling Words

bisect
triangle
universal
semicircle
biceps
bilingual
tricycle
university
semifinal
uniform

bifocals
reunion
unison
semicolon
unicorn
semiprivate
triplicate
semisweet
semiannual
biplane

Frequently Misspelled Words

doesn't
which

Home Activity Your child identified misspelled words with prefixes *bi-*, *tri-*, *uni-*, *re-*, and *semi-*. Have your child pick five list words and spell them.

Name ____

Adverbs

Directions Read the passage. Then read each question. Circle the letter of the correct answer.

Pocahontas Legends

(1) Not many historians wrote <u>accurately</u> about early events in the Jamestown, Virginia, colony. (2) Their stories are mainly myths. (3) They <u>fondly</u> include stories of the beautiful native princess, Pocahontas. (4) Captain John Smith was first ________ welcomed by Chief Powhatan, her father. (5) Then the natives captured and violently beat Smith. (6) They planned to kill him. (7) Legends say that Pocahontas hurriedly raced in to save the captain. (8) Chief Powhatan warmly adopted Smith, and for a while he treated him as a friend. (9) The colonists and the Natives <u>most happily</u> shared good relations during the next year. (10) A year later, Smith was badly injured by gunshot and had to return to England. (11) When Pocahontas <u>later</u> went to visit, the colonists told her that he had died.

1 Which question is answered by the underlined adverb in sentence 1?

- **A** How?
- **B** When?
- **C** Where?
- **D** None of the above

2 The underlined word in sentence 3 tells about which word?

- **A** stories
- **B** beautiful
- **C** princess
- **D** include

3 Which adverb best completes sentence 4?

- **A** most gracious
- **B** more gracious
- **C** graciously
- **D** greedily

4 Which best describes the underlined adverb in sentence 9?

- **A** Comparative adverb
- **B** Superlative adverb
- **C** Incorrect adverb
- **D** Not an adverb

5 Which question is answered by the underlined adverb in sentence 11?

- **A** How?
- **B** When?
- **C** Where?
- **D** None of the above

School + Home

Home Activity Your child prepared for taking tests on adverbs. Ask your child to find three adverbs in an ad or catalog and write the comparative and superlative forms for each adverb.

Name ____

Suffixes *-ate, -ive, -ship*

Spelling Words				
activate	negative	friendship	objective	representative
attractive	creative	membership	partnership	compassionate
fortunate	considerate	secretive	scholarship	restrictive
affectionate	cooperative	originate	township	relationship

Complete the Words Fill in the blanks to complete the list words. Write the words.

1. r ___ ___ t r ___ ___ t ___ v e 1. ____________________
2. ___ ___ ___ e c t ___ ___ ___ a t e 2. ____________________
3. ___ r h r ___ h i 3. ____________________
4. s ___ ___ o l ___ ___ s ___ ___ ___ 4. ____________________
5. n e ___ ___ t ___ v ___ 5. ____________________
6. ___ ___ l a t ___ ___ ___ s h ___ ___ 6. ____________________
7. c o ___ ___ a s ___ i ___ n ___ t ___ 7. ____________________
8. o ___ j ___ ___ t i ___ e 8. ____________________
9. ___ ___ r t n ___ ___ ___ h i p 9. ____________________
10. ___ o w ___ s ___ ___ ___ 10. ____________________

Synonyms Write the list word that means the same or nearly the same.

11. companionship 11. ____________________
12. start up 12. ____________________
13. lucky 13. ____________________
14. collaborative 14. ____________________
15. typical 15. ____________________
16. appealing 16. ____________________
17. begin 17. ____________________
18. private 18. ____________________
19. imaginative 19. ____________________
20. thoughtful 20. ____________________

School + Home **Home Activity** Your child has learned to spell words with suffixes *-ate, -ive,* and *-ship.* Ask your child to say and spell all list words that end with *-ive.*

Contractions and Negatives

Directions Write the contractions for the underlined words in the sentences.

1. They will come over after the wedding. ______________
2. You may have had enough cake, but I have not. ______________
3. I would really like the cake to be chocolate. ______________
4. You have been busy making plans for the wedding. ______________
5. The groom says he is not nervous. ______________
6. I did not want to be the ring bearer. ______________
7. She is wearing the wedding dress her mother wore. ______________
8. We are flying to Florida in the morning. ______________
9. I do not want to leave my grandparents' house. ______________
10. They will not put a centerpiece on the table. ______________

Directions Circle the word in ( ) that correctly completes each sentence.

11. They won't (never, ever) forget this day.
12. We didn't see (no, any) presents.
13. She won't go (anywhere, nowhere) until the party is over.
14. Didn't (anybody, nobody) catch the bouquet?
15. He wouldn't let (no one, anyone) near the cake.
16. Nobody knows (anything, nothing) about the broken chair.
17. We can't go (nowhere, anywhere) after the party.
18. Dad couldn't eat (any, none) of the food.
19. He never said (nothing, anything) about the music.
20. My parents don't (never, ever) dance at weddings.

School + Home **Home Activity** Your child reviewed contractions and negatives. Have your child read aloud a page from a familiar story and change contractions into the words they are made of as he or she reads.

Name ____________________

Words from Many Cultures

Spelling Words				
ivory	cocoa	lilac	gorilla	pretzel
safari	kayak	crocodile	fiesta	dandelion
monsoon	slalom	amateur	boutique	suede
poncho	hammock	bungalow	sequin	burrito

Word Search Find and circle ten list words in the word search. Words are down, across, up, and diagonal. Write the words on the lines.

S	H	A	L	I	T	O	U	R	S
A	A	U	P	R	E	T	Z	E	L
F	M	F	I	E	S	T	A	E	A
E	M	O	A	Z	E	L	C	P	L
R	O	T	P	R	C	A	Y	O	O
C	C	I	R	H	I	R	I	N	M
O	K	R	E	U	O	A	V	C	O
C	E	R	T	V	A	C	O	H	N
O	Z	U	I	H	A	M	M	O	K
A	E	B	U	N	G	A	L	O	W

1. ____________
2. ____________
3. ____________
4. ____________
5. ____________
6. ____________
7. ____________
8. ____________
9. ____________
10. ____________

Classifying Write the list word that belongs in each group.

11. canoe, paddle boat, ship, _____ 11. ____________

12. tsunami, hurricane, water spout, _____ 12. ____________

13. leather, denim, corduroy, _____ 13. ____________

14. tulip, daisy, lily, _____ 14. ____________

15. alligator, lizard, reptile, _____ 15. ____________

16. store, mall, shop, _____ 16. ____________

17. glitter, spangles, lace, _____ 17. ____________

18. weed, grass, plant, _____ 18. ____________

19. monkey, ape, orangutan, _____ 19. ____________

20. beginner, novice, newcomer, _____ 20. ____________

School + Home **Home Activity** Your child has learned to spell words from other cultures. Say a list word and have your child define and spell it.

Adjectives and Articles

Directions Underline the adjectives in the sentences once. Underline the articles twice.

1. Religious leaders offered help to the protestors.
2. As an American citizen, I have certain rights.
3. It was an honor to hear the eloquent speakers.
4. That stunning victory surprised everyone.
5. A crowd celebrated under starry skies.

Directions Write *a, an,* or *the* to complete each sentence.

6. Cesar Chavez suffered from ______________ aching leg and ______________ fever after the march.
7. ______________ final contract offered higher wages and better conditions.
8. Cesar Chavez drove to Beverly Hills to meet with ______________ landowners.
9. People sang ______________ victory song at the celebration.

Directions Add a vivid adjective to describe each underlined noun.

10. ______________ supporters celebrated Cesar Chavez's thirty-eighth birthday.
11. Ten thousand ______________ people arrived in Sacramento.
12. Cesar Chavez fought for the first signed contract for farmworkers in ______________ history.
13. Speakers addressed the ______________ crowd in Spanish.
14. ______________ determination paid off for Cesar Chavez and his followers.
15. Farmworkers trusted Cesar Chavez because he was ______________.

School + Home **Home Activity** Your child reviewed adjectives and articles. Have your child find three sentences with adjectives in a magazine article. Ask him or her to replace the adjectives with different adjectives.

Name ____________________

Compound Words

Spelling Words

old-fashioned	daydream	summertime	follow-up	knee-deep
foothills	nevertheless	self-control	themselves	baby-sit
make-believe	sunburn	bloodhound	fine-tune	great-grandmother
roller-skating	folklore	empty-handed	self-esteem	runner-up

Make Compound Words Match words on the left with words on the right to form compound words. Remember to add a hyphen if necessary.

1. make	skating	1.	____________
2. folk	grandmother	2.	____________
3. blood	selves	3.	____________
4. great	believe	4.	____________
5. knee	lore	5.	____________
6. self	burn	6.	____________
7. roller	hound	7.	____________
8. them	fashioned	8.	____________
9. sun	control	9.	____________
10. old	deep	10.	____________

Word Scramble Unscramble each word below to form a list word. Write the word. Remember to add a hyphen if necessary.

11. einnutef	11.	____________
12. meyddraa	12.	____________
13. dempnhdatye	13.	____________
14. tbasiyb	14.	____________
15. ohfolslti	15.	____________
16. tseelefsme	16.	____________
17. etssvenrleeh	17.	____________
18. msreteiumm	18.	____________
19. nruueprn	19.	____________
20. wpouolfl	20.	____________

School + Home

Home Activity Your child has learned to spell compound words. Ask your child to give an example of a one-word compound word and a compound word with a hyphen, spell each one, and use each one in a sentence.

Using *this, that, these,* and *those*

Directions Underline the words in ( ) that complete the sentences correctly.

1. The River yearned to leave (that, this) Earth and travel to the skies.
2. Do you want to pick some of (those, them) flowers in the meadow?
3. (Those, This) land is rich and fertile, but (those, that) land is dry.
4. You should wear (this, these) sunglasses to protect your eyes.
5. (That, Those) leopards are beautiful but dangerous.
6. Did you see (that there, that) cheetah running through the grasses?
7. Take (this, these) photo of the Sahara to show your teacher.
8. All of (these, this) African rivers have interesting names.
9. (This, Those) particles of water formed fluffy white clouds.
10. (These, That) large gorilla is the strongest of his family group.
11. I enjoyed reading (this, this here) myth about the River and the Sky.
12. I swam in some of (that, these) small lakes.

Directions Write the sentences correctly.

13. This here book explains the formation of the Sahara.

____

____

14. Mrs. Palmer read us stories about them African cultures.

____

____

15. That there herd of antelope has traveled far to reach water.

____

____

School + Home **Home Activity** Your child reviewed demonstrative adjectives. Have your child find sentences with demonstrative adjectives in a favorite book and tell whether each sentence tells about something nearby or far away.

Name ____________________

Suffixes *-ism, -age, -ure*

Spelling Words				
mileage	moisture	heroism	storage	passage
organism	journalism	failure	mixture	postage
luggage	departure	patriotism	optimism	acreage
percentage	enclosure	voltage	temperature	mannerism

Alphabetical Order Write the list word that fits in alphabetical order between the two words.

1. mango	**1.** ____________	manor
2. might	**2.** ____________	mind
3. irritate	**3.** ____________	key
4. patch	**4.** ____________	pattern
5. page	**5.** ____________	past
6. elephant	**6.** ____________	face
7. absent	**7.** ____________	article
8. routine	**8.** ____________	straight
9. popular	**9.** ____________	pound
10. patient	**10.** ____________	perfect

Antonyms Write the list word that means the opposite or nearly the opposite.

11. pessimism **11.** ____________

12. cowardice **12.** ____________

13. dryness **13.** ____________

14. success **14.** ____________

15. arrival **15.** ____________

Synonyms Write the list word that means the same or nearly the same.

16. suitcase **16.** ____________

17. electricity **17.** ____________

18. combination **18.** ____________

19. living thing **19.** ____________

20. climate **20.** ____________

School + Home **Home Activity** Your child has learned to spell words with suffixes *-ism, -age,* and *-ure.* Call out some list words and have your child spell the words, define the words, and use the words in sentences.

Comparative and Superlative Adjectives

Directions Write the comparative and superlative forms of each adjective.

Adjective	Comparative	Superlative
early	1. ____________	2. ____________
radiant	3. ____________	4. ____________
dense	5. ____________	6. ____________
enormous	7. ____________	8. ____________
bad	9. ____________	10. ____________
wet	11. ____________	12. ____________
beautiful	13. ____________	14. ____________

Directions Circle the correct form of the adjective to complete each sentence.

15. People are always looking for the (larger, largest) gold deposits in the world.

16. Panning for gold takes (greatest, greater) patience than I have.

17. The gold necklace Tim gave Becky was the (lovelier, loveliest) necklace she owned.

18. Your bracelet is (shiniest, shinier) than Pam's.

19. Sandy was (more tired, tireder) than Susan after panning for gold.

20. The boys were (dirtiest, dirtier) than the girls after exploring the mine.

21. To design jewelry, Jim used a (more sophisticated, most sophisticated) computer program than a jeweler has.

22. Tom's drawing of Pompeii was the (most colorful, colorfulest) one on the wall.

23. Marti has the (prettyest, prettiest) ring in the class.

24. This gold coin is (bigger, biggest) than that one.

School + Home **Home Activity** Your child reviewed comparative and superlative adjectives. Have your child find three advertisements in a magazine or newspaper and point out the comparative and superlative adjectives advertisers use to sell products and services.

Name ____________________

Prefixes *bi-, tri-, uni-, re-, semi-*

Spelling Words

bisect	triangle	universal	semicircle	biceps
bilingual	tricycle	university	semifinal	uniform
bifocals	reunion	unison	semicolon	unicorn
semiprivate	triplicate	semisweet	semiannual	biplane

Crossword Puzzle Use the clues to find the list words. Write each letter in a box.

Across

3. figure with three sides
5. make-believe creature
7. classmates' get-together
9. half circle

Down

1. exists everywhere
2. divide into two equal parts
4. partly private
5. as a group; together
6. airplane with two wings on each side
8. two languages

Classify Write the list word that fits in the group.

10. period, comma, _____ 10. ____________________
11. forearms, elbows, _____ 11. ____________________
12. elementary, high school, _____ 12. ____________________
13. contacts, reading glasses, _____ 13. ____________________
14. bitter, sweet, _____ 14. ____________________
15. triple, trilogy, _____ 15. ____________________
16. regional, quarterfinal, _____ 16. ____________________
17. unicycle, bicycle, _____ 17. ____________________
18. outfit, attire, _____ 18. ____________________
19. biannual, half-yearly, _____ 19. ____________________

School + Home **Home Activity** Your child has learned to spell words with prefixes *bi-, tri-, uni-, re-,* and *semi-*. Ask your child to choose a list word from Exercises 10–19 and tell a clue for the word that can be used for a crossword puzzle.

Name ______________________________

Adverbs

Directions Underline the adverb or adverbs in each sentence.

1. First, people hurriedly went to their underground shelters.
2. They had listened quite closely to weather forecasters.
3. Finally, they could climb slowly back upstairs.
4. Everywhere anyone looked, the tornado had struck catastrophically.
5. Soon residents were busily planning a new Greensburg.
6. They barely had time to look back.
7. Architects spoke hopefully of new "green" buildings.
8. Residents read the new town plan very thoroughly.
9. It's a good thing Greensburg's residents worked together so well.
10. They gratefully received volunteers to help them rebuild.
11. Later, everyone will meet outside for a celebration.
12. People now seem to be quite happy there.
13. One believes strongly that their tragedy will end well.

Directions Use the adverbs from the box to complete the sentences.

better	tomorrow	swiftly	there	eventually

14. ________________ morning a new building opens.
15. It was built ________________ by contractors.
16. ________________ will be a produce market inside.
17. It will work ________________ to bring fresh food to residents.
18. ________________ many more towns will have markets like this one.

School + Home **Home Activity** Your child reviewed adverbs. Ask your child to say three sentences using the verb *skate* and the correct forms of the adverb *badly* (*badly, worse, worst*).

Name ____

Persuasion Chart

Directions Fill in the graphic organizer with information about your persuasive essay.

Introduction: State your position or thesis.

↓

First reason

↓

Second reason

↓

Third reason (most important)

↓

Conclusion

Name ______________________________

Persuasive Words

Directions Write a sentence about your topic using each persuasive word below. Consider using these sentences in the draft of your persuasive essay.

1. **important**

____

____

____

2. **best**

____

____

____

3. **worst**

____

____

____

4. **never**

____

____

____

5. **must**

____

____

____

Using Vivid Adjectives

One way to improve your writing is to use vivid adjectives. They can clarify information and help strengthen the writer's position in a persuasive essay.

General The state has oil in its reserves.

Improved The state has abundant oil in its reserves.

Directions Add a vivid adjective from the box or your own vivid adjective to describe the underlined noun in each sentence. Write the new sentence.

magnificent ambitious economical scarce valuable

1. The Southwest is conserving supplies of water.

2. People went west to search for gold.

3. Even garbage is a resource.

4. Mud has been used to build structures.

5. Scientists look for ways to conserve energy.

Name ______________________________

Peer and Teacher Conferencing Persuasive Essay

Directions Read your partner's essay. Refer to the Revising Checklist as you write your comments or questions. Offer compliments as well as revision suggestions. Then take turns talking about each other's draft. Give your partner your notes. After you and your teacher talk about your essay, add your teacher's comments to the notes.

Revising Checklist

Focus/Ideas

- ☐ Is the persuasive essay focused on one position?
- ☐ Is the position supported by strong reasons, facts, and examples?

Organization

- ☐ Is the writer's position clearly stated in the introduction?
- ☐ Are the supporting reasons presented in a logical order, such as order of importance with the most important reason given last?

Voice

- ☐ Is the essay serious, sincere, and convincing?

Word Choice

- ☐ Does the writer use persuasive words and vivid adjectives effectively?

Sentences

- ☐ Are sentences varied in length, kind, and structure?

Things I Thought Were Good ______________________________

____

____

Things I Thought Could Be Improved ______________________________

____

____

Teacher's Comments ______________________________

____

Name ______________________________

Author's Purpose

- The **author's purpose** is the reason or reasons an author has for writing.
- Authors may write to persuade, inform, entertain, or express thoughts and feelings. They may have more than one purpose for writing.

Directions Read the following passage. Then complete the diagram and answer the question below.

Chivalry was a way of life for knights in the Middle Ages. Their code of conduct valued courage, honor, service, and the protection of women. Chivalry developed during the eighth and ninth centuries in Europe and peaked in the twelfth century. The system required a knight first to be trained as a page and then serve as a squire, or knight's aide. Chivalry inspired the popular legend of King Arthur and the Knights of the Round Table. Today when we speak of someone as chivalrous, we usually mean they are courteous.

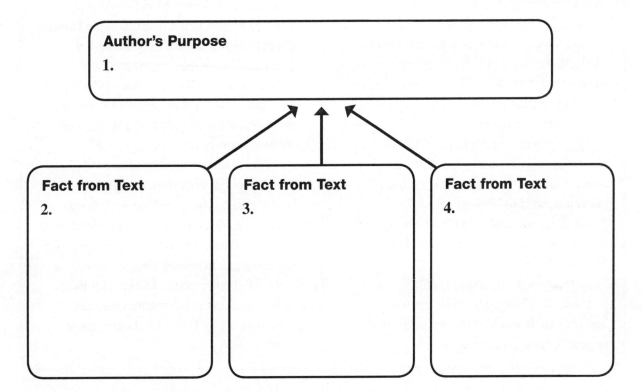

Author's Purpose

1.

Fact from Text

2.

Fact from Text

3.

Fact from Text

4.

5. Do you think the author met his or her purpose? Why or why not?

____

____

Home Activity Your child read a short passage and identified the author's purpose. Work with your child to identify the purpose of an article in a newspaper. Ask you child to explain if the author met his or her purpose.

Writing • Parody

Key Features of a Parody

- imitates a familiar story's plot, style, and language
- changes some details of the orginal story for comic effect
- may imitate the style of the orginal writer

Donna Cutie and the Energy Guzzlers

Are you one who loves tales of the future? You know, the ones where the smart girl saves the day. Beware! Those tales can drive you mad.

Sylvia Ortiz was her name—a tall, skinny girl, who wore a clouded expression, as if her heart held secret daydreams.

Indeed it did. Sylvia O. longed to live in days to come, when galactic crusaders battled for a clean, safe planet. Sylvia's room in suburban New Jersey so overflowed with books of science fiction, no one but lanky Sylvia could squeeze into it.

Sylvia buried herself in these future tales. She read day and night, until her mind snapped. "Sylvia Ortiz is no more," she announced to her astonished family. "I am the renowned fighter and champion of the environment, Donna Cutie de la Mancha."

In the garage she found a white jump suit and a toy light saber. Her hat was a shower cap. It would serve her until she got official EPA protective gear.

An energy fighter must have a noble vehicle. Donna Cutie owned an old, slightly rusted bicycle that squeaked when she climbed hills. She renamed the bicycle Agua Pura, which means "clean water."

An energy fighter must also have an assistant to make phone calls and send e-mails. Donna Cutie invited Panna Danza, the pizza store owner, who smelled of garlic and burnt toast, to come along. "Come with me, Panna," Donna Cutie said. "Within a week I will conquer the energy guzzlers on the island of Manhattan and make you the nation's energy czar."

"That sounds pretty good to me," Panna replied. "If I were energy czar, my husband could be a senator, and all my children could have great government jobs." So Panna agreed to come along. She saw no harm in seeing a bit of New York.

In the days to come, Donna and Panna would have many adventures together, if only poor Agua Pura could carry them past the driveway!

1. Underline three sensory details that draw you into the story.

2. Circle examples of language borrowed from the original story.

3. What is one key difference?

____

Vocabulary

Directions Choose the word from the box that best matches each definition. Write the word on the line.

Check the Words You Know
___lance
___misfortune
___quests
___renewed
___renowned
___resound
___squire

______________________ **1.** made like new

______________________ **2.** searches or hunts

______________________ **3.** a long, wooden spear with a sharp iron or steel head

______________________ **4.** to echo

______________________ **5.** bad luck

Directions Choose the word from the box that best completes each clue. Write the word on the line shown to the left.

______________________ **6.** Unknown is to _____ as dull is to shiny.

______________________ **7.** Knight is to _____ as blacksmith is to apprentice.

______________________ **8.** _____ is to restored as built is to constructed.

______________________ **9.** Happiness is to _____ as brightness is to dullness.

______________________ **10.** _____ are to searches as journeys are to trips.

Write a Description

On a separate sheet of paper, write a description of a knight. Show that you have visualized details about the knight's appearance and actions. Use as many vocabulary words as you can.

School + Home **Home Activity** Your child identified and used vocabulary words from *Don Quixote and the Windmills.* Read a story or nonfiction article with your child. Have your child point out unfamiliar words. Work together to figure out the meaning of each word by using other words that appear near it.

Modifiers

Adjectives, adverbs, and prepositional phrases are **modifiers**, words or groups of words that tell more about, or modify, other words in a sentence. Adjectives modify nouns and pronouns. Adverbs modify verbs, adjectives, or other adverbs. Prepositional phrases can act as adjectives or adverbs.

As Adjective The windmills on the hill were huge.
As Adverb The horse galloped up the hill.

- To avoid confusion, place modifiers close to the words they modify. Adjective phrases usually come right after the word they modify. Adverb phrases may appear right after a verb or at the beginning of a sentence.
- The meaning of a sentence can be unclear if the modifier is misplaced.

  No: We read about a knight who battled giants in class.
  Yes: We read in class about a knight who battled giants.
- The position of *only* in a sentence can affect the sentence's entire meaning. Place *only* directly before the word or words it modifies.

  Example: Only he saw giants. (Nobody else saw them.)
  He only saw giants. (He didn't do anything except see.)
  He saw only giants. (He saw nothing else.)

Directions Write *adverb, adjective,* or *prepositional phrase* to identify each underlined modifier. Write *adjective* or *adverb* to identify how a prepositional phrase is used.

1. The squire rode behind the knight. ______________________
2. Don Quixote wore pieces of rusty armor. ______________________
3. Bravely he battled the windmills. ______________________
4. The lady in his dream was named Dulcinea. ______________________

Directions Each sentence has a misplaced modifier. Rewrite the sentence and put the word or phrase where it belongs.

5. I sat and thought about knights in the kitchen.

____

6. Don Quixote only wanted Dulcinea, no one else.

____

School + Home **Home Activity** Your child learned about modifiers. With your child, read a favorite story. Ask your child to point out several adjectives, adverbs, and prepositional phrases and explain what those words or phrases are modifying.

Name ______________________________

Suffixes *-ary, -ery, -ory*

Spelling Words				
bakery	scenery	vocabulary	temporary	surgery
inventory	directory	pottery	discovery	imaginary
machinery	nursery	voluntary	honorary	satisfactory
introductory	advisory	bribery	secondary	bravery

Definitions Write a list word that matches the definition.

1. courage 1. ____________
2. the working parts of a machine 2. ____________
3. a place where young children are cared for 3. ____________
4. of second rank or importance 4. ____________
5. freely chosen 5. ____________
6. the act of giving or taking a bribe 6. ____________
7. having or conferring distinction 7. ____________
8. containing or giving advice 8. ____________
9. adequate 9. ____________
10. used to introduce 10. ____________
11. a book that lists information 11. ____________

Synonyms Write the list word that means the same or almost the same as each word below.

12. bake shop 12. ____________
13. ceramics 13. ____________
14. supply 14. ____________
15. make-believe 15. ____________
16. short-term 16. ____________
17. setting 17. ____________
18. finding 18. ____________
19. operation 19. ____________
20. words in a language 20. ____________

School + Home **Home Activity** Your child wrote words with suffixes *-ary*, *-ery*, and *-ory*. Ask your child to say five list words, spell them, and use them in sentences.

Name ____________________

Story Comparison Chart

Title A ____________________

Characters

Setting

Events

Ending

Title B ____________________

Characters

Setting

Events

Ending

Name ____________________

Vocabulary • Prefixes *re-* and *mis-*

- A **prefix** is a word part added at the beginning of a base word to change its meaning. Look for prefixes to help you figure out the meanings of unfamiliar words.
- The prefix *re-* means "again" or "do over." The prefix *mis-* means "bad" or "wrong."

Directions Read the following passage. Then answer the questions below.

A renowned knight came upon a family that had had the misfortune of meeting robbers on the road. Ronald, the knight's new squire, wanted the famous knight to be pleased with him. Ronald eagerly handed the knight his lance so he could do battle with the robbers. But Ronald tripped, causing the knight to fall from his horse. This mishap gave the robbers a chance to race off. Ronald renewed his courage. He charged off toward the robbers and overpowered them, retrieving the family's fortune. "Your deeds will resound through history," the knight told Ronald with a smile.

1. How does the prefix in *misfortune* help you to determine its meaning?

____

____

2. How does the prefix in *mishap* help you to determine its meaning?

____

____

3. How does the prefix in *renewed* help you to determine its meaning?

____

____

4. How does the prefix in *resound* help you to determine its meaning?

____

____

5. Why is it hard to use the prefix in *retrieving* to understand its meaning?

____

____

School + Home

Home Activity Your child read a short passage and used prefixes to understand new words. Work with your child to identify unfamiliar words in an article. Together, see if any of the unfamiliar words have prefixes that can help with understanding the unfamiliar words. Confirm the meanings in a dictionary.

Parts of a Book

- Understanding the **parts of a book** can help you to use books more easily.
- The **title page** gives the title, author, and publisher, and the **copyright page** tells when the book was published. It can help you to know if information in the book is recent. The **table of contents** lists the chapters, stories, or other contents of the book.

Directions Read these four pages from a book.

The History of Sixteenth-Century Spain

Second Edition

by
Matthew Allison

Real History Publishing Company
New York and London

© 2000 by Matthew Allison
All rights reserved.
Printed in the United States of America
ISBN 0-333-44444-6

Contents

Name ______________________________

Directions Use the book pages you just read to answer the following questions.

1. What is the first page on the left? What is the page on the right?

2. Who is the author of this book? On what page would you learn about the author?

3. Who is the publisher of the book? Where does the publisher have offices?

4. What year was this book published? Who holds the copyright?

5. By looking at the table of contents, how can you tell where the main part of the book begins? What is the name of the first section of the main part of the book?

6. Would this book be a good source for a report on Spanish kings in the 1500s? Explain.

7. Which chapter would you read to find out about Spain's business and trade in the sixteenth century?

8. Does this book have illustrations? How can you tell?

9. How would you locate information about King Ferdinand in this book?

10. Explain how the chapters of this book are organized.

School + Home

Home Activity Your child learned about using the parts of a book. Look at a reference book together. Ask your child to locate the publication date and publisher, as well as to explain what is on the table of contents page.

Suffixes *-ary*, *-ery*, *-ory*

Proofread an Article Circle six misspelled words. Write them correctly. Find a sentence with an unnecessary comma. Write it correctly on the line.

Spelling Words
bakery
scenery
vocabulary
temporary
surgery
inventory
directory
pottery
discovery
imaginary
machinery
nursery
voluntary
honorary
satisfactory
introductory
advisory
bribery
secondary
bravery

Our class visited a factory that makes pottary. After an introductory talk by the factory manager, we looked at the directery and decided to see the specialized machinary first. The factory workers took a timporary break to show us how the machines worked. It was a very interesting diskovery to learn about the process of making pottery. There are many steps to take from a chunk of clay to a satisfacktory product.

After the tour, we went to the bakery for a snack. This was a very educational and fun day.

1. ______________ 2. ______________

3. ______________ 4. ______________

5. ______________ 6. ______________

7. ____

____

Proofread Words Circle the word that is spelled correctly. Write it on the line.

8. secondery	secondry	secondary	8.	______________
9. nursery	nursury	nersery	9.	______________
10. volentery	voluntary	volentary	10.	______________
11. honorary	honerary	honorery	11.	______________
12. bravery	bravory	braviry	12.	______________
13. introductory	interductory	introductery	13.	______________
14. advisery	advisory	advizory	14.	______________
15. bribery	bribary	bribiry	15.	______________

Frequently Misspelled Words
whole
beginning

School + Home **Home Activity** Your child identified misspelled words with suffixes *-ary*, *-ery*, and *-ory*. Ask your child to think of a way that can make it easier to remember whether a word ends in *-ary*, *-ery*, or *-ory*.

Name ____________________________________

Modifiers

Directions Read the passage. Then read each question. Circle the letter of the correct answer.

Iditarod Start-Up

(1) The strong and handsome huskies tear down a snowy path. (2) It is the start of the famous Iditarod dogsled race in Alaska. (3) The finish line is in the harsh wilderness about 1,000 miles from Anchorage. (4) More than fifty sled drivers called "mushers" courageously participate in this challenging race. (5) The course winds up and down huge mountains with craggy peaks. (6) It passes through thick evergreen forests. (7) The mushers know that this race celebrates Alaska's pioneer spirit and colorful history

1 How many adjectives are found in sentence 1?

A 1
B 2
C 3
D 4

2 Which best describes the underlined phrase in sentence 3?

A Adjective phrase
B Adverb phrase
C Prepositional phrase
D None of the above

3 Which adverb is found in sentence 4?

A fifty
B drivers
C challenging
D courageously

4 The underlined phrase in sentence 5 describes which word?

A mountains
B course
C winds
D huge

5 Which best describes the underlined modifier in sentence 6?

A Adjective phrase
B Adverb phrase
C Prepositional phrase
D None of the above

Home Activity Your child prepared for taking tests on modifiers. Copy a paragraph from a newspaper or magazine article, leaving blanks where modifiers go. Ask your child to suggest possible modifiers for the blanks. Compare with the original paragraph.

Graphic Sources

- A **graphic source** organizes information in a way that is easy to see. Graphic sources include maps, charts, tables, pictures, and time lines.
- Use graphic sources to help you understand what you read and to preview your reading.

Directions The following map shows regions of ancient Greece. Use it to answer the questions.

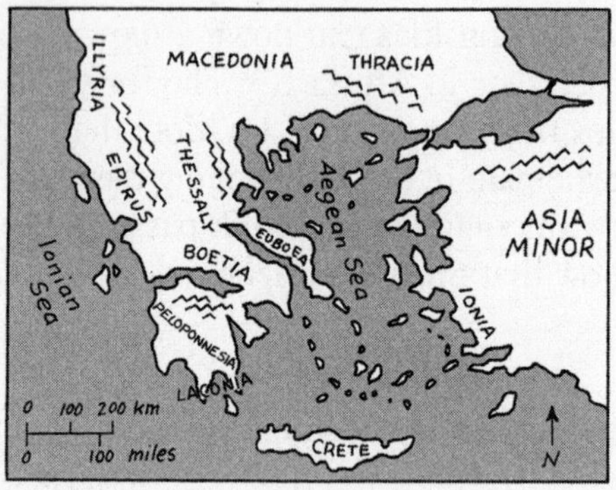

1. What does this map show?

____

____

2. What was the northernmost region of ancient Greece? the southernmost?

____

3. About how far was it from Macedonia to Crete? What bodies of water surrounded ancient Greece?

____

____

4. What can you tell about the geography and natural features of the land in ancient Greece?

____

____

5. The current border of Greece is south of Macedonia. It is also east of Thracia and west of Asia Minor. On a separate sheet of paper, draw your own map approximating Greece today. How does that map compare with the map of ancient Greece?

School + Home **Home Activity** Your child used a map to learn about ancient Greece. With your child, look over a map of an unfamiliar place, and challenge your child to explain what he or she can learn from it.

Name ______________________________

Writing • Notes

Key Features of Notes
- include most important facts and dates
- paraphrase, or restate information in one's own words
- cite, or name, original source(s)

Notes on: *Egypt* by Ann Heinrichs

"Homes, Adornments, and Games" pp. 300–301

1. Homes

Most people—simple, brick houses ate **and** slept on floor—used candles, oil lamps

Wealthy people—large, beautiful homes—had courtyards, gardens, pools

2. Adornments

Women— wore makeup—made out of plants **and** animals— black materials such as soot **and** kohl—red materials for lipstick and blush—painted fingernails—fancy combs in hair

Wealthy women—gold jewelry with precious stones

3. Clothing

Light clothing—skirts **and** robes made of linen—bare feet—scarves to cover heads

Wealthy—leather sandals, wigs

4. Games

"Ancient paintings and artifacts show how much the Egyptians loved games."

Children—leapfrog, tug of war, catch

Adults—board games: senet and "snake"

1. Use the notes to contrast the homes of most Egyptians with the homes of the wealthy people.

____

____

____

2. Make an inference about the weather in ancient Egypt, based on the clothing people wore.

____

____

____

Name________________________________

Vocabulary

Directions Choose the word from the box that best matches each definition. Write the word on the line.

Check the Words You Know

___architecture
___democracy
___empire
___ideal
___mythology

________________ **1.** a group of legends or stories about a particular country or person

________________ **2.** a group of countries or states under one ruler or government

________________ **3.** a style or special manner of building

________________ **4.** just as you would wish; perfect

________________ **5.** government that is run by the people who live under it

Directions Choose the word from the box that best matches each clue. Write the word on the line.

________________ **6.** Ancient Greece was the first example of this political system.

________________ **7.** The religion of ancient Greece included examples of this.

________________ **8.** Athens built up this kind of union of many territories.

________________ **9.** Ancient Greece made a large contribution in this field.

________________ **10.** The Greek philosopher Plato outlined this kind of government.

Write an Opinion

On a separate sheet of paper, write your opinion of an ideal civilization. Think about how it would look politically, economically, and artistically. Be specific in explaining your opinion.

School + Home

Home Activity Your child identified and used vocabulary words from *Ancient Greece*. Read a story or nonfiction article with your child. Have him or her point out unfamiliar words. Work together to figure out the meaning of each unfamiliar word by looking at other words around it.

Name ______________________________

Conjunctions

A **conjunction** is a word that is used to join words, phrases, or sentences.
Coordinating conjunctions such as *and, but,* and *or* are used to combine two or more subjects, predicates, or sentences to make compound subjects, predicates, or sentences.

Maggie and Deb are marathon runners.
Katie will run five miles or swim 50 laps tomorrow.
Gerry wanted to see the Greek play, but he was ill.

Subordinating conjunctions such as *because, if, then, when, although, before,* and *after* are used to link dependent clauses and independent clauses in complex sentences.

He gets good grades because he studies. When she speaks, everyone listens.

Directions Underline the correct conjunction in ( ).

1. Wrestling (but, and) boxing were part of the ancient Olympic games.
2. He could throw a javelin, (or, but) he could not throw a discus.
3. Were the games held in Athens (or, but) Olympia?
4. I wanted to attend the Olympic trials, (and, but) I could not get a ticket.
5. The ancient Greeks developed both a democratic system of government (or, and) a system of trial by jury.
6. Listen carefully to the words of this song, (and, or) you will learn about legendary Greek heroes.
7. Is the play a comedy (and, or) a tragedy?
8. Samantha read "The Tortoise and the Hare," (but, or) she did not like it.

Directions Underline the conjunction in each sentence. Write *CC* if it is a coordinating conjunction and *SC* if it is a subordinating conjunction.

9. If you read Aristotle's works, you will learn his ideas about happiness. ______
10. Children offered toys to Apollo and Artemis. ______
11. Although Greece was a land of democracy, people still owned slaves. ______
12. Greek men often held meetings, but the women did not attend. ______

School + Home **Home Activity** Your child learned about conjunctions. Have your child find three conjunctions in a favorite book, tell whether they are coordinating or subordinating conjunctions, and explain how he or she knows.

Name ______________________________

Related Words 2

Spelling Words

alternate	alternative	office	official	economy
economics	normal	normality	restore	restoration
indicate	indicative	gene	genetic	excel
excellence	adapt	adaptation	crime	criminal

Related Words Write the list word that is related to each list word below.

1. crime — 1. ____________
2. economy — 2. ____________
3. restore — 3. ____________
4. excel — 4. ____________
5. gene — 5. ____________
6. office — 6. ____________
7. alternate — 7. ____________

Word Definitions Write a list word to match each definition.

8. average, standard, conforming — 8. ____________
9. being a sign of, suggestive — 9. ____________
10. usual condition — 10. ____________
11. to point out — 11. ____________
12. adjustment to changes in conditions — 12. ____________
13. to be superior — 13. ____________
14. to return to a former condition — 14. ____________
15. violation of the law — 15. ____________
16. one that substitutes for another — 16. ____________
17. thrift, avoiding waste — 17. ____________
18. inherited from your parents — 18. ____________
19. place of business — 19. ____________
20. to adjust to change — 20. ____________

School + Home **Home Activity** Your child wrote related words. Use a list word in a sentence and have your child spell the word.

Name ______________________________

Topic List

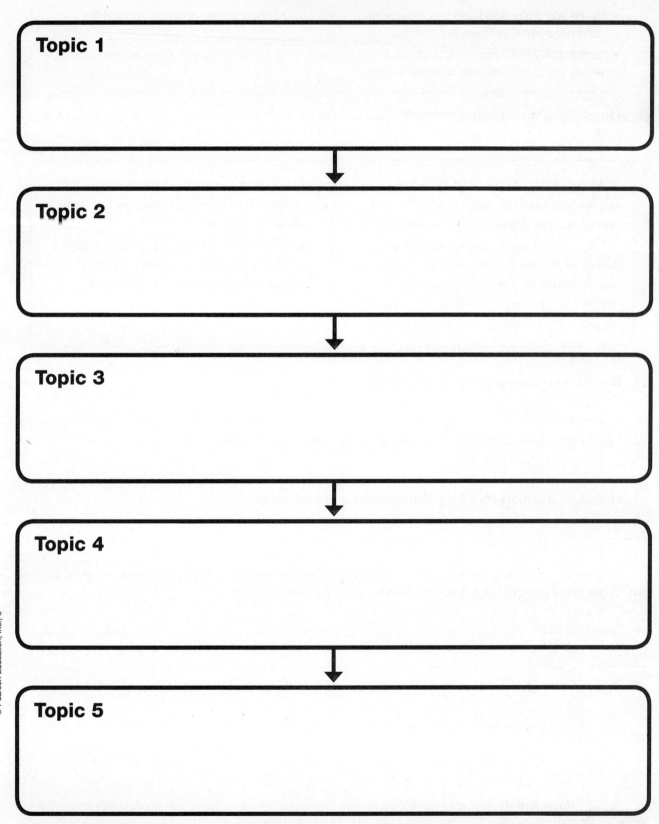

Topic 1

Topic 2

Topic 3

Topic 4

Topic 5

Name ______________________________

Vocabulary • Unfamiliar Words

- When you are reading and see an unfamiliar word, use **context clues**, or words around the unfamiliar word, to figure out its meaning.
- Context clues include definitions, explanations, and synonyms (words that have the same or nearly the same meaning as other words).

Directions Read the following passage. Then answer the questions below. Look for context clues as you read.

Archaeologists study artifacts to understand the people, customs, and life of ancient times. They go to areas where ancient civilizations such as the Greek or Roman Empire existed, and they dig for artifacts. The shrines they find might tell them about the culture's religion or mythology. Remnants of buildings tell them about the architecture of the ancient culture. Weapons and tools may tell them about the hunting and farming practices of a culture. On an ideal dig, archaeologists quickly and easily find many artifacts telling a complete story of an ancient civilization.

1. Based on the passage, what is an empire?

____

2. What clues does the passage provide about the meaning of *mythology?*

____

3. How does a context clue tell you the meaning of *architecture?*

____

____

4. What clues does the passage provide about the meaning of *culture?*

____

____

5. What can you tell from context about the meaning of *ideal?*

____

____

Home Activity Your child identified and used context clues to understand new words in a passage. Work with your child to identify unfamiliar words in an article. Then have him or her find context clues to help with the understanding of the new words. Confirm the meanings with your child.

Name______________________________________

Time Line

- **Time lines** are a way to visually present events in time order. The events may be in a story or in nonfiction information. Time lines can cover very general topics or very specific topics.
- There are many different designs for time lines, which may be read from left to right or top to bottom. Use time lines to help you understand time relationships and remember the order of events.

Directions Use this time line to answer the questions.

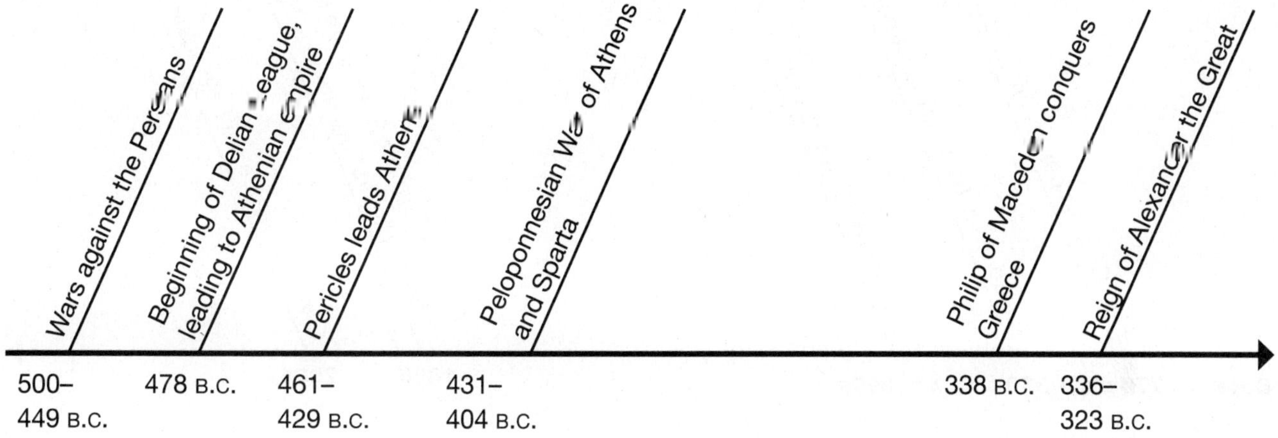

CLASSICAL AGE

1. What does this time line show?

____

____

2. How is the time line organized? How is it read?

____

3. Who is the earliest Greek leader—Alexander the Great, Pericles, or Philip of Macedon?

____

4. How many years does this time line cover?

____

5. How does the title help in understanding the information?

____

____

Name____

Directions Use this time line to answer the questions.

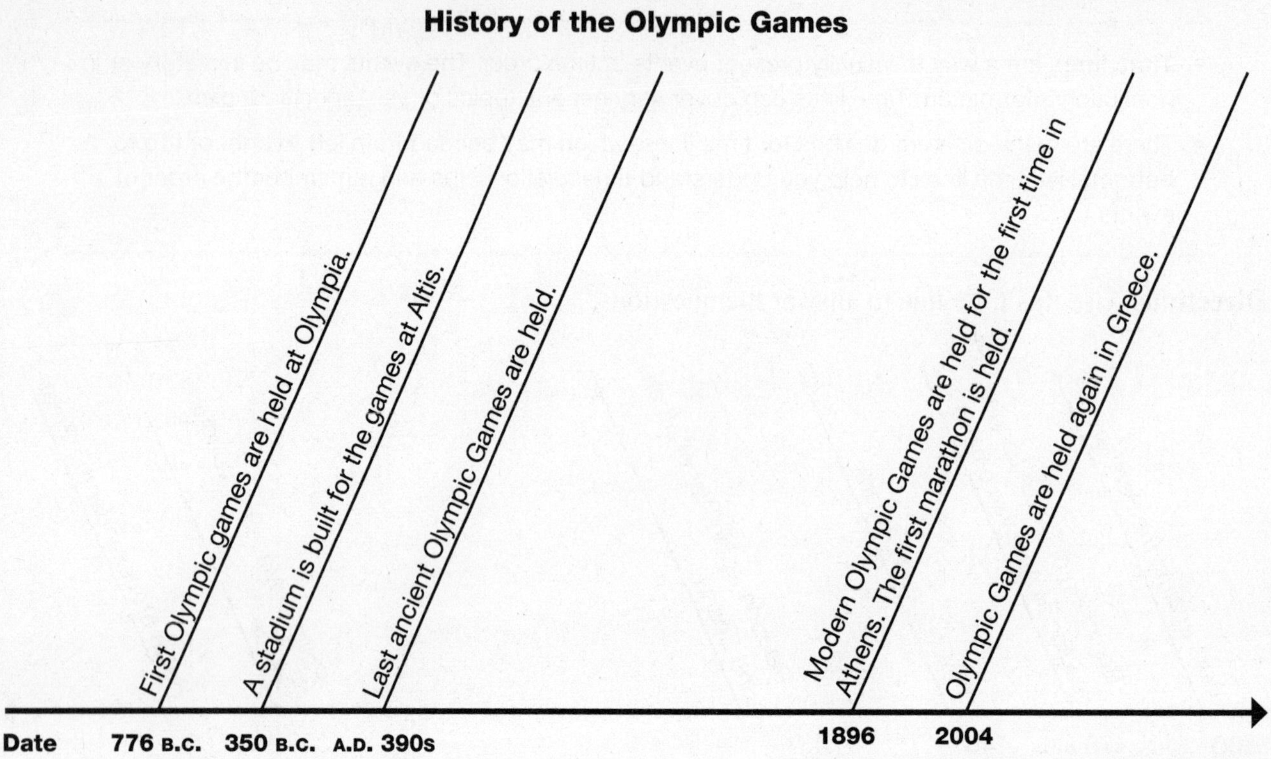
History of the Olympic Games
First Olympic games are held at Olympia.
A stadium is built for the games at Altis.
Last ancient Olympic Games are held.
Modern Olympic Games are held for the first time in Athens. The first marathon is held.
Olympic Games are held again in Greece.
Date
776 B.C.
350 B.C.
A.D. 390s
1896
2004

6. What does this time line show?

____

7. How is this time line read?

____

8. How many years does the time line cover? How long did the ancient Olympic Games last?

____

____

9. According to this time line, when were the modern Olympic Games held in Greece?

____

____

10. Explain how this time line can be used to improve understanding of the topic. What advantages does a time line have over text?

____

____

School + Home **Home Activity** Your child learned about using time lines as resources for improving comprehension. Together, look at a time line in an almanac or book. Ask your child to explain what the time line shows.

Name ______________________________

Related Words 2

Proofread an Outline Circle six spelling errors in the outline. Write the words correctly. Find a sentence with an incorrect verb form. Write it correctly.

Spelling Words
alternate
alternative
office
official
economy
economics
normal
normality
restore
restoration
indicate
indicative
gene
genetic
excel
excellence
adapt
adaptation
crime
criminal

Frequently Misspelled Words
friend
awhile

Using Heat

A. Heating systems—warm homes and buildings

1. Forced-air system—fuel heats air, which is blown through ducts and vents; other vents restor cool air to the furnace to be reheated.

B. Solar energy—alturnative energy from the sun

1. Passive solar heating use econumy of nature to move heat.

C. Heat engine—an engine that converts thermal energy into mechanical energy

1. Internal-combustion engines convert only about 26 percent of the fuel's chemical energy to mechanical energy—indicetive of inefficiency.

D. Heat mover—device that moves thermal energy from one place to another

1. Air conditioners exsel at cooling warm air.
2. Heat pumps alturnate between cooling and warming air.

1. ______________ 2. ______________

3. ______________ 4. ______________

5. ______________ 6. ______________

7. ____

____

Proofread Words Circle the word that is spelled correctly. Write it on the line.

8. genetic	ginetic	**8.**	______________
9. oficial	official	**9.**	______________
10. ecunomics	economics	**10.**	______________

School + Home **Home Activity** Your child identified misspelled related words. Spell list words and have your child tell you if you spelled them correctly or incorrectly. Make some intentional spelling mistakes and have your child spell the words correctly.

Name ____

Conjunctions

Directions Read the passage. Then read each question. Circle the letter of the correct answer.

Job Issues

(1) Maureen had a job helping the school librarian after school. (2) Most days Maureen stayed in the library and helped other students while Mr. Thompson took a lunch break. (3) Because Mr. Thompson trusted Maureen, he did not lock things up when he left. (4) Jonas was Maureen's friend, and he was also a prankster. (5) Maureen hadn't noticed that anything was missing after Jonas's visit, but Mr. Thompson did. (6) Maureen suspected that Jonas had taken from the desk both the stapler and a CD. (7) Maureen didn't want to get Jonas in trouble, or she knew she had to do the right thing. (8) After their talk, Jonas returned the stapler and the CD, ______ he apologized to Mr. Thompson.

1 Which best describes the underlined phrase in sentence 2?

- **A** Compound sentence
- **B** Compound predicate
- **C** Compound subject
- **D** None of the above

2 What change, if any, should be made in sentence 4?

- **A** Change ***and*** to **but**
- **B** Change ***and*** to **so**
- **C** Change ***and*** to **because**
- **D** Make no change

3 Which best describes the underlined phrase in sentence 6?

- **A** Compound sentence
- **B** Compound predicate
- **C** Compound subject
- **D** None of the above

4 What change, if any, should be made in sentence 7?

- **A** Change ***or*** to **but**
- **B** Change ***or*** to **so**
- **C** Change ***in trouble*** to **out of trouble**
- **D** Make no change

5 Which conjunction best completes sentence 8?

- **A** however
- **B** and
- **C** but
- **D** or

School + Home

Home Activity Your child prepared for taking tests on conjunctions. Ask your child to look through a newspaper or magazine article and find five conjunctions.

Name____

Vocabulary

Directions Choose the word from the box that best matches each definition below. Write the word on the line.

Check the Words You Know
___disgraced
___progress
___promoted
___relish
___retreat
___revolting
___unison

__________________ **1.** together; as one

__________________ **2.** raised in rank

__________________ **3.** act of withdrawing

__________________ **4.** repulsive; disgusting

__________________ **5.** a side dish to add flavor to food

Directions Choose the word from the box that best completes each sentence below. Write the word on the line shown to the left.

__________________ **6.** Appealing is to ____ as healthy is to sick.

__________________ **7.** Defeat is to ____ as win is to advance.

__________________ **8.** Criticized is to praised as ____ is to honored.

__________________ **9.** ____ is to reduced as lifted is to dropped.

__________________ **10.** Improvement is to increase as development is to ____.

Write a Journal Entry

On a separate sheet of paper, write a journal entry you might make after you attend a party or school event. Use as many vocabulary words as you can.

School + Home

Home Activity Your child identified and used vocabulary words from *The All-American Slurp*. Read a story or nonfiction article with your child. Have him or her point out unfamiliar words. Work together to try to figure out the meaning of each word by using other words that appear near it.

Commas

You already know that **commas** are used in compound sentences, after the greeting and closing in a letter, and in series of three or more words, phrases, or sentences. Here are other uses of commas.

- After an introductory word or phrase, such as *well, yes,* or *by the way*
  Well**,** I suppose that suggestion makes the most sense.
- To set off a noun of direct address
  Mrs. Gleason**,** may I take your coat? I warned you**,** Meg**,** to stay home.
- After a dependent clause at the beginning of a sentence
  When they come to visit**,** they always bring a tasty treat.
- Before and/or after an appositive—a noun or noun phrase describing another noun
  The main course**,** spicy chicken**,** was delicious.
- Before and after interrupting words or phrases
  The buffet**,** as they promised**,** was loaded with food.
- Between a day of the week and a month and between a date and a year
  Today is Tuesday**,** March 14. Their wedding was on January 17**,** 2010.
- Between the street address and the city and between the city and the state in an address. Do not use a comma before the ZIP code.
  My school is at 1432 Cross Street**,** Chicago**,** IL 60600.

Directions Read the following parts of a letter. Add commas where they are needed.

1. How is your family Mr. Gleason?
2. My parents look forward to your visit as you know.
3. Sunday April 5 2009
4. Dear Mr. Gleason

Directions Add commas where they are needed in the sentences.

5. The Lakeview an expensive restaurant requires reservations.
6. We like hamburgers milk shakes and sushi.
7. After we saw the movie we went out to dinner.
8. Our neighbors moved to 53 West Birman Street Birmingham New York.

School + Home **Home Activity** Your child learned about commas. Have your child look at a page of a favorite book, point out the commas, and explain why each comma is used.

Name ___

Easily Confused Words

Spelling Words				
proceed	precede	advise	advice	formerly
formally	further	farther	personal	personnel
immigrate	emigrate	college	collage	descent
dissent	persecution	prosecution	envelope	envelop

Words in Context Pick a list word to finish each sentence. Write it.

1. My sister is starting her first year of (college/collage) this fall. 1. ___
2. Many people (emigrate/immigrate) to the United States each year. 2. ___
3. Do you always ask such (personal/personnel) questions? 3. ___
4. I don't wish to discuss the matter any (further/farther). 4. ___
5. Political (descent/dissent) is a part of democracy. 5. ___
6. I will dress (formally/formerly) for the wedding. 6. ___
7. May I give you some (advise/advice)? 7. ___
8. We should (proceed/precede) with caution through the intersection. 8. ___
9. Put the letter in the (envelop/envelope) before you mail it. 9. ___
10. He suffered (persecution/prosecution) at the hands of his enemies. 10. ___

Word Meanings Write a list word that fits each meaning.

11. to go before 11. ___
12. to give suggestions 12. ___
13. previously 13. ___
14. more distant 14. ___
15. employees 15. ___
16. to leave one's country 16. ___
17. artwork made of various materials 17. ___
18. a downward step 18. ___
19. the act of carrying on a lawsuit 19. ___
20. to enclose or enfold 20. ___

School + Home **Home Activity** Your child learned the meanings of related words. Ask your child to use two of the similar words in a sentence.

Name ______________________________

Five-Column Chart

Name ____________________

Vocabulary • Multiple-Meaning Words

- Some words have **multiple meanings,** or more than one definition.
- Try each of the meanings in the sentence. **Context clues,** or words around the unfamiliar word, can help you to figure out the correct meaning.

Directions Read the following story about a family meal. Then answer the questions below. Look for context clues as you read.

When I was promoted to junior high, my family had a party that I'll never forget. The guests had arrived and dinner was ready to be served when the cats jumped onto the table. They started munching on the tuna salad. "That's revolting!" Aunt Ida and Uncle Sid screamed in unison. The cats looked up and moved on to the relish plate filled with deviled eggs and pickles. Dad and I chased the cats, but already the guests had begun their retreat toward the door. Suddenly they all felt ill or had urgent work to do.

After they left, Mother moaned, "We can progress in every field of human life, but we can't keep the cats off the table!" She felt disgraced that the guests left without eating and upset that the meal was ruined. "Look at it this way," said Dad. "At least we don't have to buy cat food."

1. Two meanings of *promoted* have to do with "furthering a sale by advertising" and "raised in rank." What clue in the story above helps you to determine the correct meaning?

____

2. *Revolting* can mean "uprising" or "disgusting." What clues help you to determine its meaning in the story above?

____

3. In the passage does *relish* mean "good flavor" or "a side dish"? How do context clues help you determine the meaning?

____

4. Meanings for *retreat* include "the act of withdrawing" and "a retirement for religious exercises." How do context clues in the passage help you determine the meaning?

____

5. How does the context help you determine which meaning of *progress* is used in the story, "improvement" or "to move forward"?

____

Home Activity Your child identified and used context clues to determine the correct definitions for words with multiple meanings. Read a story with your child. Encourage your child to figure out the meanings of multiple-meaning words using context clues.

Name________________________________

Instruction Manual

- **Instruction manuals** are guidebooks that give instructions on how to do something. They may be intended for immediate use or for reference.
- They usually have several parts, such as table of contents, index, sections, and graphics. Read through instructions before following the procedures.

Directions Use this excerpt from an etiquette manual to answer the questions.

Table Manners

Eating is a social activity, which means that you need to think of others when you eat. Poor table manners can disgust other people. In contrast, good table manners show you respect them.

- Put your napkin on your lap.
- Sit up straight with your elbows off the table.
- Wait to eat until everyone is served.
- Don't talk with food in your mouth.
- Chew with your mouth closed.
- Don't make loud noises when you eat.
- Don't shovel in your food.
- Ask for something to be passed rather than reaching across the table for it.
- Don't lick your knife or eat off it.
- Don't lick your fingers.

1. How would this be used as a manual?

___

2. If you wanted to locate this information on table manners, how could you find it in the etiquette manual?

___

3. Would a manual on table manners be a good place to find out which fork to use or how to put butter on your plate? Why?

___

4. How might an etiquette manual on table manners be different in a different country?

___

___

5. What aspects of table manners are covered in this passage? Which items could graphics help you understand better?

___

___

Name ______________________________

Directions Use these instructions to answer the questions below.

How to Use Chopsticks

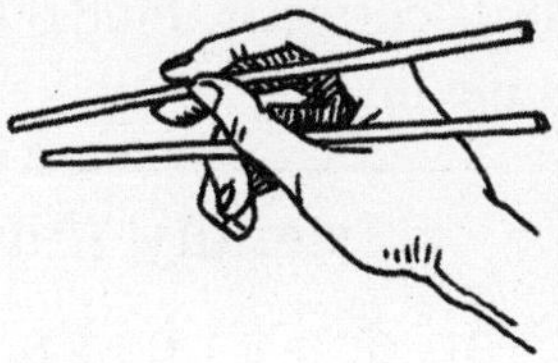

Chopsticks were developed about 5,000 years ago and are the most used utensil in China. Here are six easy steps for using chopsticks correctly.

1. Hold the chopsticks in the middle, with the ends even and not crossed.
2. Hold the top chopstick firmly between your thumb and index and middle fingers, like a pen.
3. Rest the bottom chopstick on your ring finger and hold it down with your thumb. Always keep the bottom chopstick still.
4. Move the top chopstick by guiding it with your top two fingers.
5. Pick up food by moving the top chopstick outward, straightening your index finger. As you grab the food, bend your index finger to bring the top chopstick toward the bottom chopstick.
6. Lift food between chopsticks to your mouth.

Chopstick Etiquette

- Don't wave your chopsticks in the air.
- Don't transfer food from your chopsticks to someone else's.
- Don't stab food with your chopsticks.
- Don't stick your chopsticks vertically in a dish.

1. What is the purpose of this passage?

____

2. Would the passage be for immediate use or reference? What would be a good way to use it?

____

____

3. How does the drawing improve your understanding of the procedure?

____

4. Which chopstick moves, and which one always stays still?

____

5. Does it matter if the instructions are followed in order? Why or why not?

____

____

____

____

Home Activity Your child learned about using manuals as resources. Look at a cookbook together, and ask your child in what ways it is a manual. Have your child demonstrate how to locate information and how to use the cookbook.

Name ______________________________

Easily Confused Words

Proofread a Newsletter Circle six spelling errors in the newsletter. Write the words correctly. Find a misplaced comma. Write the sentence correctly on the line.

Friendly Advise for Catching and Cooking Crabs

You don't need a collage education to go crabbing. Crabs are easy to catch. All you need is string, a net to envelope the crabs, and a large bucket or cooler. Crabs, are found around boat moorings and piers. I advize you to use fresh bait. Crabs follow the scent the bait leaves in the water.

Cooking crabs is as simple as catching them. Just deposit the live crabs (dead ones can make you sick!) in a large pot of boiling water, than add your personnel favorite spices. Wait about fifteen minutes until the shells turn crimson.

1. ____________ 2. ____________

3. ____________ 4. ____________

5. ____________ 6. ____________

7. ____

____

Spelling Words

proceed
precede
advise
advice
formerly
formally
further
farther
personal
personnel

immigrate
emigrate
college
collage
descent
dissent
persecution
prosecution
envelope
envelop

Frequently Misspelled Words

since
then

Proofread Words Circle the word that is spelled correctly. Write it on the line.

8.	proseed	proceed	8. ____________
9.	advise	advize	9. ____________
10.	formerly	formurly	10. ____________
11.	firther	further	11. ____________
12.	personnel	personel	12. ____________
13.	imigrate	immigrate	13. ____________
14.	collage	colage	14. ____________

School + Home **Home Activity** Your child identified misspelled words that are easily confused. Ask your child to pick five list words, spell them, and use them in sentences.

Commas

Directions Read the passage. Then read each question. Circle the letter of the correct answer.

Dinosaurs in the United States

(1) According to scientists, dinosaurs roamed the western United States about 150 million years ago. (2) These amazing reptiles could be found in Montana Utah Colorado and Wyoming. (3) The region was hot and moist with many lakes and swamps, a supportive climate in which these creatures could thrive. (4) There was the large *Apatosaurus*, a plant-eater with a long neck that enabled it to feed off the tops of trees. (5) *Allosaurus* was a successful predator, a carnivore with short teeth, a large head, and short front limbs. (6) In addition to the many dinosaurs that roamed the land, the skies were filled with flying reptiles that were also predators and scavengers.

1 In sentence 1, the underlined portion is an example of which?

A Direct address
B Appositive
C Introductory phrase
D Series

2 What change, if any, should be made in sentence 2?

A Insert comma after the word ***found***
B Insert commas after the words ***Montana, Utah,*** and ***Colorado***
C Insert comma after the word ***reptiles***
D Make no change

3 Which change, if any, should be made in sentence 3?

A Insert comma after the word ***moist***
B Delete comma after the word ***swamps***
C Insert commas after the words ***moist*** and ***climate***
D Make no change

4 Which sentence in this passage includes an appositive and words in a series?

A Sentence 3
B Sentence 4
C Sentence 5
D None of the above

5 In sentence 6, the underlined portion is an example of which?

A Introductory phrase
B Direct address
C Series
D Appositive

School + Home **Home Activity** Your child prepared for taking tests on commas. Ask your child to write a paragraph about trying a new food for the first time. Have your child use commas in at least three different ways.

Name ____________________

Draw Conclusions

- When you **draw a conclusion**, you form a reasonable opinion about something you have read.
- Evaluate whether your conclusions are valid. Ask yourself: Do the facts and details in the text support my conclusion? Is my conclusion valid, based on logical thinking and common sense?

Directions Read the following passage. Then complete the diagram below.

The Aztecs had many laws that covered issues from stealing to gambling to taxes. Laws even regulated the kinds of clothing Aztecs could wear. For example, nobles could wear clothes decorated in many colors, but commoners had to wear plain clothes. All laws were enforced by judges and police.

The punishment for many crimes, even lesser crimes, was death. For example, wearing the wrong type of clothing could lead to punishment of death. Anyone who broke laws protecting forests and crops could be killed as well. The laws applied to everyone—nobles, commoners, and slaves. However, since nobles were expected to behave better, they were punished more harshly for committing crimes. For example, while a commoner might have his head shaved for committing a crime, a nobleman might be put to death for the same crime.

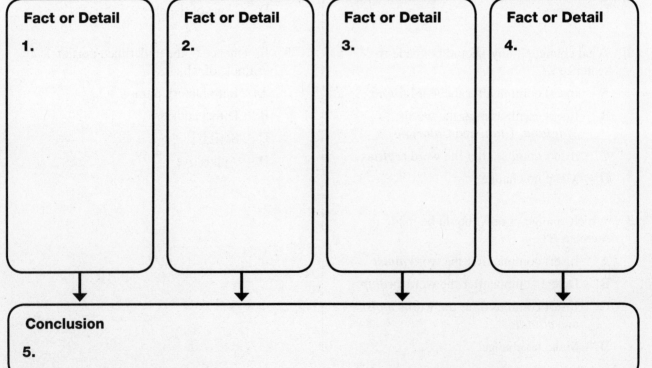

Fact or Detail

1.

Fact or Detail

2.

Fact or Detail

3.

Fact or Detail

4.

Conclusion

5.

School + Home **Home Activity** Your child made a conclusion about a nonfiction passage and supported it with details. Work with your child to draw conclusions about information in the sports pages of the newspaper. Challenge your child to support his or her conclusions with specific details.

Name ______________________________

Writing • News Article

Key Features of a News Article

- reports information about an event, idea, or person
- tells who, what, where, when, why
- includes direct quotations
- includes interesting information to capture a reader's attention

Jeepers, Peepers!

A Concerned Resident

Jeepers, Creepers! Slow Down for Peepers! This was the message on several signs that appeared along Pond Road on the afternoon of March 21. After some investigating, this reporter found out that the signs had been made by 12-year-old town resident, Jessie Bond.

A Lesson About Peepers

In an interview, Jessie explained that on the first rainy nights of spring, tiny frogs, called spring peepers, head for swamps and ponds to breed. She explained that over a few nights in March, hundreds of these pale green thumb-sized frogs climb down trees in the woods along Pond Road and attempt to cross the busy the street. Their goal is to reach water where they can mate and lay eggs.

A Success Story

Jessie said, "Last year I noticed that many of the peepers were killed by cars speeding by. I thought I'd give the peepers a little help. So far, most people have slowed down a lot. I think my signs are working." When asked why she wanted to help the peepers, Jessie said the peepers were cute, and she likes them because they eat mosquitoes!

1. Reread the selection. Why do peepers climb down trees and try to cross the street?

____

____

____

____

____

2. Jessie is quoted as saying that her signs are working. Underline the fact that supports that statement.

Name ________________________________

Vocabulary

Directions Choose the word from the box that best matches each definition below. Write the word on the line.

Check the Words You Know

___benefits
___campaigns
___comrades
___enrich
___foreigners
___invaders

________________ **1.** things that are for the good of someone or something

________________ **2.** enemies who enter with force or attack

________________ **3.** people from another country

________________ **4.** fellow workers or soldiers

________________ **5.** to make rich or richer

Directions Choose the word from the box that best completes the crossword puzzle below. Write the word in the puzzle.

Across

6. partners

7. advantages

Down

8. people who go in with force

9. a series of military operations in a war

10. to make richer

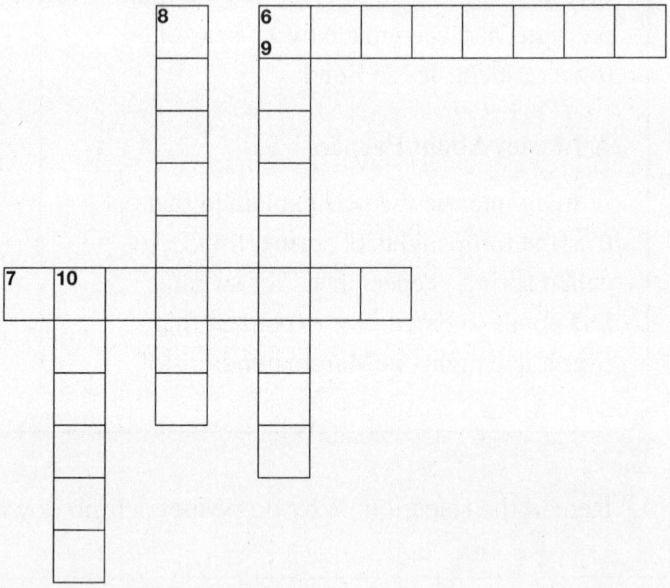

Write a Letter

On a separate sheet of paper, write a letter to a soldier. Be sure to ask questions you'd like the soldier to answer. Use as many vocabulary words as you can.

Home Activity Your child identified and used vocabulary words from *The Aztec News*. Together read a story or nonfiction article. Have him or her point out unfamiliar words. Work together to try to figure out the meaning of each word by using other words that appear near it.

Quotations and Quotation Marks

A **direct quotation** gives a speaker's exact words. Begin each quotation with a capital letter and enclose it in **quotation marks**. Use commas to set off words that introduce, interrupt, or follow a direct quotation. Place the end punctuation or the comma that ends the quotation inside the quotation marks.

"I am preparing food for the festival," she said. "What kind of food?" I asked.

Do not begin the second part of an interrupted quotation with a capital letter. Set off the interrupting phrase with commas.

"Remember," said Mother, "don't be late."

If the interrupted quotation is two complete sentences, use a period and a capital letter.

"Please make tortillas," I begged. "They taste great!"

An **indirect quotation** is a quotation that is reworded instead of being quoted directly. It does not need quotation marks.

Father said he would sing at the festival.

Directions Write *I* if the sentence is punctuated or capitalized incorrectly. Write *C* if the sentence is correct.

1. Do you live in a royal palace?" the boy asked. _____
2. "No, she replied. "I live in a whitewashed cottage." _____
3. The street vendor yelled, "Buy a tortilla pancake!" _____
4. "The pochtecas" Grandfather said, "Are merchants who may also be spies." _____
5. "Spies!" I exclaimed. "Is it dangerous?" _____

Directions Add quotation marks to each sentence as needed.

6. Take these cocoa beans to the market, Mother advised. Don't stop along the way!
7. What an adventure! declared the boy.
8. Look out your window at night, Mother said. You may see a pochteca leaving the city.
9. Are they richer than the nobles? I asked.
10. Tonight we celebrate my birthday, Sheri said. Are you coming to my party?

School + Home **Home Activity** Your child learned about quotations and quotation marks. Have your child explain the difference between a direct quotation and an indirect quotation.

Name ____________________

Word Endings *-ice*, *-ise*, *-ize*

Spelling Words				
memorize	advertise	service	realize	justice
exercise	recognize	organize	civilize	apprentice
supervise	sacrifice	sympathize	enterprise	minimize
cowardice	improvise	paradise	vocalize	compromise

Synonyms Write a list word that has the same meaning as each word or phrase below.

1. to use the voice 1. ____________
2. to make up 2. ____________
3. to lessen 3. ____________
4. business 4. ____________
5. to oversee 5. ____________
6. beginner 6. ____________
7. to put in order 7. ____________
8. to work out 8. ____________
9. to become aware 9. ____________
10. fairness 10. ____________

Words in Context Write a list word to finish each sentence.

11. My brother and I reached a ___ about using the computer. 11. ____________
12. When I grow up I want to live in a tropical ___. 12. ____________
13. Blaming others for your mistakes is a form of ___. 13. ____________
14. I ___ with your unhappy situation. 14. ____________
15. Sometimes you can help others by making a small ___. 15. ____________
16. Parents try to ___ their children. 16. ____________
17. You looked so different that I did not ___ you. 17. ____________
18. The waiters at that restaurant provide good ___. 18. ____________
19. If you want to sell something, it is good to ___ it. 19. ____________
20. I often ___ the words to my favorite songs. 20. ____________

School + Home **Home Activity** Your child wrote words ending in *-ice*, *-ise*, and *-ize*. Ask your child to pick a list word and define it.

Name ____________________

Five-Column Chart

Name________________________________

Vocabulary • Multiple-Meaning Words

- **Dictionaries** and **glossaries** provide alphabetical lists of words and their meanings.
- While reading, you may come across multiple-meaning words. If this happens, you can use a dictionary or glossary to find which meaning of the word is used.

Directions Read the following passage about Tula and the Aztec empire. Look for multiple-meaning words as you read. Use a glossary or dictionary to answer the questions below.

Tula was a young assistant to an Aztec warrior, and he and his comrades from school had been on many military campaigns. The Aztecs were often at war with other tribes. Conquering more lands would enrich the Aztec empire with more farmland. In addition, Tula knew that there were other benefits of war, such as the protection of trade, taking of prisoners, and gaining more goods and taxes from the people they ruled. In 1519, Tula and the rest of the Aztec army were surprised and confused by foreign invaders on horseback who spread disease across the land. "I have never seen such animals—they scare me," said Tula.

1. What is the meaning of *comrades* in this passage? Write two other meanings of the word.

____

____

2. What is the meaning of *campaigns* in this passage? What is another meaning of the word?

____

____

3. Which definition of *enrich* makes sense in this passage?

____

4. In this passage, what is the meaning of *benefits?*

____

5. Choose one of the multiple-meaning words from questions 1-4. Write a sentence using the word in a different way from the way it is used in the passage.

____

____

School + Home

Home Activity Your child identified and used a dictionary or glossary to identify the uses of multiple-meaning words in a passage. Read a magazine or newspaper article with your child. Work together to identify multiple-meaning words and use a glossary or dictionary to determine their meanings.

Name____

Online Newspapers

- **Online newspapers** are divided into sections, like print newspapers. They present the same type of information, but it is accessed differently.
- Finding the major stories of the day in an online newspaper is fairly easy, but finding other information is more indirect. It is necessary to click on links to move from section to section.
- Online newspapers usually charge to download information that is more than a few days old.

Directions Use this online newspaper index to answer the questions below.

***Metropolitan Times-Herald* Online**

News/Home Page	Today's Paper	Classified	Shopping
Weather/Traffic	Columnists	Find a job	Sales & deals – new
Local news	Editorials and opinion	Find a car	See newspaper ads
Nation/World news	Special sections	Find real estate	Yellow pages
Election 2012	In the community	Rent an apartment	Grocery coupons
Special reports	Obituaries	Find a mortgage	
Business/Tech	Corrections	Personals	**Using Our Site**
Leisure/Travel		Place an ad	Registration
Sports			Contact us

1. What are the main sections of the index? Under which heading would you find most news stories?

____

____

2. Which link would you use to find out about stock market news?

____

3. Which link would you use to find out about hockey scores?

____

4. How would you find today's editorials?

____

5. What types of links are featured in this index?

____

____

____

Name ____________________

Online Newspapers

Directions Use this online newspaper home page to answer the questions.

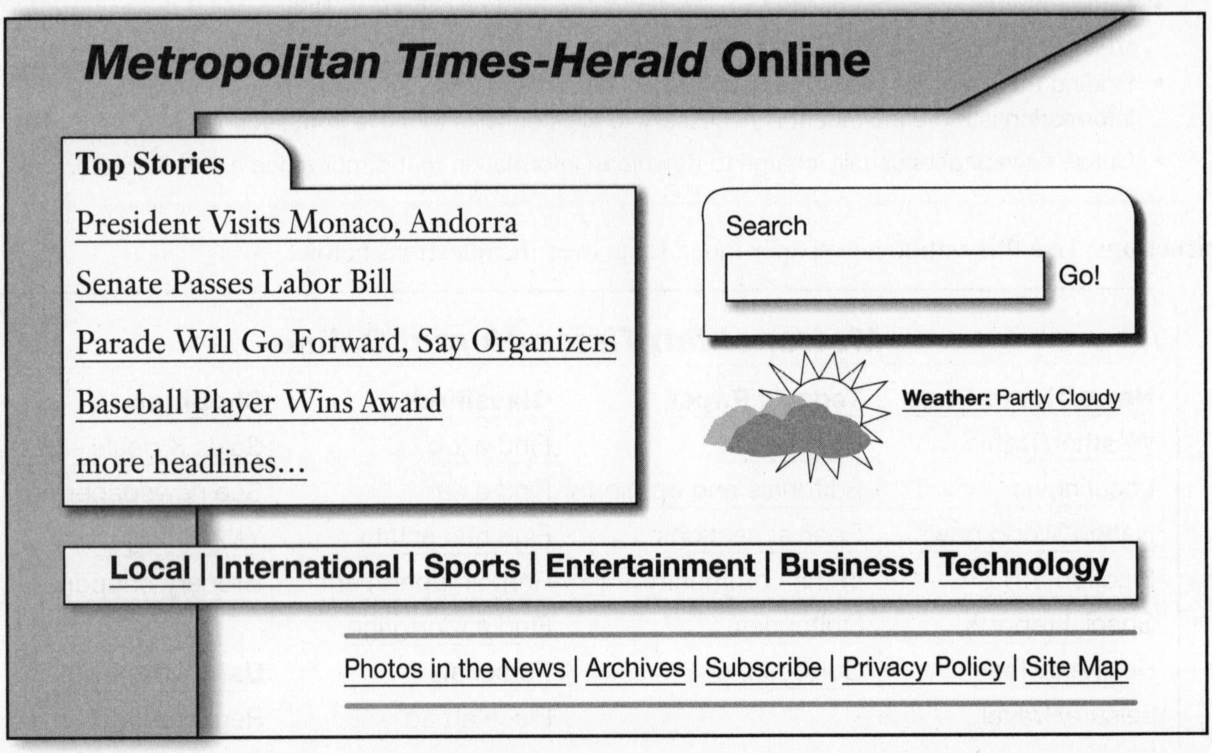

6. What are two of the day's top stories? How would you get more complete information?

7. How would you find out about current movies?

8. Would this online newspaper be a good place to look for historical information on Iran? Why?

9. How would you find recent news photographs? an article from several weeks ago?

10. Where could you enter a key word to find out about a subject in the news?

School + Home **Home Activity** Your child learned about using online newspapers as resources. Look at an online newspaper together. Ask your child to locate different types of information that you specify.

Name ____________________

Word Endings *-ice, -ise, -ize*

Proofread a List Circle six misspelled words in the list below. Write them correctly. Find an incorrect verb form. Write the phrase correctly on the line.

Conservation

Measures that can be taken to minamize loss of resources

- sacrifise by take shorter showers
- organize and supervize conservation groups
- exercize care when your using pesticides and fertilizers
- realise that you can make a difference

1. ____________ 2. ____________

3. ____________ 4. ____________

5. ____________ 6. ____________

7. ________________________________

Spelling Words

memorize
advertise
service
realize
justice
exercise
recognize
organize
civilize
apprentice
supervise
sacrifice
sympathize
enterprise
minimize
cowardice
improvise
paradise
vocalize
compromise

Frequently Misspelled Words

Florida
you're

Proofread Words Circle the word that is spelled correctly. Write it on the line.

8.	servise	service	8. ____________
9.	civilize	civilise	9. ____________
10.	simpathize	sympathize	10. ____________
11.	enterprise	enterprize	11. ____________
12.	voculize	vocalize	12. ____________
13.	cowardice	cowardise	13. ____________
14.	improvize	improvise	14. ____________
15.	paradise	paredise	15. ____________
16.	advertise	advertize	16. ____________

School + Home **Home Activity** Your child identified misspelled words ending in *-ice, -ise,* and -ize. Ask your child to pick and spell two list words that have different pronunciations for *-ice*.

Quotations and Quotation Marks

Directions Read the passage. Then read each question. Circle the letter of the correct answer.

Pancakes for Mom

(1) Henry had an "aha" moment when he realized, "Uh-oh, I forgot that today is Mother's Day!" (2) He hopped out of bed and pulled on his clothes. (3) "Dad, I want to make special pancakes for Mom this morning." "What do I have to buy?" (4) Henry left for the supermarket with his shopping list. (5) He gathered the pancake mix and blueberries, but he couldn't find the pancake syrup. (6) "I can help you, young man," said a nearby stock clerk, look over there in aisle 2." (7) Henry rushed home, and in twenty minutes the pancakes were ready. (8) "Happy Mother's Day!" he said proudly as he knocked on his mother's door. (9) "This is the best surprise I've gotten all day," said Mom happily. (10) "These are amazing pancakes, and they wouldn't be the same without syrup."

1 What change, if any, should be made in sentence 1?

- **A** Change ***"Uh-oh*** to **Uh-oh**
- **B** Change ***Day!"*** to **Day.**
- **C** Change ***realized,*** to **realized**
- **D** Make no change

2 What change, if any, should be made in sentence 3?

- **A** Change ***morning." "What*** to **morning. What**
- **B** Change ***morning." "What*** to **"morning. What**
- **C** Change ***morning."*** to **morning**
- **D** Make no change

3 What is the correct form of sentence 6?

- **A** "I can help you, young man, said a nearby stock clerk, look over there in aisle 2."
- **B** "I can help you, young man," said a nearby stock clerk. "Look over there in aisle 2."
- **C** "I can help you, young man," said a nearby stock clerk, look over there in aisle 2."
- **D** I can help you, young man," said a nearby stock clerk, look over there in aisle 2.

4 What change, if any, should be made in sentence 8?

- **A** Change ***Day!"*** to **Day!**
- **B** Change ***"Happy*** to **Happy**
- **C** Change ***door.*** to **door."**
- **D** Make no change

School + Home **Home Activity** Your child prepared for taking tests on quotations and quotation marks. Ask your child to listen to the conversation in your home and write with correct quotation marks three sentences that he or she heard.

Name ______________________________

Generalize

- **Generalize** by making a broad statement that applies to many examples.
- When you read, clues to generalizations are words such as *many, few,* and *always.* Valid generalizations are backed by supporting details and experts.

Directions Read the following passage. Then complete the chart below.

During the early twentieth century, many African Americans migrated from the South to the North. In addition, another trend was taking place. In 1910, more than 72 percent of African Americans lived in rural areas, and less than 28 percent lived in cities. In 1920, however, 66 percent of African Americans lived in rural areas, and 34 percent lived in cities. Over that period, the African American population of many cities swelled. New York City, for example, went from 91,709 citizens in 1910 to 152,467 in 1920.

Generalization

1.

↑

Supporting Details

2.

3.

4.

5. Write three questions you could ask to find out more about this subject.

____

____

____

Home Activity Your child made a generalization based on the facts of a nonfiction passage. Work together to make generalizations based on the facts in an article about a historical period. Challenge your child to support his or her generalizations.

Name ____________________

Writing for Tests

Prompt: A job posting for counselors at a local summer camp asks applicants to write an essay describing their interests and abilities. Write your job application essay. Include reasons why you are right for the job.

Application Essay: Wolverine Summer Camp

I think I would be an ideal candidate for the job of camp counselor at Wolverine Summer Camp. My abilities, experience, and interests fit perfectly with the job description, including knowledge of first aid, group leadership, sports, and outdoor activities.

I am just about to finish sixth grade at Carver Middle School, where my favorite classes are science, art, and physical education. These classes, for which I receive good grades, show that I love studying nature, have a knack for arts and crafts, and am active in the outdoors. I have also played on the Carver School Soccer Team for three years.

In addition, I have experience as a babysitter and enjoy my job watching two children, ages 5 and 9. I enjoy tutoring third graders in a reading program we have at school, so I know that I can be patient and helpful in a teaching situation. Through another school program, we all had to learn some basic first aid skills. I am hoping to learn more.

I have been a camper at Wolverine Summer Camp for the last five summers, so I know, from the kids' point of view, what makes a good counselor. I also know that a counselor's job is hard, but, as my soccer coach, Ms. Walpole, would tell you, I am responsible and hardworking. I look forward to the opportunity to use my experience, interests, and talents to make camp a fun learning experience for a new generation of Wolverines!

1. What strengths, interests, and experience does the writer mention? Underline experience, circle interests, and put a check mark over strong character traits or abilities.
2. Does the applicant convince you that he or she is the best person for the job? Explain key ways that the writer convinced you or what you feel is lacking.

____

____

____

3. What makes the conclusion in the final paragraph stand out?

____

____

____

Name____

Vocabulary

Directions Choose the word from the box that best matches each definition below. Write the word on the line.

Check the Words You Know

___burden
___conformed
___leisure
___maintenance
___rural
___sufficient
___urban

________________ **1.** were the same as

________________ **2.** free

________________ **3.** enough

________________ **4.** belonging to the country

________________ **5.** act of keeping in good repair

Directions Choose the word from the box that best completes the crossword puzzle below. Write the word in the puzzle.

Down

6. agreed

7. something carried

Across

8. of the city

9. not busy

10. not of the city

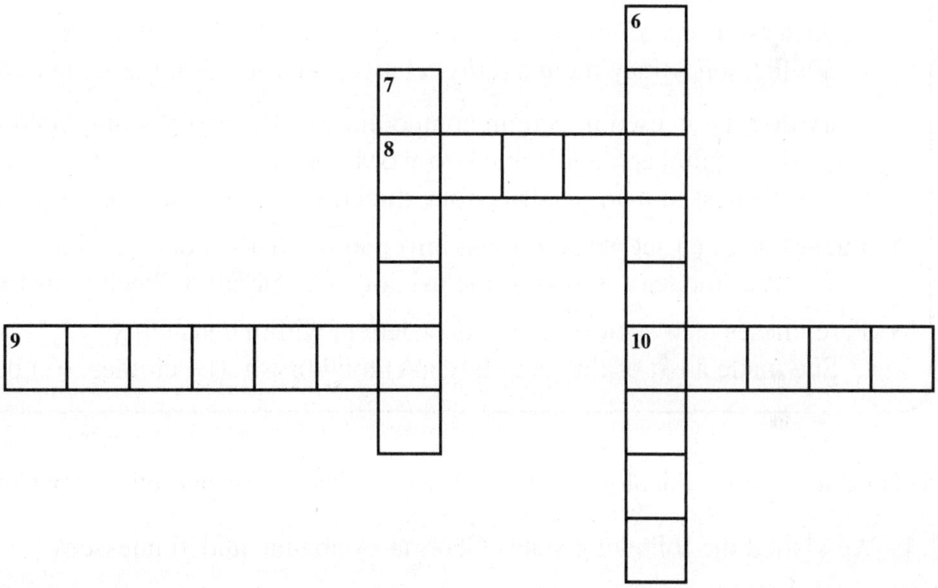

Write a Broadcast

On a separate sheet of paper, write a brief script for a broadcast about a family's journey within the United States. Use as many vocabulary words as you can.

School + Home **Home Activity** Your child identified and used vocabulary words from *Where Opportunity Awaits.* Read a story with your child. Have him or her point out unfamiliar words. Work together to try to figure out the meaning of each word by using other words that appear near it.

Name ____________________

Punctuation

You have already learned about punctuation such as commas, quotation marks, and end marks. Here are some other kinds of punctuation:

- A **semicolon (;)** can be used to separate the two parts of a compound sentence when they are not joined by a comma and a conjunction.
  Southerners migrated to the North**;** they often took the train.
- Semicolons separate items in a series if commas are already used in the series.
  The soccer team included Adam Hoyt**,** sophomore**;** Matthew Thomas**,** senior**;** and Joshua John**,** junior.
- A **colon (:)** is used after the salutation in a business letter and to separate the hours and minutes in expressions of time.
  Dear Mrs. Smith**:**   10**:**30 P.M.
- Colons also introduce a list and set off a speaker's name in a play.
  I did the following chores**:** wax the car, clean my room, and sweep the porch.
  SANDI**:** Hello there!
- A **dash (—)** sets off information that interrupts the flow of a sentence.
  Southerners**—**they included my relatives**—**suffered in the winter weather.
- A **hyphen (-)** is used in certain compound words, such as compound adjectives before nouns; spelled-out numbers; and some two-word nouns.
  a well**-**dressed man   fifty**-**four students   self**-**esteem, make**-**believe
- **Parentheses ( )** set off additional information that is not essential.
  The documentary will air on television next month. **(**Check your local listings.**)**
- Parentheses also enclose numbers or letters within a sentence.
  She made a list of things to buy: **(**A**)** toothbrush, **(**B**)** clothes, **(**C**)** books.

Directions Add semicolons, colons, dashes, hyphens, or parentheses where they belong.

1. We visited the following states Georgia, Alabama, and Tennessee.
2. The play begins at 800 P.M. See Theater Notes for more information.
3. Our neighbors were Mr. Jones, a printer Mr. Smith, a blacksmith and Mr. Heath, a butcher.
4. The Thomases lived in a crowded apartment they shared it with another family.
5. Being a free man how he loved the sound of that was a boost to his self esteem.
6. EMILY Then where did they go?

   JOHN They went to Chicago.

School + Home **Home Activity** Your child learned about punctuation. Have your child scan a page of a book and identify at least three different punctuation marks. Ask your child to explain the uses of the punctuation marks.

Name ______________________

Latin Roots 2

Spelling Words				
vision	suspect	visible	donate	spectator
visor	current	excursion	revise	pardon
prospective	provision	supervisor	inspector	spectacle
concur	recur	visitor	donor	donation

Word Meanings Write a list word to match each definition.

1. likely to come about; expected — 1. ______________
2. a gift to a charity — 2. ______________
3. a statement that makes a condition — 3. ______________
4. one who donates something — 4. ______________
5. an overseer — 5. ______________
6. a guest — 6. ______________
7. one who inspects or examines things — 7. ______________
8. to occur again — 8. ______________
9. to agree — 9. ______________
10. something to look at — 10. ______________

Word Clues Write the list word that matches each clue.

11. The ability to see is this. — 11. ______________
12. When you forgive someone you do this. — 12. ______________
13. Someone who may have broken a law is this. — 13. ______________
14. When you make changes to something you do this. — 14. ______________
15. This is a trip you take. — 15. ______________
16. Something that can be seen is this. — 16. ______________
17. People who give something to charity do this. — 17. ______________
18. Something worn to shield the eyes from sunlight is this. — 18. ______________
19. Someone who only watches is this. — 19. ______________
20. This is a swift flow of water. — 20. ______________

School + Home **Home Activity** Your child wrote words with Latin roots. Ask your child to say and spell the list words with the Latin root *vis*.

Scoring Rubric: Job Application Essay

	4	3	2	1
Focus/Ideas	Clear, focused essay addresses the prompt	Clear or focused essay, but gives too much or too little information	Vague essay that barely addresses the prompt	Rambling essay; lacks development and detail
Organization	Logical organization; good transitions and details	Some sequenced ideas with some transitions	Some details; few order words	Lacks structure and transitions
Voice	Engaging, lively, and enthusiastic writing	Language correct, but shows little personality	Little originality, personality, or involvement	Careless writing with no feeling
Word Choice	Specific, persuasive words highlight qualifications	Some persuasive words to express ideas	Generally limited or redundant language	Vague, dull, or misused words
Sentences	Varied and clear sentence structure	Some sentence variety and length	Some wordy or awkward sentences; little variety	Choppy; many incomplete or run-on sentences
Conventions	Excellent control; few or no errors	Good control; few errors	Little or weak control; many errors	Many serious errors that prevent understanding

Vocabulary • Synonyms

- You can determine the meaning of an unfamiliar word by its **context,** or the other words surrounding it.
- **Synonyms,** or words that have the same meaning, can provide context clues.

Directions Read the following passage about migrating north. Then answer the questions below.

When Jared returned home from school one day, his mother had packed up their belongings. "We're heading north with the rest," she said, lugging her burden, a load of boxes, out to the street. "Where will we live?" Jared asked. It would be an urban area, a city, not a rural area like the farm town where they lived now, his mom said. "They say there are sufficient jobs there, so I sure hope they're right and there are enough jobs for your father and me." Jared looked a little sad. "Don't you worry. With our leisure time when we're not working, we'll enjoy what the city has to offer," his mother promised. "There'll be beaches and parks—just you wait."

1. What does *burden* mean? What synonym helps you to determine the meaning?

____

____

2. What does *urban* mean? What synonym helps you to determine the meaning?

____

____

3. Does *rural* refer to the city or country? What clue helps you to determine this?

____

____

4. How would using context clues help you determine the meaning of *sufficient*?

____

5. What does *leisure* mean? How can you use context clues to determine the meaning?

____

____

Home Activity Your child identified and used context clues to understand new words of a passage. Work together to identify unfamiliar words of an article. Then your child can find context clues to help determine the meanings of the new words. Confirm the meanings with your child.

Name____

Map/Globe/Atlas

- A **map** is a drawing of a place that shows where something is or where something happened. Different kinds of maps are picture, road, political, physical, and special-purpose. A map's **legend** is a key that explains the symbols used on a map. A **compass** shows directions and a **scale** shows distance. An **atlas** is a book of maps, and a **globe** is a sphere with a map of the world on it. Because Earth is round, globes give a more accurate picture of the shape of Earth than flat maps do.

Directions Use this map of the Jones family's migration in 1917 to answer the questions.

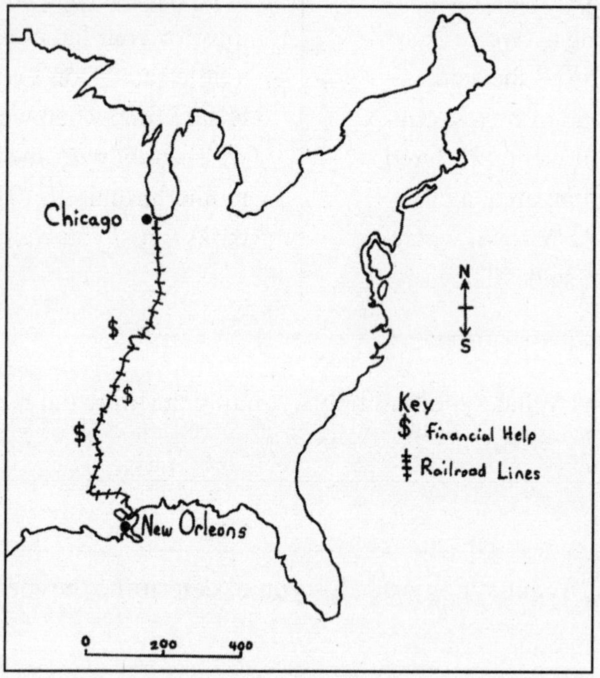

1. In which direction did the Jones family travel from New Orleans to Chicago?

____

2. Approximately what distance did the family travel?

____

3. What help did the family get?

____

____

4. What form of transportation did the family use?

____

5. What does the $ represent?

____

Name____

Directions Use this map of migration patterns for the United States in 2002.

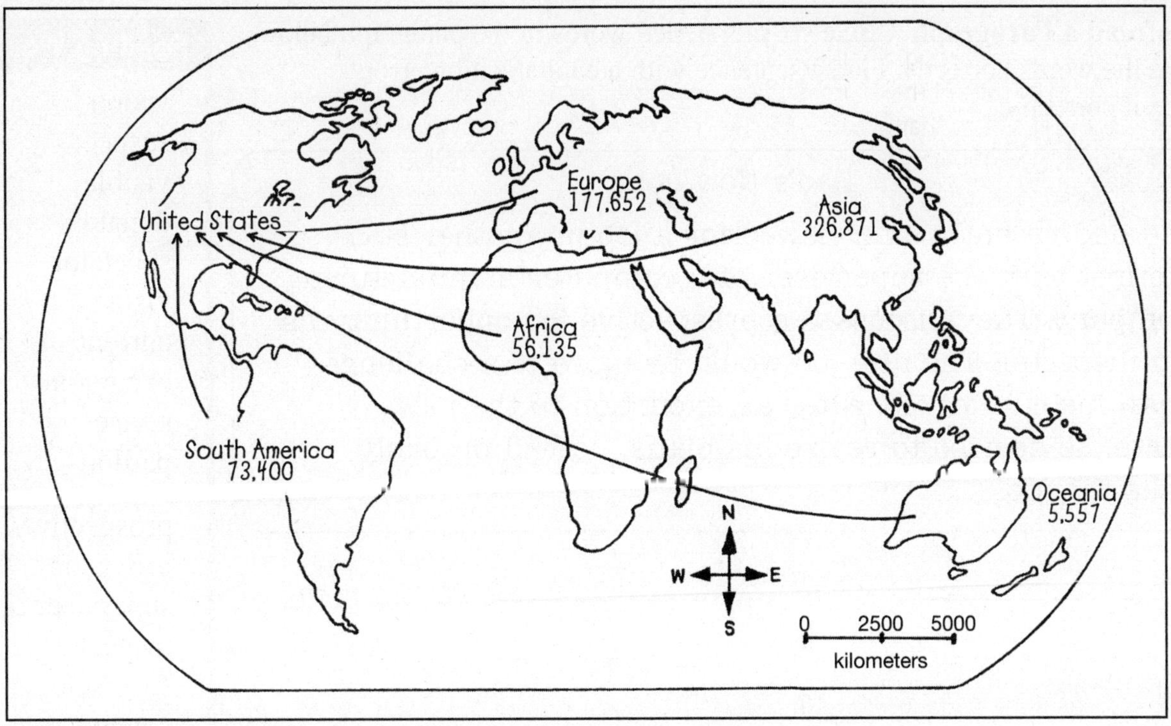

6. How many people migrated to the United States from Africa in 2002?

____

7. Approximately what distance did migrants from central Africa travel to get to the central United States?

____

8. Which part of the world had the most migrants to the United States in 2002?

____

____

9. Some migrants traveled north to the United States. Where were they from?

____

10. Explain how this map is similar to a globe.

____

____

School + Home **Home Activity** Your child learned about using maps and globes as resources. Look at a globe together. Ask your child to describe the relative sizes of different continents and oceans, as well as approximate distances between cities that you name.

Name ______________________________

Latin Roots 2

Proofread a Paragraph Circle six misspelled words in the paragraph below. Write the words correctly. Find a sentence with a capitalization error. Write it correctly.

Spelling Words
vision
suspect
visible
donate
spectator
visor
current
excursion
revise
pardon
prospective
provision
supervisor
inspector
spectacle
concur
recur
visitor
donor
donation

Frequently Misspelled Word
clothes

Dad's New Job

My dad recently interviewed for a job in another state. He met with the superviser of a computer manufacturing company. They discussed a prespective job opportunity as an inspecter. The new job would be more of a challenge than his currint job. After an excurtion to the new state, he decided to revize his plans. he will probably take the job.

1. ______________ 2. ______________

3. ______________ 4. ______________

5. ______________ 6. ______________

7. ______________________________

Proofread Words Circle the word that is spelled correctly. Write it on the line.

8.	cuncur	concur	cancur	8. ______________
9.	visor	vizor	vizer	9. ______________
10.	visible	vizible	visibul	10. ______________
11.	donur	donar	donor	11. ______________
12.	spektator	spectator	spectater	12. ______________
13.	suspekt	suspect	suspecked	13. ______________
14.	vizion	vision	visiun	14. ______________
15.	donate	donnate	doneat	15. ______________
16.	donation	doenation	donasion	16. ______________
17.	parden	pardin	pardon	17. ______________
18.	specticle	spectacle	spectecle	18. ______________

School + Home **Home Activity** Your child identified misspelled words with Latin roots. Ask your child to pick a list word, define it, and use it in a sentence.

Punctuation

Directions Read the passage. Then read each question. Circle the letter of the correct answer.

The Beale Street Music Festival

(1) Kyle planned to visit the following cities in Tennessee; Nashville, Memphis, Knoxville. (2) In Memphis—his first stop—he was excited to go to the Beale Street Music Festival. (3) This celebration of music has become one of the biggest annual galas( ) it draws people from all over the country. (4) Back in 1901 in Memphis, a musician named W.C. Handy—popular, but still little-known—wrote the first blues song. (5) Non-music events also fill the schedule at this event. (6) *The Guinness Book of World Records* says the festival has become the world's largest barbecue competition. (7) Many music fans, however, believe that you cannot appreciate the Blues without visiting the place where it was born ( ) on Beale Street in Memphis.

1 What changes, if any, should be made in sentence 1?

A Insert colon after the word ***visit***
B Delete comma after ***Memphis***
C Change ***Tennessee;*** to **Tennessee:**
D Make no change

2 In sentence 2, what is the function of the phrase *his first stop?*

A The phrase tells more about Memphis.
B The phrase explains why Kyle is going.
C The phrase tells why Kyle is excited.
D The phrase has no function.

3 What form of punctuation should replace the parentheses in sentence 3?

A Colon (:)
B Semicolon (;)
C Dash (—)
D Hyphen (-)

4 What change, if any, should be made in sentence 4?

A Replace the dashes with hyphens
B Remove the hyphen
C Insert semicolon after ***1901***
D Make no changes

5 What form of punctuation should replace the parentheses in sentence 7?

A Colon (:)
B Semicolon (;)
C Dash (—)
D Hyphen (-)

School + Home **Home Activity** Your child prepared for taking tests on punctuation. Have your child write a paragraph about his or her favorite musical genre. Ask your child to use a dash, a hyphen, a colon, and a semicolon in the paragraph.

ıffixes -*ary*, -*ery*, -*ory*

Spelling Words

bakery	scenery	vocabulary	temporary	surgery
inventory	directory	pottery	discovery	imaginary
machinery	nursery	voluntary	honorary	satisfactory
introductory	advisory	bribery	secondary	bravery

Word Group Write the list word that fits in each group.

1. costumes, lighting, stage, _____ 1. ____________
2. supermarket, restaurant, coffee shop, _____ 2. ____________
3. adequate, sufficient, enough, _____ 3. ____________
4. preschool, primary, junior high, _____ 4. ____________
5. dictionary, glossary, thesaurus, _____ 5. ____________
6. preliminary, first, initial, _____ 6. ____________
7. operation, procedure, anesthesia, _____ 7. ____________
8. willing, optional, not required, _____ 8. ____________
9. brief, momentary, fleeting, _____ 9. ____________
10. ceramics, porcelain, terra cotta, _____ 10. ____________

Word Endings Add -*ary*, -*ery*, or -*ory* to each word to make a list word. Change the spelling of the base word if needed. Write the list word.

11. bribe 11. ____________
12. honor 12. ____________
13. machine 13. ____________
14. advise 14. ____________
15. direct 15. ____________
16. imagine 16. ____________
17. discover 17. ____________
18. brave 18. ____________
19. invent 19. ____________
20. nurse 20. ____________

School + Home **Home Activity** Your child has learned to spell words with suffixes -*ary*, -*ery*, and -*ory*. Tell your child base words of the list words from Exercises 1–10. Ask your child to say the list word with the suffix and spell the word.

Name ____

Modifiers

Directions Underline the prepositional phrase in each sentence. Write *adverb* or *adjective* to identify how the prepositional phrase is used.

1. We played in the park in the afternoon. ____________
2. The sun on my head is hot and uncomfortable. ____________
3. Jorge rides his horse along the trail. ____________
4. Watch that man by the tree. ____________
5. You can see clearly in the bright light. ____________
6. The woman with the white scarf smiled warmly. ____________

Directions Underline the adjectives, adverbs, and prepositional phrases in each sentence. The number in ( ) tells how many modifiers a sentence contains. (Do not underline the articles *a, an,* and *the.*)

7. The two knights shared a meager dinner under the trees. (3)
8. Sancho slowly poured cold water into the pot. (3)
9. He made a thick stew that had very little meat in it. (4)
10. Hungry peasants quickly stuffed the bread in their mouths. (3)
11. An army of giants was marching west through the valley. (3)

Directions Identify the misplaced modifier in each sentence. Rewrite the sentence, and put the modifier where it belongs. Underline the modifier.

12. Joyce only ate the bread—no other food.

____

13. We could see cattle grazing in the distance with binoculars.

____

____

14. The man waved to me with a beard.

____

____

School + Home **Home Activity** Your child reviewed modifiers. Have your child use a magazine article to show you adjectives, adverbs, and prepositional phrases that make the writing specific and interesting.

elated Words 2

Spelling Words

alternate	alternative	office	official	economy
economics	normal	normality	restore	restoration
indicate	indicative	gene	genetic	excel
excellence	adapt	adaptation	crime	criminal

Crossword Puzzle Use the clues to find the list words. Write each letter in a box.

Across

2. a country's business affairs
4. action that breaks the law
5. to point out
7. to bring back
10. to take turns

Down

1. determines a trait
3. place of business
6. usual, ordinary
8. to be or do better than
9. to change

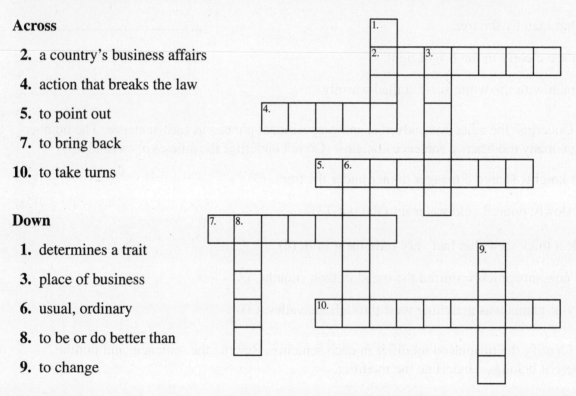

Synonyms Write the list word that means the same or nearly the same.

11. commerce	11. ______	12. adjustment	12. ______
13. rebuilding	13. ______	14. hereditary	14. ______
15. demonstrative	15. ______	16. felon	16. ______
17. option	17. ______	18. regularity	18. ______
19. authorized	19. ______	20. greatness	20. ______

School + Home **Home Activity** Your child has learned to spell related words. Ask your child to use two pairs of related words in sentences.

Conjunctions

Directions Underline the correct conjunction in ( ).

1. The modern Olympic games are held every two years, (and, before) they alternate between summer and winter.

2. My cousin was scheduled to run the marathon, (because, but) he sprained his ankle a day before the race.

3. (Before, And) you study American government, read Aristotle's thoughts about liberty.

4. Did the modern Olympics begin in 1896 (or, and) 1897?

5. Jill chose to read about Hippocrates (or, because) she wants to be a doctor.

6. Chariot races must have been exciting (but, after) dangerous.

7. (If, After) the Dark Ages ended, Athens (and, but) Sparta became powerful city-states.

8. (If, Before) Pericles came to power, only wealthy people served in government.

9. (If, When) Rome defeated the last Greek kingdom, the Hellenistic age was over.

10. We study ancient Greece today (because, but) Greek culture influenced the world.

Directions Underline the conjunction in each sentence. Write *CC* if it is a coordinating conjunction and *SC* if it is a subordinating conjunction.

11. The Greeks developed drama and literature. ______

12. I read some of Aesop's fables when I returned home. ______

13. The teacher wanted ten students for the Greek drama, but only six students volunteered. ______

14. Will you come to the Ancient Greece exhibit, or will you stay at home? ______

15. The Roman Empire grew after the Romans conquered the Greeks. ______

16. Although a fable teaches a lesson, it can still be entertaining. ______

17. She could run for miles, but she could not swim a single lap. ______

18. If you like Greek myths, you will like the one explaining why spiders weave webs. ______

School + Home **Home Activity** Your child reviewed conjunctions. Together listen to 30 seconds of a news broadcast and have your child write some conjunctions he or she hears during that time.

Name ______________________________

Easily Confused Words

Spelling Words				
proceed	precede	advise	advice	formerly
formally	further	farther	personal	personnel
immigrate	emigrate	college	collage	descent
dissent	persecution	prosecution	envelope	envelop

Word Search Find and circle ten list words in the word search. Words are down, across, and diagonal. Write the words on the lines.

P	O	P	E	R	S	O	N	N	E	L	P	E
R	A	R	O	D	I	S	S	E	N	T	R	E
E	D	I	F	A	R	T	H	E	R	G	O	P
C	N	E	O	H	O	C	E	M	E	R	C	E
O	A	V	C	E	D	G	P	I	M	A	O	R
D	D	O	E	T	A	H	O	G	U	D	L	S
P	V	L	I	L	S	E	L	R	R	V	O	E
E	R	S	L	O	O	N	E	A	O	I	L	C
R	S	O	C	E	N	P	V	T	P	C	E	U
A	C	I	C	A	R	O	O	E	C	E	I	T
G	N	N	E	E	G	T	I	O	E	L	C	I
E	F	O	R	M	E	R	L	Y	L	Y	E	O
S	F	E	N	V	E	D	E	R	L	Y	O	N

1. ______________
2. ______________
3. ______________
4. ______________
5. ______________
6. ______________
7. ______________
8. ______________
9. ______________
10. ______________

The Right Word Write a word from each pair to finish the sentence correctly.

11. proceed/precede — What letters _____ the letter *D*? 11. ______________
12. formally/formerly — Let me _____ introduce myself. 12. ______________
13. emigrate/immigrate — Did she _____ to the U.S.? 13. ______________
14. envelope/envelop — Put a stamp on that _____. 14. ______________
15. advice/advise — I _____ you not to speak. 15. ______________
16. personal/personnel — It's his _____ opinion. 16. ______________
17. prosecution/persecution — The _____ has a strong case. 17. ______________
18. further/farther — I will look _____ into it. 18. ______________
19. descent/dissent — The hill has a steep _____. 19. ______________
20. college/collage — He plans to attend _____. 20. ______________

School + Home **Home Activity** Your child has learned to spell words that are easily confused. Ask your child to pick some list words and define them.

Commas

Directions Read the following parts of a letter. Add commas where they are needed.

1. Dear Mrs. Lin
2. Superior CO 80027
3. Monday February 19
4. Thank you for the birthday gift Mrs. Lin.

Directions Add commas where they are needed in the sentences.

5. Because we didn't have any flour Mother did not make potstickers.
6. Excuse me may we have a table for four?
7. Dad got a promotion a higher salary and increased confidence.
8. Well let's draw straws to see who will set the table for dinner.

Directions Rewrite the sentences, adding commas where necessary.

9. When the waiter brought the oysters we weren't sure how to eat them.

___

___

10. I tried to read the menu but it was in French.

___

___

11. Father a systematic man tries to be prepared for all situations.

___

___

12. The waiter brought water lemon slices and extra napkins to the table.

___

___

School + Home **Home Activity** Your child reviewed commas. Choose a piece of junk mail. Ask your child to find at least three commas in it and identify how they are used.

Name ___________________________

Word Endings *-ice, -ise, -ize*

Spelling Words				
memorize	advertise	service	realize	justice
exercise	recognize	organize	civilize	apprentice
supervise	sacrifice	sympathize	enterprise	minimize
cowardice	improvise	paradise	vocalize	compromise

Word Meanings Write the list word that fits each meaning.

1. act of giving up one thing for another 1. ________
2. physical activity 2. ________
3. to reduce 3. ________
4. to put in order 4. ________
5. to share or agree with a feeling or opinion 5. ________
6. place of happiness and beauty 6. ________

Finishing Words Fill in the blank with *ice, ise,* or *ize* to finish each word. Write each word.

7. recogn _____ 7. ________
8. enterpr _____ 8. ________
9. coward _____ 9. ________
10. apprent _____ 10. ________
11. real _____ 11. ________
12. improv _____ 12. ________
13. comprom _____ 13. ________
14. memor _____ 14. ________
15. vocal _____ 15. ________
16. advert _____ 16. ________
17. just _____ 17. ________
18. serv _____ 18. ________
19. superv _____ 19. ________
20. civil _____ 20. ________

School + Home **Home Activity** Your child has learned to spell words that end with *-ice, -ise,* or *-ize.* Call out some of the list words and ask your child to give synonyms for the words.

Quotations and Quotation Marks

Directions Add quotation marks and punctuation to each sentence as needed.

1. At the party I said we will serve hot chocolate
2. Our teacher said the Aztecs knew how to throw a party
3. Your jade earrings are lovely June said
4. The musician said I will play a traditional song after the feast
5. Can you paddle a canoe she asked
6. Did you read this article about Aztec culture asked Mrs. Bennett It's very interesting
7. Beth said I read it yesterday
8. Grandmother whispered Lake Texcoco shimmers like a large emerald

Directions Rewrite each sentence, adding quotation marks, capitalization, and punctuation as needed.

9. The Aztec warriors used stones, spears, and arrows said Mr. Evans.

____

____

10. When the Spaniards fell into the lake I explained they could not swim because of their heavy armor.

____

____

11. Look at this armband the curator said you can see Aztec markings.

____

____

12. The child asked how we made the beads.

____

____

School + Home **Home Activity** Your child reviewed quotations and quotation marks. Ask your child three questions and have him or her write a response to each in the form of a quotation.

Name____

Latin Roots 2

Spelling Words				
vision	suspect	visible	donate	spectator
visor	current	excursion	revise	pardon
prospective	provision	supervisor	inspector	spectacle
concur	recur	visitor	donor	donation

Antonyms Write the list word that has the opposite or nearly the opposite meaning.

1. hidden — 1. ____________
2. keep — 2. ____________
3. oppose — 3. ____________
4. participant — 4. ____________
5. punish — 5. ____________
6. host — 6. ____________

Synonyms Write the list word that has the same or nearly the same meaning.

7. repeat — 7. ____________
8. journey — 8. ____________
9. change — 9. ____________
10. contribution — 10. ____________
11. accused — 11. ____________
12. condition — 12. ____________

Word Groups Write the list word that belongs in each group.

13. wave, splash, tide, _____ — 13. ____________
14. see, sight, look, _____ — 14. ____________
15. boss, manager, director, _____ — 15. ____________
16. giver, contributor, philanthropist, _____ — 16. ____________
17. showy, extravaganza, scene, _____ — 17. ____________
18. sunglasses, hat, shade, _____ — 18. ____________
19. examiner, checker, investigator, _____ — 19. ____________
20. probable, likely, possible, _____ — 20. ____________

School + Home

Home Activity Your child has learned to spell words with Latin roots. Say some list words and ask your child to identify the Latin root. Then ask him or her to define the words.

Punctuation

Directions Add semicolons, colons, dashes, hyphens, or parentheses where they belong.

1. The Thomas family moved to Chicago they arrived on a train.
2. His brand new job required him to be at work at 600 in the morning.
3. Train routes determined where many migrants relocated routes were called "chains."
4. Dear Mr. Harrison I would like to schedule an appointment.
5. The Thomas children study the following English, history, and science.
6. The dock workers included the following Jim, a Chicagoan Bill, an Ohioan and Tim, a southerner.
7. MARTHA What day will you be arriving?

   MARY Our train will arrive on Saturday.
8. It can take time to adjust to a new city in the end, it is worth it.
9. To whom it may concern The railroad company needs additional employees.
10. School starts promptly at 815 A.M.
11. Mr. Thomas's neighbors included David, an usher Karl, a delivery man and Mike, a shipyard worker
12. Boysenberry ice cream they sell it only at Kraft's is wonderful.
13. The immigrants they were determined to read went to night school.
14. Many southerners had family in the North they decided to move north too.
15. Chicago was a well known destination for southerners. See photographs on page 9.

School + Home **Home Activity** Your child reviewed punctuation. Have your child write a letter to a friend describing what it would be like to move to a new place. Ask your child to use two semicolons and two colons in the letter.

Name ______________________________

KWL Chart

Directions Fill out this KWL chart to help you organize your ideas.

Topic ______________________________

What I Know	What I Want to Know	What I Learned

Controlling Question ______________________________

Name ______________________________

Topic and Detail Sentences

Directions Think about the organization of your research report. Write a topic sentence and at least two detail sentences for each paragraph.

Paragraph 1
Topic Sentence ______________________________

____

Detail Sentences ______________________________

____

____

Paragraph 2
Topic Sentence ______________________________

____

Detail Sentences ______________________________

____

____

Paragraph 3
Topic Sentence ______________________________

____

Detail Sentences ______________________________

____

____

Paragraph 4
Topic Sentence ______________________________

____

Detail Sentences ______________________________

____

____

Name ______________________________

Adding Modifiers

One way to revise your writing is to add modifiers such as adjectives, adverbs, and prepositional phrases to describe, or modify, other words in a sentence.

General	Pharaohs built tombs.
More Specific	Pharaohs in ancient Egypt usually built costly tombs.

Directions Add a word or phrase from the box or your own adjective, adverb, or prepositional phrase to describe the underlined word in each sentence. Write the new sentence.

year-round	fashionable	with its white marble columns
skilled	of tropical birds	

1. The Aztecs used feathers in their headdresses.

____

____

2. Ancient Egyptian men and women wore many accessories.

____

____

3. The ancient Greeks ate bread, beans, and olives.

____

____

4. Notice the design of the Parthenon.

____

____

5. The Egyptian pyramids were built by architects and engineers.

____

____

Editing

Directions Edit this paragraph. Look for errors in spelling, grammar, and mechanics. Use proofreading marks to show the corrections.

Proofreading Marks	
Delete (Take out)	⌐
Add	^
Spelling	⬭
Uppercase letter	≡
Lowercase letter	/

The anchent Maya loved jewelry. Both men and women wear earrings, bracelets, necklaces, nose rings collars, and anklets. The most valueable jewelry were made of jade. Jade, a hard green stone with a bluish tint was the most precious material the Maya knew. They associated it with water and the maize plant, maize being there most important food. Different from the more familar chinese jade, Maya jade is slightly more harder, more opaque, and more uneven in color. With no medal tools, the Maya cutted, carved, and polished jade to make beads, jewelry ornaments, small statues, and masks. Maya Rulers were buried with many jade objects to take with him to the afterlife. Even ordinery Maya was buried with one or more jade beads in their mouths to use as a offering to the gods of the Underworld.

Now you'll edit the draft of your research report. Then you'll use your revised and edited draft to make a final copy of your report. Finally, you'll share your written work with your audience.